# Contents

Foreword by Hugh Johnson 4

Introduction 5

How to use this book 6

The region and the wines 7

- A little history 7
- Terroir 9
- The appellations 14
- The grapes 20
- Life of the vine and vinification 23
- Growers and merchants 34
- Enjoying burgundy 39
- Vintages 44
- Stars of recent years 49

Wines and villages 50

- Wines of the Yonne 50
- Côte d'Or 63
- Côte Chalonnaise 116
- The Mâconnais 128
- Beaujolais 139

A-Z of Burgundy producers 161

Index 252

# Foreword

Access to the personal files of a top professional is surely the most that any serious amateur of wine could ask. This latest generation of wine books, represented by Serena Sutcliffe's *The Wines of Burgundy*, amounts almost to such a privileged snoop.

The situation reports and critical opinions that form the basis of buying decisions are normally classified information. But wine literature has moved on with quite startling speed from the phase of enthusiastic generalisation to that of precise wine-by-wine commentary. In this book it drops its sixth, if not seventh, veil. Now we are allowed to know as much as the most experienced professionals.

Serena Sutcliffe has earned a formidable international reputation as a wine-taster of authority and decision. She is now a senior director of Sotheby's and heads the company's international wine department. From London, she travels constantly throughout the wine world, but Burgundy has always fascinated her – partly, one suspects, because it is such an enigmatic, volatile and controversial region. Everyone knows that burgundy, both red and white, can be sublime. Yet it so often fails to meet expectations. What greater challenge for an unprejudiced taster and writer than to track down the authentic and commendable, and to warn us about the rest?

Serena Sutcliffe learned her impeccable French as a translator for UNESCO in Paris. She learned her wine in the London wine trade, being one of the first women to pass the stiff examination and become a Master of Wine. Her writing is a natural gift, which was made plain to the world in 1981 when she was responsible for a totally new edition of André Simon's *Wines of the World.*

Together, these attributes make her a highly qualified guide. Her day-to-day dealings with Burgundy and Burgundians give her an up-to-date insight such as none before her has tried to pack into the convenient compass of a book of this size. It is a remarkable privilege to be able, as it were, to look over her shoulder at the sometimes hypnotising complexities of the most tantalising of all the great wine regions.

**Hugh Johnson**

# Introduction

In the second half of the 1990s, there is more really good burgundy on the market than ever before. The generally excellent vintages of the 1980s gave way to very creditable wines in the 1990s. It is fair to say that, so far, the decade has been far kinder to Burgundy than to Bordeaux. The 1990 vintage was superb everywhere and, in Burgundy, some red '91s and white '92s are exciting. The '93 reds are wonderful, while the '94s need careful selection but can be rewording. Both '95 and '96 have produced glorious red and white wines.

In fact, all burgundy needs selection. This book, I hope, will help you do it for yourself. There are more growers in it than in the previous editions and the comments may be even more trenchant! I try to assess a grower's performance over a period of recent years rather than pick out certain specific wines. If a grower is on form, and has real vinous integrity, he will do well in every year, within the context of the climate given to him.

I have arranged the book in a slightly different and, I hope, more logical order. And, where possible, I have updated statistics.

There seems, to me, to be a higher proportion of excellent growers and winemakers in Burgundy than even ten years ago. Pride and competition have both played their part in bringing this about, as well as a new generation establishing itself and gaining confidence. Greater prosperity has been used well, in sensible investment and improvements. Nevertheless, one still comes across wines that are an insult to their appellation, in some markets more than on others, indicating that mediocre houses concentrate on less-knowledgeable drinkers. There are poor wines from everywhere, but disappointing burgundy drives me mad, as I am lucky enough to know how good it can be.

If there is one plea I can make to you, the reader and consumer of burgundy, it is to be more adventurous with vintages. Even in lesser years there are good wines, usually at an attractive price, as Burgundians have learnt to differentiate more honestly between a great year and a more modest vintage.

Happy searching and – even more importantly – happy drinking. And please tell the producer, or merchant, when you find a burgundy outstanding – *pour encourager*. Equally, do not hesitate to lambast all and sundry if you drink a bad burgundy; there is no excuse!

# How to use this book

The book has three main parts: first, an introduction; second, a section on wines and villages; third, an A–Z list of producers.

**The Region and the wines**
The introductory section gives a general picture of Burgundy and its wines, and is an ideal starting point.

**Wines and villages**
This section gives a briefing on each area within Burgundy and its appellations (including soil and topography), together with profiles of selected domaines and their wines.

The five Burgundy areas (The Yonne, Côte d'Or, Côte Chalonnaise, The Mâconnais, Beaujolais), and the appellations within them, are arranged in geographical order from north to south.

To look up a particular village/appellation, turn to the area section first (eg Beaujolais) and then to the village/appellation within that section (eg Fleurie). The maps at the start of each area section show the principal ACs and can help with this. (All areas and appellations are also listed in the Index starting on page 252.)

For the Yonne, Côte Chalonnaise, the Mâconnais and Beaujolais, the description of each appellation is followed by a listing of that appellation's principal producers, with details of their holdings (where available), winemaking methods and an assessment of their wines.

For the Côte d'Or, which is by far the largest and most diverse area, a small selection of recommended producers, together with an assessment of their best wines, is included. For a comprehensive listing of the Côte d'Or producers, and details of their holdings and winemaking methods, consult the A–Z.

**A–Z of Burgundy producers**
The A–Z section is a list of over 600 producers, including growers, *négociants*, *négociant-éleveurs* and cooperatives. It can be used when looking up individual producers and also provides an index to those recommended in the 'Wines and villages' section.

A number of abbreviations have been used in this edition. Vineyard areas are expressed in hectares (shortened to ha), and yields are expressed in hectolitres (hl) or hectolitres per hectare (hl/ha). At the beginning of each area and village section, the symbols ● ○ ◑ indicate whether red, white or rosé wine is produced.

| | |
|---|---|
| AC (AOC) | Appellation d'Origine Contrôlée |
| km | kilometres |
| cm | centimetres |
| mm | millimetres |
| 1 hectare (ha) | = 2.47 acres |
| 1 hectolitre (hl) | = 22.02 gallons (Imperial)/26.45 |
| gallons (US) | = approx 11 cases of wine |
| | (12 x 75cl bottles per case) |

# The region and the wines

To many people, French and foreigners alike, the word 'Burgundy' is synonymous with wine and rollicking good living. It conjures up visions of gastronomy, *bonhomie* and rosy cheeks, berets and cellars and baggy trousers. Quite how this image came about is lost in the alcoholic fumes of time, but there is no doubt that it is there. Whether it has actually helped or hindered historic Burgundy to find its rightful place amongst the truly great wines of the world is another matter.

There is nothing homogeneous about the term. 'Burgundy' is a good chunk of eastern France, and to many who live there its frontiers are often the limits of their travels. The region covers the area from Chablis down to Lyon, encompassing much beautiful, rolling countryside which will not be of immediate interest to the wine-lover. But what will attract anyone who has ever lifted a glass of good Burgundy to his or her lips is the diversity of tastes emerging from such a disparate landscape.

Viticultural Burgundy consists of the Yonne, chiefly known for its Chablis, the Côte d'Or, the Côte Chalonnaise, the Mâconnais and Beaujolais. Chablis is an island, isolated from the rest and logically more a part of Champagne than Burgundy, but the other four defined areas form the Burgundian corridor which leads into the Rhône Valley and on down to the Mediterranean.

## A little history

Camille Rodier, writing from the fastness of Nuits-St-Georges in 1920, pours a certain amount of scorn on the theories of Pliny and Plutarch as to the origins of the vine in present-day Burgundy. The ancients would have it that the Gauls invaded Italy for its wine (a somewhat chauvinistic point of view) and when they turned tail and returned over the Alps, they took Italian vinous habits with them. The Burgundians of our days have, incidentally, made a brave attempt to illustrate Gallo-Roman living conditions by erecting a model village of that era by the Beaune service station on the Autoroute du Sud.

What does seem likely is that the vine came to Burgundy via the Greek settlement of Marseilles about 600BC, considerably predating the arrival of the Romans and their need for the grape. In the following centuries, in spite of Roman protectionism, safeguarding the Italian home product, and barbarian invasions in the fifth century, the vine flourished – so much so that in the sixth century, Gregory of Tours was singing the praises of the wines produced near Dijon.

The history of the vine in Burgundy is unalterably linked with the Church. From the end of the fifth century, monasteries were established throughout Burgundy, and the rise of what are now some of the grandest appellations of the area became inextricably bound up with royal or aristocratic gifts to the abbeys. The vastly powerful religious centre of Cluny in the Mâconnais was founded in 910; Cîteaux, on the plain near Nuits, followed in 1098. The harsh order of the Cistercians did much to discipline vine production and ensure the fame of the local wines, and they were, of course, the founders of the Clos de Vougeot. It is worth pondering the austerity of the Cistercian order as one dines now in Bacchanalian fashion with the Chevaliers du Tastevin at Vougeot.

Secular power in Burgundy was held from the 14th century for more than 100 years by the Valois dukes. At their apogee, their empire and influence included large chunks of France and Flanders; in the absence of a competent king, Duke Philip the Bold of Burgundy was certainly the most powerful man in the whole of France. Four dukes – Philip the Bold, John the Fearless, Philip the Good and Charles the Bold – presided over a state that was characterised by military strength, material wealth and artistic splendour: perfect conditions for the vine to flourish. It was at this time that the Low Countries became such good clients of Burgundian winemakers, a tradition which has continued to this day. A key figure was Nicolas Rolin, chancellor to Philip the Good, who was able to amass considerable wealth while holding this post. In 1443, he atoned for his excesses by founding the Hôtel-Dieu in Beaune, later to be supported by the donation of vineyards.

However, in the end, the scattered nature of the Burgundian empire proved to be its downfall, and with the death in battle of Charles the Bold in 1477, Burgundy became truly French under the rule of Louis XI.

The first great Valois duke, Philip the Bold, had in 1395 declared war on the Gamay grape by ordering that it be pulled up and replaced by the 'nobler' Pinot. This was a recurring theme in Burgundian viticultural history, and the first shot in what was to be a long battle between quality and quantity. But the pendulum always had a tendency to swing towards the 'generous' Gamay. In 1855, of the 26,500 hectares of vines on the Côte d'Or, 23,000 hectares were planted to Gamay, a state of affairs which needs no commentary. However, in mitigation, it must be said that yields varied between 15 and 20 hectolitres per hectare. It should also be remembered that Burgundy was ahead of Bordeaux in the selection of grape varieties.

Taking the Côte d'Or, it is interesting to note the fluctuations in the area under vine:

| | | | |
|---|---|---|---|
| ***1816*** | *24,000 ha* | ***1955*** | *8,825 ha* |
| ***1875*** | *33,745 ha* | ***1982*** | *8,600 ha* |
| ***1929*** | *12,112 ha* | ***1996*** | *9,340 ha* |

In 1929, hybrid vines were planted on 1,723 hectares of the region, while in 1955 there were 5,048 hectares of *appellation contrôlée* vines. The 1982 figure included 7,621 hectares of vines producing AC wine, with a mere 979 hectares producing *vin de table*. By the 1990s, the figure for *vin de table* was so small as to be negligible.

One of the keys to the whole enigma that is Burgundy is the multifarious ownership of the vineyards. This was originally brought about by the French Revolution of 1789, when the religious estates were broken up with all the ferocity of a zealous Henry VIII of England 250 years earlier. Aristocratic domaines were also dispersed, rarely to come together again, whereas in Bordeaux returning *emigrés* were able to carry on as before. This fragmentation of vineyard area has been exacerbated by French laws of succession: all the children inherit, not just the eldest son.

Burgundy did not escape the two natural disasters which hit the whole of viticultural France in the 19th century. The first was oidium, or powdery mildew, which began seriously to affect yields until the remedy of dusting the vines with sulphur was discovered. This method has been used, in one form or another, ever since.

The second disaster, phylloxera, was to have far more devastating effects, as shown by the dramatic drop in the area under vine between 1875 and 1929. This vine louse, or aphid, came originally from the US, and vines simply died under its attack. In the absence of accurate scientific methods, growers often resorted to superstitious folk remedies, and much time and money were lost in experiment and deliberation. Flooding, one suggested remedy, was hardly practicable on the slopes, and injecting the soil with carbon bisulphide was not a permanent solution to the invasion. Only grafting onto American vine rootstocks, immune to the activities of the pest, guaranteed complete safety, and gradually, as the 19th century turned into the 20th, this technique was adopted.

But the economic ramifications were enormous. Many growers could not afford the cost and either gave up vine-growing or left the region, and the area under vines shrank irrevocably. It was the better sites on the slopes that survived, and yields leapt forward, so the picture after phylloxera was in many ways a good deal healthier than in the past. At this time, high-yielding Pinots made their appearance. It is a distortion, however, to attribute the increase in yields entirely to new clones. Better and more intelligent vineyard husbandry played a part. The comparatively tiny yields of the past were as often the result of disease as anything else.

## Terroir

Burgundy is in eastern France, far away from maritime influence and 'enjoying' a continental climate (although sometimes that is perhaps not quite the word to use in the Siberian conditions of many a Burgundian January). What rivers there are do not make their mark on the microclimate in any significant way; the Serein in Chablis is far too tiny, and the Saône of the Côte Chalonnaise too far from the vineyard slopes. River and vineyard are closest in the Mâconnais, where the Saône breaks its banks with monotonous regularity; however, crops other than the vine usually bear the brunt of this.

Chablis, 136 kilometres (85 miles) to the northwest of Dijon, lies stranded on the way to Paris, only about 70 kilometres (44 miles) to the south of the Aube, the southernmost classified area of Champagne. Chablis forms part of the Auxerrois, with the Yonne Valley vineyards west of Chablis producing somewhat earthy wines from the communes of St-Bris-le-Vineux, Chitry,

Irancy and Coulanges-la-Vineuse. Chablis' claim to fame is its subsoil of Kimmeridge clay/limestone, to which Chardonnay is ideally suited. Nowadays, Portlandian limestone, found in some of the outlying villages around Chablis, is considered by the authorities to be just as special. Unfortunately, this island of vines is subject to particularly severe winters, with spring frost a hazard right up to the end of May. The great hill of the Grands Crus, close to Chablis itself, is a particular frost trap, while the plateau areas of Chablis are often swept by snow during the winter.

The Côte d'Or, or *la Côte* as it is known locally, stretches from Dijon 50 kilometres (31 miles) down to Dezize-lès-Maranges in the *département* of Saône et Loire, in a southerly direction until Beaune, but then veering more to the southwest. The Côte is, in fact, the eastern edge of a calcareous upland plateau which ends with the Saône river plain. The 'Golden Slope' is so described because of the fiery colours of the vine leaves in autumn. When gazing at this splendour, it is easy to forget that only two per cent of the agricultural surface of the *département* of the Côte d'Or is covered by vines, but this supports 1,750 growers and 35 per cent of salaried agricultural labour.

The vineyard area of the Côte d'Or can be divided into three distinct parts: the Côte, which comprises the Côte de Nuits and the Côte de Beaune; the Hautes-Côtes; and the plain of Beaune. The greatest wines come from the Côte and the vine here reigns supreme. The domaines are very small, averaging five hectares, mostly family-owned and often with plots in several villages.

The Hautes-Côtes, frequently ignored in the past but now worthy of serious consideration, are in the hinterland, with vines planted on the slopes of small valleys called combes. Here the vine is mixed with other fruits such as blackcurrants and raspberries, but, as growers find more economic ways to run their vineyards, confidence in wine is returning. Family properties in the Hautes-Côtes tend to be ten hectares in size and, for economic viability, the vines are mostly high-trained and wide-spaced. Some of the slopes are not as well exposed here as on the Côte itself, so good weather is needed for optimum ripeness.

The plain around Beaune is, again, not specifically viticultural, but there are now some noble grapes – Pinot Noir, Chardonnay, Aligoté and Gamay – amongst the mixed farming.

The Côte Chalonnaise is not a continuous, visible escarpment, but a series of hills, stretching southwards from Chagny, with fine slopes ideal for vine-growing. The vines are usually grown at heights of 300–335 metres (985–1,100 feet), higher than the Côte d'Or and therefore usually vintaging three or four days later. The vineyards of Rully and Mercurey are close to each other, but Givry stands on its own to the south, and, to the southwest of Chalon-sur-Saône, Montagny and Buxy are responsible for some fine white wines. The vineyards appear between fields and woods, not as predominantly eastward facing as those on the Côte d'Or.

Much of the Mâconnais vineyard area lies to the northwest of the town of Mâcon, but the finest area of the 'Pouilly satellites' is found to the southwest. To the north, where the 'bulk' Mâcon is

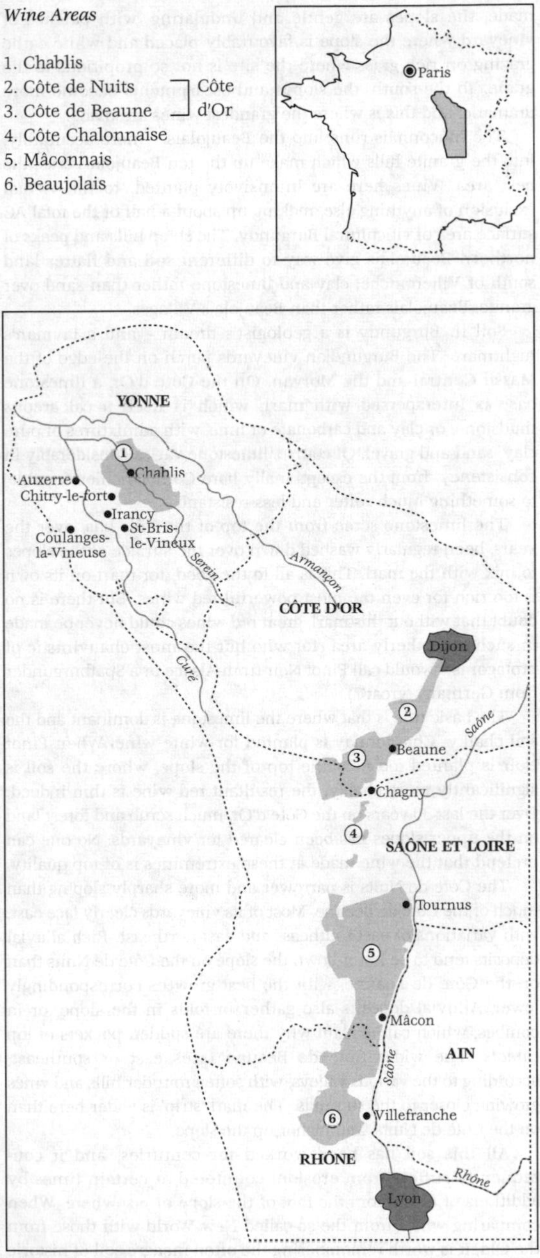
*Wine Areas*
1. Chablis
2. Côte de Nuits
3. Côte de Beaune
Côte d'Or
4. Côte Chalonnaise
5. Mâconnais
6. Beaujolais
Paris
YONNE
Auxerre
Chablis
Chitry-le-fort
Irancy
St-Bris-le-Vineux
Coulanges-la-Vineuse
Serein
Armançon
CÔTE D'OR
Cure
Dijon
Saône
Beaune
Chagny
SAÔNE ET LOIRE
Tournus
Mâcon
AIN
Saône
Villefranche
RHÔNE
Rhône
Lyon

made, the slopes are gentle and undulating, with patches of vineyard where the slope is favourably placed and white cattle grazing on rich grass where the site is not so propitious to the grape. To the south, the slopes and escarpments become more dramatic, and this is where the grandest wines are made.

The Mâconnais runs into the Beaujolais – more accurately, into the granite hills which make up the ten Beaujolais *crus*, the best area. Vines here are intensively planted, to the virtual exclusion of anything else, making up about a half of the total AC surface area of viticultural Burgundy. The steep hills and peaks of northern Beaujolais give way to different soil and flatter land south of Villefranche: clay and limestone rather than sand over granite, Beaujolais rather than Beaujolais-Villages.

Soil in Burgundy is a geologist's dream – and a layman's nightmare. The Burgundian vineyards perch on the edge of the Massif Central and the Morvan. On the Côte d'Or, a limestone base is interspersed with marl, which is itself a calcareous mudstone, or clay and carbonate of lime, with admixtures of pure clay, sand and gravel. Of course, limestone varies considerably in consistency, from the exceptionally hard Comblanchien 'marble' to something much softer and less resistant.

The limestone scree from the top of the hills has, over the years, been regularly washed down over the surface of the slopes to mix with the marl. This is all to the good, for marl on its own is too rich for even the most powerful red wines. But there is no doubt that without this marl, great red wines could never be made in such a northerly area (for who but the most chauvinistic of protagonists would call Pinot Noir from Alsace or a Spätburgunder from Germany 'great'?).

The basic rule is that where the limestone is dominant and the soil chalky, Chardonnay is planted for white wine. When Pinot Noir is planted too near the top of the slope, where the soil is significantly more chalky, the resultant red wine is thin indeed. Over the last 30 years on the Côte d'Or, much scrub and forest land on the upper slopes has been cleared for vineyards. No one can pretend that the wine made at these extremities is of top quality.

The Côte de Nuits is narrower and more sharply sloping than much of the Côte de Beaune. Most of its vineyards clearly face east, with variations of east-southeast and east-northeast. Rich alluvial deposits tend to be lower down the slope on the Côte de Nuits than on the Côte de Beaune, with the best growths correspondingly lower. Alluvial deposits also gather in folds in the slope, or in combes, which can explain why there are sudden pockets of top *climats*. The wider Côte de Beaune faces east or southeast, according to the various valleys, with softer, rounder hills and vines growing closer to the summits. The marl 'strip' is wider here than on the Côte de Nuits, and higher up the slope.

All this soil has been worked for centuries, and it consequently suffers from erosion, countered at certain times by additions of earth from the foot of the slope or elsewhere. When comparing wines from the so-called New World with those from the Old, it is worth remembering the often meagre soil of historic vineyards, where the vine must delve deep for goodness, in comparison with the fertile, 'virgin' soil of American or Australian plantations.

Who is to say that an element of soil exhaustion does not contribute to finesse? On the other hand, really tired soil in Europe is now helped by judicious fertilising or mineral additions. Drainage on the slopes is not a problem, and the process is facilitated by gravel and particles of broken-up stone, an important element in vineyards producing top quality wines.

The most vital month in the whole year, from a climatic point of view, is September. In Burgundy, the weather's performance in this crucial month can make or mar a vintage. Whereas the size of the crop is largely decided (with last-minute variations possible due to rain) by the presence or absence of spring frosts and by the relative success of the flowering, the quality of the crop is determined in September. Catastrophic rain in September ruined the 1975s on the Côte d'Or, whereas a superb September saved the situation in 1978 and thus made the wines great. In the 1990s, rain during the harvest made the difference between uniformly splendid and good.

Clearly, making red wine in such a northerly region is something of a risk, and Burgundian white wines will always show less vintage variability than reds or, to be more accurate, they will plumb the depths less often than the reds. There is a basic north-to-south difference in temperatures, with Chablis cooler than the Mâconnais, especially in the summer months. However, during this period the temperatures on the Côte Chalonnaise are lower than on the Côte de Nuits, while the Côte de Beaune suffers fewer extremes of cold and heat than the Côte de Nuits, so there is no straightforward pattern.

December, January and February are the coldest months, July and August the hottest. The strongest frosts are in January and February, but March and April frosts are usually more to be feared since the vegetation is further advanced. Snow cover is always a protection against frost damage, but unfortunately there was no snow, for instance, in the severe cold of February 1985. One way to combat frost is by a careful selection of vineyard sites – facing east and south in Beaujolais, the Mâconnais and the Côte Chalonnaise, east-southeast (generally) in the Côte d'Or, and southeast and southwest in Chablis. A warm June is critical for flowering. August and September are always hotter in Bordeaux than in Burgundy, which goes a long way towards explaining the more consistent record of Bordeaux vintages compared with those of Burgundy.

Light and sunshine are also vital to successful grape-growing, and Burgundy, situated around 47° latitude, enjoys long periods of daylight in the growing season. With its inland continental climate, Burgundy hardly lags behind Bordeaux in hours of sunshine. July is the sunniest month, followed by August, June and May. Humidity is remarkably similar in both areas as the vine develops. Rainfall is often the cause of Burgundy's undoing. The crucial factor with rain is not so much the quantity which falls, but when it falls. Regular light rain is always more desirable than storms, and when rain is interspersed with sun, the earth can warm up relatively quickly. Persistent rain in summer brings with it the risk of grey rot, the Burgundians' bogey. However, even after a seemingly lethal bout of rain in August, a dry September and early October can completely save the situation. The Côte d'Or is drier than the regions to the south, and certainly less wet than the Hautes-Côtes, partly because the climate is drier and more continental towards Dijon, and partly because the slope of the Côte affords a measure of protection from the rain-bearing winds from the west.

However, the drawback of this favoured position is that northern Burgundy is more susceptible to hail than elsewhere, and the Côte de Nuits seems particularly vulnerable, with significant damage in 1983, 1981, 1979 and 1971 (the Côte de Beaune was even worse hit in 1971). But hail is always highly localised, and part of a commune can be hit while the rest remains untouched.

As in every viticultural region, the microclimate of their own particular area (or plots, in the case of Burgundy) will concern growers far more than the general picture. Factors like position on a slope, proximity to woods and the neighbouring topography (for instance, a dip in the hill causing a current of wind) all serve to temper or aggravate an overall tendency, and can make the difference between wild success and only moderate performance.

# The appellations

To set the scene, it is as well to keep in mind the amount of wine produced in Burgundy which is covered by the *appellation contrôlée* laws. In the table below, by region, are the AC figures for the 1996 vintage.

**The 1996 Crop in Burgundy**

| Area | White (hl) | Red and Rosé (hl) |
|---|---|---|
| Regional appellations | 228,934 | 1,025,019 |
| Chablis | 230,412 | — |
| Côte de Nuits | 2,052 | 74,252 |
| Côte de Beaune | 54,935 | 126,875 |
| Côte Chalonnaise | 31,380 | 43,094 |
| The Mâconnais | 317,508 | 49,135 |
| Beaujolais Crus | — | 362,151 |
| Côte d'Or Grands Crus | 3,796 | 14,449 |
| **Total 2,563,992** | **869,017** | **1,694,975** |

The first known attempt to define Burgundy wines and guard their origins was made by King Charles VI of France in 1416. He defined the area of *Vin François*, by which he meant wine made in the region of Paris, and that of *Vins de Bourgogne*, for wines made above the bridge at Sens, including the Auxerrois and the Beaunois, and transported on the Yonne river. Things have become a little more sophisticated since then. However, at the outset, it should be reiterated that the AC system in France (and not just in Burgundy, although this region seems to receive more criticism than most) is not a guarantee of quality, much as we would like it to be. For that to happen, controls would have to be more stringent and, in the case of Burgundy, the arrangements regarding tasting dramatically overhauled. But that would be Utopia. What could be realistically hoped for would be rules and regulations created by people of integrity with great practical knowledge of growing vines and making wine in a capricious area, rather than by desk-bound bureaucrats, however worthy their motives.

What the AC laws do endeavour to do is guarantee the geographical origin of the wines, and lay down viticultural and vinification precepts which should lead to better quality.

***The specifications cover:***
Area of production
Grape varieties permitted
Minimum alcohol level before chaptalisation (page 17)
Maximum yield per hectare
Methods of planting, pruning and treating the vines
Vinification
Maturation and *élevage*

Four organisations carry out between them the work of controlling the quality and marketing of French wines:

**The INAO** (*Institut National des Appellations d'Origine*)
**The ONIVIT** (*Office National Interprofessionnel des Vins de Table*)
**The SRFCQ** (*Service de la Répression des Fraudes et du Contrôle de la Qualité*)
**The DGI** (*Direction Générale des Impôts*)

The basis for today's laws has been laid down during this century, with refinements and improvements at each stage, culminating in the 1974 revision, which offered the chance of real progress. The two 1974 Decrees stopped the 'cascade' quality rating system and ordered that all AC wines be analysed and tasted.

Before 1974, a grower who made well over the permitted yield from a Grand Cru site could obtain the Grand Cru AC for up to 30 hectolitres per hectare of what he or she had produced, and baptise the excess yield with more modest names (Premier Cru, straight or *village* wine, and right down the line to Bourgogne Rouge and *vin de table*) in descending (or 'cascading') order. All the wine was the same, but the prices changed. *Génial!*

Now the grower has to opt for the classification he or she wants for the entire crop at the time of the *déclaration de récolte.* The system starts with a *rendement de base,* or basic yield, which can be adjusted each year by the fixing of a *rendement annuel,* or annual yield for that vintage, to allow for fluctuating climatic conditions. After 1974, a *plafond limite de classement* (PLC), or classification ceiling, was also introduced, allowing a further

**1983: Allowable yields per hectare in Burgundy**

| CÔTE D'OR APPELLATIONS | Rendement de base | Rendement annuel - 1983 | Plafond limite de classement |
|---|---|---|---|
| **Grands Crus Côte de Nuits** | | | |
| Bonnes Mares, Chambertin, Chambertin Clos de Bèze, Clos de la Roche, Clos St-Denis, Clos des Lambrays, Clos de Tart, Clos de Vougeot, Musigny Rouge | 35 hl/ha | 35 hl/ha | +20% |
| Chapelle-Chambertin, Charmes-Chambertin, Griotte-Chambertin, Latricières-Chambertin, Mazis-Chambertin, Mazoyères-Chambertin, Ruchottes-Chambertin | 37 hl/ha | 37 hl/ha | +20% |
| Echézeaux, Grands Echézeaux | 35 hl/ha | 26 hl/ha | +60% |
| La Tâche, Richebourg, La Romanée, Romanée-Conti, Romanée-St-Vivant | 35 hl/ha | 15 hl/ha | +100% |
| Musigny Blanc | 40 hl/ha | 37 hl/ha | +20% |
| **1er Cru Côte de Nuits** Same figures apply as for communes below | | | |
| **AC Communes Côte de Nuits** | | | |
| Chambolle-Musigny, Côte de Nuits-Villages, Fixin, Gevrey-Chambertin, Morey-St-Denis, Nuits-St-Georges, Vougeot | 40 hl/ha | 40 hl/ha | +100% |
| Vosne-Romanée | 40 hl/ha | 24 hl/ha | +100% |
| | | | |
| **Grands Crus Côte de Beaune** | | | |
| Corton Rouge | 35 hl/ha | 35 hl/ha | +20% |
| Corton Blanc, Corton-Charlemagne, Charlemagne, Bâtard-Montrachet, Bienvenues-Bâtard-Montrachet, Chevalier-Montrachet, Criots-Bâtard-Montrachet, Le Montrachet | 40 hl/ha | 50 hl/ha | +20% |
| **1er Cru Côte de Beaune** Same figures apply as for Côte de Beaune-Villages | | | |
| **Côte de Beaune-Villages** | | | |
| Aloxe-Corton, Auxey-Duresses, Beaune, Blagny, Chassagne-Montrachet,Cheilly-lès-Maranges, Chorey, Côte de Beaune & Villages, Dezize-lès-Maranges, Ladoix, Meursault, Monthelie, Pernand-Vergelesses, Pommard, Puligny-Montrachet, St-Aubin, St-Romain, Sampigny-lès-Maranges, Santenay, Savigny, Volnay | 40 hl/ha | 40 hl/ha | +20% |
| Aloxe-Corton, Auxey-Duresses, Beaune, Chassagne-Montrachet | 45 hl/ha | 45 hl/ha | +20% |
| Cheilly-lès-Maranges, Chorey, Côte de Beaune, Dezize-lès-Maranges, Ladoix, Meursault, Monthelie, Pernand-Vergelesses, Puligny-Montrachet, St-Aubin, St-Romain, Sampigny-lès-Maranges, Santenay, Savigny | 45 hl/ha | 55 hl/ha | +20% |

| 1996: Allowable yields per hectare in Burgundy | | | |
|---|---|---|---|
| **CÔTE D'OR APPELLATIONS** | **Rendement de base** | **Rendement annuel - 1996** | **Plafond limite de classement** |
| **Grands Crus Côte de Nuits** Bonnes Mares, Chambertin, Chambertin Clos de Bèze, Clos de la Roche, Clos St-Denis, Clos des Lambrays, Clos de Tart, Clos de Vougeot, Musigny Rouge | 35 hl/ha | 42 hl/ha | +20% |
| Chapelle-Chambertin, Charmes-Chambertin, Griotte-Chambertin, Latricières-Chambertin, Mazis-Chambertin, Mazoyères-Chambertin, Ruchottes-Chambertin | 37 hl/ha | 45 hl/ha | +20% |
| Echézeaux, Grands Echézeaux, La Tâche, Richebourg, La Romanée, Romanée-Conti, Romanée-St-Vivant | 35 hl/ha | 42 hl/ha | +20% |
| Musigny Blanc | 40 hl/ha | 48 hl/ha | +20% |
| **1er Cru Côte de Nuits** Same figures apply as for communes below | | | |
| **AC Communes Côte de Nuits** Chambolle-Musigny, Côte de Nuits-Villages, Fixin, Gevrey-Chambertin, Morey-St-Denis, Nuits-St-Georges, Vougeot, Marsannay, Vosne-Romanée | 40 hl/ha | 52 hl/ha | +30% |
| Morey-St-Denis, Nuits-St-Georges, Vougeot, Côte de Nuits-Villages, Marsannay | 45 hl/ha | 59 hl/ha | +30% |
| **Grands Crus Côte de Beaune** Corton Rouge | 35 hl/ha | 42 hl/ha | +20% |
| Corton Blanc, Corton-Charlemagne, Charlemagne, Bâtard-Montrachet, Bienvenues-Bâtard-Montrachet, Chevalier-Montrachet, Criots-Bâtard-Montrachet, Le Montrachet | 40 hl/ha | 48 hl/ha | +20% |
| **1er Cru Côte de Beaune** Same figures apply as for Côte de Beaune-Villages | | | |
| **Côte de Beaune-Villages** Aloxe-Corton, Auxey-Duresses, Beaune, Blagny, Chassagne-Montrachet,Cheilly-lès-Maranges, Chorey, Côte de Beaune & Villages, Dezize-lès-Maranges, Ladoix, Meursault, Monthelie, Pernand-Vergelesses, Pommard, Puligny-Montrachet, St-Aubin, St-Romain, Sampigny-lès-Maranges, Santenay, Savigny, Volnay | 40 hl/ha | 48 hl/ha | +20% |
| Aloxe-Corton, Auxey-Duresses, Beaune, Chassagne-Montrachet, Cheilly-lès-Maranges, Chorey, Côte de Beaune, Dezize-lès-Maranges, Ladoix, Meursault, Monthelie, Pernand-Vergelesses, Puligny-Montrachet, St-Aubin, St-Romain, Sampigny-lès-Maranges, Santenay, Savigny | 45 hl/ha | 54 hl/ha | +20% |

quantity (usually 20 per cent) to be accepted. As this involves obligatory tasting, and distilling of the entire production if the PLC is refused, many growers (especially in the Beaujolais) hold back from making this request, through a profound dislike of 'busybody' visits to their cellars.

In any case, it has to be said that, given the variable Burgundian climate, this kind of yield is often a pipe-dream. In many domaines, especially where there is a good proportion of old vines, growers often do not achieve the maximum allowed for their Grands Crus. Consequently there is an argument for widening the gap between these very special wines and the Premiers Crus and *village* wines. These can stand an increase in the allowed production in good years, whereas the Grands Crus will not, and should not, be so prolific. A move towards a lighter hand on the rein was made in a decree just before the prolific vintage of 1982, but perhaps at the wrong end of the quality scale, because red Grands Crus such as Corton had their basic yield increased from 30 to 35 hectolitres per hectare, while the whites jumped further, Chablis Grand Cru from 35 to 45 and Le Montrachet from 30 to 40. Le Montrachet's 1982 *rendement annuel* was increased to 60 hectolitres per hectare, which, plus a further 20 per cent PLC, gave a total of 72. In 1983, the comparable figures were 50 hectolitres per hectare plus 20 per cent, giving 60. Large yields affect the quality of white wine less than that of red, especially with the sensitive Pinot Noir, but these very generous yields for Grand Cru wine must impair concentration and extract. But again I know of producers who did not reach these permitted yields, to their credit.

As an example of how the *rendement annuel* can alter the *rendement de base,* the tables on pages 16 and 17 show those fixed for 1983 and 1995. In 1983, certain Grands Crus such as Echézeaux, La Tâche and Romanée-Conti, and communes like Vosne-Romanée, had their basic yields greatly reduced by the *rendement annuel* – in this case because of hail damage. But at the same time they were given very high PLC limits, which allowed for more AC wine to be declared, after tasting. In 1995, permitted yields followed a more normal course, while 1983 showed that there is flexibility in the system to take account of climatic aberrations.

The tasting requirement in Burgundy, supposedly operational since 1979, works quite well on the Côte Chalonnaise (with a certain amount of self-regulation) but not on the Côte d'Or. It has proved impossible in this immensely complex and fragmented area for every wine in every grower's cellar to be tasted every year. This, of course, does not worry the majority of growers, but logistically the scheme does pose genuine problems. In any case, the plan was to taste in growers' rather than *négociants'* cellars, meaning that an enormous amount of wine would have to be tasted in the few months after the vintage, before many wines 'disappeared' into blends. What happens in reality is that random sampling is done in growers' cellars, which acts as a mild deterrent, comparable perhaps to the random search operated by Customs.

But even if the tasting is done to the letter of the decree, there is still room for switching and deception by a determined producer. The INAO controls the amount of Burgundy sold in relation to what is harvested, but obviously there is room for manoeuvre, given the fact that major roads pass through Burgundy. The INAO reputedly tastes a producer's wines at least once every three years, but it is worth stressing that there is many an AC and a VDQS wine from other regions in France that has jumped through all the tasting and analytical hoops and come out disgusting! Strict adherence to all the rules in the world will not ensure delicious wine at all times – it comes down to the integrity and intelligence of the producer and the demands of an enlightened consumer.

The *Répression des Fraudes* does make periodic prosecutions, which sometimes even bite, at least financially. Where the AC system falls down in Burgundy, at least as a credible institution, is in the hypocrisy of some of its edicts – for instance, in the case of chaptalisation (the addition of sugar to the fermenting must, or grape juice, to increase alcohol). Legally, chaptalisation is permitted to add up to two degrees additional alcohol, 1.7 kilos of sugar added to 100 litres of must, increasing the alcohol in the wine by approximately one per cent. It is not permitted to go over the addition of nine kilos of sugar per three hectolitres of must and 200 kilos per hectare. Above all, the wine must have naturally attained the minimum alcohol level for its AC before any sugar can be added to the must. It is widely known that in 1984 and 1987, for example, many wines (especially reds) did not attain the minimum level and were consequently chaptalised way beyond the permitted amount – for they all finished up around 12.8–13 per cent as usual.

Burgundy must retain the right to acidify in years that need it, especially when too much potassium is in the soil. Many burgundies need additions of tartaric acid in order to keep well. There is nothing wrong in this if done with restraint: low natural acidities are a problem in other parts of France, especially recently. However, healthy soil that is not over-treated, allied to low yields, gives a natural, better balance than heavy chaptalisation and automatic acidification. Who needs wines of 13° anyway?

The hierarchy of the ACs is as follows:

***Grand Cru***
***Premier Cru***
***AOC Communale*** (*village* wine)*
***AOC Régionale*** (generic or regional wine)

**Village* or commune wine may also be described as 'straight', eg straight Meursault. Americans tend to use the phrase 'regular' Meursault.

The last category includes Bourgogne and Bourgogne Grand Ordinaire, Bourgogne Rosé Marsannay, Bourgogne Passe-Tout-Grains, Bourgogne Aligoté, Bourgogne Hautes-Côtes de Beaune and Bourgogne Hautes-Côtes de Nuits.

# The grapes

The grape scene is relatively simple in Burgundy although, given the difficult climatic conditions, continuous work is being done on clones in order to develop resistance to misfortunes such as grey rot. As a rule, the general density of planting of vines in the Côte d'Or is 10,000 vines per hectare, whereas in Chablis it is 6,000 per hectare. These are the principle varieties:

## RED

***Pinot Noir*** This is the most tantalising of the world's noble red grapes. In Burgundy, Pinot Noir is the red grape of the Côte d'Or and the Côte Chalonnaise, with only a tiny amount grown in the Mâconnais. It achieves heights unsurpassed anywhere when at its best in Burgundy, but it travels only tentatively. The finest examples of Pinot Noir outside Burgundy come from Oregon and Australia (Victoria and Western Australia), with California (Carneros and Santa Barbara) and New Zealand (Martinborough and Canterbury). These can be isolated cases, created by brilliant winemakers. It is also grown in Alsace, Austria, Germany (where the wines are light), Switzerland, Eastern Europe and northeast Italy, and it is vital to classic champagne.

Pinot Noir both buds and ripens early, and it is susceptible to spring frost and winter cold, as well as to cold temperatures during flowering. It likes calcareous, marly soils, but dislikes unduly hot climates, where the wines lack finesse – hence its lack of success in the Napa Valley of California. The dark green leaves are thick and of medium size, with small, cylindrical bunches. The grapes are close together in the bunches, which facilitates the spread of rot, given the right humid circumstances. The berries are blue-black in colour, slightly oval, with relatively thick skins, although less thick than in the early part of this century due to clonal selection. All the colour in the wine comes from the skins, as the flesh and juice of the grape are colourless. It is encouraging that in a thin-skin year like 1984, many growers still managed to produce wines of good colour, showing improved vinification techniques.

Considerable experimentation on Pinot Noir clones was done, especially at Echevronne in the Hautes-Côtes de Beaune. The work is carried out under the auspices of the regional department of the *Association Nationale Technique pour l'Amélioration de la Viticulture* (ANTAV), which is composed of representatives from the INAO, the *syndicats et associations viticoles*, the *coopératives*, the *chambres d'agriculture* and the vine nurserymen. A vast array of Pinots is grown under controlled and identical conditions, and the resulting wines are tasted blind against each other. There are Pinots from the Côte Chalonnaise, the Jura, Champagne and Switzerland, the Pinots *fins*, *moyens* and *gros*, as well as the high-yielding Pinot *droit*. Some Pinots are named after villages on the Côte, some after growers.

Work is being done on resistance to grey rot and virus diseases such as fan leaf and leaf curl, and on the relationship between yield, alcohol and quality. It is difficult to see great red wines being produced at over 35 hectolitres per hectare, but good wines, in a healthy year, can certainly be made with a yield of 40 hectolitres per hectare. After all, not every village Burgundy should be made for lengthy laying down – just as not all Bordeaux should play the role of a classed growth. But growers should be persuaded to adopt the most successful quality clones, even if they have to renounce the highest-yielding examples. There is no excuse not to, with the prices their wines command nowadays. Good results have been seen on the Côte d'Or from two Pinot *fin* clones, numbers 114 and 115, if they are not grafted onto excessively productive rootstocks. More recently 777, 667 and 828 have been favoured.

***Gamay*** Although this is the grape *par excellence* of the Beaujolais, it probably originated in the hamlet of this name next door to St-Aubin on the Côte d'Or. It is at its best on the granite-based, sandy-schisty soil of the northern Beaujolais, where the ten *crus* are to be found. It is also successful on the richer clay and limestone soil of the southern Beaujolais (although the wines should be drunk very young). Here, over-large yields can make the wine a pale imitation of the 'real thing', but very good Beaujolais can be produced at 50 to 60 hectolitres per hectare. Recommended clones include 509, 358, 222, 282 and 656, with the recent 787 heavily tipped.

Gamay covers about one-quarter of the Mâconnais AC area, and is significant on the Côte Chalonnaise, where it contributes to Bourgogne Passe-Tout-Grains (two-thirds Gamay and one-third Pinot Noir). It has very little importance on the Côte d'Or. Gamay can be found scattered around France, in Savoie, the Loire and the Ardèche, as well as in California.

The Gamay Noir à Jus Blanc, or Gamay Beaujolais, yields well, even after spring frosts. Its juice is white, as the name implies, so the colour comes from the skins. The compact grapes are grouped in cylindrical bunches encouraging the spread of grey rot under humid conditions. The grape ripens early, but the optimum picking time must be judged carefully if the must is to have a good natural sugar content, especially if the yield is high. If rain swells the grapes near or at the vintage, it is difficult to get good colour and extract.

Two other grapes, the César and the Tressot, are allowed in the Yonne for Bourgogne, Bourgogne Ordinaire or Bourgogne Grand Ordinaire. They are earthy varieties, even a bit 'foxy'. César (or Romain) has more merit than Tressot, but both are rare and invariably mixed with Pinot.

## WHITE

***Chardonnay*** Probably the most magic grape name in the whole world, eliciting cries of joy from consumers as they drink it, but often groans of pain as they pay the bill. The name 'Chardonnay' may have come from a village in the Mâconnais, or it could have been the other way round. Chardonnay makes all the best white wines from Chablis to the Mâconnais. It is one of the classic grapes of Champagne, and has recently been grown most successfully in the Ardèche, thanks to the efforts of Louis Latour (*qv*). It also produces excellent results in California, Australia, New Zealand and many other countries, with Bulgaria and northern Italy knocking at the consumer's door at more reasonable prices.

Chardonnay adores limestone soil and, in most cases, its wine ages beautifully in bottle. The vine has large thin leaves and the bunches are not so tight as other varieties, allowing air movement and reducing the risk of rot. The early budbreak makes spring frost a danger, but relatively early maturity makes it a good choice for areas with shorter growing seasons. It is a generous producer, but is susceptible to fan leaf, or *court noué*. It is not a member of the Pinot family, as was originally thought – the erroneous name is even enshrined in a Burgundian AC, Pinot-Chardonnay-Mâcon.

Chardonnay *moyen* clones which have proved successful on the Côte d'Or are 76, 95 and 548, together with 96, 124 and 131 if not encouraged to overproduce.

***Aligoté*** This is the second white grape variety of Burgundy, but it is not in the same league as Chardonnay. However, it yields well and ripens early and, in sunny years, the wine can be most appetising. In less ripe years the results are too acid. It has no potential for ageing in bottle and should always be drunk young. The best Aligoté wines tend to be produced in the northern part of the Côte Chalonnaise and in villages like Pernand-Vergelesses and St-Aubin on the Côte d'Or, although the latter are now rare.

***Pinot Blanc*** For a long time this variety was confused with Chardonnay, and not only in Burgundy (northeast Italy often got it wrong also). It seems rather a waste to grow it in Burgundy in the place of Chardonnay, as it does not have the zest of Pinot Blanc in Alsace. The wines can be rather heavy and plain. It is probably a mutation of Pinot Noir. There are one or two good examples on the Côte de Nuits, but it is a rarity.

***Pinot Beurot*** This is Pinot Gris, or Tokay d'Alsace. Although in the same Pinot family, the wine is more stylish than Pinot Blanc when planted in Burgundy, although it may be best in a blend. It is rare indeed, but occasionally appears in the Hautes-Côtes de Beaune and in Savigny.

Melon de Bourgogne is still allowed for Bourgogne Grand Ordinaire, but I have never consciously drunk it in this form. It is the same grape variety as the Muscadet of the Loire, but that is another story. Melon is now planted, however, in the new Vézelay vineyards in the Yonne. Sacy is grown (in diminishing quantity) in the Auxerrois, where it is usually made into sparkling wine because of its high acidity and low alcohol, essential prerequisites for transformation into bubbly. Sauvignon appears here too, in the VDQS wine Sauvignon de St-Bris.

## Life of the vine and vinification

There is nothing mysterious about growing grapes – it is just fruit farming. But healthy grapes are a prerequisite for making fine wine; they are the *matière de base*. They can only be achieved through the constant vigilance and presence of the *vigneron* and, if he is the owner, by constant checking that his orders are being carried out effectively.

The planting of a new vineyard is costly indeed. The old vines are taken out, the ground is broken up, earth is moved and replaced with new earth (which should come from within the appellation area), the soil disinfected (vital in the prevention of *court noué*, or fan leaf), and the right organic and mineral balance established. Then there are grafts and stakes, posts and wire, which vary with the density of the planting – usually 8,000–10,000 vines per hectare. Of course, some grafts do not take, especially after a severe winter like early 1985, so in the second year there might be costly replacements to be made. All the time there are expensive treatments to be maintained against pests and diseases, as well as fertiliser to be added, and on top of all this are the labour costs. Not until the 'fourth leaf', or fourth year, can *appellation contrôlée* wine be made from the new vineyard.

Soil analysis is relatively new for some *vignerons*, and there is no doubt that there were periods, for instance, when too much potassium was added – one grower on the Côte de Nuits says he has not added any for over 20 years. It is always tempting to fertilise generously, but excessive potassium is a sure route to detrimentally high yields and low acidities. Nitrogen must also be added with measured care, otherwise too much vegetation is produced, causing increased humidity around the vine and therefore increased risk of grey rot. Dehydrated manure is often used. As for weedkiller, some won't touch it, others insist on it, but what clearly emerges is that it should never be used over-enthusiastically; who knows what is being stored in the soil for the future? Grass sowing between rows limits soil erosion and provides competition for the vines which then have to delve deeper for nutrition.

Infectious degeneration of the vines, *court noué* or fan leaf, has been a problem in Burgundy, and the only cure is grubbing up a vineyard and disinfection, as well as the planting of resistant clones. Sometimes growers talk proudly of their small yields, but the tell-tale yellowish, deformed leaves give the game away. Not all small crops are healthy!

Grey rot is the bogey of Burgundy and it has by no means been mastered. It is ironic that this disease is welcomed under certain conditions in Sauternes/Barsac and in Germany, for it is none other than *Botrytis cinerea*. But it is a disaster when it spreads amongst Pinot Noir or Gamay grapes, reducing yields, destroying the colour cells and imparting an unpleasant taste to the resultant wine. Burgundian growers took to regular spraying against grey rot after the shattering experience of 1975 and, for a few years, it looked as if the situation was under control, but 1983 on parts of the Côte de Nuits proved that it was not. One answer seems to be to vary the chemical formula of the spray every two years, and certainly the grower has to be there to spray at exactly the right time. One spraying too few is often a false economy. Are Septembers now more rainy than years ago, or are there other factors, such as thinner grape skins and bigger grapes packed close together, which foster the conditions conducive to grey rot? However, it has to be said that the wonderful weather in years like 1988, 1989 and 1990 gave confidence. Mildew, the downy variety, and oidium, the powdery type, are often treated with fungicides, whereas in the past a copper sulphate and lime spray (Bordeaux mixture) effectively controlled downy mildew, or peronospora. This had the side-effect of hardening the grape-skins, probably making them more resistant to the spread of grey rot. It may or may not be significant that Beaujolais still widely uses Bordeaux mixture and suffers far less from rot than the Côte d'Or – but it is also less humid in summer in the Beaujolais, so it is not an entirely fair comparison. Burgundians who tend towards a more organic approach to viticulture have come back to the use of copper sulphate and other natural products.

Red and yellow spider and various kinds of moth all need careful and regular treatment at the critical times. Alternatively, natural predators can be encouraged, which is certainly better than total reliance on chemicals. The grape caterpillar which seems most to worry the Burgundian, especially in recent years, is the *ver de la grappe*, also known as *tordeuse de la grappe, cochylis* or *eudemis*. The most dangerous period is mid-July.

## THE VITICULTURAL YEAR IN BURGUNDY

**January** It is usually too cold and the ground too frozen to do much in the vineyard and, in any case, it is often unwise to prune too early. Those who had made a precocious start were caught by the extreme cold of 1985. Snow cover, of course, can act as protection for the vines if the temperature falls really low.

**February** February and March are when the main pruning takes place. This sets the whole scene for the eventual quality of the wine, because you can prune either for indiscriminate quantity or for reasonable cropping. It is the most skilled job in the vineyard, and good pruners are highly prized. Each vine must be treated individually, bearing in mind its strength, how it may have reacted to a previous big yield, hail or cold. Experienced pruners have a feel for each vine, something almost instinctive which guides their pruning clippers as they work. The following types of pruning are used in the region:

**Guyot pruning** Single-Guyot is the most common form found on the Côte d'Or and the Côte Chalonnaise, with double-Guyot in Chablis. The main, fruit-bearing cane, pruned to six buds, is attached to the lowest of three wires supporting the shoots and vegetation. A short cane, with two buds, is also left to produce fruit but, more importantly, to grow the shoots which become the next year's two canes – hence, poor pruning can affect not only the current year's crop but also the following one.

Vines are trained low in Burgundy, about 30cm from the ground, so that any warmth in the soil from daytime sunshine can continue to help ripen the grapes at night. High training is practised in the Hautes-Côtes, which is more economical and carries less risk of spring frost.

**Gobelet pruning** This is the classic method of pruning in the Beaujolais. The vine is really a free-standing bush, with three or four 'spurs' of wood, each producing a fruit-bearing cane cut back to two buds. The vigorous vegetation is tied up around a post, or occasionally trained between wires, resulting in a less bush-like appearance.

**Cordon-de-Royat pruning** This spur-pruning is found at the southern end of the Côte de Beaune, especially in Santenay and Chassagne-Montrachet. The vine is trained horizontally, with the spurs producing fruit-bearing canes pruned to one or two buds. Skill is needed to start off the horizontal training, but once set up, the vegetation is well spread out between wires.

***Taille à queue*** This is the style of pruning seen traditionally in the Mâconnais, with the producing branch bent over in a semicircle.

One of the most evocative Burgundian sights in winter is the smoke from the wheelbarrow braziers where the *vigneron* burns the prunings as he works up and down the rows. The smoke mingles with the frosty mist and the effect is a blue haze. It also warms freezing fingers, and the soil is enriched by the ashes.

**March** The pruning is completed during this month, followed by bending the fruit-bearing canes under the lower wires, avoiding damage to the buds. If earth has been piled around the roots to protect them from severe frosts, it is dug up and spread out. This airs the soil and helps distribute fertiliser. The fertiliser options here are: manure (probably still the best choice), nitrogen for the vegetation, phosphoric acid for successful fruit development and healthiness, and potassium for increased yield, improved must and to help the vines resist disease and frost. Getting the recipe right is a difficult task. Tractors for ploughing have been used for 35 years in Burgundy now which has caused soil compaction. This is also the month for grafting, using the *greffe anglaise*, a z-shaped cut which fits the French vine graft to the rootstock. In these northern climes, there is no such thing as grafting 'in the field', and these successful grafts will be planted in the vineyard the following year.

**April** Grafting continues, usually requiring about two to three weeks to take at a temperature of 20°C (68°F) in sand or sawdust. The *vigneron* fears spring frost, as by this time the vine is really vulnerable and it is often this fear which causes him to prune 'generously'. The red spider can also make a first appearance at this time. The main cane is fixed to the lower wire and, now that the sap has risen, the wood is more pliable. New vineyards are planted out this month. There will be grapes after three years, but *appellation contrôlée* wine only after four.

**May** The frost threat continues during the first week. Weeds are dealt with by weedkillers or ploughing, and treatments against spiders, moths, mildew and oidium are applied – frequently these can be combined in one spray. The timing of these treatments is critical, and a *station d'avertissements agricoles* issues advice based on the meteorological conditions. It is a frightening thought that mildew fungi can remain incubated for several years – those of 1975 survived the dryness of 1976 to reappear alarmingly in 1977. The successful new grafts are planted out in the nursery for their year's sojourn there. In the vineyard, unwanted, non-fruit-bearing shoots are removed.

**June** This is the month when the vines flower. Ideal conditions include sun and warmth, with minimum rain and wind. Good, quick, regular flowering ensures a healthy crop, barring later calamities like hail-storms. But if the weather is poor, *coulure*, or flower abortion, occurs, substantially reducing the size of the harvest. Any straggling branches are placed between the double wire in the middle and new shoots are attached to the upper wire by metal or plastic clasps or clips. Treatments continue, although preferably not during the actual flowering.

**July** Treatments continue as before, with growers totting up the cost. Ploughing along the rows is often effected, as well as the mechanical trimming of excess foliage at the end of the branches, which only takes away nutrition intended for the grapes. This is also the time when an altruistic grower might remove excess bunches in an effort to improve quality. This could give as much as a two per cent increase in natural alcohol if a crop is reduced by a third. Understandably, growers are reluctant to do this, on the assumption that quantity equals cash (if not reputation) but in years such as 1982 and 1986 it can be necessary. However, if it is done on a regular basis, the vine compensates and the exercise enters into a vicious circle of restraint followed by even higher yields. Hail is a risk during this month, and both rockets and aircraft have been used to disperse clouds or to make the hail fall as rain. As hail often happens at night, disasters still occur – parts of the Côte de Nuits in 1983 bore witness to the fact that nature cannot be completely tamed.

**August** There will be more foliage trimming, or *rognage*, plus general maintenance, such as repairing walls and cleaning around the periphery of vineyards. This is the month of the *véraison*, or the process of the grapes softening and changing colour. In the nursery, any rootlets which have appeared on the graft are removed. All the equipment for the vintage is cleaned, with all wooden vessels being soaked and rendered watertight. Bacteria can take a real hold on equipment lying fallow for a year, and there is no doubt that the arrival of stainless steel or enamel-lined vats has simplified this work.

**September** General maintenance and preparation for the vintage continues, with one eye on the heavens. Grape ripeness depends on so many things: the weather, the age of the vine, where it is planted, how much it has been asked to produce, how it has been cared for. The optimum moment for picking is when there is the right balance between sugar and acidity, but it is usually the former quality which is deficient in Burgundy, hence the need to chaptalise. However, acidity has been on the low side if you take a general view of the past 20 years, a phenomenon noted also in Bordeaux, and considered to be due in part to excess use of chemical fertilisers. Pick early and the risks from inclement weather are reduced, but there is more sugar to make up. Pick late and the acidity can go even lower and the resultant wine can lack balance and be without much projection of fruit.

The Côte Chalonnaise usually picks a few days after the Côte d'Or, probably due to vineyards at a higher altitude, with the Mâconnais starting before them both, often at the same time as the Beaujolais. To show how widely the start of the harvest can vary, below are the dates when the *Ban de Vendange* was called on the Côte de Beaune in recent years:

| | | | |
|---|---|---|---|
| *1975* | *25 September* | *1986* | *27 September* |
| *1976* | *30 August* | *1987* | *28 September* |
| *1977* | *9 October* | *1988* | *21 September* |
| *1978* | *7 October* | *1989* | *13 September* |
| *1979* | *25 September* | *1990* | *17 September* |
| *1980* | *6 October* | *1991* | *25 September* |
| *1981* | *23 September* | *1992* | *12 September* |
| *1982* | *16 September* | *1993* | *15 September* |
| *1983* | *22 September* | *1994* | *16 September* |
| *1984* | *29 September* | *1995* | *26 September* |
| *1985* | *24 September* | *1996* | *18 September* |

It can be seen at a glance that there is no neat correlation between date of picking and quality, with a fine year like 1978 being late, and another fine year, 1989, early. There is certainly an argument now for individual quality domaines to choose their own picking times, rather than being forced to follow the official start dates for each zone.

Picking is still done almost entirely by hand in Burgundy, in sharp contrast to Bordeaux. In 1983 the Gironde topped the list with 1,050 machines, while the Yonne had 27, the Côte d'Or 25, the Saône et Loire 16, with the Rhône (Beaujolais) right at the bottom with just one. By 1986 the number of machines in the Gironde had risen to 1,500. By 1991 in Burgundy, the figure was only 400: 190 in the Saône et Loire (principally for Mâcon Blanc), 150 in Chablis and 60 in the Côte d'Or. The Gamay's *gobelet* pruning is unsuitable for machine harvesting, and there is no advance on the 1983 figure of one for the Rhône (Beaujolais). Picking by machine in Burgundy will no doubt increase, above all for white grapes on large estates in Chablis and the Mâconnais but, at the moment, there is no pressing socio-economic need for it and much of the vineyard does not lend itself to machine picking, either on account of its topography or because of the way it is divided into small, often scattered, plots. Machine-picking white grapes leads to skin contact with the juice, so it only works well on healthy, ripe grapes.

**October** The vintage finishes this month and the grower gets down to making the wine – unless the grapes are sold to a *négociant* or a cooperative. This is also when old vineyards are grubbed up, with deep ploughing, manuring and disinfecting.

**November** Winter deep ploughing is accompanied by replacing any earth which might have fallen to the foot of a slope. Pre-pruning starts, cutting off the fruit-bearing main cane and leaving two shoots on the short cane for the main spring pruning. Some growers plough a furrow of earth around the feet of the vines to protect them from winter frosts, but others aver that the process is detrimental to the vine's root system.

**December** This month sees a repetition of the activities of deep ploughing, pre-pruning, preparing new vineyard land and earth adjustments. Pre-pruning is held up if the temperature drops below freezing.

## ROOTSTOCKS

Since phylloxera the European grape varieties must be grafted onto American or American/French rootstocks. Vine and rootstock must be well matched. Just as research and experiment with grape clones has been improved and extended, so has work on rootstocks. A particular rootstock on unsuitable soil can cause the grafted vine to overcrop, produce unripe or low-sugar grapes, or create *coulure* (failed flowering).

Successful combinations have been Pinot Noir clones 115 and 114 on rootstocks Fercal and 161–49C. Growers have found that 161–49C is particularly good on calcareous soil, giving grapes which ripen well, while SO4 can produce too much wood and grapes of less sugar content on the Côte de Nuits. A Franco-American hybrid is 41B, very good in high limestone soils and on high ground. Chardonnay clones B95 and B96 have done well on 161–49C on pebbly soil.

Most of these same rootstocks are found in Beaujolais, but there is also the Vialla on granite soils, probably of pre-phylloxera origin, and the pure American 420A, which thrives at high altitude in *crus* such as Chiroubles. In Chablis, with high lime and accompanying risk of chlorosis (a disease which causes loss of colour in leaves, due to lack of iron in calcareous soil), the most common rootstocks were SO4 and 41B, but the tendency now is towards 161–49C.

# Making the wine

Winemaking in Burgundy is as idiosyncratic as one would expect from a region of individualists. If you make a tour around any given group of winemakers, you will hear almost as many theories and views on the best way to make either red or white wine. A variety of different systems coexists, particularly with regard to procedure at vinification, or fermentation, and there is no absolute blueprint for success. However, the main themes are clear. It is also worthy of note that both a particularly brilliant maker of white wine and one of red have cited cleanliness as being the most important element in the whole process.

A brief look at the structure of the grape will give a clearer idea of the raw material. The stalk or stem accounts for three to five per cent of the whole, the skin ten to 20 per cent, the pulp or fleshy part of the fruit 70 to 80 per cent, and the pips two to four per cent. Within these component parts are distributed water, cellulose, minerals such as sulphates, potassium phosphates, lime and soda, sugars (glucose and levulose), acids (tartaric, malic and citric) and tannin. The stalks contain tannin, which, in excess, gives a bitter taste, and water, which dilutes the alcohol level. A small quantity of stalks can, however, give a wine backbone. The pips contain even more tannin, so great care must be taken with crushing and pressing, or far too much astringence will appear in the wine.

But the flesh and the skins provide the basis of both the must (the unfermented juice) and the wine. The colourless juice which comes from the flesh contains the sugars and the acids, while, during fermentation, the colouring matter in the grape skins of Pinot Noir and Gamay is dissolved by the alcohol and distributed in the must.

## RED WINES

The Pinot Noir grapes (for Gamay in the Beaujolais there is a different method) are brought into the *cuverie*, sorted for unripe or rotten fruit at the best domaines, and put through a crusher-stemmer. Many winemakers put back a proportion of stalks to strengthen the structure of the wine – perhaps ten to 20 per cent. There are growers who favour a pre-fermentation cool maceration to enhance aroma and colour, sometimes lasting for five, even seven days. Fermentation vats vary considerably, both in size and material. The traditional open wooden vats are still seen in many cellars and, whereas this type of vat poses problems in Bordeaux, the coolish Burgundian Octobers rarely result in temperature-control risks. The temperature can briefly go over 30°C (86°F) at the beginning of the fermentation, but it is usually not too dangerous and at night the temperature drops sufficiently for it to be a brake. In fact, it is much more usual to have to heat all or part of the must (in steam-heated, double-lined, copper bowls), in order to get things going, for a 'stuck' fermentation is dangerous – either because of the risk of oxidation (in spite of judicious addition of sulphur dioxide) or because of contamination by bacteria. Sometimes, when the must heating has been excessive, the wine can have a slightly 'jammy' taste.

Fermentation vats in Burgundy can also be of concrete or steel; some are lined with enamel or glass, and there is a limited amount of stainless steel, especially with the largest houses. Nearly all vats, of whatever material, are open, but there are some advocates of closed vats. In many cases, the cap of skins is kept in contact with the juice, for good colour extraction, by means of wooden poles, or *piges*. There is also a certain amount of treading by men, which surprises those who think this practice is now confined to the Douro Valley of Portugal. *Remontage*, or pumping the must from the base of the vat and spraying the top, is another means to the same end. There is a fair amount of tannin in the skins and the potential for aroma, so this process is vital if a quality wine is to be achieved. The yeasts are thus also spread well, essential when reliance is on natural yeasts for turning the sugar into alcohol. Many top producers only use indigenous yeasts, although good, local cultured yeasts have now been developed. Open vats can have a system of a permanently submerged cap, attained by the use of a perforated lid, but *remontages* are still necessary.

Chaptalisation, or the adding of sugar to the fermenting must, can be effected with a *remontage*. There are those who like to do this at the beginning of the fermentation, and others who like to do it in small doses as the fermentation progresses, but great care has to be taken that no residual sugar remains at the end. For red wines, cane or beet sugar can be used, with cane sugar for white wines. Chaptalisation, of course, raises the alcohol level, but it also slightly lowers the fixed acidity of a wine. The ratio of alcohol to extract is higher in chaptalised wines, and excessive chaptalisation also tends to mask fruit and aroma. So, the conundrum remains – what to do in Burgundy when natural alcohol is deficient, owing to a sunless year. My own inclination is to settle for less alcoholic wines, destined for young drinking, and rigorously to declassify Grand Cru and Premier Cru wines to village level when the modesty of the year warrants such action. In poor years in Burgundy these grand-sounding names often fail to reflect the real nature of a top *cru*, so let us cease to pretend and simply say that, in some years, this level of achievement is not possible. Is it so shaming when we are the victim of nature? After all, there was hardly a single 1972 Bordeaux Cru Classé worthy of the name!

As for length of fermentation, or vatting time, this varies between winemakers, and it certainly varies between years. In an excessively tannic year like 1976 (admittedly a rare occurrence – but nevertheless an example), some meticulous producers actually reduced their vatting time so as to avoid an imbalance of tannin. Some people also believe in shorter fermentation when the grapes are less than healthy. On the other hand, wines produced in a year of high production or only moderately sunny conditions can often benefit from a long fermentation.

However, all the main colour extraction is achieved in the first three or four days, although the extraction of tannin continues throughout the vatting. Increased body and extract can be added to a wine which is perhaps light owing to high yields (as in 1982) through the process of drawing off a quantity of juice during the fermentation, thereby increasing the ratio of solids to liquids. This results in a good deal of non-AC rosé wine, but it is a financial sacrifice which can pay off by greatly enhancing the quality of the remaining red wine. Ideally, yields should be controlled before this stage. Vatting times in the Côte d'Or generally vary between eight and 15 days, and there is no set of rules in this respect which will guarantee automatic perfection each time.

When the wine is run off the lees, the remaining skin and pips are pressed and the first pressing is almost always added to the free-run wine. Nowadays, horizontal presses are in use: Vaslin, Mabille and Willmes. More press wine can be added if the vintage is completely healthy. The solid matter left after the pressings is later distilled into the spirit called marc. The malolactic fermentation follows, either in vat or barrel. The malic acid is transformed into lactic acid and carbon dioxide gas by this process, softening the wine and preventing a later fermentation in bottle, a misfortune which sometimes happened in the past in Burgundy. Often a cellar has to be warmed to about 17°C (63°F) to enable the malolactic fermentation to take place – very cold Burgundian cellars create difficulties. I would go so far as to say that some growers' wines are bottled too late, way after the optimum point, just because they have had to wait so long for the malolactic fermentation to be completed.

Red wine is then taken off its lees and aged in oak barrels of approximately 228 litres for anything between one year and two, depending on the type of wine, the nature of the vintage and the whim of the producer – judgement might be a kinder word. Every type of oak seems to be in service, with wood from the Allier and the Vosges often favoured for red wine, as well as that from the Jura and the Limousin. However, oak from the Tronçais and the Châtillonais, the plateau of the Côte d'Or north of Dijon at Châtillon-sur-Seine, is also seen. The proportion of new wood in a cellar varies with the financial strength of a house and the needs of a year, although that is difficult to judge since the new casks have to be ordered well in advance of the harvest. In 1994, a new oak barrel, or *pièce*, cost 2,800 francs. The Pinot Noir cannot take excessive new oak, with its overpowering tannin and vanilla flavours, so the balance of new oak against old has to be just right. Grands Crus, for example, are more suited to new barrels than village wines. The width of the oak grain, how the oak staves are dried and how the barrels are toasted are all influential on the eventual taste of the wine. New casks can be seasoned, often using water, to remove excess astringence.

Racking, or the periodic transfer of wine from one barrel to another, thereby separating it from any stale solid matter which may have fallen to the bottom of the cask, is usually done three times before bottling – in the spring after the vintage, before the following vintage, and before bottling. The tendency is for less rather than more, as excessive racking can tire and dry out a wine. Burgundian cellars are usually cold and humid, so less evaporation takes place here than elsewhere in France. Nevertheless, topping-up is a regular operation, especially as in Burgundy the bung-hole is always on top, thereby leaving room for personal expression. Of course, the wine used for topping-up should be similar, but sometimes I suspect it might be inferior. If done too enthusiastically, it could contribute to the 'house style' of certain *négociants*' wines, but, as usual, conscientious winemakers will do their honest best.

A fining to clarify the wine is usually carried out before bottling, using whites of egg, gelatine, casein (a milk protein), isinglass (a fish product) and bentonite. Whites of egg seem to be favoured for red wines, but gelatine can be used to remove excess tannin (as in 1976). These substances bring about a coagulation of any suspended matter, which then falls to the bottom of the barrel or tank, leaving the clear wine to be racked off. Usually, the wines receive a light filtering before bottling, but some domaines feel this can affect quality (less flavour, body or extract?) and avoid filtering, often signifying this by a small slip label to warn the consumer that there might be some haze or deposit in the wine. Personally, I feel that super-clarifying can detract from maximum character in a wine, but when wine is shipped around the world, deposit is disliked. However, it is ironic to note that it has always been more accepted in a Bordeaux than in a burgundy, for no valid reason, unless it is that sediment in burgundy can be more hazy and less solid than it is in Bordeaux. A conscientious grower will have a flexible attitude according to the vintage, but will prefer a policy of minimum intervention.

Bottling is vitally important, and there are still some bottling faults in burgundy, oxidation and uncleanliness being the two chief culprits. Nowadays, the wine is assembled in tanks before bottling to achieve homogeneity and avoid the cask-to-cask differences of the past. Nearly all burgundy is cold-bottled, although a few houses pasteurise. It seems to me that absolute hygiene, a great deal of running water in the cellar, and limited but sensible use of sulphur dioxide should provide all the precautions needed by a careful winemaker.

## WHITE WINES

With these wines the whole process takes place in a different order, with pressing before fermentation. The stalks are not removed, and they help 'drain' the juice from the horizontal presses, which can be pneumatic or screw type. Oxidation is a great enemy of white wine, so a speedy but gentle pressing and a judicious use of sulphur dioxide are both desirable. The murky juice is then immediately run off into vats to stand and clarify – the *débourbage*. In large concerns, centrifuges are sometimes used, as the aim is to start with a very clean must.

Fermentation then takes place, either in barrel or vat. Nearly all fine Côte d'Or wines are fermented in oak, frequently new, perhaps Allier, Vosges or Tronçais. The ideal temperature is 15–20°C (59–68°F) and the fermentation should be lengthy, to extract maximum flavour and bouquet, with periodic rousing of the lees and yeasts to regulate the process. The cask needs to be filled to the right level to allow some air for the yeasts to work, but not too much to cause oxidation. The wine stays on its lees until malolactic fermentation is complete, which could be late spring, but is then run off into clean barrels for the rest of its ageing, usually with an escalating proportion of new oak, according to the wine's place in the hierarchy. In some cases, retention of a proportion of malic acidity can give more exciting and complex aromas.

Chaptalisation is usually effected right at the beginning of fermentation. The most usual finings for white wine are casein, isinglass and sometimes bentonite for excess protein. For fine white wines only a light filtering should be necessary because fermentation in *barriques* has a 'fining' effect itself, and the wines tend to fall bright naturally from their long *élevage* in cask. Some of the best wines are bottled at 18 months of age, others before that time. Some Côte Chalonnaise wines are bottled in the spring after the vintage. In the Mâconnais, more modest wines are kept in tank and bottled when needed, usually a matter of months after the vintage, and the wines are cold-stabilised by refrigeration to avoid tartrate deposit. On the Côte d'Or, allowing very cold air into the cellars usually brings this about naturally, and it would be a travesty to overtreat very fine white wines intended for ageing. A few tartaric crystals are a sign that a wine has been treated gently, which brings joy to the heart of a committed burgundy-lover.

## ROSE WINES

Rosé does not mean much in Burgundy, except for the rosé of Marsannay. The *vin gris* method is to press the red grapes in order to give a light colour, and then to ferment as for white wine. Alternatively, and more usually, the grapes can be macerated for a day or two and the juice drawn off when the colour is right – pressing and fermentation follow.

## SPARKLING WINES

*Méthode traditionnelle* wines have been made in Burgundy since 1822, but in 1975 a superior appellation, Crémant de Bourgogne, was created. Pinot Noir or Pinot Blanc, Pinot Gris, Chardonnay and Aligoté grapes are used (Gamay, Sacy and Melon can also be included) and very gently pressed; only the first pressings are retained for Crémant de Bourgogne. Fermentation is carried out and a *cuvée* is made which must be approved by a commission chosen by the INAO before it can be admitted for bottling and the *prise de mousse*: a secondary fermentation in bottle created by adding a dose of sugar and yeast to the wine. The wine ages for nine months and goes through riddling, or *remuage*, and then *dégorgement* to eliminate dead particles of yeast which have settled out.

This is now done by freezing the necks of the bottles to solidify the sediment, which is then easily removed. The bottles are topped up, their sweetness adjusted to correspond to the type of Crémant required (Brut or Demi-Sec), re-corked and 'dressed', and rested before sale. Crémants can be *blanc*, *blanc de blancs* (made from white grapes only) or rosé. It is a pity that Crémant de Bourgogne is not better known and distributed, because the wines are fruity and fine, generally of a very high standard. France takes about three-quarters of production, but Britain is the leading importer.

Bourgogne Mousseux does not have such strict conditions as Crémant with respect to base wine (its grape varieties, which include Pinot, Gamay, César and Tressot from the Yonne, ripeness at vintage, yields, methods of transport, pressing and vinification). This appellation now only exists in its red form.

## Growers and merchants

There is a tendency nowadays to 'pigeon-hole' growers and merchants into 'Goodies and Baddies'. Of course, like everything else in Burgundy, it is far more complicated than that. There are good and bad in both camps, and there are merchants (*négociants*) who are also important domaine owners. The traditional role of the *négociant* was to buy a multitude of different lots of wine, blend them, bring them up (*élevage*) and bottle them. Now, even that has changed, with a number of merchants buying in grapes and making wine themselves – a sign of healthy progress.

Growers often sell part of their crop to *négociants*, in order to improve their cash flow, and 'domaine-bottle' a proportion, which involves 18 months to two years of stock-holding on the Côte d'Or. The domaine-bottling is done either by the grower himself or by a mobile bottling unit, such as Ninot of Beaune. There is also a good deal of *métayage* in Burgundy, a rather feudal practice which can work well. Basically, an owner who does not want to tend his vines or make wine passes this responsibility to a *métayer* or farmer, who divides the crop with the landowner. It is a system which can be successful, but naturally it further confuses the issue of wine identification in Burgundy, as two differently labelled wines can be made by the same person. It is also frustrating when long-term arrangements cannot be broken and a really fine winemaker cannot reclaim control of some of his vineyards due to *métayage* contracts. *Fermage*, on the other hand, means the vineyard is let to a winemaker who pays rent for it and so has no obligation to share the crop with others.

The *négociant* business first started to flourish in the first half of the eighteenth century; some of those companies are still well-known today. In 1996 there were 120 *négociant-éleveur* businesses in Burgundy, belonging to the Fédération des Syndicats de Négociants Eleveurs de Grande Bourgogne, with 60 of them in the Côte d'Or, 33 in Saône et Loire, 22 in the Rhône (which covers Beaujolais) and five in the Yonne. The export market took 50.5 per cent of their turnover, France 49.5 per cent. The *négociant-éleveur* is equally important in Bordeaux and Champagne, with near identical turnovers in terms of millions of francs. His role is therefore fundamental both to the health of the Burgundian economy and to the supply of large quantities of wine as required around the world. The small grower, with a handful of casks to sell, is not going to be able to supply chains of hotels, or airlines with enough Burgundy to win friends and influence people. There is a place in the mosaic of international customers for both the small grower, with 'handmade' quantities of wine to sell, and the *négociant*, with important lots available.

The Burgundian *négociants-éleveurs* sold 1.53 million hectolitres (or the equivalent of 204 million bottles) in 1996, of which 45 per cent was AC wine from Burgundy, 12 per cent other ACs (mostly Côtes-du-Rhône), with VDQS wine, *vin de pays* and *vin de table* making up the remaining 43 per cent. The estimated *vin de table* figure is now 27 per cent, a considerable, and highly desirable, improvement on the 40 per cent figure I had to report when I first

**Burgundy's statistics for 1996**

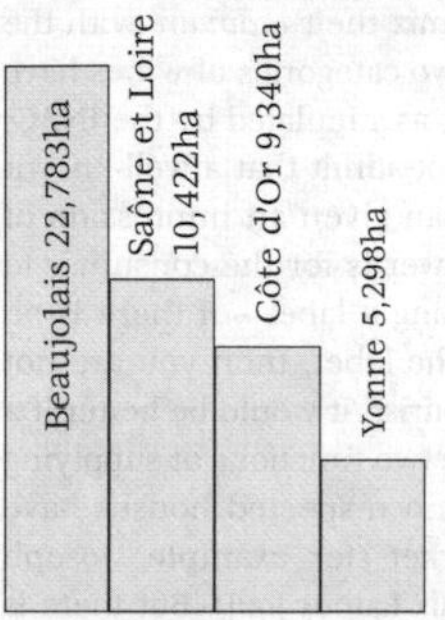


**Surface area in production 47,843ha**

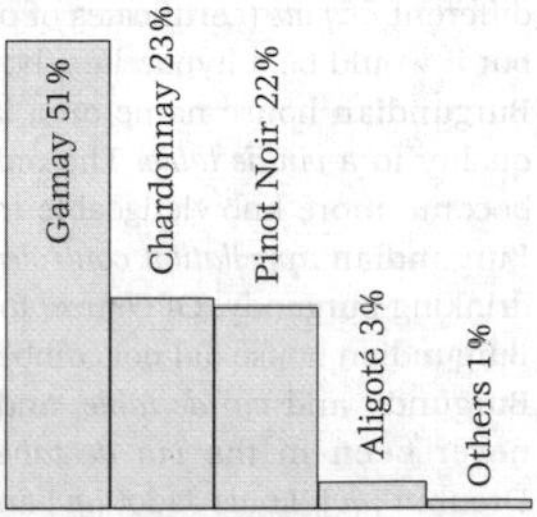


**Grape variety distribution**

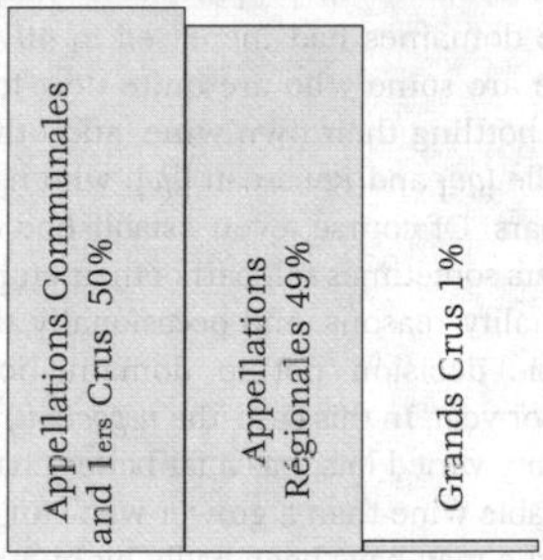


**Average production 2.5 million hl**

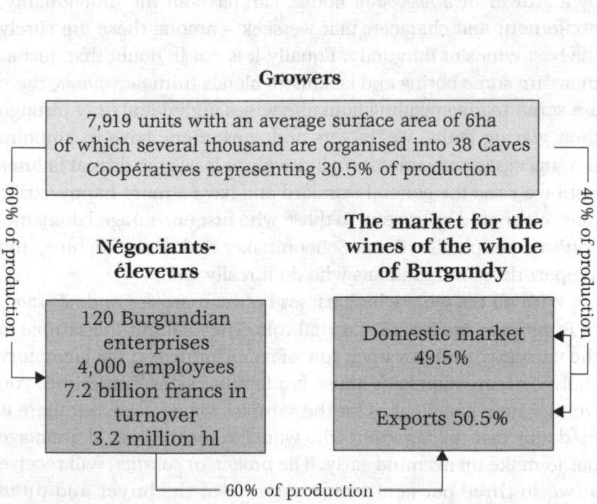

wrote this book. Nevertheless, it is still a pity that *négociants* in Beaune and Nuits sell this important amount of ordinary table wine. Is it never possible for them to mix their *ordinaire* with the AC names? Of course, nowadays the two categories of wines have different *acquits* (certificates of origin), as stipulated by the INAO, but it would be a hypocrite who did not admit that a well-known Burgundian house name on a label can given an impression of quality to a *vin de table*. The only answer is for the consumer to become more knowledgeable in reading a label – if there is no Burgundian *appellation contrôlée* on the label, then you are not drinking burgundy. Of course, to the purist, it would be better if a Burgundian house did not combine the two functions of supplying Burgundy and *vin de table*, and certain respected houses have never been in the *vin de table* market (for example, Joseph Drouhin [*qv*], Louis Jadot [*qv*] and Louis Latour [*qv*]). But there is the argument that healthy sales of *vin de table* can help to finance the costly business of buying and maturing fine Burgundy.

In 1979, 74 per cent of the Burgundian harvest was sold by *le commerce bourguignon*, or the *négociant* houses, and 26 per cent directly by the domaines or properties. In 1996, the proportion bottled by the domaines had increased to 40 per cent. In this category there are some who are quite new to the business of maturing and bottling their own wine, and others (like Gouges [*qv*], d'Angerville [*qv*] and Rousseau [*qv*]) who have been doing it for over 60 years. Of course, even established domaine-bottlers and direct sellers sometimes sell part of their crop to the *négociants* for fiscal or quality reasons, and occasionally they will take the really dramatic decision not to domaine-bottle at all in a particularly poor year. In this case, the *négociant*, with his ability to blend from many varied lots, has a far better chance of producing at least a palatable wine than a grower who can use only his own produce and who may have been badly hit by hail or rot.

There is no doubt that a fine domaine wine, whether owned by a grower or a *négociant* house, can have all the individuality, excitement and character that we seek – among these are surely the best wines of Burgundy. Equally it is not in doubt that, just as there are some boring and lacklustre blends from *négociants*, there are some really appalling domaine wines, individual only through their glaring faults. We, buyers and consumers, have to pinpoint the successes and lambast (figuratively at least) the dismal failures until we raise the general standard and have a more happy 'strike rate'. We should be grateful to those who first encouraged domaine-bottling, people like Frank Schoonmaker and Alexis Lichine, and support those Burgundians who do it really well.

With all the wine which passes between grower and *négociant* in Burgundy, brokers play a vital role. They submit the sample to the *négociant*, and row upon row of small bottles on the laboratory shelves of any merchant house is a familiar sight. Sometimes you wonder how long it takes for the samples to be tasted, but there is no doubt that the *négociant* who wants to get the best of a vintage has to make up his mind early. The broker, or *courtier*, will receive a two to three per cent commission from the buyer and up to three per cent from the grower. He never holds any stock, but it is his responsibility to ensure that the wine subsequently delivered is identical to the sample accepted.

There are also a few brokers in Burgundy who specialise in finding good domaines, grouping them together and offering a choice to foreign buyers. This is especially useful to those who do not like to wrangle over the price in French, and the best of this breed also act as a filter where wines of dubious quality are concerned. A few brokers fall into the trap of thinking that all domaine wines are by definition better than *négociant* wines, and they could add to the already swollen heads of some growers, but the most responsible perform a valuable service.

There is one other category of participant in the Burgundian wine trade that is peculiar to the region: the *commissionnaire en vins*. He is somewhere between a *négociant* and a *courtier* in that he does engineer sales between domaines and clients, but he also keeps stocks. He can hold a key position as a bridge between the somewhat hidebound, insular grower and the multifaceted export world without being weighed down by the heavy corporate structure of a fully-fledged *négociant*. Hence his prices can be keen for the relative quality of his wines – what the French would call a good *rapport qualité-prix*.

Cooperatives are singularly absent from the Côte d'Or scene apart from the well-run Coopérative des Hautes-Côtes de Beaune et Nuits. There is a good co-op at Buxy on the Côte Chalonnaise, a rather too powerful one in Chablis, others as dominant in the Mâconnais, and some reputable ones in Beaujolais, particularly in the north.

## BUYING BURGUNDY AT AUCTION

Burgundy bargains can be found at auction since the market is dominated by Bordeaux and many people do not think of the saleroom as a source of supply. However, there are frequently excellent lots of wine that sell for less at auction than they would on some wine merchants' lists. By keeping a careful eye on the catalogues, delicious burgundies can be found at affordable prices. Overall, few domaines have really made their mark in the auction room, with notable exceptions such as Domaine de la Romanée Conti (*qv*), Henri Jayer (*qv*) and Leflaive (*qv*), but many high-quality domaines appear from time to time and give burgundy-lovers a real chance to acquire their favourite wine at a moderate price. Leroy (*qv*) wines can go high, especially in the US, and de Vogüé (*qv*) is appreciated.

## THE TRADE IN BURGUNDY

Historically, Burgundy was at a disadvantage in comparison with Bordeaux when trying to sell its wines abroad, as there was no port and no direct river to the sea. The Yonne was used to some extent; wine was also taken both to Paris and Rouen for onward transportation on the River Seine. Nowadays, road tankers are used and France's fine system of *autoroutes* provides speedy travel. Hold-ups can occur at frontiers, and even more so

**Exports of burgundy in 1996**

| White burgundy | | Red burgundy | | Beaujolais | |
|---|---|---|---|---|---|
| Germany | 23.7% | Switzerland | 20.6% | Germany | 30% |
| UK | 23% | UK | 13.6% | Switzerland | 20.4% |
| US | 15% | Belgium and Luxembourg | 13.4% | US | 12.4% |
| Belgium and Luxembourg | 9% | Netherlands | 9.8 | UK | 9.5% |
| Japan | 7.3% | Germany | 9% | Netherlands | 6% |
| Netherlands | 7% | US | 8.8% | Belgium and Luxembourg | 5.7% |
| | | Japan | 6.3% | Japan | 3% |
| (Others | 15%) | (Others | 18.5%) | (Others | 13%) |

at Channel ports, but that is the fault of bureaucracy, not transportation. The Channel Tunnel has helped accessibility. Wine for the US is often taken to Le Havre, while exports to the Far East and to Australia are normally sent via Marseilles. Insulated containers should always be used in the transportation of wine to far-flung customer countries.

Exports of AC burgundy in 1996 reached a value of 2,750 million francs and 0.7 million hectolitres in volume. The principal customers around the world are broken down in the table above. While the UK and US still lead where white burgundy is concerned, it is noticeable that, overall, the primarily German-speaking markets are now vital to burgundy.

Who drinks burgundy? Both in France and in the export markets, much of the wine is sold in hotels and restaurants, especially the high-quality, very expensive wines. Here, the original cost of the wine is somewhat masked by high mark-ups, and if the hospitality is classed as entertaining, the whole thing is more easily swallowed. There is a degree of resistance to the high prices of some burgundy when it comes to the 'take-home' trade, and top burgundy is more likely to be sold by a fine-wine merchant than a high-volume supermarket. However, prices have been more sensible in recent years and many burgundy-lovers buy a good bottle and take it home to drink with simple food, rather than eat out expensively, and drink less well.

The importance of exports should make Burgundians extra-vigilant and aware of competition. The US, particularly, can fall out of love with a region just as fast as it can become enamoured of it, and the Burgundians should take care that they do not kill the golden goose. Many of the larger houses and domaines are conscious of this, but some estates, relatively new to exporting, might feel that the trend can only go upwards and that the market will absorb any wine at any price. This is not so, as numerous defections have shown in the past.

As long as burgundy delivers the quality behind the label, at a price which is not exorbitant for what the customer is getting, it will continue to keep old friends and find new ones. But greed and inconsistent quality are a certain route to failure in the long term.

## Enjoying burgundy

How do you understand Burgundy's nomenclature, and how do you translate the label on your bottle of wine? No one can be in Burgundy for long, or read a book on the subject, without noting the number of hyphens in the place-names. The simple explanation is that the wily Burgundian, at some stage, tagged the name of the best-known local vineyard on to the name of his village – hence, Gevrey-Chambertin, Morey-St-Denis, Chambolle-Musigny and right on down the Côte.

Vineyard names, or *climats,* often give an indication of their soil: Les Chaillots (siliceous pebbles), Les Grèves (small pebbles or gravel); or of the vegetation once found there. Les Charmes (yoke-elms or hornbeams), Les Genevrières (juniper bushes), Les Chênes (oaks); or even of local wildlife: Les Cailles (quails), Les Perdrix (partridges). Even walls built from stones collected in the vineyards are cited: Aux Murgers. Yes, Burgundian place-names are picturesque, designed to lure and to allure.

Burgundian spelling is often what the French would call *facultatif* – you have a choice. Thus, Dominode and Dominaude, Véroilles and Varoilles, etc. Burgundians also seem uncertain as to whether to put an 's' on the end of Passe-Tout-Grains, and Chablisien spelling can appear positively anarchic. Similarly, the use of definite articles may vary. Thus, Beaune Les Grèves is often seen as Beaune-Grèves. A vagary of Burgundian pronunciation is to say 'ss' for 'x', ie 'Fissin' (Fixin) and 'Aussey-Duresses' (Auxey-Duresses). Mercifully, none of this affects the taste of the wine. This book endeavours to give the spelling and usage chosen by the domaine itself and shown on its labels.

### BOTTLES AND GLASSES

All burgundy is in sloping-shouldered bottles, never in the square-shouldered bottles of Bordeaux. The traditional colour is a yellow-green, which the French call *feuilles mortes*. It is especially pleasing with white wines when matched with a yellow capsule;

for red wine, the capsules are red. It is rare to find magnums in Burgundy, in spite of the fact that this is the ideal size for laying down: Burgundians should be encouraged to use this large format in great years. The Domaine de la Romanée Conti (*qv*) sometimes bottles in very large formats. There was a brief experiment in the early 1980s with a 'Burgundian bottle' for AC wines, with 'AOC de Bourgogne' imprinted in the glass under the neck label. It was an aesthetic disaster and, happily for all, it died an early death.

Labels are comparatively simple in Burgundy:

| | |
| --- | --- |
| Joseph Drouhin<br>PULIGNY-MONTRACHET<br>Appellation Contrôlée<br>Mis en bouteille par<br>JOSEPH DROUHIN<br>Négociant à Beaune, Côte d'Or<br>13.5% 75cl | **Wine from a *négociant***<br>The name of the *négociant*.<br>The name of the wine.<br>Confirms AC status.<br>Bottled by Joseph Drouhin.<br>Address of the firm.<br>75cl, the standard EC and US content.<br>13.5%, the alcoholic content of the wine.<br>The vintage in this case appears on the neck label. |
| Mis en bouteille au Domaine<br>GEVREY-CHAMBERTIN<br>1er Cru Aux Combottes<br>Appellation Gevrey-Chambertin<br>1er Cru Contrôlée<br>1982 DOMAINE DUJAC<br>Morey-St-Denis (Côte d'Or)<br>13% 75cl | **Wine from a domaine**<br>Bottled at the domaine.<br>Name of the wine.<br>The fact that it is Premier Cru is mentioned in this case.<br>Confirms AC status.<br>Vintage and name of the domaine.<br>Address of the domaine owner.<br>13%, the alcoholic content of the wine.<br>75cl, the standard EC and US content. |

All the folklore and drinking songs of Burgundy might lead one to believe that the *tastevin* is the only vessel from which to drink its wine! But in reality, this dimpled, silver tasting cup (actually more like a small saucer) is only useful for seeing if a wine still in cask is clear of haze. With the *tastevin*'s wide surface, the bouquet of a wine is lost immediately, and gaining a true impression of a wine's taste is difficult against metal. So, for serious tasting and assessing, a glass is better.

The classic tulip-shaped glass is suitable for all wines, whether red or white, as is the approved tasting glass created by the INAO. But there are a few shapes widely used in Burgundy which seem to suit the particularly heady nature of the wines. It is as if burgundy needs more room in a glass to breathe and develop than Bordeaux; great burgundy has something slightly unrestrained about it, requiring space to express itself.

Below are the three glasses most often found in Burgundy:

(a) The shape most favoured by Burgundians for both red and white wine is the *ballon*, a Cognac-type squat glass, with a short stem and a huge bowl narrowing at the top to catch and hold the bouquet. It is extraordinarily reassuring to grasp a *ballon* in the hand, swirl the wine around, inhale deeply and then, finally, take a good mouthful and let it roll in over the palate.

(b) In restaurants in Burgundy, particularly, you are quite often given a kind of elegant goldfish-bowl, on a long stem. Provided the size is not too exaggerated, this can be extremely effective in showing off the qualities of red burgundy. it works well with great, rich whites, too
(c) There is another shape which I have not seen elsewhere, a large glass with a long stem and a generous bowl which tapers in only slightly towards the rim. This is a very traditional glass, and can allow a red wine to expand and open out.

(a) (b) (c)

The quality of the glass should be as fine as you can afford as it enhances the enjoyment of a wine. Riedel, the Austrian glass specialist, makes beautiful examples in perfect burgundy shapes. For all red burgundy Riedel's Vinum 416/7 is wonderful, while for mature red burgundy, in particular, the Sommelier 400/16 is unequalled. For all white burgundy try the Vinum 416/5, and for mature white burgundy I would suggest the Sommelier 400/0.

## LAYING DOWN BURGUNDY

There are two main advantages in cellaring fine burgundy: you can drink the wines when they are showing at their best; and you can buy them when they are first offered, at the keenest possible price. It is a sad fact that when a wine becomes ready to drink, it has frequently disappeared from the market, so judicious buying at an early stage is always to be recommended. Only Grands Crus from top-quality vintages should be considered for really long-term cellaring, but Premiers Crus make excellent mid-term drinking. Both Pinot Noir and Chardonnay make 'fragile' wines which are highly susceptible to temperature fluctuation, so laying down Burgundy should only be considered if you have access to a cool cellar – between 10°C and 15°C (50–59°F) is ideal.

## SERVING BURGUNDY

Burgundians almost never decant their wines. Their attitude is usually one of great simplicity: bring up bottle from cellar, draw cork, pour into glass. As their cellars are very cool this eliminates the need for a refrigerator for the whites, and the reds are left to do their developing in the glass. There is much to be said for this approach. Decanting is a controversial subject anyway, and experiments do not seem to have proved conclusively that the process is beneficial or otherwise. However, I have had young Burgundy poured into a glass carafe and served soon afterwards, with delicious results. The perfume seemed to be even more heady than usual. With old wines it can also be sensible to separate wine from deposit, but the particles in suspension can be tricky to handle and decanting needs a steady hand and a keen eye; decant just before drinking. Grand Cru Chablis can be fabulous when decanted.

Outside Burgundy, the most common fault associated with the serving of its wines is to offer the red wines too warm and the white too cold. Reds that are over-warm can be 'soupy' and really disappointing, while white burgundy, over-chilled or left too long in a refrigerator, can completely break up, taste flat and lose its flavour. Red burgundy is at its best served at 15–16°C (about 60°F), with young Beaujolais cooler, at about 13°C (55°F). White burgundy can have a bigger variation. The very finest, especially if they have some bottle age, can be served at around 13°C (55°F), but a simple Mâcon-Villages could be served a great deal cooler, at around 9–10°C (just under 50°F). But even then, don't kill it with cold – you will miss so much.

## TASTING BURGUNDY

To unlock the flavours and smells of fine burgundy is to attain a hedonist's nirvana. Trying poor burgundy is a deadening experience, with no impression of clean fruit on the palate, and either a tainted or an over-alcoholic 'mask' preventing you from seeing something true.

Both red and white burgundy possess a multitude of perfumes and tastes, and the more you find, the better the wine is likely to be. More modest wines should be attractive, straightforward and fruity, while wines from fine sites, in ripe years and made by gifted winemakers will keep you searching for adjectives to describe them until the last drop has disappeared from the glass.

All the following flavours have been ascribed to burgundy, more especially to the bouquet of fine bottles – they are not fanciful, just an attempt to try to pinpoint those heady, sensual aromas which assail the lucky drinker of good burgundy:

*Cherries, Raspberries, Strawberries, Redcurrants, Cassis, Apricots, Peaches, Figs, Prunes, Plums, Greengages, Quinces, Apples, Loganberries, Blackberries, Hazelnuts, Vanilla, Cinnamon, Acacia, Mayblossom, Hawthorn, Blackthorn, Honey, Liquorice, Laurel, Truffles, Chocolate, Tar, Grilled almonds, Roses, Violets, Hay, Toast, Wet fur, Wet leaves, Farmyards, Leather, Cocoa, Honeysuckle, Hung game, Oatmeal*

This is by no means a definitive list: the more burgundy tasted, the greater the experience and the vocabulary to express it. In addition, individual tasters differ in the qualities that impress them and the similarities that they perceive. There are other aromas, occasionally fleetingly encountered in burgundy, but which seem to me to occur more frequently in Bordeaux – tobacco and mint are examples (the influence of Cabernet, as opposed to Pinot Noir, or is it more complicated than that?).

Some descriptions are used far more often with reference to white wine than to red. Mayblossom, acacia and hazelnuts are more often associated with Meursault than with Pommard, for instance, while cherries, farmyards and raspberries are firmly in the red camp. But it would be misleading to categorise all these descriptions rigidly into red and white columns, because they do overlap and surprises have a habit of creeping up on even the most experienced taster – this is one of the joys of wine.

When starting to taste burgundy, it might be less confusing first of all to try to impress the basic scent and flavour of Chardonnay and Pinot Noir on the mind and senses. Then treat this as a canvas upon which to splash all the other sensory perceptions which present themselves. Let us hope that most of them will be positive, attractive and appetising, but inevitably there will be some less appealing odours and tastes too – perhaps dirty wood, vinegar or nail varnish. Discard those wines, but not without complaining to the supplier, and concentrate on finding those burgundies which astonish with their range of bouquet and savour. They are easy to recognise and difficult to forget!

## BURGUNDY WITH FOOD

There is a burgundy to go with virtually every type of food, with the exception of the dessert or pudding course, as there is no sweet white wine of the region. However, some of the most perfect meals finish with cheese and nuts, and this gives great scope.

Burgundian red wines, particularly the great growths of the Côte de Nuits, are superb with game, especially if it is well hung. One of the greatest gastronomic partnerships I ever experienced was in the company of that respected burgundy man, Harry Yoxall, at what was to be our last dinner together. We had roast grouse, *bien faisandé*, with a bottle of Grands Echézeaux 1952 from the Domaine de la Romanée-Conti. What was incredible was that the Grands Echézeaux had the rich, gamey smell of the grouse! Venison, hare and wild boar are also magnificent with ripe burgundy from a good year.

The combinations, of course, are infinite – mixed charcuterie with Beaujolais, Chablis with *andouillettes*, Meursault with *jambon persillé*, that splendid green-speckled Burgundian ham galantine. It was in Burgundy that the myth that eggs 'do not go with wine' was finally put to rest – what is better than a young Côte de Beaune with *oeufs en meurette*, lightly poached eggs with a red wine sauce? With the garlicky snails of the region, an Aligoté is ideal, while something like a plain sole or piece of turbot deserves a Chevalier-Montrachet or Corton-Charlemagne.

Robust dishes like *boeuf bourguignon* or *coq au vin* are more than welcome after a morning's tasting in cold cellars (or pruning on a February day), and a vibrant, even earthy burgundy is best here – perhaps a Santenay or a Mercurey. Unfortunately, some regional recipes which require a long cooking time are rarely found in restaurants, such as *potée bourguignonne* (ham, pork and sausages cooked together with vegetables), or *pouchouse*, made from fresh fish from the Saône simmered in white wine (if red wine is substituted it becomes a *matelote*, and the colour of the accompanying wine changes accordingly).

Two dishes often found in the Mâconnais are refugees from the Ain, across the Saône. *Quenelles de brochet*, or flaked-pike moulds, should really only be eaten in restaurants of impeccable reputation, otherwise you might come up against a floury, 'ersatz' version, while poached *poularde de bresse* is a dish of great subtlety, which is equally happy with either red or white burgundy.

At last: people realise that not all cheese has a miraculous effect on wine. While the soft, creamy goat cheeses of the Mâconnais and *fromage blanc* floating in cream are delicious with chilled Beaujolais, Epoisses and even Cîteaux often seem to be too strong and tangy for fine Côte d'Or. I prefer the Gruyère-related Comté or the Savoyard Beaufort, one of the great, unsung cheeses of the world.

Whatever you do, be adventurous with burgundy. It is not a delicate blushing violet, to be protected against all other flavours – on the contrary, it relishes competition! Mix the metaphors and the national cuisines. Try great Chablis with serrano ham, ripe red burgundy with Cantonese duck and one of the Montrachet satellites with steamed lobster and noodles. Experiment and learn – I do not happen to like white burgundy with caviar, but you might!

## Vintages

As with any wine area, there is a general picture for each vintage, on which there is over-painting by individual growers. A poor winemaker will not suddenly produce tremendous wine in a fine year, and a skilled winemaker can make surprisingly attractive wine in a poor one. With older vintages, the assessments really only apply to Grands Crus and the top Premiers Crus.

**1996** We are extraordinarily lucky to have this great pair of vintages, 1995 and 1996. Some give the edge to the whites in '95 and the reds in '96, but I am reluctant to generalise. In 1996, flowering was quick and successful and the summer fine, with a dry sunny September. The harvest was hugely healthy and , where excessive yields have been avoided, both red and white wines from top sites will be 'keepers'. Look for great *terroir* individuality in this vintage. Top tip: go for Chablis '96.

**1995** An exciting vintage, but one must have the financial means to acquire it! The reds have good colour, acidity and natural alcohol and the wines should develop real personality. Quantities are low, with depth, fruit and extract at top level. White burgundy is excellent, with the heat of July and August giving small, concentrated grapes. Rich musts with high natural sugar combine with ideal acidity levels – and this equals real quality, with the potential to age. Beaujolais is terrific in 1995, with a tempting quality-price ratio.

**1994** Great heat in August was followed by rain in September (particularly on the 20th) and this dashed hopes of a top-ranking vintage. There is good fruit, colour and acidity in the reds, which will develop before the 1993s. Buy up this vintage if you can – the best domaines, and their best sites – it is a year where old vines, late picking and selection in vineyard and cellar have paid off royally. The Côte de Nuits is probably more favoured than the Côte de Beaune. The whites will not be great keepers – enjoy them in young to middle-age. There are particularly good Meursaults and Corton-Charlemagnes. Beaujolais was picked early and is good.

**1993** A fairly tricky year, including hail, storms and rain but also good sun and warmth in the the day from mid-July to the end of August. Flowering was consistent and early. Hopes were very high at the beginning of September with good maturity, but intermittent rain at harvest demanded careful timing. The best wines, as always, come from skilled winemaking involving selection and controlled yields. The top reds are majestic and I am incresingly impressed with their structure and character – many are quite fabulous. The whites are more modest but many are attractive.

**1992** From May to August, every month except June had higher temperatures than normal. Flowering in June was good and early. The first half of July received 80–90 per cent of the monthly rainfall but the second half benefited from high temperatures. August was very hot and sunny, giving excellent véraison, but there was some rain in September. The white wines are undoubtedly fine throughout all the regions – I feel they may be for mid-term, rather than long-term, delight. The reds need careful selection, and are mostly soft and forward.

**1991** The weather was good right up to the harvest, and Burgundy was very little damaged by the frost which had affected so much of the rest of France on April 22nd. Some parts of the Côte de Nuits had suffered from hail in June, but the main problem was that the heavens opened on the date of the *Ban de Vendange* (25 September). The reds are variable but there are excellent, concentrated examples, and they are very good value. They will keep well. The whites are not as well defined, but many are drinking very well now. The Mâconnais and the Beaujolais benefited from the fact that the harvest in these areas was completed before the rains.

**1990** Picking took place in ideal conditions after a long, hot, dry summer. The yield was large for both red and white wines but acidities were generally better than in 1989. Chablis made excellent wines for the second year running and the Côte de Beaune whites were better balanced than many of their respective '89s, if not as exciting as the best of the earlier vintage. Although a few growers claim to have made better red wines in 1989, most of the '90 reds are more concentrated in all respects. They have a wonderful richness of fruit and an opulence of flavour similar to the '85s. Like that vintage, they will probably drink well early on, but they have the structure to keep well, too. Once again, there were delicious wines from Beaujolais and the Mâconnais, although the latter was sometimes dizzily alcoholic.

**1989** A very promising early vintage was diluted somewhat by rainfall in the fortnight before picking. Acidities were on the low side overall and – in contrast to 1988 – the yield was higher for the red wines than for the whites. As a result, the reds suffered from some dilution, but they are ripely flavoured wines with considerable charm, for relatively early drinking. The top wines have a hedonistic flavour which is very 'come-hither'! The best Chablis are outstanding as are the best Côte de Beaune whites; but some of the latter can be over-alcoholic and seriously lacking in acidity. Excellent quality in the Mâconnais, the Côte Chalonnaise and, especially, in the Beaujolais.

**1988** After a mild winter, wet spring and hot, dry summer, the harvest took place in ideal conditions. The crop was large, unexpectedly so for the white wines, and consequently some Chablis and Côte de Beaune whites tend to lack depth; others are textbook. The best reds are excellent: concentrated, firm and tannic – aromatic, flavoury wines for the long haul, with less of the lush, ripe fruit that is found in the '85s, '89s and '90s, but perhaps more power. Some very good whites from Pouilly-Fuissé that will benefit from keeping.

**1987** One of the rare years when the natural sugar level of the reds was higher than in the whites. Much depended on whether people harvested before or after the rain. Picking was late and there was some rot, but good domaines sorted out affected grapes. Most of the wines lack concentration (except when yields were very small), but there are softly attractive reds already drinking well in the mid-1990s, and whites are fresh and forward, if without a great deal to say for themselves.

**1986** A good late flowering promised well, but late summer storms encouraged rot on the plain. However, most of the vintage took place in glorious weather and the crop was nearly as big as 1982's. As a result, most reds lack concentration and definition – others appear charming, but the beauty and consistency of the '85s is not there. The white wines have style and elegance. The Côte Chalonnaise, the Mâconnais, the Beaujolais *crus* and Chablis were all most successful.

**1985** The particularly severe winter hit the headlines: in January, the temperature fell to -25˚C (-13˚F), while in February it hit a mere -15˚/20˚C (5–-4˚F). The worst damage was in Chablis and the lower parts of the Côte de Nuits, forcing considerable replanting. However, in the vital three months between the flowering and the vintage, temperature and sunshine were above average and rainfall below. September and October were glorious and, as there was so little rain, the grapes were incredibly healthy. The wines are beautifully clean, radiantly fruity and attractive, with the rich texture and seduction of a really ripe vintage. This is a luscious vintage, which appeared delicious relatively young, but which has not lasted consistently well at all levels. However, the best reds are a joy. The top whites have the balance and fat to last for years and are great wines.

**1984** Cold weather in September prevented the spread of rot, but inevitably it also precluded real ripeness, and the wines were very low in natural alcohol. As a result, chaptalisation came into its own, and there are undoubtedly unbalanced wines as a result. But it is also a pleasant surprise to see how successful some wines appear, with clean, fruity qualities. However, they do not have depth and many are past their best.

**1983** The best wines confirm that this was the finest vintage since 1978. But rot and hail stamped their imprints on a fair number of wines. Where these twin scourges were avoided, there are remarkable wines of power and concentration, with a good deal of tannin which is more penetrable than it was in 1976. This was a vintage to lay down, something for those who say modern burgundy is 'too light'. However, in the mid-1990s, almost all the reds had advanced colours; some have a tell-tale dry mousiness when tasted. The whites have great body and power, though a few seem to have too much (natural) alcohol on the nose. The best are wonderful now.

**1982** A record harvest, which had the unhappy side-effect of overcropping from Pinot Noir. Consequently, some reds were shadows of their normal selves; others were given too much of a helping hand or suffered from heating processes to extract colour. There were many fruity, gulpable wines for young drinking, and where a winemaker ran off a good deal of surplus juice during the vinification process, there was more structure. Whites were relatively forward, but delicious and easy.

**1981** Hail tainted many wines, while others just had a dry finish. A few, somewhat miraculously, tasted good and concentrated, partly due to the small yield. The whites had firm acidity, and the grandest of them showed well.

**1980** A controversial vintage, which unfortunately masked the reality of the situation. Where the grower treated wisely against rot, there were some very creditable wines, especially at reputed domaines and particularly on the Côte de Nuits. These were reds of style and fine flavour, but most should have been drunk by now. The whites did not have much character.

**1979** A large vintage, which inevitably brings an element of variability to the scene. Many wines had most attractive fruit and charm with an infinitely enticing taste, and the grandest wines are drinking splendidly now. The top Grand Cru and Premier Cru whites share these qualities.

**1978** An exceptional vintage, and a late one, where both reds and whites have concentration, complexity and real interest – they can still be splendid. There is fruit on a sound structure, giving wines which are perfect candidates for long-term cellaring. It is the flavour and individuality of each *cru* and *climat* which really impresses. They are the most 'gamey' reds I know.

**1977** The wines were not marvellous, but could have been a lot worse – only the fine September weather saved the vintage from disaster. The reds are now old and dry – only the very best wines are not marked by this characteristic. The whites were better, everywhere, but they had no real pretensions.

**1976** These wines are really atypical Burgundy, overloaded with tannin which sometimes succeeds in masking the fruit. Where the fruity character can break through, there are some exotic wines which have kept well, and there is nearly always a concentrated 'roasted' character to them. The whites were rich and low in acidity, and many were flat or blowsy at ten years old. The top Chablis were better balanced, although their fat character made them closer to the Côte de Beaune in style.

**1975** A year all but ruined by rot, and the red wines consequently had an unhealthy brown colour and a tainted taste. The whites on the Côte d'Or were slightly better, although most have now maderised. But Chablis produced wines of breed and balance, many of them gems.

**1974** Fairly firm reds, with some body to them, but many were rather dull-tasting and lacked individuality. The whites had more interest, and some improved in the bottle.

**1973** A very large vintage which produced lightish wines of charm and fruit. The whites had low natural acidity, and were generally at their best young. A risky vintage now.

**1972** The best reds developed surprisingly well throughout the 1970s and 1980s, and now many are firm and well structured, with good fruity character. Occasionally, they are a little green. The whites also suffered from lack of ripeness, but some recovered well.

**1971** A very ripe vintage, in some instances overripe, with lovely richness and opulence. The best are a heady experience, while some are too full-blown. Patches of hail on the Côte d'Or affected a few wines. Most of the whites are blowsy now, although the best balanced, including Chablis, still amaze.

**1970** A large vintage of soft, fruity wines. They were most attractive up to the mid-1980s, but both red and white should now have been drunk, except in the case of certain Grands Crus.

**1969** A superb vintage, stamped by the breed of the wines. The underlying acidity ensured that the wines lasted well, and they have that quality of great appellation character which is the hallmark of a fine vintage. All the whites, including Chablis, were exceptionally good.

**1967** When the reds were not over-chaptalised, there were some attractive bottles, and the whites had breed. All should have been drunk by now.

**1966** A highly successful year, with quantity and quality.

**1964** Very good, definite-tasting wine, both white and red.

**1962** Very good wines, with the fine balance giving them longevity. Extremely elegant whites, now mostly elderly.

**1961** Small crop of very good wines, with the concentration to taste magnificent at 25 years old and more in the best instances.

**Some older vintages of distinction:**
1959 (especially for reds), 1957, 1955, 1953, 1952 and 1950 (both better for whites than reds), 1949, 1948, 1947, 1945, 1943, 1937, 1935, 1934, 1933, 1929, 1928, 1926, 1923, 1920, 1919, 1915, 1911, 1906, 1904.

## Stars of recent years

**The 1990s** d'Angerville, Comte Armand, Château de Chambolle-Musigny, Robert Chevillon, Bruno Clair, Coche-Dury, Joseph Drouhin, Dujac, J Faiveley, Jean-Noël Gagnard, Geantet-Pansiot, Gros Frère & Soeur, Anne & François Gros, Anne-Françoise Gros, Jean Gros, Alain Hudelot-Noëllat, Louis Jadot, Henri Jayer, Georges Jayer, Michel Lafarge, Comtes Lafon, Leflaive, Leroy, Méo-Camuzet, de Montille, Jacques Prieur, André Ramonet, Domaine de la Romanée-Conti (historic wines), Joseph Roty, Emmanuel Rouget, Georges Roumier, Armand Rousseau, Sauzet, Comte Georges de Vogüé

**1989** Marquis d'Angerville, Domaine de l'Arlot, Comte Armand, Bachelet, Simon Bize & Fils, Robert Chevillon, Bruno Clair, de Courcel, Joseph Drouhin, Dujac, J Faiveley, Henri Gouges, Gros Frère & Soeur, Anne & François Gros, Anne-Françoise Gros, Jean Gros, Alain Hudelot-Noëllat, Louis Jadot, Henri Jayer, Robert Jayer-Gilles, Michel Lafarge, Comtes Lafon, Leflaive, Olivier Leflaive Frères, Leroy, Méo-Camuzet, Georges Mugneret, Mugneret-Gibourg, Ponsot, Domaine de la Romanée-Conti, Emmanuel Rouget, Armand Rousseau, Tollot-Beaut & Fils, Comte Georges de Vogüé

**1988** Domaine de l'Arlot, Denis Bachelet, Robert Chevillon, Joseph Drouhin, Dujac, J Faiveley (especially Clos des Cortons), Henri Jayer, Michel Lafarge, Leflaive, Méo-Camuzet, Alain Michelot, Domaine de la Romanée-Conti, Armand Rousseau

**1987** Joseph Drouhin, Dujac, Jean Gros, Henri Jayer, Michel Lafarge, Comtes Lafon (white), Armand Rousseau

**1986** Michel Colin-Deléger, Henri Jayer, Michel Lafarge, François & Jean-Marie Raveneau (Chablis), Domaine de la Romanée-Conti (attractive and good value)

**1985** Robert Ampeau, Robert Chevillon, de Courcel, Joseph Drouhin, Jean Gros, Henri Jayer, Michel Lafarge (Volnay Clos du Château des Ducs bigger than most '85s), Comtes Lafon, Leflaive, Ponsot, Daniel Rion & Fils, Domaine de la Romanée-Conti, Armand Rousseau

**1984** Domaine de la Romanée-Conti, Rousseau

**1983** All the great whites: try comparing the Corton-Charlemagnes of Bonneau du Martray and Louis Latour; of Leflaive and Etienne Sauzet. Bruno Clair, J Faiveley, Alain Hudelot-Noëllat, Louis Jadot, Henri Jayer, Michel Lafarge, Louis Latour, de Montille, Pousse d'Or, Domaine de la Romanée-Conti, Armand Rousseau

**1982** Simon Bize & Fils, Bonneau du Martray (white), Bruno Clair, Joseph Drouhin, Jean Grivot, Jean Gros, Bernard Hudelot, Henri Jayer, Jacqueline Jayer, Michel Lafarge, Leflaive, Comtes Lafon, Parent, Armand Rousseau

**1981** Domaine de la Romanée-Conti, Rousseau

**1980** Dujac, J Faiveley, Henri Jayer, Domaine de la Romanée-Conti, Armand Rousseau

# Wines and villages

In this section, detailed information is given on each of the five Burgundy areas and their villages/appellations, setting the accompanying profiles of selected domaines and their wines in context in terms of soil, topography, climate and history.

The areas and the villages/appellations within them are arranged in geographical order, from north to south. (The maps at the beginning of each area section show the principal villages/appellations and can be a quick source of reference.)

For the Yonne, Côte Chalonnaise, the Mâconnais and Beaujolais, the area's principal producers are profiled. For the Côte d'Or, because of its sheer size and the variety contained within it, a personal selection of producers from each village/appellation has been included, with a discussion of their best wines. For fuller details and a more comprehensive listing of Côte d'Or producers, refer to the A–Z of Burgundy producers.

The symbols ● ○ ◑ denote red, white or rosé wine is produced. Figures for holdings *en metayage* or *en fermage,* in the entries, are in addition to the main holdings figure.

# Wines of the Yonne

## ○ CHABLIS

Chablis produces stupendous wines and contentious people. They can never quite agree among themselves which villages and slopes should fall within the appellation and which should not, whether Portlandian limestone is as good as Kimmeridgian, whether or not to use wood in the *élevage* of the wines, whether to hand or machine harvest (although 85 per cent now opt for the latter), and even whether the aspersion method of frost protection (*see* page 51) is ultimately beneficial – the man who, in my view, makes the best Chablis today has serious reservations about the practice.

The one aspect of the Chablis saga that has never been in dispute is the status of the Grands Crus, which have remained inviolate since the creation of the AC in 1938. All seven Grands Crus are on the slopes of the huge hill over the little Serein river from Chablis itself. They are:

| | | | |
|---|---|---|---|
| *Blanchot* | *12.72 ha* | *Preuses* | *11.44 ha* |
| *Bougros* | *12.63 ha* | *Valmur* | *13.20 ha* |
| *Les Clos* | *26.05 ha* | *Vaudésir* | *14.71 ha* |
| *Grenouilles* | *9.38 ha* | | |

The name La Moutonne is used for wine from a 2.35 hectare parcel of Preuses and Vaudésir, so it is considered as a Grand Cru.

The Premiers Crus area is currently being expanded, and here there is serious contention. It is difficult to judge these new plantings until the vines are older, although interested parties already think the quality is of sufficient standard. The nomenclature of Premiers Crus in Chablis has always been complicated, with a mass of alternative names. The principal Premiers Crus are listed overleaf and, with them, where applicable, are the vineyards which have the right to call themselves by the better-

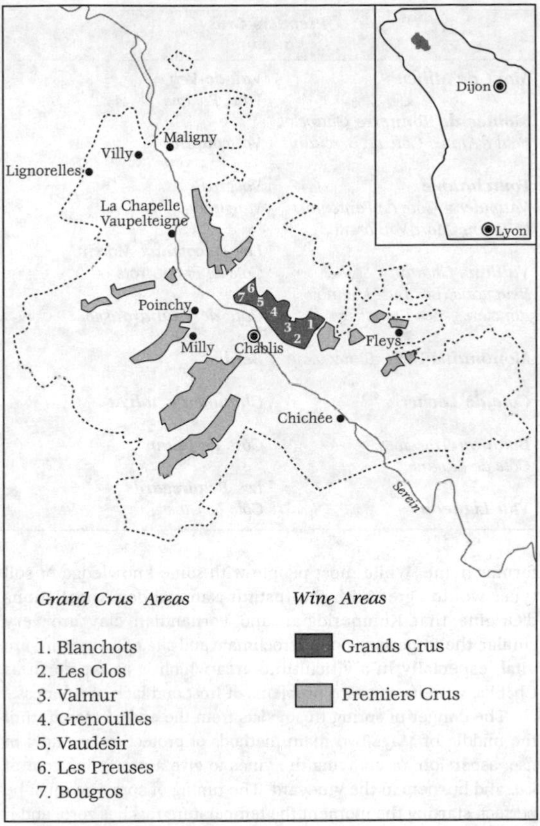


known name. It is worth remembering here that Chablisien spelling is notoriously idiosyncratic. Nowadays, the majority of wines are gathered under the main Premier Cru titles, which certainly makes for ease of marketing.

Naturally, there is far greater disparity of quality between the Premiers Crus than between the Grands Crus, which are in another category as far as richness and concentration are concerned. The Premiers Crus are scattered over a clutch of villages, some of them outlying. These villages include Fyé, Fleys, La Chapelle-Vaupelteigne, Poinchy, Fontenay, Maligny, Milly, Chichée and Beines, as well as the town of Chablis itself. Vau-de-Vey, situated in the commune of Beines, is in fact a new Premier Cru.

The villages which gained most from the extension of the vineyard area are Maligny, Lignorelles and Villy; at Maligny, particularly, much vineyard area hitherto defined as Petit Chablis was upgraded to Chablis, contributing to the decline of the

| ***Premiers Crus*** *Vineyards* | |
|---|---|
| ***Mont de Milieu*** | ***Vau-de-Vey*** *Vaux Ragons* |
| ***Montée de Tonnerre*** *Chapelot, Pied d'Aloue, Côte de Bréchain* | ***Vaucoupin*** |
| ***Fourchaume*** *Vaupulent, Côte de Fontenay, l'Homme Mort, Vaulorent* | ***Vosgros*** *Vaugiraut* |
| ***Vaillons*** *Châtains, Séchet, Beugnons, Les Lys, Mélinots, Roncières, Les Epinottes* | ***Les Fourneaux*** *Morein, Côte de Prés Girots* |
| | ***Côte de Vaubarousse*** |
| ***Montmains*** *Forêt, Butteaux* | ***Berdiot*** |
| ***Côte de Léchet*** | ***Chaume de Talvat*** |
| ***Beauroy*** *Troesmes, Côte de Savant* | ***Côte de Jouan*** |
| ***Vau Ligneau*** | ***Les Beauregards*** *Côte de Cuissy* |

former name. While most people with some knowledge of soil types would agree with the Institut National des Appellations d'Origine that Kimmeridgian and Portlandian clay are very similar, the importance of microclimate and site of a vineyard are vital, especially in a viticultural area which is as far north as Chablis, with its constant problems of frost and lack of ripeness.

The danger of spring frost exists from the end of March until the middle of May. Two main methods of protection are now in use: aspersion, or spraying the vines to give a protective coat of ice, and burners in the vineyard. The timing of spraying must be perfect, starting the moment the temperature reaches zero, and it must be uninterrupted, continuing until the temperature rises above zero again – a blocked sprinkler can be disastrous. Wind, also, can blow the water off course. The installation of such a system is expensive, but labour costs are low. Spraying equipment can easily be seen on the hill of the Grands Crus and over large parts of Fourchaume, but the two methods of protection often exist side by side. The oil burners can now be filled automatically but they still have to be lit manually, so fuel and labour costs are the main disadvantages here. In both cases, efficacy is increased by accurate frost forecasts from the nearest *station météorologique* – the most dangerous moments are usually in the early hours of the morning.

The risk of frost has also been lessened by the use of weedkillers (fewer weeds mean less humidity and therefore less frost and, as the soil does not need to be worked, it exudes less humidity). Also, there are now not so many isolated vineyards – both frost and birds seem to descend more often when vines are interspersed with uncultivated land. No one would pretend that frost in Chablis has been conquered, but its effects have been mitigated. To people who knew the region in the 1950s, the change is nothing less than dramatic.

Most growers now ferment in stainless steel or lined cement vats, but opinion varies as to the best material for ageing Chablis. There are advocates of both new and old oak, and others who prefer that their wine sees no wood at all. In general, it appears to me that Grands Crus and Premiers Crus from ripe years, particularly the former, benefit enormously from some wood-ageing (and the age of the wood seems, on tasting, to matter less than the absolute cleanliness of the casks), while straight Chablis can be delicious bottled younger and straight from the vat. Some more traditional winemakers keep their wine in vat until the spring following the vintage, when it should have finished its malolactic fermentation, and then age the wine in barrel for about a year. These casks, now, are more likely to be 225-litre *pièces* than the traditional smaller Chablis *feuillettes* of 132 litres. Naturally, new oak barrels are expensive, but that should probably not be a consideration where Grands Crus are concerned. However, care should be taken that no oxidation occurs when ageing in wood, which entails rigorous topping up, or *ouillage,* and that the wine does not take on too strong a taste of oak. Chablis supports this much less than a richer, fatter Meursault or California Chardonnay – even in a Grand Cru from Chablis there should be some underlying 'nerve' or steel: the true appellation character.

Fresh, youthful, straight Chablis need not see any wood – this is the kind of delicious *grande brasserie* wine one chooses with a dozen oysters. But just as winemakers should guard against over-heavy Chablis, they should also take care not to produce wines that are too neutral and that fade away a year or two after their birth. As with most things, a judicious mixture of the two methods, a winemaking compromise, probably produces the most memorable Chablis.

Commercially, the most significant change in Chablis has been in the greater control of its own destiny apparent during the last 25 years. Although Chablisiens still like to blame the *négociant* houses of Beaune for the wild fluctuations in price and the unsatisfactory balance between supply and demand too frequently encountered in the region, the fact remains that they now have more control over their own affairs than ever before. *Négociant* houses sold 55 per cent of the Chablis produced in 1992, with the growers selling the remaining 45 per cent. And as the producers of Chablis have a commodity which is in worldwide demand, they can very much call the tune as to the prices they charge. Obviously, it is difficult to have a stable situation when annual production figures vary as much as they do in Chablis, but the region has always been known for allowing prices to soar when there is little wine to sell of whatever quality, and for selling its wine too quickly and too cheaply when there is a prolific vintage. If only some of the stock could be sensibly blocked until the result of the following vintage is known, and the sale spread over a longer period.

The following table gives an indication of the irregular nature of the yields in Chablis. Unusually low yields are almost always the consequence of severe spring frosts or poor flowering.

**Yields of Chablis** (hectolitres)

| Year | Grand Cru | Premier Cru | Chablis | Petit Chablis | Total |
|---|---|---|---|---|---|
| 1979 | 6,124 | 33,988 | 66,126 | 7,989 | 114,227 |
| 1980 | 5,113 | 25,491 | 46,601 | 5,359 | 82,564 |
| 1981 | 2,864 | 15,686 | 22,749 | 1,723 | 43,022 |
| 1985 | 2,693 | 25,650 | 65,294 | 6,218 | 99,855 |
| 1986 | 4,676 | 32,339 | 65,602 | 5,811 | 108,428 |
| 1989 | 5,149 | 36,623 | 95,293 | 10,688 | 147,753 |
| 1990 | 5,223 | 40,138 | 114,609 | 14,209 | 174,179 |
| 1991 | 5,072 | 39,870 | 102,670 | 11,325 | 158,937 |
| 1992 | 4,994 | 42,539 | 138,300 | 21,224 | 207,057 |
| 1993 | 4,734 | 39,735 | 134,744 | 23,716 | 202,929 |
| 1994 | 4,330 | 36,702 | 128,943 | 19,819 | 189,794 |
| 1995 | 5,731 | 44,891 | 160,523 | 28,096 | 239,241 |
| 1996 | 5,318 | 42,298 | 154,990 | 27,806 | 230,412 |

As an illustration of how the number of hectares under vine is increasing, here are comparable figures showing the 11-year difference between 1982 and 1992.

| Hectares under vine | 1982 | 1992 |
|---|---|---|
| Chablis Grand Cru | 92 | 93 |
| Chablis Premier Cru | 477 | 717 |
| Chablis | 989 | 2,321 |
| Petit Chablis | 110 | 360 |

## *The Principal Chablis Producers*

### Christian Adine

*Rue Restif de la Bretonne, Courgis, 89800 Chablis. 17ha*
***Chablis 1ers Crus:*** *Montmains; Butteaux.* ***Chablis***
Very good wines can be found here, some of which are produced to conform with 'biological' regulations as laid down by the Bio-Bourgogne group.

### Domaine Baillard

*Route d'Auxerre, 89800 Chablis. 15ha*
***Chablis 1ers Crus:*** *Fourchaume; Vaillons; Montmains; Montée de Tonnerre.* ***Chablis***
Jean Servin makes correct, machine harvested Chablis.

### Cave Coopérative La Chablisienne

*8 boulevard Pasteur, 89800 Chablis. 1150ha*
***Chablis Grands Crus, Chablis 1ers Crus: Chablis, Petit Chablis, AOC Régionales:*** *Bourgogne Blanc and Aligoté; Bourgogne, Rouge Epineuil; Bourgogne Grand Ordinaire; Bourgogne, Passe-Tout-Grain; Crémant de Bourgogne*

This is the somewhat coy name for the omnipresent cooperative at Chablis. It has great influence on annual pricing policy; it swallows nearly a third of the appellation's total production and has 187 *adhérents* who bring must, not grapes, to the cellars. The policy of sometimes using growers' names on labels is justifiably criticised in some quarters, as it gives the impression of being domaine wine although it came from a co-op vat. But La Chablisienne also sells in bulk to *négociants* in Chablis and Beaune, as well as abroad in bulk and bottle. As with any co-op, selection is the key to success in buying, but there is no doubt that many Chablis and Premiers Crus are very good buys; I have had excellent Grand Cru Grenouilles.

## Domaine Jean Collet & Fils

*15 avenue de la Liberté, 89800 Chablis. 31.3ha*

***Chablis Grand Cru:*** *Valmur.* ***Chablis 1ers Crus:*** *Mont de Milieu; Montée de Tonnerre; Montmains; Vaillons.* ***Chablis***

Fine-quality, well-constituted Chablis with the distinctive 'stony' imprint of the appellation and great depth of flavour. The wines are fermented in stainless steel, with Valmur, Montée de Tonnerre and Mont de Milieu usually being *élevés* in one-third new wood. One problem for the consumer, however, is that there is no reliable pattern for what is aged in new wood and what is not. Montmains is sometimes quite oaky; some *cuvées* of the Grand Cru Valmur see no new wood at all... as there is no indication on the label, there is no way of knowing. That said, Collet's wines are often a revelation.

## Domaine Daniel Dampt

*89800 Milly. 17ha*

***Chablis 1ers Crus:*** *Vaillons; Côte de Léchet; Faurchaume; Beauroy.* ***Chablis***

This domaine has impressed recently, making wines that are the essence of Chablis style.

## Domaine Jean Dauvissat

*3 rue de Chichée, 89800 Chablis. 8ha*

***Chablis Grand Cru:*** *Les Preuses*

***Chablis 1ers Crus:*** *Montmains; Vaillons*

Usually good-quality Chablis, stainless-steel fermented and aged using a very small proportion of new wood (ten per cent maximum). The son-in-law of René Dauvissat is making Chablis with the verve and 'steel' I like in this appellation.

## Domaine René & Vincent Dauvissat

*8 rue Emile-Zola, 89800 Chablis. 9ha*

***Chablis Grands Crus:*** *Les Clos; Les Preuses.*

***Chablis 1ers Crus:*** *La Forest; Séchet; Vaillons.* ***Chablis***

René Dauvissat and his son are gifted winemakers. These Chablis are really exemplary, combining the fruit and 'nerviness' we should find in this appellation, and the kind of flavour which just makes you go 'mmmm'. This is how it is done: pressing; *débourbage* or clarifying of the must; slow fermentation at low temperature (achieved by cooling) in vat, where the wine stays until after the malolactic fermentation. However, ten per cent of the must is fermented in oak barrels. The wine is aged in oak casks from April to November, and then bottled from December to March after refrigeration and light filtration. The wines keep beautifully; they go to Parisian and provincial restaurants, private customers and all around the world. Since 1950, the property has quadrupled in size, and there have been modern innovations alongside the traditional methods. These are wines of great beauty, perfectly balanced, with just the right amount of oak. Luscious Les Preuses and Les Clos, elegant La Forest and Vaillons. The epitome of all that Chablis should be about. I only wish the Dauvissats could expand even further, and then there would be more wine for us devotees! The wines are also found under the name Dauvissat-Camus and the 1992s and 1994s are excellent.

### Domaine Jean Defaix

*Milly, 89800 Chablis. 8ha*

Clean, unoaked and well-made wines; light but good.

### Domaine Jean-Paul Droin

*16 bis, rue Jean-Jaurès, 89800 Chablis. 4ha (16ha en métayage)*

***Chablis Grands Crus:*** *Blanchot; Les Clos; Grenouilles; Valmur; Vaudésir.* ***Chablis 1ers Crus:*** *Côte de Léchet; Fourchaume; Montée de Tonnerre; Montmains; Vaillons; Vaucoupins; Vosgros* ***Chablis. Petit Chablis***

Prior to 1986, no new wood was used at this domaine. Currently the Grands Crus are fermented in a mixture of new and one-year-old wood and the Premiers Crus in one- to four-year-old wood; both are then aged for six months in casks that are not new. Chablis and Petit Chablis are made entirely in vat. Well-made, pretty and flowery wines.

### Maison Joseph Drouhin

*7 rue d'Enfer, 21200 Beaune. 35.3ha in Chablis*

The firm of Drouhin is both owner in Chablis and *négociant* in Beaune. Splendid wines, very much influenced by wood, and often fat and concentrated. Consequently, they last very well in bottle. *See also* A–Z.

### Domaine Duplessis

*5 quai de Reugny, 89800 Chablis. 5ha*

***Chablis Grand Cru:*** *Les Clos.* ***Chablis 1ers Crus:*** *Fourchaume; Montée de Tonnerre; Vaillons; Montmains*

These wines are fermented in vat and aged for up to 18 months with about six months' wood-ageing in old *fûts*. The '90s seem to be better than the '80s.

### Jean Durup/Domaine de l'Eglantière

*4 Grand-Rue, Domaine de l'Eglantière, Maligny, 89800 Chablis*

*150ha Vines in communes of Maligny; Villy; Beines; Fyé; Chablis*

***Chablis 1ers Crus:*** *Fourchaume; Montée de Tonnerre; Montmain; Vau de Vey.* ***Chablis. Petit Chablis***

A highly efficient domaine, which is just as well, given its size. M Durup has been at the forefront of the Chablis expansion policy, although his family has been in Maligny for five centuries. There is no oak in the cellars here, but the vinification is *la plus proche possible de la nature*. Pneumatic presses are very gentle on the grapes, and the concrete vats are lined with fibreglass or enamel. The resulting wines are pretty and floral, rarely deep in flavour but always elegant, and totally uninfluenced by oak. They can be labelled Château de Maligny, Domaine de l'Eglantière, Domaine de Paulière and Domaine de Valéry.

## Domaine William Fèvre/Domaine de la Maladière

*Domaine de la Maladière, 14 rue Jules-Rathier, 89800 Chablis. 60ha*
***Chablis Grands Crus:** (18ha) Blanchots; Bougros; Les Clos; Grenouilles; Preuses; Valmur; Vaudésir. **Chablis 1ers Crus:** (20ha) Beauroy; Fourchaumes; Côte de Léchet; Les Lys; Mont de Milieu; Montmains; Montée de Tonnerre; Vaillons; Vaucoupin; Vaugiraut; Vaulorent. **Chablis** (20ha). **Petit Chablis** (2ha)*
An important domaine, with more Grand Cru Chablis than any other grower. The wines have finesse and style; the best are lanolin-smooth from ageing in new oak barrels. Until 1987, all Fèvre's wines spent some time in wood, but since 1988, his Petit Chablis, Chablis and Premier Cru wines from the west bank of the River Serein have received no wood contact at all. The Grands Crus, and Premiers Crus Vaulorent, Montée de Tonnerre and Fourchaumes are vinified and matured in oak, 25% being new. The wines are often outstanding, combining all the minerally flavours and keen backbone of acidity that should characterise good Chablis. Top wines should be given at least five to ten years to develop their exceptional potential. In addition to the two names above, wines are also sold under the Ancien Domaine Auffray and Jeanne Paule Filippi names.

## Vincent Gallois/Domaine de la Vallée aux Sages

*Lignorelles, 89800 Chablis*
Excellent, unoaked, straight Chablis and Petit Chablis: concentrated, pure and vivid.

## Domaine Alain Geoffroy

*4 rue de l'Equerre, Beine, 89800 Chablis. 42ha*
***Chablis Grand Cru:** Le Clos. **Chablis 1ers Crus:** Beauroy; Fourchaume; Vau-Ligneau. **Chablis***
Alain Geoffroy is a great supporter of the expansion of the vineyard area at Beine, and he himself certainly proves that fine Chablis can be made there. New wood is now used. The wines are sold young, but keep well in bottle for those who have the foresight to lay some down. I like the stylish, fresh character, which is instantly recognisable as Chablis. Judges at competitions must like the wines from this domaine, too, as they scoop up medals with great regularity. I am not always in accord with the verdicts of these august juries, who often see wines when they are very young and miss the faults that develop later in the bottle, but in this case, I approve! If I did not, it probably would not worry them greatly.

## Domaine Jean-Pierre Grossot

*Fleys, 89800 Chablis. 12 ha*

***Chablis 1ers Crus:*** *Vaucoupin; Mont de Milieu; Fourchaume; Troêsmes; Les Fourneux.* ***Chablis***

Very good 1994s have set the tone at this young domaine. Oak is intelligently used.

## Domaine Thierry Hamelin

*Lignorelles, 89800 Chablis*

Pretty '89 Premier Cru Vau Ligneau: quite correct, no highlights, but bang-on.

## Lamblin & Fils

*Maligny, 89800 Chablis. 7ha*

***Chablis Grand Cru:*** *Valmur.* ***Chablis 1ers Crus:*** *Beauroy; Fourchaume; Mont de Milieu.* ***Chablis***

*Négociants* and vineyard owners, with all the trappings of modern vinification. Clean wines – but a touch too neutral?

## Domaine Laroche

*L'Obédiencerie, 22 rue Louis-Bro, 89800 Chablis. 76ha (21ha en métayage)*

***Chablis Grands Crus:*** *Les Blanchots; Les Bouguerots; Les Clos.* ***Chablis 1ers Crus:*** *Côte de Léchet; Les Beauroys; Les Fourchaumes; Les Montmains; Les Vaillons; Vau de Vey.* ***Chablis. Petit Chablis***

This is a big operation, with over 90ha of vines as well as the *négociant* business of Bacheroy Josselin. There is also the Domaine Laroche and its *sous marque* Domaine La Jouchère. The winemaking is of the most modern, with some limited new oak for the Grands Crus only. There are some fine separate bottlings of Vieilles Vignes such as Fourchaumes and Les Blanchots, but some of the wines seem a might too neutral in comparison with the very best.

## Domaine Long-Depaquit

*45 rue Auxerroise, 89800 Chablis. 60ha*

***Chablis Grands Crus:*** *Les Blanchots; Les Clos; Les Preuses; Les Vaudésirs.* ***Chablis 1ers Crus:*** *Beugnons; Les Lys; Vaillons; Vaucopins.* ***Chablis***

The Beaune *négociants* Bichot (*qv*) are behind this well-run domaine, which has a large part of La Moutonne, Grands and Premiers Crus as well as straight Chablis – some of the latter is bottled in Beaune. Impressive wines on the whole, the Grands Crus in particular.

## Domaine des Malandes

*63 rue Auxerroise, 89800 Chablis. 7ha (15ha en métayage)*

***Chablis Grands Crus:*** *Les Clos; Vaudésir*

***Chablis 1ers Crus:*** *Côte de Léchet; Montmains; Fourchaume; Vau de Vey.* ***Chablis. Petit Chablis***

Lyne and Jean-Bernard Marchive make wines entirely without wood which have great style and can always be recommended.

## Domaine des Marronniers

*Préhy, 89800 Chablis. 15ha*

Straight Chablis with a clear-cut mineral flavour and vivid acidity; taut, racy Montmains, both mouth-wateringly good and typical. Bernard Legland created this domaine in 1977 from AC land his father had planted with cereals. He has a very clear idea of what good Chablis should taste like and knows just how to make it. Most of his wine is unoaked, but he puts a small amount in ten to 30% new wood for a year... and indicates that it is oaked on the label. He started without any inherited baggage and seems to have absolutely the right ideas. I can see why his '90 Chablis won a gold medal at the 1991 Mâcon fair!

## Domaine Louis Michel/Domaine de la Tour Vaubourg

*9–11 boulevard de Ferrières, 89800 Chablis. 20ha*

***Chablis Grands Crus:*** *Grenouilles; Les Clos; Vaudésir.*
***Chablis 1ers Crus:*** *Fourchaume; Montée de Tonnerre; Montmain; Vaillons.* ***Chablis***

This is a very fine fourth-generation domaine, founded in 1870. The must goes through *débourbage* and fining, leaving absolutely clean material to be worked on. Fermentation takes place in vats at low temperature (18–20°C/64–68°F), and the malolactic fermentation is prolonged as long as possible; in other words, no measures are taken to speed it up. The wines are bottled in September. There is no wood in the process, but the slow, natural winemaking, plus yields which are not exaggerated, mean that the wines remain young, fresh and full of bouquet for years, always with that yellowish-green light to them which is so characteristic of Chablis. Of the production, 80% is exported, with 20% going to private clients and restaurants in France. There is a fine array of elegant, fruity Premiers Crus, wines almost with a sheen to them, as well as the Grands Crus and straight Chablis. These are beautifully balanced, stylish Chablis wines, a tribute to what can be achieved by ageing in stainless steel alone.

## J Moreau & Fils

*Route d'Auxerre, 89800 Chablis. 40ha*

***Chablis Grands Crus:*** *Blanchot; Clos des Hospices; Les Clos; Valmur; Vaudésir.* ***Chablis 1er Cru:*** *Vaillons.* ***Chablis***

Significant producer and *négociant* was acquired by Boisset (*qv*) in 1997. Wood has no part in the vinification, and after the fermentations the wines are kept for three to six weeks on healthy lees before being racked. The pride of the pack is the Chablis Grand Cru Clos des Hospices (within Les Clos) which, it is said, combines a bouquet of hazelnuts with a steely or flinty quality coming from the soil, and a vanilla or lemony nose from the Chardonnay – and no wood influences these aromas. The other Grands Crus can also be serious wines, but I have had disappointments at lesser levels. The *vin de table* Moreau Blanc has nothing to do with Chablis but, as with Mouton Cadet, there is sometimes confusion in the public mind, not helped by the fact that the labels and the wording of the advertising are so similar.

### Domaine Civile de la Moutonne

*89800 Chablis. 2.35ha*

Bichot (*qv*) owns most of the Société Civile with a small proportion controlled by Drouhin. La Moutonne is a majestic wine, enormously concentrated in great years. The celebrated plot lies in the Grands Crus of Vaudésir and Les Preuses, but does not officially have Grand Cru status itself.

### Baron Patrick

*89800 Chablis*

Baron Patrick is one of the brand names under which Patrick de Ladoucette – best known for his Comte Lafond Sancerre and Ladoucette Pouilly-Fumé – markets Chablis. Straightforward, unoaked Chablis. *See* A Régnard & Fils.

### André Philippon

*Fleys, 89800 Chablis*

Quality Chablis and Premier Cru Mont de Milieu, stainless steel-fermented and briefly aged in wood, very little of which is new.

### Domaine Pinson

*5 quai Voltaire, 89800 Chablis. 10ha*

***Chablis Grand Cru:*** *Les Clos*

***Chablis 1ers Crus:*** *Forêts; Montmains; Mont de Milieu*

Wines that are fermented in vat and aged in old wood. Some very good Chablis, concentrated and minerally, but sometimes the taste of 'old wood' intrudes.

### Domaine François & Jean-Marie Raveneau

*9 rue de Chichée, 89800 Chablis. 2ha (5ha en métayage)*

***Chablis Grands Crus:*** *Blanchot; Les Clos; Valmur*

***Chablis 1ers Crus:*** *Butteaux; Chapelot; Montée de Tonnerre; Vaillons; Mont Mains; Forêt*

Son Jean-Marie makes these wines, the most complex in Chablis. Classic Grands and Premiers Crus, wood-aged and built for long life in bottle. They have style and enormous interest. Stupendous examples of the genre as shown by a Vaillons 1986 drunk at eight years old. Are very recent vintages quite as spectacular? We shall have to wait and see.

### A Régnard & Fils

*28 boulevard du Docteur-Tacussel, 89800 Chablis*

*Négociant specialising in:*

***Chablis Grands Crus:*** *Vaudésir; Valmur, Les Clos*

***Chablis 1er Cru:*** *Fourchaume*

This purely *négociant* house, bought by Patrick de Ladoucette in 1984, is still run by Michel Rémon (*qv*), and the wines are still also sold under Rémon's own name as well as that of Albert Pic. The wines are stainless-steel fermented and have very little oak-ageing, but a later bottling than some. In spite of limited wood-ageing, a few Premiers Crus and Grands Crus in the mid-1980s had more than a hint of old wood in their flavour. That said, consistent quality has improved under the eye of M Ladoucette. The complete range of Chablis is covered by this house, and if you tasted no other you would have a very good idea of the appellation. Pic's Les Clos 1983, drunk in 1994, was stupendous.

## Domaine Guy Robin

*13 rue Berthelot, 89800 Chablis. 10ha*

***Chablis Grands Crus:*** *Blanchot; Valmur; Vaudésir*

***Chablis 1ers Crus:*** *Butteaux; Montée de Tonnerre; Vaillons*

A little wood is used in the winemaking for the Grands Crus; the Premiers Crus see no wood at all. Difficult to judge here, as form has been so erratic.

## Domaine Ste-Claire

*Préhy, 89800 Chablis. 50ha (16ha en métayage)*

***Chablis 1er Cru. Chablis. AOC Régionales:*** *Sauvignon de St-Bris; Bourgogne Irancy; Bourgogne Rouge, Blanc and Aligoté*

Most of Jean-Marc Brocard's production is Chablis *tout court* (35ha), stainless-steel fermented and with no wood-ageing. It is honest, straightforward wine. The Sauvignon de St-Bris lacks a little breadth, even for St-Bris, but the Chardonnay de St-Bris has a zesty northern freshness to it.

## Domaine Servin

*Francois Servin, 89800 Chablis. 32ha*

***Chablis Grand Crus:*** *Blanchot; Les Clos; Preuses; Bougros*

***Chablis 1ers Crus:*** *Montée de Tonnerre; Vaillon; Les Forêts.* ***Chablis***

The harvesting and pressing are done with Domaine Baillard, but these promising wines are made separately. Top *crus* are aged in oak, while others reside in stainless steel to maintain crisp freshness. The Servin family strongly recommend decanting Grands and Premiers Crus.

## Simonnet-Febvre

*9 avenue d'Oberwesel, 89800 Chablis. 5ha*

***Chablis Grand Cru:*** *Preuses*

***Chablis 1er Cru:*** *Mont de Milieu.* ***Chablis***

This is a small domaine, but Simonnet-Febvre is an important *négociant-éleveur* who buys in must and vinifies it for young bottling. The house was founded in 1840 and Jean-Claude Simonnet is the fifth-generation member of the family now in charge. The firm also makes a speciality of other Yonne wines, such as Irancy and Coulanges. Bottled under several other labels, the wines see no wood at all and are straightforward in flavour – at best.

## Domaine Gérard Tremblay/Domaine des Iles

*12 rue de Poinchy, 89800 Chablis. 28ha (5ha en métayage)*

***Chablis Grand Cru:*** *Valmur.* ***Chablis 1ers Crus:*** *Beauroy; Côte de Léchet; Fourchaume; Montmains.* ***Chablis. Petit Chablis***

At best, this domaine produces full, fruity wines which mostly sees no wood-ageing at all. However, there is lack of consistency, even in the occasional use of oak.

### Domaine de Vauroux/Olivier Tricon

*Route d'Avallon, 89800 Chablis. 28ha*
***Chablis Grand Cru:*** *Bougros*
***Chablis 1ers Crus:*** *Montée de Tonnerre; Montmains.* ***Chablis***
Olivier Tricon specialises in straight Chablis, which accounts for nearly 25 of his 28ha. His wines are stainless-steel fermented with the Grand Cru and Premiers Crus aged for a few months only in wooden casks. Fruity wines with attractive definition and pure Chablis character. The Olivier Tricon label is mostly for non-domaine wines.

### Domaine Vocoret & Fils

*40 route d'Auxerre, 89800 Chablis. 30.4ha*
***Chablis Grands Crus:*** *Les Clos; Valmur; Blanchots*
***Chablis 1ers Crus. Chablis***
Here, the usual process is reversed – the wines are fermented in large oak barrels but aged in stainless-steel vats. The wines are textured and full, and there is a generous span of them in all categories. They benefit from time in bottle and usually age well.

## OTHER WINES OF THE YONNE

No one would pretend that these wines are much seen on export markets (except for the Sauvignon de St-Bris), but they are fun to track down while on holiday in the area and rewarding to drink in local restaurants at some of the most modest prices in the whole of Burgundy.

**Irancy** By far the best known of the Yonne red wines, it has had its own appellation since 1977 and is now made mostly of Pinot Noir, with small quantities of César. Undoubtedly, the Pinot Noir contributes finesse, while the César is more rustic. The soil is Kimmeridgian, and the vineyard area is prey to the twin dangers of frost and hail, although Irancy has a favoured microclimate. Some Bourgogne Rosé is also produced here. The individual vineyard Palotte is, in fact, in the neighbouring village of Cravant and therefore can only be called Bourgogne Rouge; it is the same for the wines from the commune of Vincelottes. The best growers are Léon Bienvenu, Bernard Cantin, Jean-Pierre Colinot, Roger Delaloge, Gabriel Delaloge, Jean Renaud and Jean Podor, whose Irancy Les Mazelots is probably the top wine of the appellation. Much Irancy goes to the Chablis *négociants*, with Simonnet-Febvre (*qv*) making a speciality of the appellation. There is also the Domaine de Pérignon, run by the Nuits-St-Georges firm of Chauvenet (*qv*), which produces Passe-Tout-Grains from Pinot Noir and Gamay.

**Coulanges-la-Vineuse** Wine from Coulanges is only classed as Bourgogne but, rather strangely, Coulanges-la-Vineuse may appear on the label. The wine is similar to Irancy, although usually lighter, and it is made entirely from the Pinot Noir. The principal growers are Raymond Dupuis, Serge Hugot, André Martin & Fils and Pierre Vigreux, while the Chablis *négociants* of Bacheroy Josselin and Simonnet-Febvre (*qv*) also sell Coulanges.

**St-Bris-le-Vineux** It is the Sauvignon de St-Bris that has the regional denomination *Vin Délimité de Qualité Supérieure*, although the Aligoté can be good in ripe years. Pinot Noir, Gamay, a little César, Chardonnay and Sacy are also grown, which gives scope for the production of Bourgogne Rouge and Blanc, Passe-Tout-Grains, Bourgogne Grand Ordinaire and Crémant de Bourgogne. The best growers, whose wines can also sometimes be seen abroad, are Louis Bersan & Fils, now run by the two sons, Jean Brocard, Robert Defrance, Michel Esclavy, Patrice Fort, Jean-Hugues Goisot, Domaine Félix and Domaine Verret.

**Chitry-le-Fort** Chitry has the same array of grape varieties as St-Bris, with especially good Aligoté, and Bourgogne Blanc made from Chardonnay, which shares the Kimmeridgian soil of Chablis and some of its characteristics. Very good Aligoté Côtes de Chitry comes from Léon Berthelot, Jean-Claude Biot, Paul Colbois (much better than his Sauvignon) and Gilbert Giraudon. Joel Griffe and Roland Viré are other reliable names. Many of the growers of Chitry and St-Bris belong to the agricultural collective of the SICAVA, which makes Crémant de Bourgogne. Wine is also made at Tonnerre, Epineuil and Vézelay. The Caves de Bailly is a good source of Crémant de Bourgogne, Sauvignon de St-Bris and Aligoté – SICA du Vignoble Auxerrois, Bailly, 89530 St-Bris-le-Vineux. The SICA La Vézelienne dominates the Vézeley wine district. Go there for Bourgogne Blanc and Rouges. The great chef, Marc Meneau of L'Espérance sends his grapes to this cooperative. Good red Epineuil from Pinot Noir is made by Jean-Claude Michaut and the best Bourgogne Chardonnay and Bourgogne Pinot Noir from the Tonnerre area comes from the Caveau des Fontenilles.

# ●○◐ Côte d'Or

The Côte d'Or is the heart of Burgundy, golden in name and in reputation. Although historic Dijon is by far the largest town on the Côte, the pivotal centres for the wine trade are Beaune and Nuits-St-Georges. As with any wine area, there is a complex web of *négociants*, growers and brokers who make and sell the wines, each jealously guarding his position in the line of supply. But the Côte d'Or is the most democratic of wine regions, its vineyards divided into hundreds of small plots which are either inherited or acquired by a diplomatic marriage. Some growers see their job as suppliers of grapes, leaving the *négociant* houses to do their own vinifications, while others like to control the whole process right up to the sale to the customer. There is a large number of growers who both make their wine, and sell a part of it to the *négociants*, via the brokers, to finance the proportion they wish to mature and bottle themselves. Somewhere in all this lurk magnificent winemakers who have made Burgundy the most show-stopping word in wine vocabulary; on page 66 is a list of the Côte's Grands Crus and their villages. Others, who are less skilled or less caring, unfortunately have access to the same labels. The greatest red and white burgundies are made on the Côte d'Or, particularly if you take a wine's ability to age as a criterion of quality. It is awesome to remember this if you drive from Dijon to Beaune, with the slope of the Côte on your right, an imposing presence all along the way. Do this in autumn, when the leaves are changing colour, and let the vineyards create their magic. This is the Côte d'Or, where some of the most intoxicating taste sensations in the world are created.

## ●◐○ MARSANNAY

**1996 production:**
***AOC Communale* ● *7,905hl***
***AOC Communale* ○ *1,350hl***
***AOC Communale* ◑ *3,520hl***

In 1987, the new appellation of Marsannay was created, covering 250ha in the communes of Chenôve, Marsannay-la-Côte and Couchey. It applies to white, red and rosé wines. Two *climats* in Chenôve, formerly very famous, Le Clos du Roi and Le Clos du Chapitre, are now part of the new appellation Marsannay. Bourgogne Aligoté, Blanc and Passe-Tout-Grains are also produced on a small scale. Much less rosé is produced now, with only about 15% on offer, but this quantity does vary with the quality of the vintage – in good years, growers tend to opt for making red. On the better slopes, growers concentrate on making red wine, which has improved as the plantings have aged. The rosé should be drunk young, when it has a hint of strawberries, and is excellent in hot weather, when a red burgundy tastes flat and 'soupy'. Red Marsannay is frank and gamey, slightly earthy in character, with good concentration if the year is propitious and the vines old.

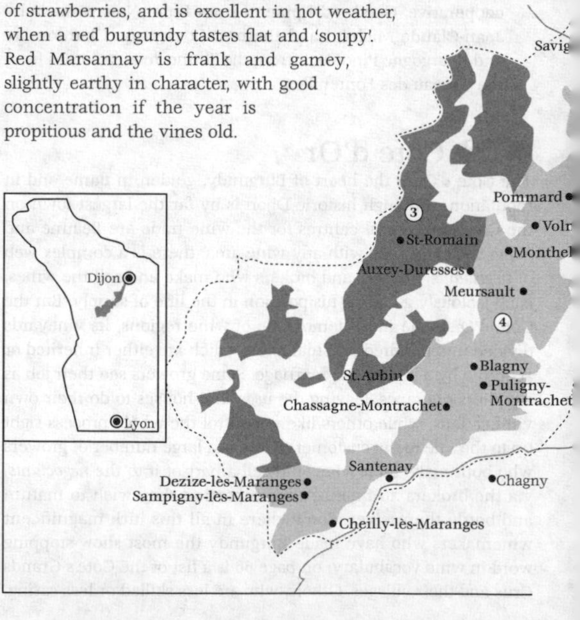

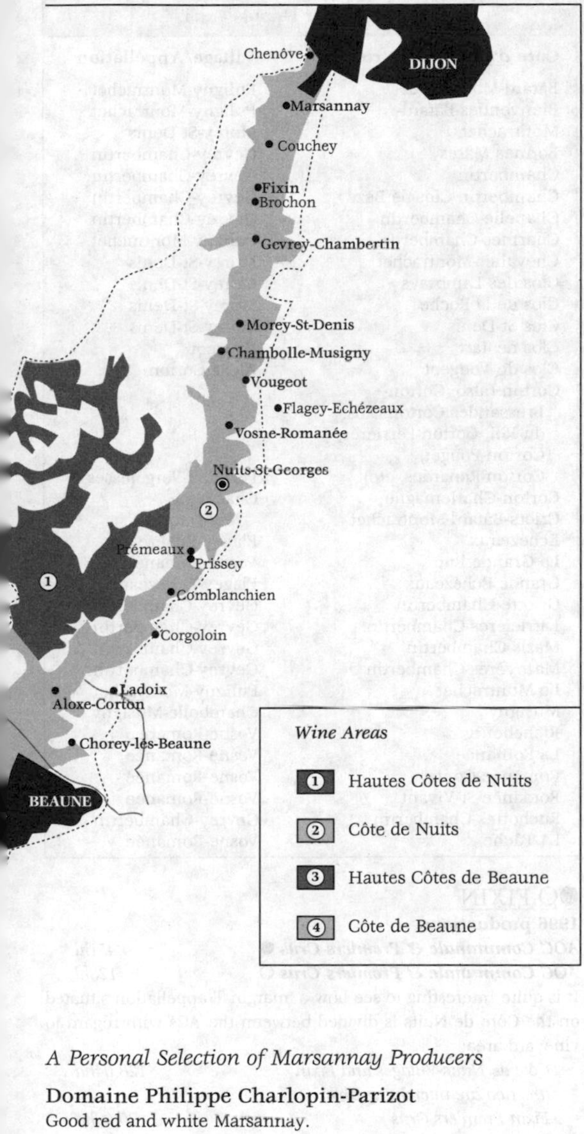


### *A Personal Selection of Marsannay Producers*

### Domaine Philippe Charlopin-Parizot

Good red and white Marsannay.

### Domaine Bruno Clair

The domaine makes a perfumed rosé and Bourgogne Rouge with a bouquet of 'wet dog' (which is very pleasant, I assure you) and a taste of redcurrants.

**The Côte d'Or Grands Crus**

| Côte d'Or Grands Crus | Village/Appellation |
|---|---|
| Bâtard-Montrachet | Puligny-Montrachet |
| Bienvenues-Bâtard-Montrachet | Puligny-Montrachet |
| Bonnes Mares | Morey-St-Denis |
| Chambertin | Gevrey-Chambertin |
| Chambertin Clos de Bèze | Gevrey-Chambertin |
| Chapelle-Chambertin | Gevrey-Chambertin |
| Charmes-Chambertin | Gevrey-Chambertin |
| Chevalier-Montrachet | Puligny-Montrachet |
| Clos des Lambrays | Morey-St-Denis |
| Clos de la Roche | Morey-St-Denis |
| Clos St-Denis | Morey-St-Denis |
| Clos de Tart | Morey-St-Denis |
| Clos de Vougeot | Vougeot |
| Corton (also: Corton-Bressandes Corton Clos du Roi, Corton-Perrières, Corton-Pouget, Corton-Renardes, etc) | Aloxe-Corton |
| Corton-Charlemagne | Pernand-Vergelesses |
| Criots-Bâtard-Montrachet | Chassagne-Montrachet |
| Echézeaux | Flagey-Echézeaux |
| La Grande Rue | Vosne-Romanée |
| Grands Echézeaux | Flagey-Echézeaux |
| Griotte-Chambertin | Gevrey-Chambertin |
| Latricières-Chambertin | Gevrey-Chambertin |
| Mazis-Chambertin | Gevrey-Chambertin |
| Mazoyères-Chambertin | Gevrey-Chambertin |
| Le Montrachet | Puligny-Montrachet |
| Musigny | Chambolle-Musigny |
| Richebourg | Vosne-Romanée |
| La Romanée | Vosne-Romanée |
| Romanée-Conti | Vosne-Romanée |
| Romanée-St-Vivant | Vosne-Romanée |
| Ruchottes-Chambertin | Gevrey-Chambertin |
| La Tâche | Vosne-Romanée |

## ●○ FIXIN

**1996 production:**

***AOC Communale & Premiers Crus* ●** *4,451hl*

***AOC Communale & Premiers Crus* ○** *128hl*

It is quite interesting to see how a 'marginal' appellation situated on the Côte de Nuits is divided between the ACs with regard to vineyard area:

| | |
|---|---|
| *Côte de Nuits-Villages and Fixin (the two are interchangeable)* | *128.04ha* |
| *Fixin Premiers Crus* | *20.00ha* |
| *Appellation Bourgogne* | *56.84ha* |
| *Bourgogne Grand Ordinaire* | *37.91ha* |

***Premiers Crus:*** *Les Meix-Bas (part), Le Clos du Chapitre (part), Aux Cheusots (part), La Perrière (part), Les Arvelets (part), Les Hervelets (part), Suchot, Queue de Hareng*

The Premiers Crus are on the upper part of the slope, which goes up to 350m (1,150ft), on a base of Bajocian limestone. Le Clos du Chapitre is on a marked slope, with Bathonian brown soil very rich in pebbles. La Perrière is above it, on a 12–14 per cent gradient, with its share of pebbles. Aux Cheusots, within which lies the Clos Napoléon, is virtually without a slope. Les Hervelets and Les Arvelets, once the same *climat*, lie between Fixin and Fixey on Bajocian limestone and, in spite of only a mild slope, there is in places barely 25cm (ten inches) of soil over the base. Where limestone is predominant, the wines have more finesse, but deeper soil with more clay content tends to give tougher, more tannic wines.

La Perrière and Clos du Chapitre fight for front ranking at Fixin. Both can be kept safely for a decade, when from good years. In youth the taste is somewhat *sauvage* and gamey, with blackcurrant flavours. Les Hervelets and Les Arvelets are thought more 'feminine', although in these days of *égalité* one should say that the fruit is softer. Aux Cheusots should have some finesse, although in the past I have been treated to some hefty Clos Napoléons which perplexed me somewhat. I think things are a little more healthy nowadays.

## *A Personal Selection of Fixin Producers*

### Domaine Bruno Clair

White Fixin from the Pinot Blanc, vivacious when young, heavier after a few years in bottle – but I still wonder whether Chardonnay would not be better. Excellent red Fixin, partly from 40-year-old vines, so the yield is not big: pure raspberries.

### Domaine Pierre Gelin

This domaine produces Fixin which has that *sauvage* character, even at five years old. Big, gutsy burgundy, without being 'blackstrap', so the fruit holds it own against the weight, but often it could take a decade in bottle.

### Domaine Philippe Joliet

Clos de la Perrière which can give please in good vintages, but perhaps could be better.

## ● GEVREY-CHAMBERTIN

**1996 production:**

***Grands Crus:***

| | |
|---|---|
| *Chambertin* | *629hl* |
| *Chambertin Clos de Bèze* | *563hl* |
| *Chapelle-Chambertin* | *199hl* |
| *Charmes-Chambertin/Mazoyères-Chambertin* | *1,184hl* |
| *Griotte-Chambertin* | *161hl* |
| *Latricières-Chambertin* | *346hl* |
| *Mazis-Chambertin* | *345hl* |
| *Ruchottes-Chambertin* | *134hl* |

***AOC Communale & Premiers Crus,*** *19,676hl*
***Premiers Crus*** *Les Véroilles, Village St-Jacques known as Le Clos St-Jacques, Aux Combottes, Bel-Air, Les Cazetiers, Combe aux Moines, Etournelles, Les Gémeaux, Lavaux, Poissenot, Champeaux, Les Goulots, Issarts, Les Corbeaux, Cherbaudes, La Perrière, Clos Prieur-Haut, Fonteny, Champonnet, Au Closeau, Craipillot, Champitenois known as Petite-Chapelle, En Ergot, Clos du Chapitre (part)*
No commune in Burgundy has more Grands Crus than Gevrey – it could be compared to Pauillac boasting three first growths, only more so. A peculiarity is that Chambertin Clos de Bèze may be called Chambertin, but the reverse does not apply. Charmes-Chambertin can also be styled Mazoyères-Chambertin – the two names are interchangeable. Spelling runs riot at Gevrey: Les Véroilles alternates with Les Varoilles, Griotte sometimes sports an 's' at the end, and Etournelles can become Estournelles. But behind a certain disorganisation in nomenclature, lies an array of some of the most seductive tastes in Burgundy.

The vineyard rises to 350m (1,150ft), although the line of Grands Crus is below 300m (980ft) on a gentle slope. They lie on a base of Bajocian limestone covered with thin debris, brown chalky soil with clay particles. Small pebbles play an important part, especially in the top section of Chambertin. Griotte and Chapelle-Chambertin have very thin soil, with the rock base even coming through in some places. Mazoyères and Charmes have gravelly soil of no more than 30–35cm (12–14in) in depth, a poor covering over the rock. Latricières and Ruchottes are on white oolite and everywhere there are outbreaks of the hard geological foundations. The Grands Crus shelter under the woods of the Montagne de la Combe Grisard, a good barrier against the winds from the north and also helping against hail. There are woods above the Premiers Crus, with Les Véroilles, one of the very best, right among them and possessing a microclimate of its own. The vines are picked later here than in the Grands Crus. Clos St-Jacques, often the equal of the Grands Crus, and Les Cazetiers share a very similar situation, but Champonnet has the unusual distinction of facing north to northeast.

Unusually for the Côte, the *village* appellation extends over the Route Nationale and towards the railway. There is barely any slope, so good drainage depends on the subsoil. Here there are layers of pebbles, so this aspect is satisfactory. I have come to the conclusion that when I have had mediocre wines from this part of the commune, it was not because of the soil, but due to over-production or bad winemaking.

The whole palette of aromas and flavours can come into top Gevrey. When the wines are young, there are strawberries and raspberries, violets, undergrowth, and game in the rich wines. As they mature, flavours of liquorice develop with some intensity. Amazingly enough, Griotte really can be marked by cherries! Chambertin combines finesse with power, needing years to develop – the best-bred is never too generous with itself in youth. If there is a difference between Chambertin and Clos de Bèze, it is difficult to spot, as often winemaking techniques or the respective ages of the vines overrides any innate variation. Then, there is the one-way interchangeability of the two names, so you have to be sure of what you are tasting. The best way to do this is when the wine is still in barrel and the winemaker describes the origin of each 'lot'. Latricières seems to have the most exquisite lacy quality, long and lingering but hardly ultra-powerful. Charmes-Chambertin can be less tannic and ready sooner than the other Grands Crus, while Chapelle-Chambertin can be very fruity.

Among Premiers Crus, Clos St-Jacques has wonderful animal scents and a sturdy attack when young, while Clos des Varoilles (the Premier Cru's entire six hectares is composed of this *clos*) is tannic when young, mouthfilling when more mature. Liquorice is a feature of many wines, especially in years of over-ripeness. Straight Gevrey should be silkily soft and perfumed, and easy to recognise.

## *A Personal Selection of Gevrey-Chambertin Producers*

### Domaine Bachelet
Denis Bachelet is doing splendid work here, right up to Charmes-Chambertin level. There is finesse, class and great perfume.

### Domaine Alain Burguet
Straight Gevrey-Chambertin and Vieilles Vignes, both with a lovely bouquet, but sometimes a trifle too 'big' on the palate for the seductive style of the appellation to dominate. Vieilles Vignes is usually a keeper.

### Domaine Charlopin-Parizot
The '90s have produced excellent Charmes.

### Domaine Bruno Clair
Rich Clos St-Jacques of great elegance and aromatic persistence, as well as textbook Cazetiers.

### Maison Joseph Drouhin
Griottes which is always very good indeed, a mixture of breeding and balance... and those cherries.

### Domaine Claude Dugat
Very impressive, rich wines, full of heady scent and flavour. They will find their way into my cellar!

### Domaine Dujac
Aux Combottes which shows that Jacques Seysses is as at home here as in Morey-St-Denis. Usually only a medium-keeper.

### Domaine Michel Esmonin
Real interest and complex flavour, across the board.

### Maison J Faiveley
La Combe aux Moines Premier Cru has a true Gevrey bouquet of violets and warm earth, and a taste of redcurrants, cherries and violets. Also Grands Crus to die for – but be patient.

### Domaine Geantet-Pansiot
The very attractive Premier Cru Le Poissenot boasts a cherry fruit bouquet along with some richness on the palate. The '90 Charmes-Chambertin is fabulous – but then, all the '90s here are superb.

### Domaine Denis Mortet
Les Champeaux that is quite impressive.

### Domaine Georges Mugneret
Superb Ruchottes that really keeps.

### Domaine Ponsot
Chambertin and Griotte which tend to be big and rich, sometimes jammy; most last well.

### Domaine Philippe Rossignol
This domaine makes straight Gevrey-Chambertin which is exemplary, if you want to know what the appellation is about at a non-grandiose level.

### Domaine Rossignol-Trapet
Excellent, stylish Grands Crus, although the estate is so young that we have yet to see aged bottles.

### Domaine Joseph Roty
A small domaine, but where the Charmes usually lives up to expectations, as does the rich and spicy Gevrey-Chambertin Premier Cru Les Fontenys.

### Domaine Georges Roumier/Christophe Roumier
This estate produces Ruchottes which can be quite splendid – at its best, it is among the stars of the Côte de Nuits.

### Domaine Armand Rousseau
The Clos St-Jacques made here always needs time, with its tight kernel of fruit – *une splendeur*! As if that weren't enough, Rousseau also produces excellent Cazetiers, Ruchottes, Charmes, Mazy-Chambertin and Clos de Bèze. No serious burgundy cellar should be without them.

### Domaine Christian Sérafin
Gevrey-Chambertin *vieilles vignes* that is currently a great buy.

### Domaine Jean Taupenot-Merme
Lovely Charmes, with breed and style. This grower resists the temptation to 'bump up' in lighter years. Drink quite young.

### Domaine des Varoilles
A range of Gevrey wines; lasting, classy bottles. There is velvety fruit intermingled with the structure. Clos des Varoilles is superb and concentrated.

## ●○ MOREY-ST-DENIS

**1996 production:**

***Grands Crus* ●**

| | |
|---|---|
| *Clos de la Roche* | *600hl* |
| *Clos de Tart* | *290hl* |
| *Clos St-Denis* | *291hl* |
| *Clos des Lambrays* | *366hl* |
| *Bonnes Mares* | *602hl* |
| ***AOC Communale & Premiers Crus* ●** | *4,401hl* |
| ***AOC Communale & Premiers Crus* ○** | *119hl* |

***Premiers Crus:*** *Les Ruchots, Les Sorbés, Le Clos Sorbés, Les Millandes, Le Clos des Ormes (part), Meix-Rentiers, Monts-Luisants, Les Bouchots, Clos de la Bussière, Aux Charmes, Les Charrières, Côte-Rôtie, Calouères, Maison-Brûlée, Les Chabiots, Les Mauchamps, Les Froichots, Les Fremières, Les Genevrières, Les Chaffots, Les Chénevery (part), La Riotte, Le Clos Baulet, Les Gruenchers, Les Façonnières*

Morey-St-Denis considers that it is not sufficiently well known, sandwiched as it is between Gevrey and Chambolle; as a result, there can be relative bargains here, especially among the Grands Crus. It is not very well publicised that there are two small cooperatives at Morey which now vinify their grapes and sell the results to the *négociants*. But some of the greatest tastes in the whole of Burgundy can come from Morey-St-Denis, and luckily for us, there is a handful of vineyard owners in the commune who are interested in achieving perfection, in spite of what the elements sometimes do to thwart them.

It is a considerable feat to have five Grands Crus in one commune, although only 1.5ha of Bonnes Mares lies in Morey – the remaining 13.5ha fall in the commune of Chambolle-Musigny. Clos des Lambrays was made a Grand Cru in 1981; in 1979, the estate had been sold to new owners after considerable time in the doldrums. Both Clos des Lambrays and Clos de Tart are in the hands of a single proprietor, which is a rare occurrence on the Côte d'Or. Clos de Tart and the Premier Cru Clos de la Bussière are typical abbey *clos* of the Middle Ages, completely surrounded by walls and with the buildings attached.

The slope of Morey-St-Denis lies next to that of Gevrey and shares the same geological makeup. The base is Bajocian limestone for the Grands Crus. The highest part of the Morey vineyard is Monts-Luisants at 350m (1,150ft) on Bathonian limestone, with very poor, gravelly soil – the lack of clay and iron content makes it suitable for making the unusual white wine of the same name. The limestone rock is very evident, although Clos de la Roche probably refers to one rock which may have existed between Latricières-Chambertin and Clos St-Denis and which was used in Celtic or druidical rites. The calcareous vein comes from Bonnes Mares, crosses east-facing Clos de Tart and goes to the upper part of Clos des Lambrays, which is a little more sandy. Clos de Tart and Bonnes Mares have a very visible topsoil of calcareous debris, while Clos de la Roche and Clos St-Denis are on brown limestone soil with few pebbles, but benefiting from a good, sheltered microclimate.

These Grands Crus lead us into the realm of truffles, wild cherries and redcurrants. Clos de Tart may be the most tannic wine when young, but that derives as much from the winemaking techniques of virtually no destalking and long vinification with the skins immersed as from anything else. Clos de la Roche has perfect structure and composition, the 'bonework' covered by rich fruit, which makes it ideal for ageing – total seduction.

The breed in this *cru* is again evident in Clos St-Denis, which combines finesse and charm with a certain chewy quality, *mâche*. It is difficult to place Clos des Lambrays at this precise moment, as about a third of the vineyard was replanted in 1980 and gradually a proper rotation of new plantations will have to be created. Under the previous owners, nothing had been done for decades, and the average age of the vines was 70 years, a most unhealthy state of affairs. The wines are already fruity and attractive, but we hope they will gain in depth in future years, depending also on what selections are made. Bonnes Mares from Morey is very limestone influenced, and can appear quite hard and taut when young, full of breed and opening out with age.

Most of the Premiers Crus are on the northern side of Morey; they share characteristics with the Grands Crus, but lack their richness and staying power, while offering immense flavour and earthy scents. It is said that the taste is of almonds and cherry-stones. The straight Morey appellation even tips over a little on to the eastern side of the Route Nationale. The wines can be delicious and redolent of red fruits.

## *A Personal Selection of Morey-St-Denis Producers*

### Pierre Amiot

Grand Cru Clos de la Roche with vibrant fruit, tastes of plums and lingering flavours. But stay will the good years.

### Domaine Dujac

A domaine run with the greatest intelligence by Jacques Seysses who, not being born Burgundian, perhaps finds it easier to try out innovations in his quest for quality. The Morey-St-Denis Premier Cru is always splendid – strawberries and redcurrants – while the Clos de la Roche has glorious projection of fruit and complexity – farmyards and violets! Sometimes the colours are not deep, but the flavours will overwhelm and there is never excess alcohol. Also fine Clos St-Denis and Bonnes Mares.

### Domaine Georges Lignier

This domaine very often produces the 'essence of the grape' taste: beautiful, clear wine. The Clos des Ormes is always a fine bottle, full of liquorice flavours, and there is also Clos St-Denis, Clos de la Roche and Bonnes Mares.

### Domaine Hubert Lignier

Elegant, textured Clos de la Roche combining great richness of fruit with distinct minerally spice.

### Mommessin/Clos de Tart

Solely owned by the Mommessin family, this *clos* can produce remarkable wines. When young, they have a nose of violets, later a fascinating mixture of leather, humus and spices. The taste is of redcurrants and vanilla when young (100% new barrels are used) and has spicy concentration when mature. Only occasionally has there been a certain clumsiness and perhaps an excess of alcohol. These are burgundies to lay down.

### Domaine Ponsot

Clos de la Roche which always needs many years to develop; one-dimensional in youth, it has a lovely scent and distinction when mature. Occasionally there has been oxidation, perhaps caused by a bottling fault.

### Domaine Georges Roumier

Clos de la Bussière which takes its time to develop, as it is all raw fruit when young.

### Domaine Armand Rousseau

Charles Rousseau's magic touch rarely deserts him – the wines are brimming with scent and class and luscious fruit. Clos de la Roche which is really superb, especially if given five to ten years, even in good to moderate vintages, and then swirled in the glass.

### Domaine Bernard Serveau

Premier Cru Les Sorbets which needs time in good years, but there is texture to match the framework.

## ●○ CHAMBOLLE-MUSIGNY

**1996 production:**

***Grand Cru***

| | |
|---|---|
| *Musigny* ● | *388hl* |
| *Musigny* ○ | *21hl (usually approx 20hl)* |
| *Bonnes Mares (part)* ● | *See Morey-St-Denis for hl* |
| ***AOC Communale & Premiers Crus*** ● | *7,239hl* |

***Premiers Crus:*** *Bonnes Mares (part), Les Amoureuses, Les Charmes, Les Cras (part), Les Borniques, Les Baudes, Les Plantes, Les Hauts-Doix, Les Châtelots, Les Gruenchers, Les Groseilles, Les Fuées, Les Lavrottes, Derrière-la-Grange, Les Noirots, Les Sentiers, Les Fousselottes, Aux Beaux-Bruns, Les Combottes, Aux Combottes, Les Chabiots, Les Carrières, Aux Echanges (part), La Combe d'Orveaux*

The Grands Crus are Musigny, of which there is a tiny amount of white wine, and Bonnes Mares, 13.7ha of which fall in this commune. The vineyards of Chambolle-Musigny lie at between 250 and 300m altitude (820–980ft) on a variety of debris materials, from red alluvial soil to brown limestone. Musigny itself is on an important gradient, varying between eight and 14%, necessitating frequent replacing of earth from the bottom to the top of the slope. The subsoil is white oolite on the upper parts, Comblanchien limestone farther down. There is up to 20% pebbles, permeable limestone (giving good drainage and finesse) and some red clay, which gives richness. Musigny is on the southern, Vougeot side of Chambolle, while Bonnes Mares borders Morey-St-Denis to the north. Les Amoureuses, lying just below Musigny, has a subsoil full of geological faults, so that some of the roots reach a depth of ten metres (33ft).

The top wines of Chambolle should have supreme scent and lacy delicacy. The light soil should lead to perfume, elegance and 'femininity', rather than Nuits-type power and earthy splendour. The great complexity of the tastes should creep subtly up on you, not knock you for six with a sledgehammer. Of course, the fascinating comparisons are between Musigny and Bonnes Mares, or Musigny and Les Amoureuses, especially when the wines are made by the same person. Musigny combines a well-constructed framework, underlying body, with enormous subtlety and silky finesse. Bonnes Mares tends to have the more visible body and fat, while Les Amoureuses should be the epitome of elegance. Bonnes Mares has a bouquet which veers entrancingly from violets to the scent of undergrowth, a very Burgundian trait. Overall, in the wines of Chambolle-Musigny, raspberries and spices are often intermingled. The wines should never be robust (if they are, you have reason to be suspicious), but they should have both projected scent and tenacity of flavour.

### *A Personal Selection of Chambolle-Musigny Producers*

**Domaine Bernard Amiot**
Straight Chambolle with all the bouquet and charm which one should get from this appellation.

**Domaine Ghislaine Barthod-Noëllat**
Straight Chambolle and Les Charmes which are floral, spicy and well worth buying. Les Cras is always a winner.

**Château de Chambolle-Musigny/JF Mugnier**
Scented, lacy Les Amoureuses, and wonderfully fine-textured Musigny with a glorious 'peacock's tail' finish.

**Domaine Robert Groffier**
Perfumed, spicy, elegant Les Amoureuses as well as rich, ample Bonnes Mares.

**Domaine Alain Hudelot-Noëllat**
Straight Chambolle and Les Charmes which can be explosively good, with great breed and long finish. Just occasionally, there has been too rapid oxidation of the wine after opening, which could indicate a bottling problem (sulphur dioxide level too low). Everything else with these wines is absolutely lovely.

**Domaine Mugneret-Gibourg/**
**Domaine Georges Mugneret**
Premier Cru Les Feusselottes which is classy, delicate and lingering. Worth the hunt for it!

### Domaine Christopher Newman
Bonnes Mares of depth and flavour in recent years.

### Domaine Georges Roumier/Christophe Roumier
Straight Chambolle which is pure fruit and shows great style. There is also a particularly floral Musigny and Bonnes Mares as well as stylish Amoureuses.

### Domaine Bernard Serveau
Really excellent, infinitely silky Les Chabiots. Other producers might learn from this little-vaunted domaine.

### Domaine des Varoilles
Rich, fat and glossy Bonnes Mares – exemplary wine which ages in grand style.

### Domaine Comte Georges de Vogüé
Les Amoureuses which is floral and sometimes ethereal. On occasions, the Musigny is not so very much better, which it should be for the price; at other times, it is magical. Bonnes Mares can combine voluptuousness with backbone. The Musigny Blanc, made from Chardonnay, is good, but the rarity justifies the price more than anything else. However, I do not agree with those who say you could think it was a red wine if blindfolded!

## ●○ VOUGEOT

**1996 production:**

***Grand Cru* ●**

| | |
|---|---|
| *Clos de Vougeot* | *1,791hl* |
| ***AOC Communale & Premiers Crus* ●** | *569hl* |
| ***AOC Communale & Premiers Crus* ○** | *138hl* |

***Premiers Crus:*** *Les Petits Vougeots, Les Cras (part), Clos de la Perrière*

The Grand Cru is Clos de Vougeot, and this can only be red, whereas the modest quantity of Premiers Crus and appellation Vougeot wine includes a small amount of white.

The Grand Cru dominates the commune, both by reputation and through sheer size: it covers 50ha and accounts for more than four-fifths of the land under vines in Vougeot. Except for the fact that historically it is a *clos* surrounded by walls, all this land would almost certainly not be classed as Grand Cru, for the soil types and positions on the slope are amazingly disparate. The other drama is that if the Clos were in Bordeaux, it would almost certainly be in the hands of one owner, not of just over 80. The single proprietor could then select the best *cuvées*, from the real Grand Cru parts of the Clos, and make a genuine *grand vin*, perhaps creating a second wine for the rest. However, this is not to be.

The Clos lies at an altitude of 240–270m (785–885ft), with a gentle three to four per cent gradient. The vineyards go right down to the Route Nationale, making it the only Grand Cru so low on the Côte. It is this that is especially worrying for those who do concern themselves about genuine Grand Cru status in Burgundy, because the soil here is deeper, on alluvial deposits, and not particularly well-drained. It is impossible to make wines of intrinsic breed from soil of this type, but it is just the quality one seeks in a Grand Cru.

The top part of the Clos is on Bathonian oolitic limestone, with a covering of pebbles and little clay. In the middle of the slope it changes to Bajocian limestone with much more clay, but the pebbles help provide good drainage. There is no doubt that to have a hope of an element of real 'class' in your Clos de Vougeot it would be as well to choose proprietors with vineyards in the upper part of the Grand Cru. Unfortunately, however, it is not as simple as that. The hand of man counts, as always, for a great deal, and much also depends on the size of the parcel owned, as vinifying a small amount of wine is always difficult and a certain 'mass' is necessary for really satisfactory results. To this end, people with several plots in various parts of the Clos will put their grapes together to make one *cuvée*. This is sometimes beneficial when all the plots are well placed, but in other cases it 'dilutes' the 'real' Grand Cru plot by mixing it with grapes from a piece of land which would barely merit Premier Cru status in another commune.

Locally, the difference between the upper and lower parts of the Clos has always been recognised; apparently, before World War II, there was even talk of taxing the two parts separately, but the idea was not realised. Certainly, the most reputed *climats* (Musigny de Vougeot and Grand Maupertuis are examples) are in the higher part of the Grand Cru, although judicious blending between complementary plots of land can produce wines of great interest.

Clos de Vougeot should be rich, sometimes even chocolatey, with a powerful background. Some wines have violets on the nose and a liquorice finish, while the very ripe vintages can be redolent of roasted pecans. There should be good flesh and generosity, and a long, long finish, but the wine should not be overwhelming – no burgundy should. The aim is to overpower with flavour and texture.

The Premiers Crus share some similarities with Chambolle-Musigny, with finesse and attraction, but without the body of the Clos. The Clos Blanc de Vougeot produces white wines and is in the hands of one owner; thus, it is difficult to judge if its lack of excitement is due intrinsically to the plot or to the winemaking.

Straight Vougeot does not show style, but can be pleasant; many a beginner has mistaken it for Clos de Vougeot, a problem of complicated Burgundian nomenclature.

## *A Personal Selection of Vougeot Producers*

### Domaine Robert Arnoux

Clos de Vougeot of a very high standard and which does justice to its favoured position in the Clos. Rich, truffley and textured.

### Domaine Bertagna

Recent vintages seem to be on the up: lovely Vougeot Premier Cru, with wonderful bouquet and fruit, and good Clos de la Perrière with chocolatey overtones. About half of this vineyard was replanted in the mid-1960s, so it has now come of age.

### Domaine René Engel

Now making some of the very best examples of the genre.

### Domaine Jean Grivot

Clos de Vougeot of fine quality and real Grand Cru character. My money is on the '93 for the future.

### Domaine Gros Frère et Soeur

Bernard Gros makes really commendable Clos Vougeot.

### Domaine Anne et François Gros

The young vintages of Clos Vougeot are most promising.

### Domaine Jean Gros

Really superb Clos Vougeot, classic and rich. Impressive.

### Domaine Mongeard-Mugneret

Beautifully placed in the Clos, the wines are usually most honourable, although they can occasionally be a bit blunt.

### Domaine Georges Mugneret

Excellent Clos Vougeot, often needing time.

### Domaine Daniel Rion & Fils

Clos de Vougeot which can be really good.

### Domaine des Varoilles

These are classic Clos Vougeots, wines which are big, rich and need time to develop.

## ● FLAGEY-ECHEZEAUX

**1996 production:**

**Grands Crus**

| | |
|---|---|
| *Echézeaux* | *1,365hl* |
| *Grands Echézeaux* | *337hl* |

There are no Premiers Crus as such, although the two Grands Crus can be declassified, and the *village* wine from Flagey is sold as Vosne-Romanée. But the glory is in the two Grands Crus. These are really *lieux-dits* which are above Clos de Vougeot and not near the village of Flagey at all. The upper part of Echézeaux is certainly the best section of the vineyard, but the very size and disparity of this large area means that it sometimes does not reach the standard of the more homogeneous Grands Echézeaux.

The rock structure that underpins Echézeaux is immensely complicated, with lower Bathonian and upper Bajocian limestone in constant interplay. The vineyard of Echézeaux is placed high for a Grand Cru, but the soil has good pebbles, and is deep enough, for the classification to be justified. However, there is great diversity, with excessive limestone in places but rich clay and brown chalk in others. There is an enormous difference in gradient between the two Grands Crus, with the upper part of Echézeaux at between 13-14 per cent and Grands Echézeaux at only three to four per cent.

When tasting a number of Echézeaux against Grands Echézeaux, you tend to think that the difference between the two is rather overstated. As always in Burgundy, it seems, the hand of man counts for so much, and I have had many Echézeaux which were better than their grander brothers. In principle, Grands Echézeaux should live longer, with the power and structure to outlast the more elegant Echézeaux. But judicious new wood can give both wines full body and, as for finesse, that really can be gained or destroyed forever in the fermenting vat. Still, you should find a touch more complexity of bouquet in mature Grands Echézeaux.

*A Personal Selection of Flagey-Echézeaux Producers*

**Domaine Georges Clerget/Christian Clerget**
Echézeaux of usually fine quality.

**Maison Joseph Drouhin**
Grands Echézeaux and Echézeaux which have always impressed; earthy, spicy, superb and long-finishing.

**Domaine René Engel**
Grands Echézeaux and Echézeaux to covet.

**Domaine Jean Grivot**
The wines from this estate are Echézeaux with which to reckon – preferably as often as possible.

**Domaine Henri Jayer**
Jayer produces wonderful unfiltered Echézeaux, which is difficult to resist in its comparative youth because of the glossy fruit and structured balance which inhabits the palate – even though you know full well that you should keep it.

**Domaine Mongeard-Mugneret**
Both the Grands Crus are found at this domaine, and very fine they are too – not the ultimate breed, perhaps, but some big wines nonetheless.

**Domaine Mugneret-Gibourg/**
**Domaine Georges Mugneret**
Bang-on Echézeaux, here: the 1989 has bitter-cherry flavour in abundance and terrific persistence.

**Domaine de la Romanée-Conti**
Echézeaux usually matures at a faster rate than Grands Echézeaux does. Both the '89s at this estate are, frankly, fabulous: the Echézeaux is full of red fruits, while the Grands Echézeaux is truffley, with more glycerol and fat. The Echézeaux '84 is gamey and very good value. Both wines can last very well, as witnessed by the Echézeaux '62 which was drunk recently. The '85s are lovely from now on.

## ● VOSNE-ROMANEE

**1996 production:**

| | |
|---|---|
| **Grands Crus** | |
| *Romanée-Conti* | *50hl* |
| *La Romanée* | *31hl* |
| *La Tâche* | *225hl* |
| *Romanée-St-Vivant* | *339hl* |
| *Richebourg* | *274hl* |
| *La Grande Rue* | *57hl* |
| ***AOC Communale & Premiers Crus*** | *7,325hl* |

***Premiers Crus:*** *Aux Malconsorts, Les Beaux Monts, Les Suchots, Les Gaudichots, Aux Brûlées, Les Chaumes, Aux Raignots Le Clos des Réas*

There is an element of shared vineyards between Vosne and Flagey-Echézeaux, as the straight appellation Vosne-Romanée comes from both communes. But the splendour of Vosne is its Grands Crus, a matchless yardstick by which to measure other great wines from the Côte de Nuits.

However, it sets itself a tough task, since now that the potential of these great growths is known, they are also measured against the best that they themselves can do. If we find them lacking, we have every right to say so, just as the producers feel they have every right to charge very high prices.

The Grands Crus are on the middle part of the slope, where the limestone/clay/pebble mixture is at its most balanced. The ideal size of these pebbles, or small broken stones, is between two millimetres and one centimetre in diameter. Their presence facilitates good drainage, and the larger ones store heat during the day and help to stop the temperature descending too far at night. Romanée-Conti has brown, chalky soil, with a clay and iron content – giving wines of finesse, depth and complexity. Romanée-St-Vivant has far deeper soil, with clay but also rich in limestone. Aux Raignots, above La Romanée, has sandier soil, but the limestone rock is close to the surface, so much so that 30 years ago they used explosives to break it up and prevent chlorosis of the vines.

The degree of slope changes, with La Romanée having a gradient of about 16% and Aux Raignots and the top part of Aux Malconsorts between 14–15%. The lower part of La Tâche is not on such a marked slope, but the pebble/small stone content ensures perfect drainage. The Vosne vineyard goes up to about 350m (1,150ft).

The tasting differences between the five Grands Crus are, naturally, studied at length; decision-making of this sort is one of the least painful parts of the wine business even if it may hurt financially. Romanée-Conti and La Tâche seem to change positions according to the year – in one vintage Romanée-Conti runs away with the honours, in others it is La Tâche which sails straight to the top. What you find in both, in good years, is an explosive array of sensations on the nose and great persistence on the palate. Truffles, undergrowth, wet earth, sheer voluptuous texture and flavour are all hallmarks of these two Grands Crus. There are also extraordinarily rich Richebourgs, velvet come to life, and astonishing La Romanée and Romanée-St-Vivant, but they may not possess quite such a brutal amount of aromas and tastes. If you like your senses assailed, these are the wines for you – ascetics stay away. Rubens would have loved them.

La Grande Rue lies between La Tâche and the Romanée wines, but does not display such depth and breeding. As it is in the hands of one owner, it is difficult to say if it has the potential to rise higher – perhaps it could. Aux Malconsorts can have great finesse, and Les Suchots and Les Beaux Monts hints of violets. Overall, the top wines of Vosne have an element of spiciness which is perhaps unique in Burgundy. It must be that irony, reddish soil. Straight appellation Vosne is usually perfumed and elegant; it should not be clumsy and thick. There is often a smell of cocoa and chocolate.

## *A Personal Selection of Vosne-Romanée Producers*

### Domaine Robert Arnoux

Romanée-St-Vivant and Les Suchots which mix oak, red fruits and violets. Much seems to be going right here.

### Domaine Sylvain Cathiard

Now a good source for Vosne Premiers Crus.

### Domaine Jean Grivot (now includes Domaine Jacqueline Jayer)

Les Beaux-Monts and village Vosne are nearly always rewarding.

### Domaine Jean Gros

Clos des Réas with a stunning bouquet, a real mouthful of flavour. I always seem to strike lucky with this estate.

### Domaine Alain Hudelot-Noëllat

Some formidable wines emerge from this domaine, including some juicy, fat Les Suchots, Romanée-St-Vivant with a spicy, cocoa nose and a taste of toast – an exotic, spice-bazaar wine with great length – and incredible, rich, velvety Richebourg. *A ne pas manquer*.

### Maison Louis Latour

Romanée-St-Vivant Les Quatre Journaux has always been a favourite; some wonderful, flavour-packed wines to keep.

### Domaine Leroy

Leroy makes Richebourg and Romanée-St-Vivant of extraordinary, even essence-like concentration. A specific style, but what mouthfuls of wine!

### Domaine Manière-Noirot

Manière-Noirot comes up with Les Suchots, which is earthy and *sauvage* with lots of spicy appellation character. The wines can age well.

### Domaine Méo-Camuzet

Rich, scented Les Brûlées, and Cros Parentoux I feel is Grand Cru quality in fine vintages, so great is its depth of flavour and aromatic complexity. The use of 100% new wood makes these wines enticing even when young, for there is always enormous fruit extract as well.

### Domaine Moillard-Grivot

Les Malconsorts has pleased me more than any of the wines from this estate, because it has that Vosne minerally taste and balance and is not just 'big'.

### Domaine Mongeard-Mugneret

There is a rustic side to these wines, but Les Suchots has spiciness on the nose and definite quality on the palate.

### Domaine Mugneret-Gibourg/Georges Mugneret

Excellent Echézeaux, well worth the wait for it to mature.

### Domaine Daniel Rion & Fils

Patrice Rion makes very good wines, with a wonderful trio of vintages in '88, '89 and '90. The charm is in comparing Les Chaumes with Les Beaux Monts. The Chaumes often has a classier bouquet, but the Beaux Monts is long and seductive on the palate.

### Domaine de la Romanée-Conti

Superlatives abound here, and most of them are justified. When these wines are on form, they do have that something extra. The 1980s and the '82s are very pretty right now; Richebourg '79 is a recent stunner. Avoid the '75s (which are no worse than any one else's); the '69s are good but could have been even better. Romanée-Conti '78, '66, '61, '55, '53, '52, '29, '28 and '21, all tasted at the domaine, could be the greatest burgundies ever made. If a wine could have a soul, it would be a Romanée-Conti. La Tâche '62 and '52 are of those experiences made in heaven. Romanée-Conti was replanted in 1947 – previous vintages were on un-grafted vines – and '52 was the first vintage after the replanting. The '85s are undoubtedly great, as are the '88s, '89s and '90s. The '91s should not be missed and the '93s will be giants.

### Domaine Emmanuel Rouget

Echézeaux from a good stable, as well as the fine Clos Parantoux. (Now makes all the Jayer wine, too.)

## ●○ NUITS-ST-GEORGES

**1996 production:**

***AOC Communale & Premiers Crus* ●** *14,515hl*

***AOC Communale & Premiers Crus* ○** *145hl*

***Premiers Crus:*** *(in the commune of Nuits) Les St-Georges, Les Vaucrains, Les Cailles, Les Porrets, Les Pruliers, Les Hauts Pruliers (part), Aux Murgers, La Richemone, Les Chaboeufs, Les Perrières, La Roncière, Les Procès, Rue de Chaux, Aux Boudots, Aux Cras,*

*Aux Chaignots, Aux Thorey (part), Aux Vignes Rondes, Aux Bousselots, Les Poulettes, Les Crots (part), Les Vallerots (part), Aux Champs Perdrix (part), Perrière-Noblot (part), Les Damodes (part), Chaines-Carteaux (part), Aux Argillats. (Premiers Crus in the commune of Prémeaux) Clos de la Maréchale, Clos Arlot, Les Argillières, Les Grandes Vignes, Aux Corvées, Les Forêts, Les Didiers, Aux Perdrix*

Nuits-St-Georges may be the most evocative name in Burgundy. It certainly is for me. A Nuits-St-Georges Les Argillats ensnared me for ever, led me to realise what wine and taste could be, and taught me to link the brain with the senses. It also made me love Burgundy, the whole blend of landscape and people and history. Perhaps most important of all, it helped me to reject wines which do the region no honour.

The top *crus* are on the southern side of Nuits towards Prémeaux, but that should not overshadow those other good vineyards on the northern side towards Vosne-Romanée.

The nuances of taste between the most exciting of the Premiers Crus (which some would class as Grands Crus should there ever be a 'reshuffle') follow the subtle shifts in soil makeup. The overall picture is marl, intermingled with sand and pebbles which have come away from the hard calcareous summit of the slope. Mid-slope is where the silt and scree over marl formula works best, so here lie the best growths. In the Nuits-Prémeaux area, the subsoil is Bathonian limestone with outcrops of Bajocian limestone covered with clay. The two vineyards nearest the outskirts of Nuits, Rue de Chaux and Les Procès, have significant clay content and are also pebbly. La Roncière is on lighter, more gravelly soil, leading to earlier ripening (clay is a cold soil). The subsoil here is composed of a vein of Comblanchien hard limestone. Les Porrets and Les Cailles have deep clay soil with few pebbles; Les Perrières is higher with more pebbles. Les St-Georges has more sand in the mixture, less heavy soil than at Les Porrets, while Les Vaucrains combines heavy, rich soil with considerable sand and pebbles for balance.

The northern Nuits vineyards veer more to Vosne in soil type. There are outcrops of Bajocian limestone with some alluvial soil. La Richemone has lighter, pebbly soil, while Aux Chaignots possesses more clay with the pebbles – this is further accentuated as you go towards Nuits and the soil becomes heavier. Les Damodes looks towards Vosne in the type of wine it produces. Aux Argillats faces due south, while the general exposure of this area is southeast.

This, then, is the nursery of those great, rich, intoxicating Nuits wines. They have a severe backbone to them, an 'irony' structure and a minerally gaminess which makes no compromises. That is why anodyne, soupy Nuits is a travesty; good Nuits is not merely meant to soothe, it is meant to challenge. Les Vaucrains is the slowest to mature, the most tannic and closed when young, but oh, so majestic when mature. Les St-Georges is the most complete wine, combining finesse with power, positively brambly and multidimensional in bouquet and taste. Les Porrets is known for its pure Nuits *goût de terroir*, earthy, irony, wild, but generous and all-enveloping underneath. Les Cailles is more elegant, balanced and rich in texture, while Les Pruliers has strong Nuits character, softening with bottle age. Les Perrières and La Roncière (the proof that blackberries are not just fanciful!) may not have the colour of their neighbours, but make up for that with a touch more delicacy. On the other side of Nuits, there is wonderful flavour, if less breed. Aux Chaignots and Aux Boudots give lovely bottles, wines of body and character. There is less flesh but plenty of olfactory interest in La Richemone and Les Damodes, more subtly Vosne, less sturdily Nuits.

## *A Personal Selection of Nuits-St-Georges Producers*

### Domaine de l'Arlot

Premier Cru Clos des Forêts '89 with lots of earthy fruit, and an '89 white Premier Cru Clos de l'Arlot of beautiful, fresh nuttiness. These are highlights, but consistency is all here.

### Domaine Robert Chevillon

Les Vaucrains and Les Cailles which usually match up to your expectations (if not your dreams) of Nuits, with strong black cherries and structure.

### Joseph Faiveley

It is sometimes quite difficult to spot the difference between a Faiveley domaine wine and one from their important *négoce* business, as the word 'Domaine' does not actually appear on the label. But Clos de la Maréchale, Premier Cru, is solely owned by the Faiveley family and is a cornerstone of their extensive estate. The wine is always powerful, fleshy and loaded with Nuits character and earthy flavour.

### Domaine Henri Gouges

A visit to the Gouges cellars is a liquid lesson in how this appellation should taste. Rich and fruity Les Pruliers, earthy, enveloping Clos des Porrets, deep, tannic Les Vaucrains, and sublime Les St-Georges. There is also the strong and forceful white La Perrière, made from a white mutation of the Pinot Noir and not at all like Chardonnay. The domaine is now back to formidable form.

### Domaine Jean Grivot

Pruliers which is true Nuits and village wine often of great quality.

### Domaine Henri Jayer

Straight Nuits-St-Georges, unfiltered, with a stunning colour, power and lots of raw fruit; these wines need years.

### Domaine Bertrand Machard de Gramont

The wines are usually stylish, going for flavour and elegance rather than massive body. The Hauts Pruliers is most successful.

### Domaine Alain Michelot
Aux Chaignots which is good and earthy, and excellent Les St-Georges.

### Domaine Daniel Rion & Fils
Fine bottles are made here: an earthy yet elegant Nuits-St-Georges Clos des Argillières, and especially the Hauts Pruliers, a strong and muscular wine with a marked minerally character when young, mellowing beautifully with age.

### Domaine Jean Tardy
Explosively good Les Bondots.

## ●○ PREMEAUX
The fate of Prémeaux is inextricably linked with that of Nuits-St-Georges, and the vineyard area is broken down into the following proportions:

| | |
|---|---|
| *Nuits-St-Georges Premiers Crus* | *42.25ha* |
| *Nuits-St-Georges* | *11.79ha* |
| *Côte de Nuits-Villages* | *4.97ha* |

There are a large number of *clos* among the Premiers Crus (listed under Nuits-St-Georges). Differences in taste exist between the Premiers Crus, but too often these are difficult to detect as the style seems to be 'solid *négociant*' rather than subtle and distinctive; these *clos* tend to be monopolies owned by the important *négociant* houses of Nuits. In principle, Clos des Argillières is often the most complete wine, combining structure with elegance – the vineyard is on rock with thin soil. This occurs again at the Clos Arlot, part of which is on a steep slope, whereas the Clos de la Maréchale is practically flat with deeper soil. Aux Corvées is on clay-limestone soil. There are many old vines in the area.

## ●○ COTE DE NUITS-VILLAGES
**1996 production:**

| | |
|---|---|
| *Côte de Nuits-Villages* ● | *8,171hl* |
| *Côte de Nuits-Villages* ○ | *172hl* |

The villages which make up this appellation are: Brochon, Comblanchien, Corgoloin, Fixin and Prémeaux (Prissey). Of these, only Fixin can choose to sell its wines either under the name of Fixin itself or Côte de Nuits-Villages. There has long been discussion and political manoeuvre as to whether Marsannay, Couchey and even Chenôve should have the right to the Côte de Nuits-Villages appellation, but so far promotion has been resisted. This is a pity, if only because this higher recognition would help to prevent the ever-spreading mushroom growth from Dijon of supermarkets, garages and all the other paraphernalia deemed necessary for comfortable modern living. Pessac in the Graves is under the same threat from the city of Bordeaux.

The wines can be quite blunt and tannic when young, but the graph of development is more rapid than with a better appellation, so at three to five years they are usually at their most appealing. The danger is that most Côte de Nuits-Villages is a blend of wines from varying sources, so you can end up with a very neutral brew. Daniel Chopin-Groffier is an excellent producer.

For those interested in marble quarries, and their unsightly tips, they are spread out by the side of the road and up the Côte between Prémeaux and Ladoix. Comblanchien marble is a pink-beige colour. It was used to build the Paris Opéra, the Palais de Justice in Brussels and, more recently, Orly Airport.

## ●○ HAUTES-COTES DE NUITS AND HAUTES-COTES DE BEAUNE

**1996 production:**

| | |
|---|---|
| *Hautes-Côtes de Beaune* | *24,898hl* |
| ● | *20,045hl* |
| ○ | *4,853hl* |
| *Hautes-Côtes de Nuits* | *30,050hl* |
| ● | *25,072hl* |
| ○ | *4,978hl* |

These are the villages which have the right to the Bourgogne Hautes-Côtes de Beaune appellation: Baubigny, Bouze-lès-Beaune, Cirey-lès-Nolay, Cormot, Echevronnne, Fussey, Magny-lès-Villers, Mavilly-Mandelot, Meloisey, Nantoux, Nolay, La Rochepot and Vauchignon. In Saône et Loire, the following villages are included: Change, Créot, Epertully, Paris l'Hôpital and part of Cheilly-lès-Maranges, Dezize-lès-Maranges and Sampigny-lès-Maranges.

Much of this area is plateau. However, between Mavilly-Mandelot and La Rochepot, the vineyards are on slopes at an altitude of 350–450m (1,170–1,470ft). As a result, picking on the Hautes-Côtes is about a week later than on the Côte d'Or. The geological debris favours vine-growing and the slopes face east-southeast, which is very important at such heights. The plateau of Meloisey has brown limestone soil and is well sited for making wines of quality.

The following villages have the right to the Bourgogne Hautes-Côtes de Nuits appellation: Arcénant, Bévy, Chaux, Chévannes, Collonges-lès-Bévy, Curtil-Vergy, L'Etang-Vergy, Magny-lès-Villers, Marey-lès-Fussey, Messanges, Meuilley, Reule Vergy, Villars-Fontaine, Villers-la-Faye.

Some of the best communes are on gentle slopes, sheltered from the west winds; examples are Villers-la-Faye and Magny-lès-Villers. At Villers there is deep, brown limestone, which gives quality. It must be said that vineyards hovering round the 400-metre mark (1,300ft) are at a disadvantage when it comes to consistent quality production, and they need the benefit of the best possible site to compensate for this. The wines from these two areas have the right to the basic Bourgogne appellation; only after tasting can the Hautes-Côtes label be awarded.

### *A Personal Selection of Hautes-Côtes Producers*

**Domaine François Charles**

Lovely raspberryish Hautes-Côtes de Beaune from Nantoux.

### Domaine Guy Dufouleur

Vibrant, fruity Hautes-Côtes de Nuits, reminiscent of loganberries.

### Les Caves des Hautes-Côtes Groupement de Producteurs

The cooperative now vinifies about 25% of the total production, and the quality is very good. Recently I have been impressed by its wines from the two Hautes-Côtes, and consider them some of the best value in Burgundy.

### Domaine Bernard Hudelot/Domaine de Montmain

Splendid Hautes-Côtes de Nuits from Villars-Fontaine, and good Chardonnay, too.

### Domaine Patrick Hudelot

Hautes-Côtes de Nuits Les Genevrières with plenty of backbone and flavour.

### Domaine Lucien Jacob

A leading figure in the Hautes-Côtes, with much official clonal experimentation at his estate at Echevronne. He also finds time to make good Hautes-Côtes de Beaune (and Savigny, too).

### Domaine Jean Joliot & Fils

Hautes-Côtes de Beaune from Nantoux, with a scent of violets and the fruit and body to be delicious at four to five years old.

### Domaine Henri Naudin-Ferrand

Commendable Hautes-Côtes de Nuits from Magny-lès-Villers and very good Hautes-Côtes de Beaune. Really reliable.

### Domaine Michel Serveau

This grower in La Rochepot makes superb Hautes-Côtes de Beaune, gloriously scented and fruity. Exemplary for the appellation.

### Domaine Thévenot-le-Brun & Fils

Hautes-Côtes de Nuits Clos du Vignon which is attractive and very easy to drink.

## ●○ PERNAND-VERGELESSES

**1996 production:**

| | |
|---|---|
| **Grand Cru** | |
| *Corton-Charlemagne* | *2,223hl* |
| ***AOC Communale & Premiers Crus* ●** | *3,729hl* |
| ***AOC Communale & Premiers Crus* ○** | *1,532hl* |

***Premiers Crus:*** *Ile des Hautes Vergelesses, Les Basses Vergelesses, Creux de la Net (part), Les Fichots, Caradeux (part)*

This pretty village, in the shadow of the *montagne* of Corton, has rather a schizophrenic existence, sharing as it does the red Grand Cru Corton and the white Grand Cru Corton-Charlemagne with the villages of Aloxe-Corton and Ladoix-Serrigny. Pernand also shares with Aloxe-Corton the currently unused white Grand Cru appellation Charlemagne. The Pernand-Vergelesses side of the great hill of Corton is better suited to producing great white wines than red. The soil is less ferruginous, with a higher limestone content in the marl, and a fair idea of what should be planted where on the Corton hill can be obtained by the naked eye – where the soil is redder, it should be Pinot Noir, where it is more chalky white, the Chardonnay is unsurpassed.

The 'nervy' character of Corton-Charlemagne is undoubtedly due to vine roots going down into the rock to a depth of two metres (seven feet) or more, with slight differences in the ultimate taste according to whether the soil is blue or white marl, the former a touch richer and more perfumed, the latter more dry and flinty. The best site is farther away from the village, facing south-southwest. Les Vergelesses comes from soil with about one-third clay in its content, leading to firmer red wines than those of lesser *crus*.

Corton-Charlemagne is probably the slowest to mature of all Burgundian white wines, and it is nearly always drunk too young. With bottle-age, its great bouquet, often slightly peppery in youth, turns to grilled almonds and cinnamon. There is a tautness about top Corton-Charlemagne which is not found in the richer, more unctuous Le Montrachet. White Pernand-Vergelesses is, naturally, much softer and should be drunk relatively young. Red Corton is, of course, a *vin de garde* to rival the Grands Crus of the Côte de Nuits, but red Pernand-Vergelesses at Premier Cru level is much softer, more seductive, with its bouquet of raspberries and violets, sometimes with a taste of quince jelly on the palate. Together with Savigny-lès-Beaune, these are the prettiest wines of the Côte de Beaune. Straight *village* Pernand is more earthy and less charming, even harsh in some years, but usually good value. Pernand has long made a speciality of its Aligoté, planted on marly, well-sited slopes which give it a round, full taste.

## *A Personal Selection of Pernand-Vergelesses Producers*

### Domaine Bonneau du Martray

Lying at the very heart of Pernand-Vergelesses and Aloxe-Corton, and probably the original estate of the Emperor Charlemagne, this is a remarkable domaine with fabulous Corton-Charlemagne. It even makes stunning wine in medium-quality years.

### Domaine Maurice Chapuis

Delicious Corton-Charlemagne, not as long-lived as some.

### Domaine P Dubreuil-Fontaine Père & Fils

Red Clos Berthet is perfumed and tempting at four to five years, while the white is absolutely lovely at two to four. This is a delicious pair of wines.

### Domaine Jacques Germain

Superb white Pernand, here, all rich cinnamon and honey – utterly delicious.

### Domaine Michel Juillot

Michel Juillot's first vintage of Corton-Charlemagne – from vines *en fermage* – was in 1986. This is a beautifully scented, taut and concentrated wine of authority and length, and worth seeking out.

### Domaine Laleure-Piot

This domaine is really a white wine specialist, including very good Aligoté; but this should not denigrate the reds.

### Maison Louis Latour

Consistently fine Ile des Vergelesses, often with violets and strawberries. Exemplary Corton-Charlemagne, built to last, as my own cellar attests.

## ●○ LADOIX-SERRIGNY

**1996 production:**

| | |
|---|---|
| ***AOC Communale & Premiers Crus*** ● | *4,054hl* |
| ***AOC Communale & Premiers Crus*** ○ | *759hl* |

***Premiers Crus:*** *La Micaude, La Corvée, Le Clou d'Orge, Les Joyeuses, Bois Roussot, Basses Mourettes and Hautes Mourettes*

The appellation name is really that of two villages, of which Ladoix is more important viticulturally. With Pernand-Vergelesses, it marks the northern end of the Côte de Beaune. This is another of Burgundy's schizophrenic appellations, because much of its production can be classified as Grand and Premier Cru Aloxe-Corton, and it is rare to see Ladoix-Serrigny on a label. This wine is more often than not declassified into Côte de Beaune-Villages.

Brown limestone soils are suitable for production of red wines, whereas white marl is better for the Chardonnay. Gréchons and Les Fautrières, facing east-southeast and high up on the slope, produce good white wines. The best-placed *climats* of Ladoix provide wines of body and character, derived from microclimate and a favourable position on the slope. Perhaps they are the bridge between the two Côtes. Names to trust are those that make good Aloxe, but there are some terrible 'apologies' for fine burgundy in this area. Domaine Chevalier makes honourable Ladoix; the Pierre André '92 white Ladoix and the '90 red are two respectable domaine wines. I also recommend Domaine Prince Florent de Mérode (there has been marked improvement) and Domaine Michel Mallard.

## ●○ ALOXE-CORTON

**1995 production:**

| | |
|---|---|
| **Grand Cru** | |
| *Corton* ● | *3,882hl* |
| *Corton* ○ | *100hl* |
| ***AOC Communale & Premiers Crus*** ● | *5,980hl* |
| ***AOC Communale & Premiers Crus*** ○ | *28hl* |

***Premiers Crus:*** *(in the commune of Ladoix-Serrigny) Les Maréchaudes, La Toppe au Vert, La Coutière, Les Grandes Lolières, Les Petites Lolières, Basses Mourettes. (Premiers Crus in the commune of Aloxe-Corton) Les Valozières (part), Les Chaillots (part), Les Fournières, Les Maréchaudes (part), Les Paulands (part), Les Vercots, Les Guérets*

The small village of Aloxe-Corton nestles beneath the Massif du Corton, with the vines so close to the houses that you would not be surprised to see them creeping through the doorways. The village has a share in the two glittering Grands Crus of Corton and Corton-Charlemagne, while the Premiers Crus and the straight village wine spill over into Ladoix-Serrigny.

A further elaboration of the appellation edicts allows the following vineyards to use the distinguished label Corton. In Ladoix-Serrigny: Les Vergennes (part), Le Rognet-Corton (part); in Aloxe-Corton: Le Corton, Le Clos du Roi, Les Renardes, Les Bressandes, Les Maréchaudes (part), Les Paulands (part), Les Chaumes, La Vigne au Saint, Les Meix Lallemand, Les Meix (part), Les Combes (part), Le Charlemagne (part), Les Pougets (part), Les Languettes (part), Les Chaumes et la Voierosse, Les Fiétres, Les Perrières, Les Grèves; in Pernand-Vergelesses: Le Charlemagne (part) (red wines only).

The parts of this great bluff reserved for making red Corton are those where the soil is red and irony, while the white is made from more calcareous marl. As the base is rock and the soil is poor and thin, yields are not big. Corton-Bressandes is partly on an old quarry, always a feature of very hard limestone. Corton-Charlemagne is produced on the top of the hill, where the soil is whiter, with the Chardonnay planted right up to the Bois de Corton. Of course, the subsoil has an origin of lava, as can be seen in *crus* such as Clos du Roi or Les Perrières. In many of the Premiers Crus, such as Les Maréchaudes, Les Valozières, Les Chaillots, Les Fournières and Les Vercots the soil is somewhat ferruginous and deeper. The straight Aloxe-Corton wines come from quite deep, red-brown soil, with more sand in the subsoil due to an alluvial influence. These three famous appellations are spread over the three communes as the figures in the table below show.

| | Hectares | Ares |
|---|---|---|
| **In Aloxe-Corton:** | | |
| Appellation Aloxe-Corton | 89 | 71 |
| Appellation Aloxe-Corton 1er Cru | 29 | 12 |
| Appellation Corton | 120 | 50 |
| Appellation Corton-Charlemagne | 48 | 57 |
| **In Pernand-Vergelesses:** | | |
| Appellation Pernand-Vergelesses | 137 | 63 |
| Appellation Pernand-Vergelesses 1er Cru | 56 | 51 |
| Appellation Corton, Corton-Charlemagne & Charlemagne | 34 | 50 |
| **In Ladoix-Serrigny:** | | |
| Appellation Ladoix-Serrigny* | 117 | 91 |
| Appellation Ladoix-Serrigny 1er Cru | 14 | 38 |
| Appellation Aloxe-Corton 1er Cru | 8 | 46 |
| Appellation Corton & Corton-Charlemagne | 28 | 47 |

* The wines from this area of production may also be named Côte de Beaune-Villages.

Red Corton is the most powerful, often the most tannic of all the Côte de Beaune red wines. It needs time for its bouquet to develop and for a certain youthful hardness to soften. There is almost a thickness to it, a texture of mouth-coating body and richness. Corton Clos du Roi is very structured in youth, even quite severe, but opens out majestically. Corton-Bressandes is rounder and fatter, with enormous flattering flavour on the palate. Corton-Renardes is meant to have a *côté animal*, which just might be auto-suggestion, but there is a raw, gamey side to it, and always punchy flavour, which is a feature of these top growths. Truffles, too, can be detected in the top red wines from ripe years.

The Premiers Crus do not have this depth or richness, but some have finesse and elegance. It is a mistake to 'make' them big when that quality is not intrinsically theirs, but there should be a pleasant fullness in good years. After all, a Premier Cru such as Les Valozières is just a path's distance away from Corton-Bressandes. Straight Aloxe-Corton will obviously have less style, but can be a good, generous bottle.

The sheer, flinty glory of Corton-Charlemagne is extolled under Pernand-Vergelesses: nothing can replace that heady, honeyed bouquet and molten taste (perhaps there is volcanic richness in it). White Aloxe-Corton is a rarity; Domaine Daniel Senard (*qv*) makes it from the Pinot Beurot (Pinot Gris or Tokay d'Alsace). Planted here, the wine is round, powerful and alcoholic, not at all like Chardonnay.

## *A Personal Selection of Aloxe-Corton Producers*

### Domaine Bonneau du Martray

Often not very deep in colour, this Corton nevertheless shows lovely Pinot Noir character and lingering flavour. Recently, it has been gaining more depth.

### Domaine Hubert Bouzereau-Gruère

The Corton-Bressandes and Corton Clos de Roi here are of great depth and interest.

### Domaine Chandon de Briailles

Corton-Bressandes which can have glorious fruity depth and Clos du Roi which is for the 'long haul' in terms of longevity. Greatly increased quality.

### Domaine P Dubreuil-Fontaine Père & Fils

Corton-Bressandes and Clos du Roi which do not impress by their colour but most certainly do by their flavour.

### Domaine Joseph Faiveley

Corton Clos des Cortons that is quite stupendous, truly imposing and demanding bottle age.

### Domaine Michel Gaunoux

Corton-Renardes which is usually very big, strapping wine – some people think this is bliss, I think it is merely good.

### Maison Louis Jadot
Corton-Pougets displays good, juicy fruit, sometimes with a taste of strawberries. Corton-Bressandes is just as reliable.

### Maison Louis Latour
Château Corton-Grancey is the jewel in the crown, and there are some fine vintages, beautifully gamey and flavoursome; others are more dull. Corton Clos de la Vigne au Saint has more finesse and satiny sheen, and there are some superb bottles. Aloxe-Corton Les Chaillots can taste of plums.

### Domaine Moillard-Grivot
Have patience with the Clos du Roi. Corton-Charlemagne with a nose of may-blossom and cardamom and a texture of honey – it usually develops far more quickly than that of Louis Latour (*qv*).

### Domaine Parent
Corton-Renardes with character and a kernel flavour to it.

### Domaine Tollot-Beaut & Fils
Straight Aloxe-Corton which is a very good mouthful.

## ●○ SAVIGNY-LES-BEAUNE

**1996 production:**

***AOC Communale & Premiers Crus* ●** *14,611hl*

***AOC Communale & Premiers Crus* ○** *1,513hl*

***Premiers Crus:*** *Aux Vergelesses, Bas Marconnets, Les Jarrons (formerly Les Hauts Jarrons and La Dominode), Basses Vergelesses, Les Lavières, Aux Gravains, Les Peuillets (part), Aux Guettes (part), Les Talmettes, Les Charnières, Aux Fourneaux (part), Aux Clous (part), Aux Serpentières (part), Les Narbantons, Les Hauts Marconnets, Les Hauts Jarrons, Redrescut (part), Les Rouvrettes (part), Petits Godeaux (part)*

Technically, it should always be Savigny-lès-Beaune, with the accent, as *lès* comes from the Latin *latus*, presumably 'at the side' of Beaune. Savigny is a beautiful Burgundian village, to be glimpsed from the autoroute, but only to be savoured if visited at leisure. After Beaune and Santenay, Savigny produces more red wine than anywhere else on the Côte de Beaune, and although the wines do not have the staying power of the best examples of its rivals in size, there are some exquisite bottles of Savigny.

The village itself is at the entrance to the lovely valley of Fontaine-Froide. The vineyards can be neatly divided into two parts – those on the Pernand-Vergelesses side and those on the Beaune side. The former group forms a broad sweep under the charmingly named wooded summit of the Bois de Noël, facing due south, and including Aux Vergelesses, Les Lavières, Aux Gravains, Aux Serpentières and Aux Guettes. Here the soil is rough and gravelly, with irony oolite above. Below Les Lavières it is straight appellation territory, with reddish-brown limestone, some clay and few pebbles; the drainage is thus less good, the wines a little blunter. On the opposite hillside, on the slopes of

Mont Battois, the vineyards include Les Narbantons, Les Jarrons, Les Marconnets and Les Peuillets, facing east-northeast. Here the soil is more sandy and less pebbly, with deeper debris at the foot of the slopes.

The great mark of good Savigny is a heady perfume, a searing scent of violets, raspberries, flowers and red fruits. There is sometimes an enchanting lightness of touch in Savigny, an enticing quality that is particularly seductive when the wines are quite youthful. The wines of the Pernand side, Premiers Crus such as Les Lavières and Aux Guettes, should often be drunk young to see this unforgettable charm, while the Premiers Crus on the Beaune side, Les Narbantons, Bas Marconnets, Les Peuillets and La Dominode are more solid, they have a bit more 'stuffing' and that bouquet might take a few more years to reach its apogee. A great deal depends, as always, on the age of the vineyard. I remember drinking remarkable 20-year-old La Dominode from venerable vines. The rare whites can be charming and floral when drunk young. Some were thought to be made from Pinot Blanc, but it now seems more likely that the plants were Chardonnay all along.

### *A Personal Selection of Savigny-lès-Beaune Producers*

**Domaine Simon Bize & Fils**
Copybook wines which could provide a valuable lesson to some other producers. The son of the house, Patrick Bize, makes Les Vergelesses, Les Marconnets and Aux Guettes – the latter redolent of violets. These are true, frank, fruity wines, delicious at four to five years old.

**Domaine Chandon des Briailles**
Lovely straight Savigny, particularly from 1993 onwards.

**Domaine Bruno Clair**
Savigny-lès-Beaune La Dominode from a clayey soil, yielding a firm, concentrated, long-lasting wine.

**Domaine Maurice Ecard Père et Fils**
The Serpentières is highly recommended, both for value and pure pleasure.

**Domaine Pierre Guillemot**
Outstanding examples of Savigny, including a white which is immensely flowery and enchantingly full of fresh fruit.

**Domaine Jean-Marc Pavelot**
Attractive straight Savigny and Aux Guettes, as well as serious La Dominode.

**Domaine Tollot-Beaut & Fils**
Champ-Chevrey with a rich, sweet, old-style Pinot nose, and lovely depth and length on the palate.

## ●○ CHOREY-LES-BEAUNE

**1996 production:**

***AOC Communale* ●** *6,442hl*

***AOC Communale* ○** *169hl*

The vineyards of Chorey-lès-Beaune lie on each side of the Route Nationale, but more to the east on a plain of geological debris – the height is only 230m (755ft) and the soil is predominantly alluvial. There are no Premiers Crus, but a few *climats* are recognised. Les Champs-Longs and Pièce du Chapitre are among the best, on sandy alluvial topsoil, strong in iron content and more pebbly on the slope. Les Beaumonts, Les Ratosses, Les Crais and Poirier-Malchaussée are also good sites. Logically, it would seem that Les Beaumonts and Les Ratosses are more Savigny in type, while Les Champs-Longs resembles an Aloxe-Corton from the plain, and Poirier-Malchaussée and Les Crais, on marl, have good structure. Drink relatively young to enjoy their fruity charm.

The three domaines which do honour to Chorey are: Jacques Germain of the Château de Chorey, Tollot-Beaut and Maillard Pere et Fils. The two brothers at the Domaine Gay also make good wine from old vines; less refined and more rustic than the more noted domaines, but well worth buying. In fact, the overall value at Chorey is not to be denied. Much of the wine made at Chorey is sold as Côte de Beaune-Villages.

## ●○ BEAUNE

**1996 production:**

***AOC Communale & Premiers Crus* ●** *16,805hl*

***AOC Communale & Premiers Crus* ○** *1,520hl*

***Premiers Crus:*** *Les Marconnets, Les Fèves, Les Bressandes, Les Grèves, Les Teurons, Le Clos des Mouches, Champs Pimont, Clos du Roi (part), Au Coucherias (part), En l'Orme, En Genêt, Les Perrières, A l'Ecu, Les Cent Vignes, Les Toussaints, Sur les Grèves, Aux Cras, Le Clos de la Mousse, Les Chouacheux, Les Boucherottes, Les Vignes Franches, Les Aigrots, Pertuisots, Tiélandry or Clos Landry, Les Sizies, Les Avaux, Les Reversées, Le Bas des Teurons, Les Seurey, La Mignotte, Montée-Rouge (part), Les Montrevenots (part), Blanche Fleur (part), Les Epenottes (part), Clos de la Feguine*

To many, Beaune is the hub of Burgundy, and certainly it must feel so to the bevy of historic firms which make up *le négoce beaunois*. It is everything a provincial town should be: an historic and artistic centre, a vibrant market town and an active business community. Wine has made it international and even those who will never visit it utter its name with awe. And yet the remarkable ramparts seem to keep its essential spirit to itself. The summer streets may be crowded with cars bearing foreign numberplates, and for three days each November the Hospices de Beaune Auction is a magnet for both the wine trade and amateur wine-lovers; but for the rest of the year, Beaune is quiet, even sleepy, with everyone battened down in their homes by nightfall. People work hard in Beaune, and wine is a serious business. The Hospices Sale engenders a heady atmosphere of pushing and bustling, with lights over the cobbled streets and cafés brimming; but a more typical Beaune scene is to see that same Auction Hall transformed into the Saturday morning market, full of fruit, vegetables, cheese and *charcuterie*.

After having visited the magnificent Hôtel-Dieu, and seen tapestries, flamboyantly tiled roofs and beautiful woodwork, just wander through the streets looking at the fine town houses and the handsome churches. By day you will see the intricate stonework, by night the most lovely buildings and churches are suffused with soft light. This is when Beaune is magical, with the air smoky and cold and your heels on the cobbles the loudest sound in the air. These cobbles hide endless arched cellars, where the liquid wealth of Beaune matures and breathes and the walls blacken with age and humidity. When stones and architecture hold no more fascination for you, go out into the vineyards, which come right down to the perimeter of Beaune.

The slope of the Beaune vineyards is divided in two by the Route Nationale 470 (the Route de Bouze, which is amusing for English speakers). On the northern side of Beaune, near the border with Savigny, the Autoroute slashes through the top vineyard, Les Marconnets, but apparently the original plan was to route it through Le Montrachet so perhaps we should heave a sigh of relief. The vineyards go up to about 330m (1,080ft) and the soil is basically limestone debris. There are the usual nuances between the *climats*, and even within the *climats* themselves: Le Clos des Mouches, for example, is planted with Chardonnay on the upper part, and Pinot Noir below where the soil is browner and heavier. There is clay and less gravel in Les Boucherottes and Les Chouacheux, while Les Grèves, naturally, has gravel and faces southeast. Les Bressandes and Les Fèves are on marked slopes, while the thin soil of Les Marconnets, Les Fèves and Clos du Roi, and the fact that the roots have to dig deep, contribute to the wines' longevity.

As a generalisation, the Premiers Crus on the northern side of the Montagne de Beaune are the wines which take the longest to mature, while the vineyards to the south of the Route de Bouze are more delicate and show their beauty a little sooner. In a series of Beaune wines, one might begin with a Clos de la Mousse, go on to Beaune Teurons, then Marconnets, and finally Grèves, which combines finesse with depth. Clos du Roi is usually more robust than Cent Vignes.

Finally, it is often said in a somewhat derogatory manner that the Beaune vineyards are nearly all owned by the Beaune *négociants*, who combine that exacting role with being very important domaine proprietors. Personally, the exact social and commercial status of a vineyard owner has never concerned me over-much; it is the quality of the wine in the bottle that counts, and there are many superb Beaune Premiers Crus from these historic owners that have stood the test of time and given much pleasure. Unadorned *village* Beaune is usually straightforward and without complication, produced on deeper soil with more clay, more often susceptible to frost than the Premiers Crus. The whites have an earthy touch and seem best when quite young, when their fruit and flavour are at their apogee, and the reds, too, are sturdy and almost crunchy in youth – drink them at about five years old, and then go on to the Premiers Crus.

*A Personal Selection of Beaune Producers*

**Robert Ampeau & Fils**
Clos du Roi of structure and character.

**Domaine Besancenot**
An amazing array of Premiers Crus, including Grèves of finesse, rich Cent-Vignes, robust Theurons, mouthfilling Clos du Roi. I have been lucky, but choose carefully.

**Bouchard Père & Fils/ Domaines du Château de Beaune**
The largest owner of Beaune Premier Cru vineyards, there is a magnificent range of vineyards here, culminating in the splendid Grèves Vigne de l'Enfant Jésus, a satiny beauty of power and longevity. An excellent introduction to Beaune would be the Beaune du Château, a non-vintage Premier Cru blend in both red and white. Opt for the young vintages here.

**Chanson Père & Fils**
Recently I have liked young vintages of Bressandes, Clos du Roi and Grèves, which have all had style and fruit, but my experience of mature bottles has been less favourable.

**Domaine Joseph Drouhin**
Both the red and white Clos des Mouches are of high quality. I have a particular weakness for the white, which is rich and musky, with flesh and a taste of hazelnuts – a wonderful mouthful. There is often more than a hint of cherries in the red wines of Drouhin.

**Domaine Jacques Germain**
Wine of finesse and perfume from Château de Chorey, Chorey-lès-Beaune, through to Cent-Vignes, Vignes-Franches and Les Teurons – highly recommended. Look out for Premier Cru Domaine de Saux.

**Maison Louis Jadot**
The Clos des Ursules, an enclave within Les Vignes Franches, is usually a very good, sturdy bottle of Beaune, but I have often found the firm's Theurons and Boucherottes even better.

**Domaine Michel Lafarge**
Grèves which takes time to develop, but is worth the wait.

**Maison Louis Latour**
Vignes Franches which is robust and straightforward when young, developing more complexity and texture with bottle-age.

### Domaine Chantal Lescure (bottled and distributed by Labouré-Roi)

Well-made Chouacheux, with character and impact.

### Domaine Machard de Gramont

Truly beauteous Les Chouacheux, all raspberries and flavour and impeccable balance.

### Domaine Bernard Morey

Really top-class Les Grèves has appeared successful to me, if not in the top flight.

### Domaine Albert Morot

Impressive Teurons which is usually a great treat.

### Domaine Parent

Les Epenottes, sometimes 'jammy' but always honourable.

### Domaine Tollot-Beaut & Fils

Grèves with a wonderful bouquet, the kind that revives memories of past great bottles. There is always body and concentration in these wines, sometimes a dash too much alcohol for sheer perfection, but the standard here is consistently high.

## HOSPICES DE BEAUNE

The Sale of the Hospices' wines is held on the third Sunday of November. It is far too early after the vintage to give really definite pronouncements on taste, especially in the case of the white wines, which are always shown with a considerable amount of residual sugar, but the date remains immutable. Since the wines are sold for the benefit of the Hospices, in a welter of publicity, and the Burgundians do genuinely feel they are supporting their local charity, prices are artificially high and do not always reflect the real market situation.

The Hospices Sale prices tend to increase regardless of the quality of a particular vintage; therefore it follows that it is better value to buy at the Hospices in a good year than in a mediocre one. Two recent exceptions to this were in 1986, when there was a 40 per cent fall in the average price per *pièce* from 1985, and in 1990, when the fall was 25 per cent from the 1989 prices. While worldwide recession partly accounted for the softening of prices for the excellent 1990s, in both years there was certainly a reaction to and a correction of, the overheated bids for the '85s and '89s. In 1995, prices were 4.62 per cent higher for the reds than in 1994, and 17.1 per cent for whites.

The *cuvées* produced by the Hospices are named after its benefactors and are nearly all blends of several vineyards in one village. The current list is shown on page 97. There are now three wines from the Côte de Nuits: Mazis-Chambertin Madeleine Collignon, first auctioned in 1977, and two *cuvées* of Clos de la Roche, Georges Kriter and Cyrot-Chaudron, both auctioned for the first time in 1991.

The Sale itself is interminably long – quite unlike the snappy pace at which business is done at, say, Sotheby's in London and New York. In addtion, many of the Beaune *négociants* are faithful buyers and often out of *politesse*, I feel, their foreign agents are mentioned as co-buyers.

**Hospices De Beaune vineyards and benefactors**

**Red wines**

| Appellation | Benefactor's Name | Hectares* |
|---|---|---|
| Clos de la Roche | Cyrot-Chaudron } | 0.45 ha |
| Clos de la Roche | Georges Kriter } | |
| Corton | Charlotte Dumay | 3.50 ha |
| Corton | Docteur Peste | 3.00 ha |
| Pernand-Vergelesses | Rameau-Lamarosse | 0.60 ha |
| Savigny-lès-Beaune | Forneret | 1.66 ha |
| Savigny-lès-Beaune | Fouquerand | 1.13 ha |
| Savigny-lès-Beaune | Arthur Girard | 1.18 ha |
| Beaune | Nicolas Rolin | 2.70 ha |
| Beaune | Guigone de Salins | 2.40 ha |
| Beaune | Clos des Avaux | 2.00 ha |
| Beaune | Brunet | 2.37 ha |
| Beaune | Maurice Drouhin | 2.20 ha |
| Beaune | Hugues & Louis Bétault | 2.30 ha |
| Beaune | Cyrot-Chaudron | 0.99 ha |
| Beaune | Rousseau-Deslandes | 2.39 ha |
| Beaune | Dames Hospitalières | 2.49 ha |
| Pommard | Dames de la Charité | 1.59 ha |
| Pommard | Cyrot-Chaudron | 1.83 ha |
| Pommard | Billardet | 1.89 ha |
| Volnay | Blondeau | 1.73 ha |
| Volnay | Géneral Muteau | 1.73 ha |
| Volnay-Santenots | Jehan de Massol | 1.50 ha |
| Volnay-Santenots | Guavain | 1.80 ha |
| Monthelie | Lebelin | 0.88 ha |
| Auxey-Duresses | Boillot | 0.75 ha |
| Mazis-Chambertin | Madeleine Collignon | 1.50 ha |

**White wines**

| Appellation | Benefactor's Name | Hectares* |
|---|---|---|
| Corton-Charlemagne | François de Salins | 0.25 ha |
| Corton-Vergennes | Paul Chanson | 0.25 ha |
| Meursault-Genevrières | Baudot | 1.41 ha |
| Meursault-Genevrières | Philippe le Bon | 0.60 ha |
| Meursault-Charmes | de Bahèzre de Lanlay | 0.90 ha |
| Meursault-Charmes | Albert Grivault | 0.50 ha |
| Meursault | Jehan Humblot | 0.70 ha |
| Meursault | Loppin | 0.60 ha |
| Meursault | Goureau | 0.86 ha |
| Bâtard-Montrachet | Dames de Flandres | 0.30 ha |

*The figures are approximate as the actual area of vines used for winemaking may vary considerably according to how and when parcels are replanted. No wine from vines under eight years old is used in Hospices de Beaune *cuvées*.

Monsieur André Porcheret took over the direction of the Hospices wine in 1977, and there was an immense improvement in all aspects of the winemaking during his ten years in the post. M Bruley, who succeeded him in 1987, stayed only until September 1988, after which M Roger Coussy was in charge. However, in early 1994, André Porcheret returned as winemaker, reducing yields (with 35hl/ha the intended upper limit) and practising rigorous grape selection. Twenty two full-time *vignerons* are employed in the vineyards, and both vine treatments and the amount of fertiliser put in the ground (dehydrated manure) are strictly controlled. No weedkillers are used and pruning is not over-generous. Wine made from vines under eight years of age is not sold at the Sale but labelled differently under the name Centre Hospitalier. A new *cuverie* was built outside Beaune in time for the 1994 vintage, computers control fermentation in 48 stainless-steel vats, and an underground chai for new barrels is the pride of the Côte. Longer vatting times are practised. All wines are removed by their buyers, in their new oak casks, by mid-January.

So, at the level of the Hospices itself, everything that can possibly be done to achieve quality is set in motion, and the standard of winemaking at present is very high indeed. But, as always, the quality of your Hospices de Beaune wine will depend to a very large extent on the people responsible for its *élevage*, or maturing. They can make or mar a wine. The rule is always to find out, in shop or restaurant, who did the *élevage*. Then follow the names you trust: if you do not normally like Maison X's style of wine, do not buy an Hospices wine matured by the same house, because it most certainly will have left its mark on it. All the *cuvées* are either Grand Cru or Premier Cru, with the exception of Pommard *cuvée* Cyrot-Chaudron and Meursault *cuvée* Loppin, which are village wines.

## ● POMMARD

**1996 production:**

***AOC Communale & Premiers Crus*** *15,454hl*

***Premiers Crus:*** *Les Rugiens Bas, Les Rugiens Hauts (part), Les Grands Epenots, Les Petits Epenots (part), Clos de la Commaraine, Clos Blanc, Les Arvelets, Les Charmots, En Largillière, Les Pézerolles, Les Boucherottes, Les Saussilles, Les Croix Noires, Les Chaponnières, Les Fremiers, Les Bertins, Les Jarolières, Les Poutures, Clos Micot, La Refène, Clos de Verger, La Platière (part), Les Chanlins Bas (part), Les Combes Dessus (part), La Chanière (part)*

Pommard can be over-priced and over-alcoholic, but when the best *crus* are made by the most gifted winemakers, they are probably the most exciting of the Côte de Beaune. Unfortunately, an easily pronounceable name has given the appellation added impetus on some markets and many less scrupulous producers and *négociants* have profited from this.

Leaving Beaune to the south, the seeker after Pommard practically falls into its vines. Many of them are somewhat hidden behind strong vineyard walls and there are a number of important *clos* (current law on the use of the word *clos* insists that the named vineyard must be completely surrounded by a wall, unless the *clos* has been known as such for more than one hundred years). With the exception of the Premiers Crus Clos Micot and Les Combes Dessus, all the vineyard between the two roads N74 and N73 is straight appellation Pommard. The greatest Premiers Crus, Les Epenots and Les Rugiens, are on either side of the village of Pommard, Les Epenots nearest Beaune and Les Rugiens nearest Volnay. Within Les Epenots, which faces south-southeast, there is the Clos des Epeneaux, and also the Clos des Epenots and Le Clos de Cîteaux. Les Arvelets, Les Petits Noizons (a village wine ) and Les Charmots face south, while Les Rugiens Bas is beautifully sited facing south-southeast. The Premiers Crus are mostly mid-slope and the clay-limestone (about 30% limestone) is red in colour, becoming very pebbly and white at the top of the appellation. Les Rugiens Hauts slopes more and is on a rocky subsoil, while Les Rugiens Bas is on a subsoil of Argovian limestone covered with a thick layer of fine marly-calcareous debris. All this leads to good drainage and wines of excellent colour and structure, more tannic than most wines of the Côte de Beaune. The straight appellation Pommard between the two roads has far more clay and is less stony, except for Les Perrières and La Levrière, which are on pebbly debris.

If I had the joyous task of awarding two new Grands Crus to the Côte de Beaune, they would have to be Les Grands Epenots and Les Rugiens Bas. Both have the capacity to age with true grandeur, which is one of the prerequisites for Grand Cru status. Les Rugiens Bas benefits from a superb microclimate which often enables the grapes to attain great ripeness. Here you can feel the power and richness in the wine, with concentration and intense perfume of liquorice and violets, and a colour reminiscent of the glowing red of the earth. Les Epenots also has fine character and construction, often more fruity and less hard in youth than Les Rugiens.

## *A Personal Selection of Pommard Producers*

### Robert Ampeau & Fils

Straight Pommard of character and flavour.

### Domaine Comte Armand

The Clos des Epeneaux, owned in its entirety by Comte Armand, is for those who say that present burgundy is too light. This wine always takes years to open out, with power, structure and great flavour.

### Domaine Henri Boillot

Les Jarolières with an excellent scent and, in good years, powerful structure – wine with the ability to age.

### Domaine de Courcel

Yves Tavant makes exemplary Epenots and Rugiens, with depth of bouquet and taste, real class, and a flavour of pure red fruits.

### Domaine Michel Gaunoux

Gaunoux makes Grands Epenots which is rich and spicy – the wines always seem to have the body to last, and there are many old bottles to prove it.

### Domaine Bernard et Louis Glantenay

Even the straight Pommard at this domaine is usually built to last.

### Domaine Lejeune

This estate makes En Largillière, which has a deep bouquet of strawberries and ageing potential. Rugiens of good colour and power, always an excellent mouthful.

### Domaine Machard de Gramont

Stylish, elegant Le Clos Blanc.

### Domaine de Montille

Stupendous Rugiens, immensely long on the palate, and Pézerolles rich in glycerol and fruit. Both are made for keeping – if you can.

### Domaine Parent

Elegant, fruity wines, with delicious Pinot Noir character and the flavour of the appellation, without perhaps the sheer richness of the very best.

### Domaine Pothier-Rieusset

Excellent Epenots, Rugiens and Clos de Verger. The style is luscious fruit backed by firm tannin.

## ●○ ST-ROMAIN

**1996 production:**

| | |
|---|---|
| ***AOC Communale* ●** | *1,922hl* |
| ***AOC Communale* ○** | *2,326hl* |

There are no Premiers Crus in St-Romain. This is really a forgotten little village, on a steep slope, and formerly belonging to the Hautes-Côtes rather than to the Côte de Beaune. With cliffs and rocks all around, little of the area is planted with vines. The basic soil is calcareous clay with some pebbles. Slightly more red than white wine is produced, although the white has a wider reputation. Certain sites are better suited to the Chardonnay, such as the marly Sous Roches and the chalky Les Jarrons, facing from southeast to west. La Combe Bazin has rather irony red soil at the foot of the slope (above it is always more limestone-marl), Les Poillanges on the opposite slope has roughly the same soil makeup, facing east like the pebbly Sous le Château. The best sites have good sun exposure, protection from wind and lack of humidity.

The red wines of St-Romain have a strong cherry flavour and a certain *goût de terroir*. The whites are fresh and fruity, developing quite quickly, and are best when they have a sprightly taste and attack.

## A Personal Selection of St-Romain Producers

**Domaine Alain Gras/René Gras-Buisson**
Elegant white and delicious red St-Romain, with a nose of crushed violets and a taste of violet creams and redcurrants.
Joseph Drouhin and Jean Germain also bottle some excelent white St-Romain.

## ● VOLNAY

**1996 production:**
***AOC Communale & Premiers Crus*** *10,288hl*
***Premiers Crus:*** *Les Caillerets, Cailleret Dessus, En Champans, En Chevret, Frémiets, Bousse d'Or, La Barre or Clos de la Barre, Clos des Chênes (part), Les Angles, Pointes d'Angles, Les Mitans, En l'Ormeau, Taille Pied, En Verseuil, Carelle sous la Chapelle, Le Ronceret, Carelles Dessous (part), Robardelle (part), Les Lurets (part), Les Aussy (part), Les Brouillards (part), Clos des Ducs, Pitures Dessus, Chanlins (part), Les Santenots (red), Le Village (part)*
Volnay has some of the most beautiful old Burgundian houses on the Côte, reassuringly solid with their deep roofs and sense of permanence. However, only about 400 people live here, and most of them seem to be called Rossignol! The village sits proudly above its vineyards, which face east and south, with the Premiers Crus situated over a wide variety of soils. Les Santenots lies in the commune of Meursault, but becomes Volnay-Santenots when planted with Pinot Noir, which does splendidly on the Bathonian limestone covered with reddish earth and a fair amount of pebbles.

Les Caillerets also straddles the two communes, again with reddish soil, pebbly and beautifully sited, with the top part of both En Champans and Cailleret Dessus sitting firmly on a rocky base. Above them, the Clos des Chênes is situated on Bathonian limestone, with poor, pebbly soil having difficulty clinging to the marked slope, but benefiting from a beautiful east-southeast position. Taille Pied, Bousse d'Or and the Clos des Ducs are right up against the village, but here the soils are made up of white Argovian limestone.

One is fairly safe in saying that Les Caillerets is probably the grandest of all the Volnays, and the most likely of any of them to reach a superb old age in ripe years. Although you are never looking for power in Volnay, but rather fragrance and elegance, there can often be fine structure in a Caillerets. Clos des Chênes is sometimes more lean than Caillerets, with finesse and a certain tautness when young but, with Champans, ageing well given the chance. All can have the typical Volnay scent of violets and (sometimes) redcurrants. Taille Pied will not have the flesh of Caillerets; instead, it will be delicate, while flowery Frémiets, in spite of being near Pommard, does boast the characteristic Volnay fragrance. The Clos de la Bousse d'Or possesses good potential for ageing, as does Clos des Ducs. Santenots, meanwhile, can last in bottle exceptionally well – especially from Les Santenots du Milieu.

*A Personal Selection of Volnay Producers*

### Domaine du Marquis d'Angerville

Clos des Ducs is the epitome of Volnay elegance, but with depth too, and Champans show the influence of non-greedy yields.

### Domaine Bernard et Louis Glantenay

Beautifully structured wines, at least from ripe years. They generally need time.

### Domaine Michel Lafarge

Clos des Chênes which is all satin and silk, showing the charm of Volnay, but with excellent depth of fruit. But they are magicians at every level.

### Domaine des Comtes Lafon

Volnay Santenots du Milieu of concentration and breeding, which develops outstandingly in bottle.

### Domaine de Montille

Maître Hubert de Montille is almost a sorcerer among winemakers – the tastes he conjures out of the vine! Floral Taille Pieds, Mitans tasting of cloves and chocolate, and brilliant, complex, long-lasting Champans with its bouquet of roses. These wines are the living, breathing example that excessive alcohol is not necessary to make superlative burgundy: he prefers 12.1–13%.

### Domaine de la Pousse d'Or

Gérard Potel makes satiny wines, full of fruit and flavour, especially the Caillerets Dessus Clos des 60 Ouvrées and Clos de la Bousse d'Or. He even makes a success of less propitious years, and there seems to be new life in recent vintages. Great crunchy fruit.

### Domaine Régis Rossignol-Changarnier

Straight Volnay and Les Brouillards with lovely vibrant, vivid fruit; real breed and violets in the latter.

## ●○ MONTHELIE

**1996 production:**
***AOC Communale & Premiers Crus*** ● *5,151hl*
***AOC Communale & Premiers Crus*** ○ *321hl*
***Premiers Crus:*** *Sur La Velle, Les Vignes Rondes, Le Meix Bataille, Les Riottes, La Taupine, Le Clos Gauthey, Le Château-Gaillard, Les Champs Fulliot, Le Cas Rougeot, Les Duresses (part)*

Monthelie is really the forgotten little sister of Volnay, sharing many of this appellation's characteristics but in more muted form. The span of life is shorter, and Monthelies are generally at their most delectable when relatively young. Sandwiched between Volnay and Meursault, it is another lovely Burgundian village, with old stone houses flanking the sloping streets. The vines, too, are on the slopes above Meursault, and it is only comparatively recently that Monthelie's wines have had an identity completely their own. The appellation is virtually all red wines – whites can be made, but they have a tendency to maderise easily, and the growers feel that white wine is best left to Meursault, next door.

There are, in fact, two distinct viticultural areas at Monthelie: the Coteau de Volnay, above the village, where the Premiers Crus are found – the vineyards face south or southeast, on Bathonian limestone, with reddish earth and marl on the summit; and the Vallée d'Auxey-Duresses, at the foot of the village along the north-south valley, with the vines thus facing west and east, and white Argovian limestone soil.

Good Monthelie, like Volnay, can have a tempting, scented bouquet and a sheen on the texture. It should never be heavy-weight, but the best sites produce wines of good structure. It is generally considered that the wines from the Coteau de Volnay have more finesse than those from the Coteau de la Vallée d'Auxey, where the wines can be broader. The Premiers Crus certainly have character and, when they have the balance, they can age well, too.

### *A Personal Selection of Monthelie Producers*

### Château de Monthelie

Eric de Suremain sells his red Monthelie under the château name and over the years it has proved to be the best of the appellation.

### Domaine Monthelie-Douhairet

The Monthelie Premiers Crus keep well here – start drinking them at five years.

## ●○ AUXEY-DURESSES

**1996 production:**

| | |
|---|---|
| ***AOC Communale & Premiers Crus* ●** | *4,982hl* |
| ***AOC Communale & Premiers Crus* ○** | *1,906hl* |

***Premiers Crus:*** *Les Duresses, Bas des Duresses, La Chapelle, Reugne, Les Grands-Champs, Climat du Val known as Clos du Val (part), Les Ecusseaux (part), Les Bréterins*

Auxey-Duresses is tucked in behind Monthelie, in a fertile valley at the foot of Mont Melian, and surrounded by slopes covered with vines. The appellation produces about one-third white wine to two-thirds red, but the areas of their production are quite well divided, with the white coming from the Coteaux du Mont Melian, an extension of Meursault and Puligny, and the red from the Montagne du Bourdon, an extension of Monthelie and Volnay. Les Duresses, on the Montagne du Bourdon, sits on a very pebbly, marly-calcareous base, with more soil at the foot of the slope than on the top. It faces east and southeast. La Chapelle is very similar to Duresses, with a little more marl than calcareous matter. The Clos du Val is magnificently situated facing due south, very calcareous, with more marl and pebbles than Les Duresses and La Chapelle and very little soil on the upper slopes. The soil on the Montagne du Mont Melian is even thinner, far better suited to making white wine than red.

Les Duresses produces fruity wine with some finesse, with notes of raspberry and good colour. La Chapelle can have more body and take longer to develop, with Clos du Val more powerful still, both leaning towards cassis. White Auxey has a lovely biscuity flavour, but should be drunk relatively young – it develops more quickly than Meursault.

### *A Personal Selection of Auxey-Duresses Producers*

#### Domaine Robert Ampeau & Fils

Soft, warmly earthy red wine, fruitily charming when young.

#### Domaine Jean-Pierre Diconne

Wood is very evident in both the red and the white wines, with Les Duresses therefore needing some time to emerge from the ageing. The white Auxey is lanolin-smooth and very rich. Drink young when the pleasure is at its optimum.

#### Domaine Alain Gras

Very reliable red. He also vinifies for René Gras (*qv*), and there is a good, mild white Auxey under this label.

#### Domaine Leroy

The headquarters of the Leroy empire, but it also owns vineyards in Auxey. The wines are always big and long-lasting.

#### Domaine du Duc de Magenta

Fine white wine, and usually good red.

#### Domaine Michel Prunier

Good white which is full of character, and supple, flavoury red Clos du Val with real class.

#### Domaine Pascal Prunier

Stylish, quite steely whites and reds for ageing.

## ●○ BLAGNY

**1996 production:**

| | |
|---|---|
| ***AOC Communale* ●** | *309hl* |
| ***AOC Communale* ○** | *negligible* |

This little village, squeezed in between Puligny-Montrachet and Meursault, has always posed a problem for the legislators, but the essential fact is that the appellation is for red wine only, although wine of both colours is made. White wine from the *climats* of La Pièce sous le Bois, La Jeunelotte and Sous le Dos d'Ane can be called Meursault Premier Cru, but red wine would be Blagny Premier Cru. White wine made from the *climats* of Sous le Puits, La Garenne, Hameau de Blagny and Le Trézin can be called Puligny-Montrachet, but the red must be Blagny.

Red Blagny has a very distinctive taste, slightly earthy, slightly gamey. It can really 'attack' the palate when young, but it is this very lack of neutrality which is so alluring. White wine from

Blagny is usually very fruity, very accessible – good value in restaurants, as it shows that someone has had the courage to leave the better-known *climats* of Meursault and Puligny-Montrachet, and you thus pay for a delicious taste rather than an overworked name. As for recommended producers, they are those who make their wine well in the neighbouring two appellations.

## ●○ MEURSAULT

**1996 production:**

| | |
|---|---|
| ***AOC Communale & Premiers Crus*** ○ | *18,102hl* |
| ***AOC Communale & Premiers Crus*** ● | *873hl* |

***Premiers Crus:*** *(red and white wines) Les Crus (part), Les Caillerets (part), Les Charmes-Dessus, Les Charmes-Dessous, Les Perrières Dessus (part), Aux Perrières, Les Perrières Dessous (part), Les Chaumes des Perrières (part), Les Genevrières Dessus, Les Chaumes de Narvaux (part), Le Poruzot Dessus, Les Poruzots Dessous, Les Genevrières Dessous, Les Bouchères (part), Les Gouttes d'Or, Le Poruzot (part). (White wines) Les Santenots Blancs, Les Plures (part), Les Santenots du Milieu, La Jeunelotte, La Pièce sous le Bois (part), Sous le Dos d'Ane (part), Sous Blagny (the last four in the commune of Blagny)*

When the Santenots are planted with Pinot Noir, the wines are called Volnay-Santenots, but the two hectares which are planted to Chardonnay are called Meursault-Santenots.

Many people's image of the perfect white burgundy is based on their tasting impressions of Meursault. It usually has an imposing bouquet, slightly nutty with overtones of cinnamon, and strong, persistent flavour. The best wines are also rich and fat with a long finish, all of which adds up to happy memories. The 'village' itself is large and prosperous, a real county town, dominated by a tall and elegant church spire. Many of the Premiers Crus may produce both red and white wines, but the vast majority have opted for white.

The first slope of Meursault at the Combe de St-Aubin is of Bathonian limestone, while calcareous marl and pure marl dominate the middle part of the vineyard area, and there is a good deal of debris on the upper part of the slope. On the Blagny-Meursault side, there is brown calcareous soil over Callovian limestone, as well as white Argovian marly limestone. The vineyard rises to 300m (984ft), with its southeast-facing position giving a microclimate that is very favourable to quality. There is no doubt that the worldwide demand for white wine has led to some planting of the Chardonnay on parcels which are better suited to making red wines, and these are probably the heavy Meursaults without finesse.

Les Perrières could be considered as the Meursault which has the most class and refinement, particularly from Les Perrières Dessus, where the vines frequently attain great ripeness, giving power, but the rock base of the site gives the distinguished nose. A tiny path separates Les Perrières from Les Genevrières, which also has its partisans. Elegant, scented, with the real bouquet of hazelnuts, Genevrières produces immensely pretty and seductive wines. Les Poruzots is solid with a flinty nose, with excellent keeping potential, while Les Gouttes d'Or, as the name suggests, has a beautiful golden colour and a great capacity for ageing: robust rather than delicate. The steep slope compensates for the less well-exposed site. Les Charmes is at its best from Les Charmes-Dessus (which includes the middle part of the slope); Les Charmes-Dessous is on deeper soil, with attractive round, fruity qualities.

## *A Personal Selection of Meursault Producers*

### Domaine Robert Ampeau & Fils

Superb Perrières and Charmes, which last beautifully in bottle. Also good Blagny La Pièce sous le Bois.

### Domaine Jean-François Coche Dury

Perrières of glorious lanolin texture and true breeding. But all the wines are marked by the master's touch.

### Domaine Albert Grivault

Refined, subtle, flinty Perrières, and Clos des Perrières (from the very heart of the *climat*) that has a hazelnutty bouquet and a long, luscious flavour followed by a splendid *arôme de bouche*.

### Domaine François Jobard

Superb Premiers Crus which often need eight to 12 years in bottle to show at their glorious best.

### Domaine des Comtes Lafon

Superb Meursault, from Perrières to Clos de la Barre, beautifully constructed and ageing in bottle to perfection. No filtering takes place here.

### Maison Louis Latour

The firm makes splendid selections in straight Meursault, Meursault Château de Blagny and Genevrières.

### Domaine du Duc de Magenta

Usually good and stylish straight Meursault.

### Domaine Joseph, Pierre et Thierry Matrot

Structured wines which can age well and which have real flavours and the character of each *climat*.

### Domaine Michelot

Usually, terrific wines. Big, rich Charmes – everybody's idea of fine Meursault – and Genevrières to die for.

### Domaine Jean Monnier & Fils

Wines of elegance and finesse, including delightful Genevrières.

### Domaine Pierre Morey

Perrières of absolutely top quality.

### Domaine Guy Roulot
Excellent wines made by Jean-Marc Roulot, with velvety Charmes and fat Perrières. The Tessons makes the bridge between a straight *village* wine and the Premiers Crus.

## ●○ ST-AUBIN

**1996 production:**

***AOC Communale & Premiers Crus* ●** *2,836hl*

***AOC Communale & Premiers Crus* ○** *4,311hl*

***Premiers Crus:*** *the situation is extremely complicated, with 16 climats encompassing 29 lieux-dits. In practice, several lieux-dits are grouped together under the same Premier Cru, the most frequently used being: La Chatenière, En Remilly, Les Murgers des Dents de Chien, Les Champlots, Le Charmois, Le Village, Les Castets, Sur le Sentier du Clou, Les Cortons, Les Frionnes, Sous Roche Dumay, Les Perrières*

Perhaps this is one of the 'undiscovered' gems of Burgundy, since the growers here seem to be particularly conscientious and the wines uniformly good. Recent tastings have produced extremely few disappointments and many delectable bottles, at prices which are not as exorbitant as in other parts of the Côte d'Or. St-Aubin is a tiny village behind Puligny-Montrachet and Meursault, near the hamlet of Gamay, with the vineyards facing in all directions from southeast to southwest. The soils vary, as there are really two distinct parts of St-Aubin: the vineyards below Gamay on the Roche du May, which is the end of the Côte d'Or slope, and those on the Montagne du Ban which runs westwards. Here, the steep slopes contain much limestone, affecting Premiers Crus such as Frionnes, Sentier du Clou and Castets, while the Roche du May, Champlots, La Chatenière, Sous Roche Dumay and Dents de Chien are on marl covered by calcareous debris, brown clay and chalk.

It is not deleterious to St-Aubin to say that its wines are slightly lighter, fresher versions of grander appellations. The reds can resemble Chassagne-Montrachet, with less body, and the whites veer more towards Puligny than Meursault, with less intense perfume and fat. I have found that many of the reds have a taste of strawberries, and there are inevitable nuances between the Premiers Crus – Sous Roche Dumay tends to have more body and tannin in youth, while the limestone of Les Castets gives finesse. The best whites often come from La Chatenière and Les Murgers des Dents de Chien. Here, the hazelnuts bouquet is very marked.

### *A Personal Selection of St-Aubin Producers*

### Domaine Jean-Claude Bachelet
Delicate whites, redolent of hazelnuts and mayblossom.

### Domaine Gilles Bouton
Gilles Bouton, the grandson, makes white En Remilly which is rich and oaky in a rather broad style.

### Domaine Marc Colin
White La Chatenière, aromatic and with a taste of rose petals.

### Maison Louis Jadot
Has good white St-Aubin.

### Domaine Hubert Lamy-Monnot
Excellent red Castets, built to last, while the white Frionnes mixes acacia with oak in a very stylish way.

### Domaine Henri Prudhon & Fils/Gérard Prudhon
Les Frionnes with a clear strawberry Pinot bouquet, a gently earthy flavour and very nice aromatic persistence. Good whites, too.

### Domaine Roux Père & Fils
Meticulous winemaking produces lovely whites of finesse, especially La Chatenière, and cherryish reds.

### Domaine Gérard Thomas
White St-Aubin that gives much pleasure.

## ●○ PULIGNY-MONTRACHET

**1996 production:**

| | |
|---|---|
| ***Grands Crus*** ○ | |
| *Le Montrachet* | *353hl* |
| *Bâtard-Montrachet* | *523hl* |
| *Bienvenues-Bâtard-Montrachet* | *177hl* |
| *Chevalier-Montrachet* | *335hl* |
| ***AOC Communale & Premiers Crus*** ○ | *11,152hl* |
| ***AOC Communale & Premiers Crus*** ● | *269hl* |

***Premiers Crus:*** *Le Cailleret, Les Combettes, Les Pucelles, Les Folatières (part), Clavoillon, Le Champ Canet, Les Chalumeaux (part), Les Referts, Sous le Puits, La Garenne, Hameau de Blagny, Les Truffières*

An innocent visitor to Puligny-Montrachet would never believe that it is the centre of what many would call the greatest dry white wines of the world. There are days when even the proverbial dog does not bark to break the silence. It is another of those slightly schizophrenic communes in Burgundy, rivalling Aloxe-Corton and Pernand-Vergelesses, because some of its most famous Grands Crus are shared with the neighbouring village of Chassagne-Montrachet. Chevalier-Montrachet and Bienvenues-Bâtard-Montrachet are entirely within the boundaries of Puligny-Montrachet, but Le Montrachet and Bâtard-Montrachet share their favours with Chassagne-Montrachet, whereas Les Criots lies entirely within Chassagne-Montrachet.

These fabled Grands Crus are the result of perfect micro-climates, so sheltered and positioned on the slopes that they frequently give very ripe grapes, whereas elsewhere the sugar levels might be only adequate. Le Montrachet lies on a base of hard Bathonian limestone covered by debris, with an iron-oxide content. Chevalier-Montrachet is on Bajocian marly limestone, and Bâtard-Montrachet is composed of brown limestone rich in gravel. Bienvenues-Bâtard-Montrachet is virtually an enclave within Bâtard-Montrachet, with the same soil and facing east-southeast. Chevalier-Montrachet has a more marked slope, situated above Le Montrachet. The lower part of Le Montrachet has slightly deeper soil.

The sheer imposing glamour of the Grands Crus should not cause us to forget the Premiers Crus, which are of remarkable beauty at Puligny-Montrachet. Les Combettes is on pure rock with very thin soil, except where there are faults in the rock which allow the depth of the soil to jump from a matter of centimetres to metres. Les Referts and Clavoillon have very similar soil, while Les Folatières is on a more marked slope, with white limestone debris near the top; there is always the risk of erosion here. Le Cailleret shares many characteristics with Le Montrachet, but it is more pebbly and the orientation is not quite as good as for the Grand Cru. The Premiers Crus are divided from the *village* wines by the Sentier de Couches, which continues into Chassagne and Santenay.

In Puligny, the cellars cannot be built underground, as is usually the case in Burgundy, because of the area's relatively high water table.

So, what is all the fuss about? Why are Le Montrachet and its satellites 'the best'? Without doubt, if you drink any of these wines too young, particularly Le Montrachet, you will ask yourself this very question. The bouquet, particularly, takes time to develop, and it is really a vinous crime to drink Le Montrachet at under ten years of age. The colour begins as greenish yellow and deepens to a splendid gold in bottle, while with the years the taste gains in depth and complexity. Honey, almonds, hawthorn and great textured richness are all found in Le Montrachet, provided the wine is served at no less than 13°C (about 55°F), which is perfect cellar temperature, and not refrigerator frozen.

There are those who would put Chevalier-Montrachet next in the hierarchy, followed by Bâtard, Bienvenues and Criots. Certainly I have had stupendous Chevalier, sometimes even surpassing Le Montrachet, for the hand of the winemaker counts just as much in this hallowed ground as anywhere else in Burgundy. The first two wines, particularly, need nearly as long to develop as Le Montrachet, and all are rich and mouthfilling. White burgundy of this rank is almost a food as well as a wine, it is so multidimensional and nutritious, powerful and fleshy.

Among the Premiers Crus, Les Pucelles usually develops more slowly than Les Combettes, which can be soft in some years, less nerveux than other Premiers Crus. It has a certain hazelnutty quality which makes you think of neighbouring Meursault and is broader in taste than Clavoillon and Les Folatières, which both show great finesse. Le Cailleret has a good deal of body, but Le Champ Canet and Les Chalumeaux are lighter and ready for drinking earlier.

## *A Personal Selection of Puligny-Montrachet Producers*

### Robert Ampeau & Fils

Les Combettes of great beauty and ability to age.

### Domaine Louis Carillon
Luscious, honeyed Bienvenues; not wholly top class, but very good.

### Domaine Henri Clerc
Chevalier-Montrachet that can be almost top class.

### Maison Joseph Drouhin
Folatières not from the domaine, but delicate and acacia-soft.

### Maison Louis Jadot
The fabulous Chevalier-Montrachet Les Demoiselles is shared with Louis Latour (*qv*). I always like the non-domaine Les Referts.

### Maison Louis Latour
Chevalier-Montrachet Les Demoiselles is positively exotic, rich, oaky and a great keeper. Splendid non-domaine Les Folatières and Les Referts, all almonds and mayblossom.

### Domaine Leflaive
This domaine makes some of the best white wines in all Burgundy – ergo, the whole of the world. There are few things more pleasant in life than trying to decide if the Bienvenues, the Bâtard or the unbelievable Chevalier is reminiscent of hawthorn, blackthorn or mayblossom. At the last attempt, I detected lavender honey in the Chevalier. Then there is floral Les Pucelles, rich Les Combettes. Greengages appear in young Clavoillon and limetree blossom in the straight Puligny. Always undeniable quality and breeding.

### Olivier Leflaive
Absolutely bang-on wines, from the company's own vineyards, or from bought-in grapes skilfully vinified.

### Domaine Joseph, Pierre et Thierry Matrot
Les Chalumeaux with lovely fruit marrying with oak, sometimes needing bottle-age to 'fatten'.

### Domaine Paul Pernot et ses Fils
Beautifully crafted Les Folatières with a creamy richness in good vintages, always long and elegant. Remarkable Bienvenues.

### Domaine de la Romanée-Conti
Le Montrachet of great style, simply crying out for bottle-age in order to show its voluptuous paces. The domaine made no Montrachet in 1992, missing a potentially fine year.

### Etienne Sauzet
Glorious Les Combettes, with a bouquet of woodsmoke and greengages, backed up by oak. Grands Crus to ravish the palate.

### Société Civile du Domaine Thénard
Le Montrachet from this domaine is marketed by the firm of Remoissenet (*qv*) and the wine is usually very fine and stylish.

## ●○ CHASSAGNE-MONTRACHET

**1996 production:**

***Grand Cru* ○**

| | |
|---|---|
| *Criots-Bâtard-Montrachet* | *64hl* |
| ***AOC Communale & Premiers Crus* ●** | *7,047hl* |
| ***AOC Communale & Premiers Crus* ○** | *8,908hl* |

***Premiers Crus:*** *(red wines) Clos St-Jean (part), Morgeot (part), Morgeot known as Abbaye de Morgeot (part), La Boudriotte (part), La Maltroie (part), Les Chenevottes, Les Champs Gain (part), Les Grandes Ruchottes, La Romanée, Les Brussonnes (part), Les Vergers, Les Macherelles, En Cailleret (part). (White wines) Morgeot (part), Morgeot known as Abbaye de Morgeot (part), La Boudriotte, La Maltroie, Clos St-Jean, Les Chenevottes, Les Chaumées, Les Champs Gains, Les Petits Clos, Grandes Ruchottes, La Romanée, Les Brussonnes, Les Vergers, Les Macherelles, Chassagne or En Cailleret, Vide-Bourse, Vignes Blanches*

Many of the best wines of Chassagne are made by members of three families: the Gagnards, the Delagranges and the Moreys. It is the second-to-last of the important villages on the Côte de Beaune, with only Santenay to follow. Naturally, the white wines are world famous, but the reds represent very good value and are frequently forgotten in the rush to get a more fashionable name. If the Grands Crus are white, the finest Premier Cru wines are red. The Clos St-Jean, surrounded by walls, possesses very gravelly soil, while Les Vergers, Les Macherelles and Les Chenevottes have red soil, clay with little gravel. Morgeot, the lower part of La Boudriotte, Les Champs Gain and Les Petits Clos are on white marl above and red gravelly earth lower down. The subsoil is oolitic limestone, grey, beige and pink and, when it is polished, it looks like marble and makes beautiful flagstones and fireplaces in the local houses. There is still a quarry above Clos St-Jean. Truffles grow on a base of Bathonian limestone debris, on the edge of the vineyards and on uncultivated land, although I have not seen (or eaten) any evidence of this.

There are those who make the distinction between the Puligny part of Montrachet, facing southeast, and the Chassagne part which faces more due south, following the turn of the slope. The Puligny section is meant to have the edge in terms of finesse and sheer distinction, but to my knowledge this has never been proved at some meticulously organised tasting. As always, the hand of the winemaker probably makes the difference between fine and divine.

The one Grand Cru lying entirely in Chassagne, tiny Les Criots (annual production less than 800 cases), has all the body and structure of its fellows. Of the white Premiers Crus, Les Ruchottes, Morgeot, Cailleret, Vignes Blanches and Les Champs Gains tend to have more body, while Les Vergers, Les Macherelles, Les Chenevottes and Les Chaumées are very fragrant and floral. La Boudriotte and Morgeot are the two most powerful reds, built for lasting in ripe years, reputed to have a taste of kirsch, and certainly the basis for the analogy with cherries is very detectable. Clos St-Jean often has softer fruit and matures a little earlier – prunes, peaches and violets can all be seen in these wines, while some are earthy in youth. Chardonnay, however, is invading the Clos.

## *A Personal Selection of Chassagne-Montrachet Producers*

### Domaine Amiot-Bonfils

White Premiers Crus here are rewarding.

### Domaine Blain-Gagnard

Connected with Delagrange-Bachelet (*qv*), this is a son-in-law making honeyed Bâtard, needing time for its full potential to emerge, and white Morgeot of full, robust flavour.

### Domaine Michel Colin-Deléger

White Les Chaumées (classed as Premier Cru, but one of the *lieux-dits* which usually disappears inside a better-known name) with a glorious honeyed nose: alluring, heavenly. Real *race et finesse.*

### Domaine Fontaine-Gagnard

White Chassagne-Montrachets which are impressive: oaky, with a bouquet of acacia, mayblossom and woodsmoke leading to a smooth, firm taste. The young red is a mixture of loganberries and wood which promises well.

### Domaine Jacques Gagnard-Delagrange

Monumental Grands and Premiers Crus which last well in bottle.

### Domaine Jean-Noël Gagnard

The Bâtard-Montrachet of this brilliant winemaker opened my senses to white burgundy, many years ago, and for that I shall always be grateful. He is still making stunning wine, rich, explosive of taste and beautiful enough to silence conversation. There is also white Les Caillerets, Morgeot and straight Chassagne, as well as a range of reds – I recommend that you try his Morgeot.

### Domaine du Duc de Magenta

Nearly all vinified and sold by Louis Jadot – the white Abbaye de Morgeot Clos de la Chapelle is worth finding.

### Domaine Marquis de Laguiche (Joseph Drouhin)

The must is sent into Beaune for Drouhin to do the vinifying, *élevage*, bottling and selling. Le Montrachet of enormous charm and fruit, balanced and luscious. The estate also makes terrific straight white Chassagne.

### Domaine Bernard Morey

Red Chassagne which has a lovely frank taste of crunchy strawberries. White Les Caillerets often takes a few years to open out, while Les Baudines softens sooner. There is also white Les Embrazées at this domaine.

### Domaine Pierre Morey
Incredibly good Bâtard-Montrachet, tight at first, then full, rich and toasty.

### Domaine Michel Niellon
An exemplary array of wines, from Bâtard and Chevalier down to straight Chassagne-Montrachet, all full, fat and strong on aromas and flavour.

### Domaine Ramonet
It is thanks to that great American wine-lover, Bipin Desai, that I tasted the most complete range of Ramonet wines ever shown. There are great whites, even in less-fashionable years, in other words, the exotic '74 Bâtard. The Bâtard '69, '76, '79 and '87 are classics. Le Montrachet '78 and '85 have to be touchstones of the genre, but occasionally I have been shown Ramonet Montrachets which do not bear the stamp of the Grand Cru – mysterious and worrying. Les Ruchottes can be a 'bargain' – the '83 and '86 are amazing. So are the Bienvenues '82, '83 and '86. I wish I had some Montrachet '88 and '89 to lay down, not to mention the Caillerets '89. This is a remarkable family which has created a legend – may they always honour it.

## ●○ SANTENAY
**1996 production:**

| | |
|---|---|
| ***AOC Communale & Premiers Crus*** ● | *14,728hl* |
| ***AOC Communale & Premiers Crus*** ○ | *1,574hl* |

***Premiers Crus:*** *Les Gravières, Le Clos de Tavannes, La Comme, Beauregard, Passetemps, Beaurepaire, La Maladière, Le Petit Clos Rousseau (part), Le Clos des Mouches, Le Clos Fauhard, Le Grand Clos Rousseau*

Coming from the south, this is where the Côte de Beaune begins. Wits say that this is where water and wine meet, since Santenay is also a thermal resort. It is certainly a suitable port of call for those with digestive, liver or gout problems. And where there is a *station thermale*, there is always a casino... The soil is somewhat varied, with the Premiers Crus of La Comme and Les Gravières, on the northern slope of Santenay, having a topsoil of gravel over marly limestone. Whereas Les Gravières is nearly flat, La Comme and the very pebbly Beauregard are on the side of the slope. The appellation is essentially red, but within Les Gravières there is a plot producing white wine, including the very good Clos des Gravières. On the south side of Santenay, the soils are either brown limestone or deep in character, and the wines are inevitably more earthy here.

Santenay's reds are often marked by a *goût de terroir* and can be quite tannic and hard in youth with a marked earthy quality. Les Gravières has the greatest finesse, while La Comme is more robust. La Maladière can be elegant and supple and ready for drinking sooner. Violets, chestnuts, strawberries and almonds have all been found on the nose, while the whites can have a youthful bouquet of hazelnuts and ferns.

*A Personal Selection of Santenay Producers*

**Domaine Adrien Belland**
I have had good Santenay and even better robust Santenay Comme from this estate.

**Domaine Hubert Bouzereau-Gruère**
Exemplary Santenay – gamey, 'wet dogs', crushed strawberries.

**Maison Joseph Drouhin**
Very good selections in the appellation, and appealing value.

**Domaine Guy Dufouleur**
The Clos Genêts of this domaine has very good, earthy Santenay character, it is a full wine, but fruity and frank, and not over-alcoholic and soupy.

**Domaine Jacques Girardin**
Good for straight Santenay. Also good from Yves Girardin.

**Domaine Vincent Girardin**
Les Gravières is the top wine, with very good keeping potential.

**Domaine Louis Jadot**
Makes a lovely, full Clos de Malte of real impact. This one is Jadot's latest acquisition.

**Domaine Lequin-Roussot**
A sizeable domaine, with a good spread of Premiers Crus. Wines made to last and full of character. There is also a delicious Santenay Blanc made from Pinot Blanc. René and Louis Lequin have, since 1993, split the domaine between them and these are the two labels that are now appearing.

**Domaine Mestre Père & Fils**
Earthy and fruity Santenay Clos Faubard. This is a large domaine, important in the Premiers Crus. Less than half the wine made is domaine-bottled.

**Domaine Bernard Morey**
Superb Grand-Clos-Rousseau, with new wood and sheer finesse.

**Domaine de la Pousse d'Or**
Clos de Tavannes and Les Gravières from this domaine can be among the appellation's best wines.

**Domaine Prieur-Brunet**
Particularly attractive Santenay-Maladière, with just a touch of new wood in the flavour.

**Domaine Roux Père & Fils**
Santenay made with a St-Aubin hand, and very fruity, too!

## ●○ MARANGES

**1996 production:**

| | |
|---|---|
| ***AOC Communale & Premiers Crus*** ● | *9,246hl* |
| ***AOC Communale & Premiers Crus*** ○ | *211hl* |

***Premiers Crus:*** *Le Clos des Rois, Les Clos Roussots, La Fussière, Le Clos de la Boutière, La Crois aux Moines, Le Clos des Loyères*

The Maranges appellation was officially recognised on May 23rd 1989. It brings together under one name the wines of Cheilly-lès-Maranges, Dezize-lès-Maranges and Sampigny-lès-Maranges. The appellation is immediately to the west of Santenay; indeed it is not officially on the Côte d'Or, but just over the border in Saône-et-Loire. The vineyards face south and southeast, on well-protected hillsides, and the soil contains a high proportion of Liassic clay. Hence, the wines tend to be quite tough and powerful – well-suited to ageing, indeed needing time to mellow. Recommended producers are Bernard Bachelet et Fils and Domaine Chevrot.

## ●○ COTE DE BEAUNE

**1996 production:**

| | |
|---|---|
| ***AOC Communale*** ● | *992hl* |
| ***AOC Communale*** ○ | *603hl* |

This is really a redundant appellation of 52ha, with only about 30ha under vine. It covers the area of Beaune itself, as well as the following *lieux-dits*: Les Mondes Rondes, Les Monnières, Les Pierres Blanches, Les Topes-Bizot, and La Grande Châtelaine, which is owned by the *négociant* Louis Max.

Worth finding among these wines is a white Côte de Beaune from the Lycée Agricole et Viticole at Beaune, which owns 19.3ha of vineyards and rents another 9.6ha, covering a range of appellations.

## ●○ COTE DE BEAUNE-VILLAGES

**1996 production:**

| | |
|---|---|
| *Côte de Beaune-Villages* ● | *1,157hl* |
| *Côte de Beaune-Villages* ○ | *0 hl* |

This appellation covers the following 16 villages: Auxey-Duresses, Blagny, Chassagne-Montrachet, Cheilly-lès-Maranges, Chorey-lès-Beaune, Dezize-lès-Maranges, Ladoix, Meursault, Monthelie, Pernand-Vergelesses, Puligny-Montrachet, St-Aubin, St-Romain, Sampigny-lès-Maranges, Santenay, Savigny-lès-Beaune.

All of these villages can sell their wine under their own name but, especially in the case of the lesser-known villages or in communes where the white wines are paramount, it is more advantageous to use the Côte de Beaune-Villages label. This is, in fact, an appellation sold mostly by the *négociants*, who can make a more satisfactory wine by inter-village blending.

There is another option, rarely seen, when the producer puts on the label the name of the village appellation followed by the term Côte de Beaune in letters of the same size. The red wines can be quite structured and tannic, needing a few years in bottle to soften.

# ●○ Côte Chalonnaise

The region known as the Côte Chalonnaise stretches from the valley of the Dheune near Chagny in the north to St-Gengoux-le-National, southwest of Chalon-sur-Saône, in the south. Vines cluster on slopes, but it is by no means an uninterrupted viticultural landscape. The basic soil types are limestone or calcareous clay, although variations between the villages and appellations are based more on subtleties of microclimate than of soil. However, the Chardonnay should ideally be planted where there is high limestone content, and the Pinot Noir where there is more clay, as this helps provide stronger colour. Often the calcareous matter has a tendency to fall to the foot of the slopes. Pinot Noir is the most important grape variety on the Côte Chalonnaise, with 65% of the vineyard area, while Chardonnay covers 14%, Aligoté 12% and Gamay nine per cent. The best vineyard sites face east, southeast or south, but they can be planted up to a height of 350m (1,150ft), which means later picking than on the Côte d'Or. This, coupled with the fact that it can be slightly cooler here in the summer months than around Dijon, means that in less than perfect years lack of ripeness can be a problem. But when fate is kind, the wines of the Côte Chalonnaise are not just mini-replicas of the Côte d'Or – they have real regional character and a great deal to say for themselves. Given the current price of many wines from the Côte d'Or, they also represent excellent value-for-money burgundy. Since 1990, Bourgogne Côte Chalonnaise has existed as an appellation, although not many wines appear under this label.

## ●○ BOUZERON

**1996 production:**

*Bourgogne Aligoté de Bouzeron* *3,969hl*

The Aligoté wine produced in this village close to Chagny and Rully had long been appreciated as something exceptional, and in 1979 the appellation Bourgogne Aligoté de Bouzeron was created. The wines are often richer, spicier and fuller than elsewhere and make a very worthwhile bottle for those who can be lured away to something less usual. Very good domaines for Aligoté de Bouzeron are those of Aubert and Pamela de Villaine (*qv*), the Clos de la Fortune of Chanzy Frères (*qv*) and Bouchard Père et Fils (*qv*). Delorme (*qv*), also, is known for its particularly well-made Aligoté.

### *The Principal Bouzeron Producers*

### Domaine Chanzy Frères/Domaine de l'Hermitage

*Bouzeron, 71150 Chagny*

***1er Cru:*** *Mercurey Clos du Roy (red and white)*

***AOC Communales:*** *Rully (red and white); Mercurey Carabys*

***AOC Régionales:*** *Bourgogne Aligoté de Bouzeron: Clos de la Fortune, Les Clous; Bourgogne Clos de la Fortune (red and white)*

A range of red and white wines from the Côte Chalonnaise (Mercurey and Rully), but the Bourgogne Aligoté is its best wine, and its basic Bourgogne Clos de la Fortune (red and white) is good.

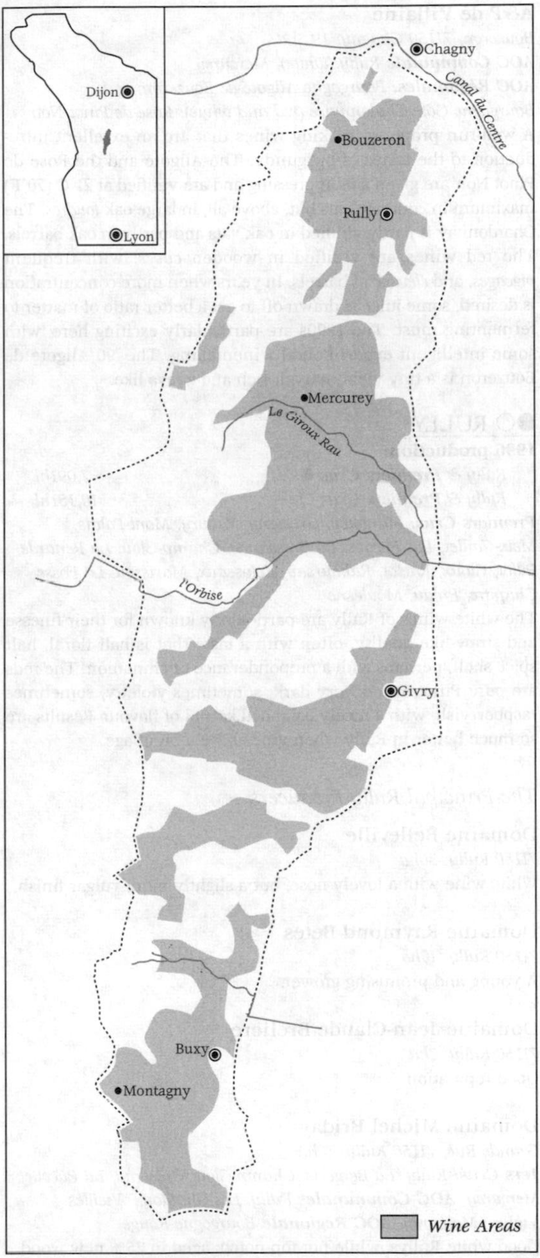
Dijon
Lyon
Chagny
Canal du Centre
Bouzeron
Rully
Mercurey
Le Giroux Rau
l'Orbise
Givry
Buxy
Montagny
Wine Areas

### A&P de Villaine

*Bouzeron, 71150 Chagny. 19.5ha*
***AOC Communale** Rully (white), Mercurey*
***AOC Régionales:** Bourgogne Aligoté de Bouzeron;*
*Bourgogne Côte Chalonnaise (red and white); Rosé de Pinot Noir*
A well-run property, making wines that are an excellent introduction to the tastes of burgundy. The Aligoté and the Rosé de Pinot Noir are given a light pressing and are vinified at 21˚C (70˚F) maximum in concrete vats but, above all, in large oak *foudres*. The Chardonnay is partly vinified in oak vats and partly in oak barrels. The red wines are vinified in wooden *cuves*, with frequent *pigeages*, and *élevage* in barrels. In years when more concentration is desired, some juice is drawn off to get a better ratio of matter to fermenting must. The 1990s are particularly exciting here, with some intelligent experimental winemaking. The '90 Aligoté de Bouzeron is a tiny yield marvel, rich and guava-like.

## ●○ RULLY

**1996 production:**

| | |
|---|---|
| *Rully & **Premiers Crus** ●* | *7,091hl* |
| *Rully & **Premiers Crus** ○* | *10,151hl* |

***Premiers Crus:** Margotey, Grésigny, Vauvry, Mont-Palais, Meix-Caillet, Les Pierres, La Bressande, Champ-Clou, La Renarde, Pillot, Cloux, Raclot, Raboursay, Ecloseaux, Marissou, La Fosse, Chapitre, Préau, Moulesne*
The white wines of Rully are particularly known for their finesse and straw-like quality, often with a taste that is half floral, half spice shelf, perhaps with a preponderance of cinnamon. The reds are pure Pinot, never very dark, sometimes violetty, sometimes raspberryish, with a nicely balanced kernel of flavour. Results are so much better in Rully when vines have a bit of age.

## *The Principal Rully Producers*

### Domaine Belleville

*71150 Rully. 30ha*
White wine with a lovely nose, but a slightly more vulgar finish.

### Domaine Raymond Bêtes

*71150 Rully. 10ha*
A young and promising grower.

### Domaine Jean-Claude Brelière

*71150 Rully. 7ha*
Good reputation.

### Domaine Michel Briday

*Grande Rue, 71150 Rully. 10ha*
***1ers Crus:** Rully: La Bergerie, Champ-Clou, Grésigny, La Pucelle; Mercurey. **AOC Communale**s Rully: Les Chailloux, Vieilles Vignes; Mercurey. **AOC Régionale** Bourgogne Rouge*
Good white Rullys, while not top-notch; aged in 25% new wood.

### Emile Chandesais

*SCEA Champs Perdrix, St-Nicolas, 71150 Fontaines. 11ha*
**AOC Communale:** *Rully Les St-Jacques*
**AOC Régionales:** *Bourgogne Côte Chalonnaise (red and white)*
An important *négociant* based on the Côte Chalonnaise. While most of the wines are just good – no more – the firm always buys at the Hospices de Beaune and I have been impressed by some of its *élevages*, which are usually silky and give evidence of new wood. I have also liked the Passe-Tout-Grains, but not the Rully wines. The domaine wines receive careful vinification, the reds in stainless-steel vats, with total destalking and maturing in oak barrels, some of which are new. The whites are fermented in new oak barrels. Domaines whose wines they distribute include the Château de Néty (Beaujolais-Villages), Domaine Hermitage (Rully Rouge and Blanc, Mercurey and Bourgogne), and Domaine Gouffier (Bourgogne, Mercurey and Bourgogne Aligoté). Chandesais is now part of the Picard group in Chagny.

### Domaine Pierre Cogny

*Bouzeron, 71150 Chagny. 13ha*
The red and white Rully here is slightly rustic, and there is also Aligoté from Bouzeron.

### Domaine Jean Coulon

*71150 Rully.*
Rully Blanc Grésigny of real interest.

### André Delorme

*Rully, 71150 Chagny. 70ha, two-thirds owned by J-F Delorme, the rest by members of his family*
**1ers Crus:** *Rully: Grésigny, Les Cloux, La Fosse, Marissou; Givry-Clos du Cellier aux Moines*
**AOC Communales:** *Rully: La Bergerie, Chaponnière, La Chaume, La Martelle, Monthelon, Montmorin, Les Thivaux, Varot; Mercurey: Les Chenaults, Les Clos, Les Crêts, Les Lamberots, Les Monthelons, Les Murgers, Les Velles, Ropiton; Montagny-l'Epaule*
**AOC Régionales:** *Bourgogne Aligoté de Bouzeron, Crémant de Bourgogne*
Jean-François Delorme has done much for the renaissance of the Côte Chalonnaise and he has greatly extended his vineyard holdings of the Domaine de la Renarde (*qv*). As the vines have aged, the quality visibly has improved. The white grapes are pressed very slowly to avoid any bitterness, and then go through a *débourbage*, or clarifying of the must, at low temperature to concentrate the aromas. The reds are partially destalked, with the aim of achieving finesse and fruit. Rully Varot, principally planted to Chardonnay, is an 18ha parcel and yields wines which have a seductive, cinnamon quality. The *négociant* business of Delorme-Meulien/André Delorme makes very good selections, especially a Bourgogne Rouge La Croix-Lieux, and the house is renowned for its Crémant sparkling wines made from Pinot Noir and Chardonnay.

### Domaine Dureuil-Janthial

*71150 Rully. 6ha*

***1er Crus:*** *Puligny-Montrachet les Champs-Gains*

***AOC Communales:*** *Rulley, Mercurey*

***AOC Régionales:*** *Bourgogne Rouge, Blanc, Passe-Tout-Grains*

No destalking and long fermentation for the reds; the whites are made from very old vines. Both are aged in up to 20% new wood, the whites for six to nine months, the reds for considerably longer. Solidity rather than subtlety.

### Domaine Duvernay Père et Fils

*71150 Rully*

Good, straightforward white wines.

### Domaine de la Folie

*71150 Chagny. 16ha (2ha en métayage)*

***1ers Crus:*** *Rully: Clos du Chaigne, Clos St-Jacques*

***AOC Communales:*** *Rully: red, white, Clos Roch (white), Clos de Bellecroix (red), En Chaponnière*

***AOC Régionale:*** *Rully Passe-Tout-Grain*

This well-run domaine produces both red and white wines. Jérôme Noël-Bouton believes in long vattings at low temperature in order to make wines which will keep, but I have always found these wines to be extremely pleasant even when comparatively young. Sales are made to French restaurants, direct to private clients and to the export markets. The red Clos de Bellecroix can be both fruity and gamey. The white Clos St-Jacques has elegance and charm.

### Domaine Paul & Henri Jacqueson

*71150 Chagny. 8.5ha*

***1ers Crus:*** *Rully: La Bressande, Clouds, Grésigny, Marissou-St-Jacques, Mont-Palais, La Pucelle, Rabourcé, Vauvry; Mercurey Naugues*

***AOC Communales:*** *Rully Les Chaponnières; Mercurey*

***AOC Régionales:*** *Bourgogne Aligoté; Bourgogne Passe-Tout-Grains*

This small, meticulously run domaine was created by Henri Jacqueson and is now run by Henri and his son, Paul. The family is of Welsh origin, owing to the fact that, in the 15th century, the personal guard of Marguerite de Bourgogne was Welsh, and the Jacquesons are descended from this line. Exports account for 65% of sales, with private customers also an important element. The predominantly red wines are made with grapes which have not been destalked, with treading morning and evening to keep the skins in contact with the juice – the vinification lasts 15–22 days and the wines are intended for keeping. The whole white grapes are pressed immediately in horizontal presses (for two hours), then the juice clarifies naturally in tanks for eight to ten hours before fermentation at a cold temperature. *Elevage* is conducted in oak barrels, 30% new each year, and bottling takes place at the end of September. The result is some very attractive wines which are a credit to the Côte Chalonnaise.

### Domaine Ninot

*Cellier-Meix-Guillaume 71150 Rully. 12ha*

Good white Rully Grésigny and red Mercurey, grown and made by Delorme.

### Domaine de la Renarde

*Rue de la République, 71150 Rully. 35ha (32ha en métayage)*

Jean-François Delorme has built up a very important domaine at Rully owning, among other things, all of the 18-hectare Varot vineyard, which produces elegant white wine with a scent of newly mown grass. What is unusual in Burgundy is to have 18ha in one parcel, rather than in scattered plots. The red Rully has greatly improved as the vines have aged and now both raspberries and strawberries spring to mind when tasting. The range of Delorme wines generally represents a very good, as they say, *rapport qualité-prix*.

### Château de Rully

*71150 Rully*

Red Rully which is fairly chewy, needing time in bottle; exceptionally good, lightly-oaked, elegant, buttery white with considerable finesse for the AC.

*See also* Antonin Rodet, Mercurey.

### Domaine de Rully St-Michel

*Rue du Château, 71150 Rully. 10ha*

***1ers Crus:*** *Rully (white): Les Cloux, Raclot, Rabourcé;*
*Rully (red): Champs Clouds, Les Cloux*
***AOC Communale*** *Rully Clos de Pellerey (red)*

Softly fruity reds and very classy white Rullys abound here. The Rabourcé is outstanding.

## ●○ MERCUREY

**1996 production:**

| | |
|---|---|
| *Mercurey & **Premiers Crus*** ● | *26,849hl* |
| *Mercurey & **Premiers Crus*** ○ | *3,405hl* |

***Premiers Crus:*** *Clos-du-Roi, Clos-Voyen or Les Voyens, Clos-Marcilly, Clos-des-Fourneaux, Clos-des-Montaigus, Les Criochots, La Cailloute, Les Combins, Champs Martins, Clos des Barraults, Clos des Myglands, Clos l'Evêque, Grand Clos Fortoul, Les Naugues, Les Crêts, Clos Tonnerre, Les Vasées, Les Byots, Sazenay, La Bondue, Le Levrière, La Mission, Griffâeres, Les Velley, Clos Château de Montaigu, La Chassière, Les Ruelles Clos de Paradis*

Mercurey produces almost exclusively red wines and they are the biggest, most structured wines of the entire Côte Chalonnaise. They can be solid and quite earthy, and they certainly last longer than the red wines of the other Côte Chalonnaise appellations. Sometimes there is more than a hint of *terroir* in the taste, derived from the marl and limestone soil which predominates here. At their best, these wines are robust and frank, with an attractive 'wet earth' bouquet; at their worst, they are dry and rustic. These wines can be a mite clumsy.

## *The Principal Mercurey Producers*

### Domaine du Château de Chamilly

*Chamilly, 71510 St-Leger-sur-Dheune. 16ha*

Louis Desfontaine makes wines which have very good appellation character. They have body, bouquet and balance, and a good deal of earthy fruit. I have had some unhappy experiences, though, so tread (or drink) warily.

### Domaine du Château de Chamirey

*71640 Mercurey. 35ha. Mercurey (red) 25ha, Mercurey (white) 10ha*

The Château de Chamirey red and white wines are now both made and distributed by the *négociant* firm of Antonin Rodet (*qv*). The grapes are mechanically harvested and both wines are vinified in stainless steel before being aged for nine to 12 months, one-third in new wood, one-third in old wood and one-third remaining in vat. Increasingly good quality, especially the white which is particularly successful and has given me much pleasure. It is supple, elegantly textured, ripe and flowery, with hints of mayblossom. The red is firm with a chewy, cherry fruit and distinct earthiness of flavour – a wine which definitely needs time to mellow.

### Domaine Faiveley (qv)

Very important holdings in Mercurey, and exemplary red, velvety wines, packed with fruit and flavour. La Framboiserie is full of auto-suggestive raspberry flavour. The wines are made and matured at Faiveley's Domaine de la Croix Jacquelet.

### Domaine Jeannin-Naltet Père & Fils

*71640 Mercurey. 8ha*

Ripe and earthy Premier Cru Clos des Grands Voyens, a monopole.

### Domaine Michel Juillot

*71640 Mercurey. 32ha*

***Grands Crus:*** *Pernand-Vergelesses: Corton-Charlemagne; Aloxe-Corton: Corton-Perrières.* ***1ers Crus:*** *Mercurey: Clos des Barraults, Clos Tonnerre, Les Champs Martins (red and white), Les Combins.* ***AOC Communales:*** *Aloxe-Corton Les Caillettes; Mercurey (red and white)*

***AOC Régionales:*** *Bourgogne Côte Chalonnaise (red and white)*

There is a wealth of experience behind the skills of Michel Juillot – his has been a family of *vignerons* since 1404, and his grandfather became a master grafter of vines at national level, something much needed following phylloxera. Vinification is in open *cuves*, after total destalking. There is always one-third new wood in the cellars, and no barrel is more than three years old. Bottling is carried out after 18–24 months of *élevage*. There is often a scent of ripe, wild fruits in the reds. White Mercurey with a *goût de terroir* and a touch of liquorice and new oak. The reds are excellent – benefiting from about one-third new barrels in the cellar – scented, fruity and well made. The Clos des Barraults is usually a more complete and more tannic wine than the Champs Martins, taking longer to mature (five to eight years).Michel Juillot also makes very fine Corton-Charlemagne.

## Domaine Marceau

*71640 Mercurey*

Another well-regarded domaine.

## Jean Maréchal

*71640 Mercurey. 10ha*

Very good-quality 'typical' Mercureys. Both red and white are aged in 20% new wood.

## Domaine du Meix-Foulot/Yves de Launay

*Clos du Château de Montaigü, 71640 Mercurey. 17ha*

***1ers Crus:*** *Mercurey: Clos du Château de Montaigü, Les Biots, Les Veleys.* ***AOC Communales:*** *Mercurey (red and white)*

***AOC Régionale:*** *Bourgogne Aligoté*

A family domaine planted around the ruins of the medieval Château de Montaigu, and making good to very good wine. The grapes are destalked, and vatting lasts eight to ten days, with treading. The wines are left in vats for six months, with no heating of the cellars, so that the malolactic fermentation can take its own time. Ageing is in oak barrels, where the wines stay for six months to a year, depending on the character of the vintage and the *cuvée* – thus, some wines are bottled just before the following harvest, but more between March and June of the next year, which gives a total ageing of 18 months. The wines are often not filtered. Both the red, and the small amount of white, can keep well. If you are passing through Mercurey and decide that you want to visit the domaine, it is as well to ask for careful directions, as it is somewhat hidden, isolated amid the vine-covered slopes.

## Domaine de la Monette

*71640 Mercurey. 9ha*

Pierre-Emmanuel Granger makes mainly red Mercurey and just a little white. The red is aged in 20% new oak for 18 months, and both the straight Mercurey and the Premier Cru are delicious examples of the appellation.

## Domaine Maurice Protheau & Fils /Domaine François Protheau & Fils

*Le Clos l'Evêque, 71640 Mercurey. 38ha (55ha en métayage)*

***1ers Crus:*** *Rully Les Grésigny; Mercurey: Clos l'Evêque, Les Vellées*

***AOC Communales:*** *Rully: Rully La Chatalienne, Rully (white); Mercurey: Clos des Corvées, La Fauconnière, Les Ormeaux, Mercurey (red)*

***AOC Régionale:*** *Bourgogne Vigne de Champrenard*

An important Côte Chalonnaise domaine, with the wines distributed by the *négociant* François Protheau & Fils. The Protheau family has been a family of growers in Mercurey since 1720, but created a new vineyard in Rully in 1976. The red grapes are completely destalked, vatted for eight to ten days and aged in oak barrels for 12 to 14 months. Clos l'Evêque and Clos des Corvées are treated to new oak. The reds tend to be tannic and slow-maturing. The white Mercurey attains richness with age. Switzerland is the leading client and Philippe Protheau is the man in charge.

## Domaine Jean Raquillet

*71640 Mercurey. 8ha*

A very good source of supply, with meticulous cellar work.

## Antonin Rodet

*71640 Mercurey. Domaine du Château de Chamirey 32ha, Domaine du Château de Rully 36ha, Château de Mercey/Domaine Rodet 65ha*

This important *négociant* firm is now owned by the group, Worms, but Bertrand Devillard continues to run the company with great dynamism. Considerable expansion has taken place here since the mid-1980s. In 1986 Rodet started to make and distribute the wines of the Château de Rully (*qv*) (including Domaine Monassier); in 1988 it acquired half of Domaine Jacques Prieur (*qv*) half of whose production Rodet also sells, and in 1989 it purchased the Château de Mercey at Cheilly-lès-Maranges, where interesting vine canopy experiments are taking place. Rodet vinifies most of its white wines from must bought from Meursault, Puligny, Chassagne and Chablis, and the recent white wines certainly show the great progress made both in selection and in methods of *élevage*. The white Château de Rully and Château de Chamirey are particularly good value. Rodet exports 55% of production to most parts of the world and is certainly one of the most improved Burgundy houses of the last few years.

## Domaine Fabien & Louis Saier

*71640 Mercurey. 25ha*

***1er Cru:*** *Mercurey Les Champs Martins*

***AOC Communales:*** *Mercurey (red and white)*

***AOC Régionales:*** *Bourgogne Rouge; Bourgogne Passe-Tout-Grains*

Les Champs Martins, which can be lovely young drinking, but I have found that the quality here is not very consistent. However, they are not alone in this failing.

## Domaine de Suremain

*71640 Mercurey. 22ha*

This domaine used to be a reliable source of Mercurey with scent and regional character: a cherry-fruited straight Mercurey and a bigger, firmer Clos-Voyen. At the moment, while there are some good wines, quality is patchy, and other wines are distinctly rustic. A disappointment.

## Domaine Emile Voarick

*71640 St-Martin-sous-Montaigu, Mercurey*

***1ers Crus:*** *Mercurey Clos du Roy (red.)* ***AOC Communales:*** *Beaune (red), Mercurey (red and white), Givry (red and white)*

Now owned by Michel Picard of the *négociant* house Picard Père et Fils, this domaine has made noticeable improvements and is well worth watching.

## ●○ GIVRY

**1996 production:**

*Givry* ● *9,154hl*
*Givry* ○ *2,043hl*

There is now a somewhat controversial list of Premiers Crus: Clos Jus, Clos Charlé, Clos de la Servoisine, Clos du Cellier aux Moines, Petit Marole, Vaux, Marole, Bois Chevaux, Petits Prétants, Clos St-Pierre, Clos St-Paul, Clos Salomon, Grands Prétants, Clos de la Barraude, En Vignes Rouges, Bois Gauthier, Le Vigron, Les Grandes Vignes, Clos Marceaux, Clos du Vernoy, Les Berges, Clos du Cras Long.

Known somewhat strangely on some labels as the 'preferred wine of King Henri IV' (when it was thought he was more closely associated with Jurançon in the Pyrenean foothills of southwest France), Givry can have a lovely fragrance and a delicious, lingering Pinot Noir charm. The wines do not have the body of Mercurey, they boast a more delicate flavour, but if, as it is rumoured, the king's mistress did in fact have a vineyard at Givry, that is all as it should be.

### *The Principal Givry Producers*

### Domaine Jean Chofflet-Valdenaire

*Russilly, 71640 Givry. 11ha*

Smoky Pinot fruit on the nose, a touch of violets, and an earthy, raw-truffles flavour. Frank Pinot without the style of the classiest Givry.

### Domaine Michel Derain

*St-Désert, 71390 Buxy. 6ha*

Good white Givry and traditionally vinified reds. Very good Bourgogne Rouge, too.

### Propriété Desvignes

*Poncey, 71640 Givry*

Correct red Givry.

### Domaine du Gardin

*16 rue de Clos-Salomon, 71640 Givry. 6.8ha*

Produces Clos Salomon of subtlety, charm and fruit.

### Domaine Joblot

*71640 Givry. 13ha*

Vincent and Jean-Marc Joblot take their vineyards and wine-making very seriously. They make 80% red and 20% white, using 40–80% new wood. It is a tribute to the quality of the grapes and vinification that the wines do not taste too oaky. Well-balanced, harmonious and true-to-type with an impressively rich, elegant red Clos de la Servoisine.

## Domaine Thierry Lespinasse

*71390 Rosey. 3ha*

Gently earthy, savoury red Givry en Choué, and a fresh, delicate white – lovely wines needing bottle-age. M Lespinasse matures his wines in one-third new oak, the red for 12–18 months, the white for eight months. Also makes a delicious Crémant de Bourgogne.

## Domaine Gérard Mouton

*Poncey, 71640 Givry. 10ha*

Very good oak-aged (25%) red and white Givry.

## Domaine Ragot

*Poncey, 71640 Givry. 7.5 ha*

White Givry can be good, rich and nutty, but the quality is not always consistent.

## Domaine de la Renarde

*Rue de la République, 71150 Rully*

Red Clos du Cellier aux Moines can have a fascinating nose of toasted bread; at other times it smells of all the herbs of Provence. The taste is always very Pinot and long-lingering.

## Société Civile du Domaine Thénard

*7 rue de l'Hôtel-de-Ville, 71640 Givry. 23.8ha*

***Grands Crus,*** *Flagey-Echézeaux: Grands Echézeaux; Aloxe-Corton: Corton Clos du Roi; Puligny-Montrachet: Le Montrachet*

***1ers Crus:*** *Pernand-Vergelesses Ile des Vergelesses; Chassagne-Montrachet Clos St-Jean; Givry Cellier aux Moines, Givry Clos St-Pierre, Givry Les Bois Chevaux.* ***AOC Communales:*** *Givry (red and white)*

Best known for its substantial holding of Le Montrachet, but the more modest Givrys are good, too, especially the Clos St-Pierre. The wines are distributed by the Beaune *négociant* Remoissenet (*qv*), but there is some domaine-bottling.

# O MONTAGNY

**1996 production:**

*Montagny (white only)* *15,781hl*

In the past, all the vineyards here had the right to the appellation Premier Cru, provided that the wines reached 11.5% alcohol before chaptalisation. Now there are 53 registered Premiers Crus! It is thus better to choose your Montagny by grower than by *cru*, as is so often the case in Burgundy. The vineyard area has grown enormously.

The vineyards of the appellation Montagny are spread over the villages of Montagny itself, Buxy, St-Vallerin and Jully-lès-Buxy. The wine was meant to be that preferred by the monks of Cluny, as opposed to royalty. It is also said that it keeps the mouth fresh and the head clear. Be that as it may, cool white Montagny is absolutely delicious. It is a mite fuller and fatter, sometimes broader, than white Rully, which can have more breeding and elegance. There is more almondy honey in Montagny, and more straw and cinnamon in Rully. It is interesting to note that there is Kimmeridgian limestone at Buxy.

*The Principal Montagny Producers*

## Cave des Vignerons de Buxy

*71390 Buxy*

This large cooperative is the source of supply for many people, both in the French and the British trade. Naturally, there is variation among the *cuvées*, but the best are most worthy of the name of Montagny. The cooperative also makes red and white Bourgogne, Passe-Tout-Grains and Aligoté, generic appellations commonly produced on the Côte Chalonnaise. The reds have been given a real boost by the development of an innovative punching down system.

## Domaine du Château de Davenay

*71390 Buxy. 31ha*

***1ers Crus:** Montagny and Rully. **AOC Communale** Rully*

***AOC Régionales:** Bourgogne Aligoté, Bourgogne Pinot Noir, Bourgogne Hautes-Côtes de Beaune*

The proprietor, Michel Picard, is pursuing quality and – happily – obtaining good results for his efforts. I have been impressed by the Montagny.

## Domaine Lucien Denizot

*Bissey-sous-Cruchaud, 71390 Buxy*

Frank, fruity Bourgogne Rouge, redolent of cherries and cassis. One was Chante-Flûté, which is the Côte Chalonnaise version of Tasteviné. (A jury selects a high quality wine which is then given a numbered label, bearing the name of the producer, the vintage and the words *Chante-Flûté*).

## Domaine Michel Goubard

*Basseville, 71390 St-Désert. 22.5ha*

***AOC Régionales:** Bourgogne Côte Chalonnaise; Bourgogne Blanc and Aligoté; Bourgogne Passe-Tout-Grains*

The Goubard family has been on the Côte Chalonnaise since 1600. Two-thirds of the vineyards they now have are on marked slopes, beautifully facing southeast for maximum sun exposure. The Bourgogne Rouge is fruity and charming, made by a semi-carbonic maceration method and meant for relatively young drinking. Half the production is sold direct and half is exported. This is very good-value burgundy and the Côte Chalonnaise Mont Avril is a lovely expression of Pinot Noir.

## Maison Louis Latour

*18 rue des Tonneliers, 21200 Beaune*

The famed Beaune shipper, Louis Latour, always makes superb selections of Montagny.

## Domaine Bernard Michel

*St-Vallerin, 71390 Buxy. 10ha*

Graceful Les Coères with a slight earthiness in its flavour. Go for the whites here.

### Château de la Saule/Domaine Roy-Thévenin

*Montagny-lès-Buxy, 71390 Buxy. 13ha*
***AOC Communale*** *Montagny*
***AOC Régionales:*** *Bourgogne Aligoté; Bourgogne Passe-Tout-Grains*
This is a very reliable domaine, with labels under the names of both Alain and Marcel Roy-Thévenin. The grapes for the Montagny are pressed rapidly and then the clarified must ferments in *foudres*, enamel-lined tanks, and a part in oak barrels. The wines are then racked in March/April for an early bottling. The result is fresh and youthful, and always in balance. The Aligoté is quite worthy, too. The wines are now nicely spread in France and on the export markets.

### Domaine Jean Vachet

*St-Vallerin, 71390 Buxy. 8.5ha*
Broad, polished Les Coères; whites better than reds.

## ●○◑ The Mâconnais

Geologists love the Mâconnais, because there are some fascinating cliff formations in the southern part, and visitors love it no less for the pretty green countryside and the wealth of Romanesque churches. If you can tear yourself away from the fruit and nut trees, the small brown goats and the white cattle dappling the hillsides, the wines are very rewarding as well.

The whole district covers about 50km (31 miles) from north to south but is only 15km (nine miles) wide. The area is determined to the east and west by the two valleys of the Saône and the Grosne, but the line of hills runs from north-northeast to south-southwest. The site and altitude of the vineyard is critical to ultimate quality, because although the summers can be very hot in the Mâconnais, the winters are cold with frost a danger until the four days (May 12–15) of the Ice Saints are past.

There are two main soil types: low-acid, calcareous soil for the Chardonnay, an excellent combination for making fine white wine; and more acid, clay, sand or siliceous soil for white wines destined for very young drinking and for the Gamay for Mâcon Rouge. The most impressive slopes, magnificently exposed to the sun (hence the frequent high natural alcohol levels), are in the southern part of the region, the hills of Pouilly, Solutré and Vergisson. Indeed, the last two are really cliffs, formed by the same Jurassic strata found in the Côte d'Or, but in rather more dramatic shape. The Chardonnay dominates in the Mâconnais, covering 68.5% of the vineyard area, with the Gamay occupying 31.3% and the Pinot Noir 0.2%. The grape variety proportions reflect the fact that it is far easier to sell white Mâcon than red. In the Mâconnais, there are 5,425ha of AC vineyard under vine.

Most Mâcon Blanc is made without seeing any wood – it is kept in vat and bottled young. Of course, there are individual growers who bottle their wines, especially in Pouilly-Fuissé, and here there are hogsheads and even wooden vats in the cellars, but as the cooperatives handle about 70% of all the wine, logistics demand modern methods. About 72% of wine going through the cooperatives is white, and 28% red. Much Mâcon Rouge is made by the *macération carbonique* method (for a description of this, *see* the section on Beaujolais), which is an attractive way of treating the Gamay if the wine is not intended for keeping. The Pinot Noir can be made into Bourgogne Rouge or be included in Passe-Tout-Grains, and it is sometimes vinified by a semi-*macération carbonique* process, which means that the wine should definitely be drunk young.

I somehow feel that the Mâconnais is the proverbial 'gateway to the south' – the grey north gives way to the ochre Midi. The houses are covered with warm-coloured, curvy tiles, reminiscent of Provence, and they have verandahs running the length of them, indicating sunny days. That might be difficult to believe in the grip of a glacial winter, but the summer gives you a vision of France in all its rural splendour.

## ●○◑ MACON

**1996 production:**

*Mâcon/Mâcon-Villages* *282,260hl*

Here the appellation is Mâcon-Villages or Mâcon with one of 43 village names. This might sound baffling, but in practice the following villages are most often seen: Clessé, Lugny, Prissé, La Roche-Vineuse, Vinzelles, Viré, and Chardonnay, which may or may not have given its name to the grape variety.

On the whole, these wines are at their best at one to two years old, when all their fruit and blossomy scents are at their most tantalising. The two enemies of good Mâcon Blanc are lack of freshness and a certain vulgarity, usually brought about by a rustic approach to winemaking. A charming characteristic is a smoky muskiness, coming from the Chardonnay clone used in the area. Widespread machine-picking leads to wines that should be drunk young – hand-picked wines last better.

### *The Principal Mâcon Producers*

### Bénas Frères

*Serrières, 71960 Pierreclos. 12ha*

Mâcon Blanc with some muskiness on the nose, broad and fat on the palate. Good red Mâcon-Serrières.

### Domaine André Bonhomme

*71260 Viré. 9.5ha*

Exemplary Mâcon-Viré year in, year out; vivid wines of delicious texture and length which spend up to six months in 25% new oak.

### Domaine Paul Broyer (Eventail)

*71960 Solutré, Soâne-et-Loire*

Lovely, fruity, plump Mâcon Solutré.

### Domaine Jean-Noël Chaland

*71260 Viré*

Lanolin-smooth Mâcon-Viré; a good bottle.

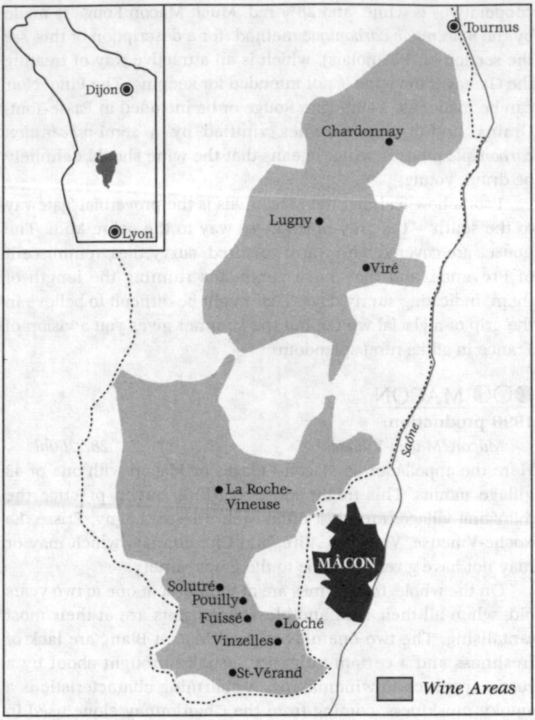


## Domaine des Chazelles

*71260 Viré*

This quite small domaine producing a particularly opulent Mâcon-Villages of much higher quality than its modest appellation would suggest.

## Domaine de Chervin

*Burgy, 71260 Lugny*

Mâcon-Burgy made by Albert Goyard of the Domaine de Roally (*qv*) family. Delicate, pretty wines of finesse.

## Cave Coopérative de Clessé

*71260 Clessé*

Light, straightforward whites and reds; the supple Blanc de Blancs *méthode traditionnelle* is probably the best of the range.

## Domaine de la Condemine

*71260 Péronne. 4.5ha*

Véronique and Pierre Janny make good, nutty Mâcon-Villages at this estate – that is, when they do not use too much sulphur dioxide in the process.

## Domaine des Heritiers Bernard Coron

*8 bd Bretonnières, 21200 Beaune. 8.61ha*

*Pouilly-Fuissé Château de Loché; Pouilly-Loché Château de Loché; Pouilly-Vinzelles Château de Loché; Mâcon-Villages Château de Loché, Le Clos du Château*

Coron produces both domaine and *négociant* wines under the same name. I am not keen on them, although, to be fair, I have not seen a domaine wine recently.

## Domaine Jacques Depagneux

*69400 Villefranche-sur-Saône*

Domaine distributed through the SVGC (*qv*).

## Domaine André Depardon (Eventail)

*71570 Leynes*

Mâcon Solutré and Mâcon Blanc Villages Les Condemines with racy acidity and style.

## Domaine des Gandines

*71260 Clessé*

Unoaked Mâcon-Clessé, lemon-fresh and delicious young, but keeps well, too.

## Domaine Emilian Gillet

*Quintaine, 71260 Clessé*

Good, fruity Mâcon-Clessé and Mâcon-Viré.

## Domaine des Granges

*71570 Chaintré*

Jean-François Cognard makes good Mâcon-Chaintré and a prize-winning Beaujolais Blanc.

## Château de la Greffière

*La Roche-Vineuse, 71960 Pierreclos. 18ha*

Mssrs Greuzard make broad, perfumed Mâcon-Villages (although the château's '90 La Roche-Vineuse was tired by the time it was a year old). There is also a lovely Bourgogne Rouge Pinot Noir.

## Domaine Adrien Guichard

*Montbellet, 71260 Lugny*

Mâcon-Villages which is always tempting.

## Domaine Guillemot-Michel

*71260 Clessé. 6ha*

Mâcon-Clessé Quintaine that is light, flowery and stylish. Quintessential Quintaine!

## Cave Coopérative d'Igé

*71960 Igé. 286 ha*

Because of the suitability of the local soils for red grapes, this cooperative produces more red than white wine. Among the whites there is a deliciously full and round Mâcon-Igé, Château

London from a particularly well exposed *lieu-dit*, and a classy St-Véran. The red Mâcons are sturdy without being coarse, and the two Pinot Noirs are very successful for the level: a vividly fruity basic Bourgogne Pinot Noir, and a more substantial *fût de chêne cuvée* where the oak is well-integrated and not overdone.

### Domaine Henri Lafarge

*Le Bourg, Domaine de la Combe, 71250 Bray. 14ha*

Wonderful floral, acacia nose and great elegance and balance in these white Mâcon wines.

### Cave Coopérative de Lugny

*71260 Lugny. 1,150 ha*

One of the few local co-ops that, sensibly, does not attempt an 'oaked' *cuvée*. Its range of whites is very well made, with noticeably pure apple-and-melon Chardonnay flavours. Particularly good are the Mâcon-Lugny Les Charmes, which is elegant and smoky with good acidity, and the supple, fruity Mâcon St-Gengoux. The red Mâcons are better value than the Bourgogne Pinot Noirs. The co-op, the largest in Burgundy, is well worth a visit. It has an attractive reception area, good tasting facilities, and it produces about four million bottles a year – so there will be some for you.

### Domaine Pierre Mahuet

*La Roche-Vineuse, 71960 Pierreclos*

Mâcon-La Roche-Vineuse with a nose of almonds – excellent fresh wine.

### Domaine Manciat-Poncet

*71850 Charnay-lès-Mâcon*

Very perfumed, full, immensely seductive Mâcon-Charnay, and excellent Pouilly-Fuissé. The latter's Vieilles Vignes is the only oaked wine, spending six months in 50% new wood. Devoted hand-harvesting.

### Olivier Merlin

*71960 Pierreclos. 6ha*

Merlin makes lovely Mâcon La Roche Vineuse from the village of this picturesque name.

### Domaine René Michel

*71260 Clessé*

Concentrated Mâcon-Clessé with a nice nuttiness.

### Château de Mirande

*71260 Lugny. 27ha*

Baron Patrice de l'Epine makes elegant, delicious Mâcon-Villages, with a lovely nose of acacia and mayblossom.

### Domaine du Prieuré

*71260 Lugny*

Very well-made Mâcon-Villages.

### Domaine de Roally

*71260 Viré. 3.5ha*

Henri Goyard makes Mâcon-Viré (and fights the dominance of the cooperative!) and succeeds admirably. Wonderful acacia nose, hazelnuts, excellent fresh wine. On the neck label he says *Raisin Cueilli à la Main* – the grapes were picked by hand, and thus the wine lasts well in bottle.

### Société Coopérative des Viticulteurs de Saône et Loire

Nutty wines, full and fat.

### Domaine Talmard

*71700 Uchizy. 31ha*

Of Paul and Philibert Talmard's 31ha of vines, 28ha are planted with Chardonnay, from which they make a deliciously clean and flavoursome Mâcon-Uchizy. A personal favourite where machine harvesting seems to have no adverse effects.

### Jean Thévenet/Domaine de la Bon Gran

*Quintaine, 71260 Clessé. 15ha*

Good Mâcon-Clessé from low yields and slow fermentation. In a hot year, the Domaine de la Bon Gran Cuvée Tradition weighs in at 14.5%, with super-ripe appley, peachy flavours and huge concentration. Occasionally, Thévenet makes a Sauternes-style Mâcon-Clessé from botrytised Chardonnay grapes.

### Domaine de Thurissey/Les Vieux Ceps

*Thurissey, 71260 Montbellet*

Robert Bridon makes scented wines with a big, broad taste.

### Trenel & Fils

*71850 Charnay-lès-Mâcon*

*Négociant* producing a consistently good range of Mâconnais, Beaujolais and Beaujolais *cru* wines.

### Verget

*71960 Sologny*

*Négociant* business started by Jean-Marie Guffens (*qv*) in 1990. He buys grapes from growers whose vineyards he has helped supervise during the year, and pays a premium for the quality of the fruit as judged by yield, sugar-acid balance, health and cleanliness. So far, he only makes white wines, in a purpose-built winery at Sologny in the Mâconnais. The wines start their fermentation in stainless-steel vats and finish in barrel. For *négociant* wines, finest results look very promising indeed. They are fresh and clean, with plenty of flavour and good *typicité* for blends within an appellation.

### Cave Coopérative de Viré

*71260 Viré. 400ha*

The cooperative makes reliable wines right across the range: fresh, lemony Mâcon-Viré, consistently good Crémant de Bourgogne from pure Chardonnay, and two nicely balanced 'oaked' *cuvées* of Mâcon-Viré and Bourgogne Rouge which are successful because only 20% new wood is used and the flavour of the wines is enhanced, not masked.

Other excellent wines include Mâcon-Villages Laforêt of Joseph Drouhin (*qv*), Mâcon-Prissé of Georges Duboeuf (*qv*), Mâcon-Viré of Louis Jadot (*qv*), Mâcon-Lugny Les Genièvres of Louis Latour (*qv*).

White Mâcon, made from Pinot Blanc or Chardonnay, can also be called Pinot-Chardonnay-Mâcon which, in these days of greater accuracy with regard to grape varieties, is slightly old-fashioned. There is also a small amount of red labelled Mâcon, plus the village name, then *Villages*.

The Supérieur denotes one per cent more alcohol for both the red and white wines: in other words, the minimum level of alcohol before chaptalisation for Mâcon Supérieur Rouge is ten per cent and for Mâcon Supérieur Blanc, 11%. The white wines of this category can be 'declassified' into Bourgogne, providing a valuable source of supply for many a merchant.

I have to say that most Mâcon Rosé wines which have come my way have been very unappealing, with the exception of one from the Maison Mâconnaise des Vins (Société Coopérative des Viticulteurs de Saône et Loire [*qv*]).

Good Mâcon Rouge or Mâcon Rouge Supérieur comes from: Henri Lafarge (*qv*), Cave Coopérative de Lugny (*qv*), Cave Coopérative de Prissé (*qv*), the Domaine des Provenchères of Maurice Gonon, Jean-Claude Thévenet, and Mâcon-Serrières from Bénas Frères (*qv*). (This is different soil and the wine is not Beaujolais in type; it is traditional, needing time, and is more 'Pinot Noir' in character with age.)

The co-ops generally maintain a good standard, although as always, the art is in selection and some could do better. They are based at Aze, Bissey-sous-Cruchaud, Buxy, Chaintré, Chardonnay, Charnay-lès-Mâcon, Genouilly, Igé, Lugny, Mancey, Prissé, Sennece-lès-Mâcon, Sologny, Verzé, 'La Vigne Blanche' at Clessé, Vinzelles and Viré.

## O POUILLY-FUISSE

**1996 production:**

| | |
|---|---|
| *Pouilly-Fuissé* | *44,478hl* |

There are no Premiers Crus, but sometimes a vineyard name is added to the wine label, particularly when a site has become known, over the years, for producing fine wine. The villages producing Pouilly-Fuissé are Pouilly, Fuissé, Solutré, Vergisson and Chaintré. There are nuances in taste between the villages, with Pouilly making a bid for top position and Solutré for the wines with more body, but probably the hand of the winemaker, and perhaps the age of the vines, is more important.

The actual rock of Solutré is somewhat menacing, especially when you know that at its feet lies nearly a hectare of the bones of wild horses driven over the cliff by 'Solutréen Man' 15,000–12,000BC. It is quite a surprise to see the escapades of this creature so well documented on the other side of France, in the Museum of Prehistory at Les Eyzies in the Dordogne. But the wine of Solutré singularly lacks menace. It is a rich, full, even earthy Chardonnay, not infrequently attaining 13–14% alcohol naturally. There is not the steeliness and 'nerve' of Chablis, nor the finesse or breeding of, say, Puligny-Montrachet, but there is plenty of flavour. Dangers can be excessive sulphur dioxide and misjudgements with barrels.

## *The Principal Pouilly-Fuissé Producers*

### Domaine de l'Arillière

*71960 Fuissé*

Stylish and fruity Pouilly-Fuissé, rather than rich and full. *See also* Société Civile du Château de Fuissé.

| | | |
|---|---|---|
| **Mâcon Supérieur Rouge** | 1996 production: | *43,707 hectolitres* |
| **Mâcon Supérieur Blanc** | 1996 production: | *12,493 hectolitres* |
| **Mâcon Rouge and Rosé** | 1996 production: | *5,428 hectolitres* |
| **Mâcon Blanc** | 1996 production: | *1,676 hectolitres* |

### Auvigue-Burrier-Revel et Cie

*Le Moulin du Pont, 71850 Charnay-lès-Mâcon. 5ha*

*Pouilly-Fuissé: Les Bouthières, Les Chailloux, La Frairie*

Pouilly-Fuissé that is always good when found in top French restaurants. The best *cuvées* spend four months in new wood. This is both a small *négociant* and a domaine.

### Daniel Barraud

*Vergisson, 71960 Pierreclos.*

Good St-Véran; rich, oaky Pouilly-Fuissé Vieilles Vignes.

### Château de Beauregard

*Fuissé, 71960 Pierreclos. 34ha*

*Pouilly-Fuissé; St-Véran; Mâcon-Villages; Beaujolais: Fleurie*

Good wines, with the St-Véran usually better value – but that is often the case except for the most exciting Pouilly-Fuissés. Ageing in up to one-third new oak.

### Domaine Bressand

*71960 Fuissé*

Well-made wines.

### Domaine Cordier Père et Fils

*71960 Fuissé. 11ha*

Plenty of finesse and complexity on the nose, here, while the taste is good but not as exciting as the bouquet. However, the wines are 'on the up', with evidence of wood-ageing.

### Domaine Corsin

*71960 Fuissé. 11.5ha*

*Pouilly-Fuissé; St-Véran; Mâcon-Villages (white); Mâcon Supérieur (red)*

Very reliable, down the line Pouilly Fuissé and St Véran.

### Domaine Louis Curveux

*71960 Fuissé. 6ha*

*Pouilly-Fuissé; Mâcon-Villages: Mâcon-Fuissé, Mâcon-Chaintré*

Wines of excellent fruity character and dimension. The Mâcon wines are vinified and aged in stainless steel only; the Pouilly-Fuissé sees a small proportion of new wood.

### Roger Duboeuf

*Chaintré, 71750 La Chapelle-de-Guinchay. 5ha*

Small-scale producer making a good Pouilly-Fuissé Les Plessis, oak-aged with a small proportion of new wood.

### Domaine Jeanne Ferret

*Fuissé, 71960 Pierreclos. 15ha*

Outstanding Pouilly-Fuissé from old vines, low yields and modest use of new wood.

### Domaine Michel Forest

*71960 Vergisson. 2.8ha*

Terrific winemaking with a gloriously fruity and succulent Les Crays and a very elegant but more austere La Roche. Excellent examples of the genre, in the camp of the oak barrel, with judiciously employed new wood.

### Société Civile du Château de Fuissé

*71960 Fuissé. 30ha. Pouilly-Fuissé; St-Véran; Mâcon-Villages; Morgon; Juliénas*

Jean-Jacques Vincent (*qv*) vinifies and ages his various *cuvées* according to the age of the vines and their vineyard location. The St-Véran, Pouilly-Fuissé Première Cuvée and Domaine de l'Arillière (*qv*) are vinified principally in tank and bottled early; the Château Fuissé is aged in 20% new oak, and the Château Fuissé Vieilles Vignes is a selection of *cuvées* from vines with an age of 30 years and more. Compare the elegant Combettes, the more powerful Brûlées, and Le Clos which combines it all. The Château Fuissé wines have attained record price levels, but they are an experience in intense flavour. The apogee is attained with the Vieilles Vignes in a really ripe year – positively mindblowing. These are keepers.

Jean-Jacques Vincent is, in my opinion, one of the most brilliant makers of white burgundy. His Pouilly-Fuissé Vieilles Vignes easily rivals the Côte d'Or's best. There has been much research on different types of oak, and the sheer dimension of the greatest vintages almost defies description.

### Domaine Guffens-Heynen

*79160 Vergisson. 3ha (1ha en métayage)*

*Pouilly-Fuissé (various lieux-dits);*

*Mâcon-Villages: Mâcon-Pierreclos (white), Mâcon-Pierreclos (red)*

Belgian Jean-Marie Guffens owns and runs this remarkable little property, in addition to the *négociant* Verget (*qv*), which he founded in 1990. The domaine whites are refined examples of their appellations; the product of old vines, very low yields and meticulous winemaking. Subtle Pouilly-Fuissés which age well for six to eight years; very good white Mâcon-Pierreclos which is best at three to four years. The whites ferment and age in one-third new oak. The red Mâcon-Pierreclos, pure Gamay, spends eight to nine months in 50% new wood. It has extract and tannin, yes, but charm and drinking appeal? No.

### Domaine Roger Luquet

*71960 Fuissé. 17ha*

Pouilly-Fuissé en Chatenet with fruit, elegance and style. A really conscientious domaine and a splendid source of supply.

### Domaine Gilles Noblet

*71960 Fuissé. 9ha*

Excellent, ample Pouilly-Fuissé, and a rare Loché.

### Domaine Jean-Paul Paquet

*71960 Fuissé. 12ha*

Full and broad with some complexity of bouquet.

### Domaine Roger Saumaize

*Vers-la-Croix, 71960 Vergisson. 2ha (5ha en métayage)*

Light and lively unoaked Mâcon-Villages and Pouilly-Fuissé Vignes Blanches; more 'serious' Pouilly-Fuissé Clos de la Roche and Ronchevats which spend some time in new wood and benefit from bottle-age. These are well-made wines – worth looking out for.

## ○ POUILLY-VINZELLES AND POUILLY-LOCHE

**1996 production:**

*Pouilly-Vinzelles and Pouilly-Loché* *4,738hl*

These two satellite appellations would make good alternatives to the expensive Pouilly-Fuissé if the quantity produced were more significant. Slightly more earthy than the best Pouilly-Fuissé, but the best have definition and character, and make interesting bottles.

## *The Principal Pouilly-Vinzelles and Pouilly-Loché Producers*

### Domaine Mathias

*71570 Chaintré. 8ha*

Fine, fruity Pouilly-Vinzelles.

Excellent selections of Pouilly-Vinzelles are made by Georges Duboeuf (*qv*). Leave the professionals to make the selections at the Vinzelles cooperative.

## ○ ST-VERAN

**1996 production:**

*St-Véran* *35,167hl*

An appellation created in 1971, virtually replacing Beaujolais Blanc (Louis Jadot (*qv*) is one of the few still to make a speciality of it). Confusingly, the village of St-Vérand is within the appellation St-Véran, as are Chânes, Chasselas, Davayé, Leynes, Prissé, St-Amour and Solutré (part). Although maturing slightly quicker than Pouilly-Fuissé, wines are nearly always better at two years than one, with more interest and complexity.

### *The Principal St-Véran Producers*

**Château de Coreaux**
*Leynes, 71570 La Chapelle-de-Guinchay*
Full, pure and fruity.

**Domaine André Depardon (Eventail)**
*Leynes, 71570 La Chapelle-de-Guinchay*
Clean, lively St-Véran which gains richness with age. Really intelligent winemaking.

**Domaine des Deux Roches**
*71960 Davayé. 34ha. St-Véran: Les Terres Noires, St-Véran, Pouilly-Fuissé; Mâcon Villages (white), Mâcon (red)*
Broad, buttery St-Véran. The best *cuvées* ferment in 20–50% new wood, and they can taste fairly 'oaky', but without being overdone.

**Domaine Duperon**
*Chasselas, 71570 La Chapelle-de-Guinchay*
Good-quality St-Véran, ripe and full.

**Domaine Thierry Guerin**
*71960 Vergisson*
Well-made, fairly full St-Véran, and Pouilly-Fuissé of weight and finesse, especially the *cuvée* La Roche.

**Domaine Maurice Martin**
*Davayé, 71960 Pierreclos*
Good quality St-Véran.

**Domaine Michel Paquet**
*Davayé, 71960 Pierreclos. 9ha*
Nutty, lanolin wine, no 'sparks' but nice St-Véran.

**Groupement de Producteurs de Prissé**
*Prissé, 71960 Pierreclos. 330ha*
The white wines are light but well made, although the St-Véran *élevé en fût de chêne* makes little sense as the wood quite obliterates essential fruit flavours. The Mâcon Rouge is a good, savoury Gamay and the co-op makes an appealing unoaked Bourgogne Pinot Noir.

**Martine & Jean-Luc Tissier/**
**Domaine des Crais (Eventail)**
*Les Vessats, 71570 Leynes. 7.6ha. St-Véran; Mâcon (white); Beaujolais-Villages; Crémant de Bourgogne*
The St-Véran Domaine des Crais is an elegant wine, the flavour of which gives an indication of the chalky soil.

**Domaine Vincent**
*Fuissé, 71960 Pierreclos.*
The estate makes rich, full wines – everything one would expect from Jean-Jacques Vincent.

## ●○◑ Beaujolais

About 23,000ha are under the vine in the Beaujolais, in a region which is 55km (34 miles) long and 12 to 15km (seven to nine miles) wide, with an average altitude of 300m (984ft). There are a few large domaines, but many small family properties of four to five hectares (around 2,500 properties of one to four hectares, and 1,400 properties of four to seven hectares).

The system of *vigneronnage* is very strong in the Beaujolais, in which the *vigneron* cultivates the owner's vineyards, while the owner may provide the *vigneron's* house, but certainly the vinification equipment, vine plants and treatment materials. The vineyard worker usually provides the vineyard equipment, and does the work. Usually, the profits on the wine are shared. About 50% of Beaujolais properties are worked by *vignerons*.

The Gamay Noir à Jus Blanc covers 98% of the Beaujolais vineyard area. It is interesting to note that the ten Beaujolais *crus* can be declassified into Bourgogne, so if you drink a red burgundy made in these areas, it will be Gamay, and not Pinot Noir, wine, somewhat different from a Bourgogne Rouge from the Côte Chalonnaise.

*La taille courte*, or Gobelet pruning, is found in the northern area of the *crus* and of Beaujolais-Villages, while *la taille longue*, simple Guyot pruning on wire, is practiced in Beaujolais Sud. In both cases, however, there must never be more than 12 buds on a vine, and the density of vine plants is between 9,000 and 10,000 plants per hectare. New clones and too generous rootstocks can lead to excessive yields, that implacable enemy of quality Beaujolais.

In red wine vinification, the main difference between the Beaujolais and the rest of Burgundy is that the Gamay is never crushed – there is no *foulage* – and the grapes are thus whole. They are put into fermentation vats, which are usually of wood *chez le vigneron*, but often of concrete at the cooperatives. The *cuves* are not completely filled, so that the accumulation of carbonic gas in the empty space can act as a break on the speed of the fermentation and protect against acetic contamination. Vats of 60hl are ideal, but in cooperatives they tend to be much larger. The weight of the grapes on top causes some juice to run at the bottom of the vat and this is then pumped over, and sometimes warmed, to get the fermentation going. Sugar to increase the alcohol and sulphur dioxide (an antioxidant) are added at this time.

The optimum extraction of bouquet (one of the great charms of Gamay that has been vinified in this way) occurs at 25–28°C (77–82°F), and the fermentation period lasts four to six days, depending on the ambient temperatures and the way in which the yeasts are working.

In effect, a fermentation takes place within each whole grape, induced by the $CO_2$ released by the fermenting juice at the bottom of the vat. This is a variation of a pure carbonic maceration fermentation, when the vat is saturated with added $CO_2$ and a ten- to 12-day maceration follows; but the typical Beaujolais procedure described above is both natural and ideally suited to Gamay. The grapes are pressed to extract the rest of the juice, the wine is put into *cuves* to settle down, and then into *fûts*, where a month later the fermentation is usually completed. These casks vary enormously in the Beaujolais, from 216 litres, 110 litres or 50–55 litres, to six hectolitres or a *foudre* with an average capacity of 50hl (this can also be made of concrete in a cooperative).

Before bottling, usually in the spring following the vintage where the *crus* are concerned, some wines are put through a flash-pasteurisation for total stability. But small growers do not have these facilities, and firms like Duboeuf (*qv*) prefer to use membrane filters and cold sterile bottling in order to preserve maximum fruit.

The worst faults of Beaujolais are usually an excess of alcohol, with the 'fumes' masking the fresh, fruity aromas, and the over-bolstered body disguising the frank, clean taste. Some *négociants* foster a hard, beefy, strong *négoce* style, while some growers' wines are casky and dirty. In large vintages, some wines are often naturally very pale and weak, as the growers give very short *cuvaisons*, or vattings, due to shortage of space. But today, more than ever before, there are examples of pure, lilting Beaujolais just waiting to be selected by wise wine-buyers who recognise good quality.

Beaujolais Nouveau, or Beaujolais Primeur, was a comparatively new phenomenon on the export markets which became increasingly popular during the 1970s. Now, there is evidence that the season for drinking Beaujolais Nouveau is growing ever shorter – the wine is released for sale in shops and wine bars on the third Thursday in November but before Christmas most people have lost interest in this vinous diversion, and the signs now are that sales of Nouveau are falling off as December advances. Prices are more sensible in the late 1990s.

There are many excellent Nouveau wines each year, and the problems of stability in a wine so rapidly prepared are largely overcome. However, it is a pity when good Beaujolais, and even more good Beaujolais-Villages, with the potential to be even better in the following year, is sold and drunk as Nouveau.

Nearly 50 per cent of the production of Beaujolais is exported throughout the world. There could not be a more seductive flagship for French exports than this delectable, lively wine.

## ●○◑ BEAUJOLAIS

**1996 production:**
*Beaujolais & Beaujolais-Villages*
*& Beaujolais crus* *1,400,538hl*

Nearly all Beaujolais is red, although there are very small amounts of white and rosé. Most straight Beaujolais is produced south of Villefranche, on clay and limestone, although it can come

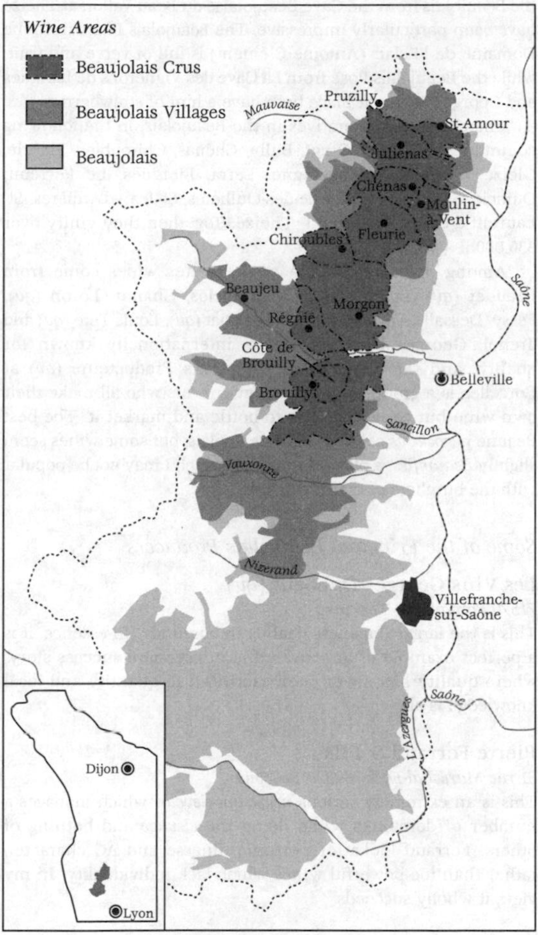


from anywhere in the region. Beaujolais Supérieur is rarely seen – it simply means that it must have one per cent more alcohol than Beaujolais *tout court*. Essentially, simple Beaujolais is best in the year after its birth – then the wise wine-drinker moves on to Beaujolais-Villages.

The following growers all produce delicious Beaujolais: Château de Bel-Air which is made at the Lycée Viticole de Belleville, Jean-Paul Brun at Charnay, with astonishing, raspberry-flavoured wine, Lucien Charmet at Le Breuil, Château Gaillard of Jacqueline and Jean-Louis Riche at Denicé, Philippe Jambon at Corcelles, René Riottot at Denicé, Pierre Jomard at Fleurieux-sur-l'Arbresle and René Marchand at Cogny. Among the cooperatives, the Beaujolais from the Cave Beaujolaise du Beau Vallon at Theizé have been particularly impressive. The Beaujolais Blanc from the Domaine de l'Eclair (Antoine Clément) is full of verve and fruit, while the Beaujolais Rosé from La Cave des Vignerons de Liergues and Georges Texier at Blacé both have a hint of strawberries.

There are 19 cooperatives in the Beaujolais, in the following communes: Le Bois-d'Oingt, Bully, Chénas, Chiroubles, Fleurie, Gleizé, Juliénas, Lachassagne, Létra, Liergues, Le Perréon, Quincié, Sain-Bel, St-Etienne-des-Oullières, St-Jean-d'Ardières, St-Laurent-d'Oingt, St-Vérand, Theizé. Together, they vinify over 330,000hl a year.

Among *négociants*, some of the better wines come from Beaudet (*qv*), Les Caves de Champclos, Chanut, Loron (*qv*), Fessy/Dessalle, Ferraud (*qv*), Gobet, Piat (*qv*), Louis Tête (*qv*) and Trenel. Georges Duboeuf (*qv*) is internationally known for quality, and the Eventail de Vignerons Producteurs (*qv*) at Corcelles is a group of independent growers who all make their own wine but come together to bottle and market it. The best Beaune *négociants* select well in Beaujolais, but some wines seem slightly *Beaunifiés*, a play on words for which I may not be popular with the burghers of that lovely town.

## *Some of the Principal Beaujolais Producers*

### Les Vins Georges Duboeuf (*qv*)

*71570 Romanèche-Thorins*

This is the largest business dealing in burgundy. In essence, it is a perfect example of an extraordinary *négociant* success story, where quality has never been sacrificed to quantity and local knowledge is all.

### Pierre Ferraud & Fils

*31 rue Maréchal-Foch, 69220 Belleville*

This is an extremely serious *négociant-éleveur*, which manages a number of domaines while doing the *élevage* and bottling of others. Ferraud looks for perfume, finesse and AC character, rather than too-powerful wines which lack individuality. In my view, it wholly succeeds.

### Mommessin et Thorin

*71850 Charnay-lès-Mâcon*

The second-largest Beaujolais-Mâconnais business, now owned by Boisset.

### Les Vins Mathelin

*69830 Châtillon-d'Azergues*

Prizewinning red and white Beaujolais.

### SVGC

*Les Chers, 69840 Juliénas*

Chanut, Dépagneux, Gobet and Sarrau are now grouped under this organisational hat.

## ●○ ST-AMOUR

**1996 production:**

*St-Amour* *18,212hl*

It may be facetious to say that this is the wine for St-Valentine's Day, but there can be few more pleasurable ways of cementing a relationship than by drinking a bottle of St-Amour *à deux*! It is perhaps best not to go into the reputed origins of the name, since it reflects somewhat badly on the clerics of times past. Suffice it to say that here we are still on a granite base, although it is the only *cru* of the Beaujolais entirely in Saône-et-Loire. The white wine made in the commune can be called St-Véran. The wines have a certain sprightliness, which is intriguing, combined with fruit and delicacy; they need sunny years to give them the necessary ripeness. Light vintages can be drunk young, but when conditions are good, a St-Amour of two to three years old is all the more interesting. Unfortunately, there is not a great deal of St-Amour to go around.

### *The Principal St-Amour Producers*

**Domaine des Duc**

*71570 St-Amour-Bellevue. 27ha*

Reliable, rich St-Amour and Chénas.

**Domaine Dufour**

*39160 St-Amour*

The highly regarded St-Amour produced here gives a very good lesson in appellation taste.

**Domaine Elie Mongénie**

*39160 St-Amour*

St-Amour that keeps well in ripe years.

**Domaine de Mongrin**

*39160 St-Amour. 27ha*

The Duc brothers are responsible for this pretty, soft, flowery wine.

**Domaine du Paradis (Duboeuf)**

*71570 St-Amour-Bellevue. 9ha*

Vines of a good age on sandy, gravelly topsoil here produce a rich St-Amour of finesse.

**Domaine Guy Patissier Les Poulets (Eventail)**

*39160 St-Amour*

Marked by strong regional flavour, this wine really packs a punch, but through its depth of taste, not through its alcohol imbalance.

**Domaine Jean-Michel Patissier /Vigne de la Côte Besset (Eventail)**

*71570 St-Amour-Bellevue*

Has an equally high reputation – lovely wines with bite and attack – as has Jean-Bernard Patissier with Les Bonnets.

### Domaine Francis Saillant

*39160 St-Amour*

Very creditable, easy-to-drink St Amour.

### Pierre Siraudin/Château de St-Amour

*71570 St-Amour-Bellevue. 13ha (8ha en métayage)*

*St-Amour; Beaujolais-Villages St-Vérand (red)*

The Château de St-Amour is a perfect example of the appellation, fermented for seven to ten days, according to the year, and keeps well. The Beaujolais-Villages from St-Vérand ferments for six to eight days, again in order to make a wine which is not ephemeral.

### Paul Spay/Domaine de la Cave Lamartine

*Domaine de la Cave Lamartine, 71570 St-Amour-Bellevue*

*0ha. St-Amour, Beaujolais St-Amour (red); Juliénas Côte de Bessay.*

This domaine possesses good sites, facing south and southeast. It is increasing its sales and exports to all the usual markets. The vinification is classic, the aim to make wines with regional character and fruit, delicious for two to three years after the harvest. But Paul Spay is against laying down the *crus* – 'leave that to the Côte d'Or and Bordeaux'! Quality seems patchy but worth investigating.

### Georges Duboeuf (St-Amour)

*Romanèche-Thorins, 71570 La Chapelle-de-Guinchay*

Good Duboeuf bottlings in the appellation include the Domaine des Sablons and the Cuvée Poitevin (this is not a wine which has escaped from the other side of France – M Poitevin is the *vigneron* and the *vinificateur*). The latter is produced from clay-limestone topsoil, balanced and elegant and capable of ageing with grace.

## ● JULIENAS

**1996 production:**

| | |
|---|---|
| *Juliénas* | *34,601hl* |

Near St-Amour, the high vineyards of Juliénas give wines which are really the epitome of what Beaujolais *crus* are all about. They are wonderfully sturdy, oozing purple fruit when young, positively crunchy in the mouth, but with a backbone that promises further development if you resist pulling the cork straightaway. There is granite and schist, and the wines have the *charpente* or structure of the soil. This is the most northerly *cru* of the Rhône *département* and it includes some vineyards from the villages of Jullié (about 80ha) and Pruzilly. The slopes of Jullié are very steep, comparable to those of Chiroubles – no picking machine can venture up this kind of gradient. Some Juliénas has intriguing spicy overtones (cinnamon, cloves) to add to its glossy richness.

*The Principal Juliénas Producers*

### Caves des Producteurs de Juliénas

*69840 Juliénas. 350 ha*

A serious co-op, founded in 1961. The firm sells to *négociants* direct, and on the export markets – and it does a very good job.

## Château de Juliénas /François Condemine

*69840 Juliénas. 33ha*

Owned by François Condemine, this is always remarkable wine, with a scented, delicate nose but immense crunch and bite on the palate – even irony. It keeps beautifully.

## Cave Coopérative de Liergues

*69400 Villefranche. 500ha*

Founded in 1929, this is the oldest cooperative in the region. It is a great Beaujolais Primeur specialist, concentrating on producing this fast-turnover, charming wine. It may be fashionable to knock the stuff, but it is still a lovely shot in the arm every November! The firm produces fairly light wines including a delicious roses-and-strawberries pink Beaujolais.

## Domaine Jean-Marc Monnet

*Les Chers, 69840 Juliénas. 5.5ha*

A very good source of supply, from excellent vineyards.

## Domaine René Monnet (Eventail)

*69840 Juliénas*

This is part of the Château de Juliénas vineyard – the vines face south-southeast and therefore attract the best of the sun. The wine is very fruity, with that Juliénas structure behind it.

## Domaine Pelletier (Eventail)

*69840 Juliénas*

Les Envaux and Les Fouillouses are consistently among the best Juliénas: full of fruit and *élan*. André and Bruno Pelletier are brilliant winemakers.

## Château des Poupets (Duboeuf)

*69840 Juliénas*

Solid wine, *gardé en fûts*, with character and flavour.

## Domaine PBI Sarrau

*69840 Juliénas. 6ha. Fleurie Grand Pré; Morgon Château Gaillard*

These two properties are owned by Pierre, Bernard and Isabelle Sarrau. The wines are bottled at the domaine and sold through the firm of Sarrau – an exercise in keeping it in the family! Of production, 65% is exported, 35% sold in France. It practices the same style and vinification methods as at the other properties in the Sarrau group.

## Domaine de la Seigneurie de Juliénas (Duboeuf)

*69840 Juliénas*

A domaine which is part of the Château de Juliénas (*qv*) and under the same ownership. Not surprisingly, the Condemine-Duboeuf connection produces fine wine, with body and even some tannin (an unusual quality for a Beaujolais), so a few years in bottle suits it admirably.

## ● CHENAS

**1996 production:**

*Chénas* *16,448hl*

Chénas produces less wine than any of the other Beaujolais *crus* and so it is the least known. The name comes from the word *chênes*, as this area used to be covered by a forest of oaks, but now the vine has taken over. The vineyards lie on granite between Chénas and La Chapelle-de-Guinchay, on either side of the valley of the Mauvaise and northwest of Moulin-à-Vent. Les Rougemonts is a Chénas site which is much appreciated. The wines have pronounced character and repay keeping for a few years in ripe vintages. They share some qualities with Moulin-à-Vent but do not have the silkiness of the 'ultimate'. However, Chénas is generous and fruity, not quite as robust as Morgon – they say it has a bouquet of peonies, but I myself have yet to detect that characteristic.

### *The Principal Chénas Producers*

**Château Bonnet**

*71570 La Chapelle-de-Guinchay. 16ha*

Pierre Perrachon here makes wine with good, fruity, definite bouquet – perhaps even better than the impression on the palate.

**Domaine Guy Braillon**

*69840 Chénas. 6.3ha*

Fruity wine, remaining youthful in bottle, with lots of body.

**Domaine des Brureaux**

*69840 Chénas*

Ample, mouthfilling and impressive Chénas from Daniel Robin.

**Domaine Louis Champagnon**

*69840 Chénas. 15ha*

Champagnon produces Chénas from the village of Les Brureaux. This is superb wine, deep-coloured and full of fruit, all rose petals and crushed grapes.

**Château de Chénas (Eventail)**

*69840 Chénas. 265ha*

Lovely crunchy fruit – magnificent taste.

**Domaine Michel Crozet**

*Romanèche-Thorins, 71570 La Chapelle-de-Guinchay*

Chénas from the Coteaux des Brureaux with vibrant fruit, roundness and body.

**GFA Domaine Desvignes**

*71570 La Chapelle-de-Guinchay*

The Château des Jean Loron has belonged to the Desvignes family since 1816. The Desvignes are keen on preserving aromas so that the wine also has fruity charm and slips down easily.

### Manoir des Journets (Duboeuf)

*69840 Chénas*

Old vines at this property yield a wine that is 'a bouquet of flowers lying in a velvet basket' – a fanciful description, but one with which I would agree. Basically, it means delightful floral aromas and a velvety texture.

### Domaine Hubert Lapierre

*Les Gandelins, 71570 La Chapelle-de-Guinchay. 7.5ha*

Wines with good, fruity bouquet and ripe power, which is not the same as excessive alcohol. Lapierre also makes a special new oak-aged *cuvée* of Chénas which needs time.

### Domaine Santé Père et Fils

*71570 La Chapelle-de-Guinchay. 9ha*

Fruity, bouncy, frank Chénas.

### Domaine Georges Trichard

*71570 La Chapelle de Guinchay. 14ha*

Really competent Chénas – and St-Amour, too.

## ● MOULIN-A-VENT

**1996 production:**

| | |
|---|---|
| *Moulin-à-Vent* | *38,571hl* |

This is the grandest of the ten Beaujolais *crus*, the wine, it is said, which most resembles a Pinot Noir from the Côte d'Or when it is aged in bottle. Perhaps this was true with the '47s. Much of the vineyard has a soil of crumbly pink sand over granite, but the special ingredient is manganese – there is an old mine under Romanèche-Thorins. Whether this contributes to the silky power of the wine is a moot point. But fine Moulin-à-Vent has real breeding allied to structure and length. The appellation does not take its name from a village, but from a sail-less windmill perched on the granite hillock of the Poncier in the hamlet of Les Thorins. Don't be surprised if Moulin-à-Vent has little bouquet when a year old – it needs time in bottle to develop, especially if made in the traditional, submerged *châpeau* way.

*The Principal Moulin-à-Vent Producers*

### Domaine Ghislaine Belicard /Les Burdelines (Eventail)

*69430, Lancié, Lyon*

Rich, opulent Moulin-à-Vent.

### Domaine Jean Brugne /Le Vivier (Eventail)

*69820 Fleurie*

Straightforward fruit rather than sheer Moulin style is the rule at this domaine, producing wines which are deliciously rich, ripe and velvety. Son Michel Brugne has a separate – and equally good – bottling.

### Domaine des Caves/Famille Delore

*Chénas, 69840 Juliénas*

The sloping vineyards, facing south-southeast, give a powerful, generous wine, well able to age.

### Domaine Louis Champagnon

*69840 Chénas*

Consistently excellent Moulin-à-Vent which has the balance to age well.

### Domaine Diochon

*Le Moulin-à-Vent, 71570 Romanèche-Thorins. 7ha*

Rich, flamboyant Moulin-à-Vent needing a few years' bottle-ageing.

### Château des Jacques

*71570 Romanèche-Thorins. 27ha Moulin-à-Vent, 9ha Beaujolais-Villages Blanc*

In 1997, Louis Jadot (*qv*) bought this famous property and we are sure to see exciting wines in the future, worthy of the domaine's past reputation. Equipment is modern, but there will be some ageing in barrels. The white Grand Clos de Loyse will also be one to watch.

### Domaine Jacky Janodet

*Les Garniers, 71570 Romanèche-Thorins. 10.5 ha*

Very old vines produce rich, glorious bottles.

### Maurice Labruyère

*Les Thorins, 71570 Romanèche-Thorins. 9ha*

Moulin-à-Vent Clos du Carquelin is a renowned name in Moulin-à-Vent. Maurice Labruyère represents the fourth generation of his family to produce the wine here and he is also president of the Union des Viticulteurs du Moulin-à-Vent.

### Clos du Moulin-à-Vent

*Les Garniers, 71570 Romanèche-Thorins. 10.5ha*

Right in the shadow of the windmill, this is a Moulin which can age and take on the flavours of Pinot Noir.

### Château du Moulin-à-Vent

*71570 Romanèche-Thorins. 31ha*

Owned by the Bloud family, this is one of the three largest estates in the appellation. Wood-ageing. Textbook Moulin-à-Vent, ideal for laying down. Depth and richness.

### Moulin-à-Vent des Hospices

The Bourisset family manages the vineyards of the Hospices de Romanèche and the wine is usually quite hefty.

### Château Portier/Michel Gaidon

*71570 Romanèche-Thorins*

I have found this wine rather alcoholic, at least in some vintages.

### Domaine de la Tour du Bief/ Comte de Sparre (Duboeuf)

*69840 Chénas*

Georges Duboeuf does a domaine-bottling of this wine from the commune of Chénas. The soil is sandy, the style is full and robust. The Domaine de la Rochelle is in the same family.

## ● FLEURIE

**1996 production:**

*Fleurie* *48,040hl*

Fleurie is blessed with the most evocative name of all the ten Bcaujolais *crus*, easy to say, even easier to drink. The wines are charming and full of fruit – and there are enough of them to go round. Between Chiroubles and Moulin-à-Vent the underlying granite gives Fleurie its *ampleur* – a fine bottle is at its most seductive between 18 months and three years old. Flcurie's perfume and crushed fruit should jump out of the glass at you.

*The Principal Fleurie Producers*

### Domaine Paul Bernard

*69820 Fleurie*

Rich, full and sweetly juicy Fleurie.

### Domaine Berrod

*Les-Roches du Vivier, 69820 Fleurie. 22ha*

Top quality Fleurie, Moulin-à-Vent (aged in small oak barrels) and Beaujolais-Villages. Drinking these bottles produces a *frisson* of pure pleasure which seems peculiar to the best wines of the Beaujolais.

### Domaine Michel Chignard

*Le Pont du Jour, 69820 Fleurie. 8ha*

Les Moriers is a good wine, full of crunchy fruit.

### Cave des Producteurs de Fleurie

*69820 Fleurie. 440ha*

A well-run cooperative, with good, true Fleurie. Its two top *cuvées* are the Cuvée Presidente Marguerite (named after a wonderful lady, Mlle Marguerite Chabert, who used to preside over the Cave), a perfumed, 'feminine' Fleurie, and the Cuvée du Cardinal Bienfaiteur, which is more powerful and can take some bottle-age.

### Domaine André Depardon (Eventail)

*71570 Leynes*

La Madone that is concentrated and rich.

### Domaine Monrozier

*Les Moriers, 69820 Fleurie. 9ha*

The domaine borders the *cru* of Moulin-à-Vent, north of the commune of Fleurie. This is a property which makes Fleurie designed to keep for a few years, rather than for instant drinking. A Swiss *négociant* takes a good chunk of the production.

### Domaine de Montgenas (Eventail)
*69820 Fleurie*

Really copybook Fleurie, full of ripe fruit and juicy texture.

### Domaine du Point du Jour
*Le Pont du Jour, 69820 Fleurie. 7.5ha*

Guy Depardon makes clean, enticing appellation-character wine.

### Domaine des Quatre Vents (Duboeuf)
*69820 Fleurie. 18ha*

Owned by Dr Darroze, this exemplary Fleurie is distributed by Duboeuf and a Swiss *négociant*, but bottled at the property.

### Domaine André Vaisse (Eventail)
*69820 Fleurie*

Grille-Midi of structure and keeping potential.

### Georges Duboeuf (Fleurie)
*71570 Romanèche-Thorins*

Fleuries, bottled and sold by Duboeuf, are Clos du Point du Jour, Château Couhard, Château des Déduits, Domaine de Fanfotin, Domaine du Haut-Poncié, Clos du Pavillon and 'La Madone'. This last is an important *climat* of 50ha with 20 owners, beautifully sited overlooking the village of Fleurie on sandy topsoil – the statue of the Virgin Mary is perched on a little chapel in view of the whole vineyard. Here, the nose is meant to be of peaches and peonies, but it is true crushed red fruit.

### Other Fleurie sites
These include La Chapelle des Bois and La Roilette. Mostly the wines are very good, but some are spoilt by excessive alcohol, as if the winemakers have sought to gild the lily. A pity, as it destroys the essential fruit character of Fleurie, indeed, of all Beaujolais. Recently, the situation has improved greatly, with alcohol levels tightly controlled. The Fleuriatons have a fine reputation, worth guarding, and they must 'keep out of temptation'.

## ● CHIROUBLES
**1996 production:**

| | |
|---|---|
| *Chiroubles* | *21,100hl* |

This is the most ethereal of all the *crus*, light and fragrant, as airborne as the height of its vineyards. It is the *cru* you drink first of all the ten – I have nostalgic memories of downing bottles of it in February and March in the Paris bistros where returning skiers met to swap stories of derring-do on the slopes.

Chiroubles is ready before all the other *crus*, with developed bouquet and enormous charm when the rest are still at the dumb stage. There is a marvellous viewpoint at La Terrasse de Chiroubles where, from a height of 750m (2,460ft) you can see the whole of the Beaujolais, the River Saône and, on the horizon, the Jura topped by the snowy Alps and even Mont Blanc on clear days. The Terrasse and surrounding hills are themselves often dusted with snow in January and February. Although this is the highest in altitude of the *crus*, the vineyards are still firmly based on granite. All in all, the Chiroublons are very lucky to have such a delicious commodity which 'sells itself' at such a young age.

### *The Principal Chiroubles Producers*

#### Domaine Cheysson

*Clos les Fargues, 69115 Chiroubles. 26ha*

Archetypal Chiroubles, which means it is delicious and *gouleyant:* utterly gulpable.

#### La Maison des Vignerons à Chiroubles

*69115 Chiroubles*

Delicious, light, textbook Chiroubles – quaff it in huge quantities when it is six months to a year old. Terrific for other *crus*, too.

#### Domaine Desmures Père & Fils (Duboeuf)

*69115 Chiroubles*

Another jewel in the Duboeuf crown, a triumph of teamwork between a family of growers and winemakers and the perfect technique and cleanliness of professional bottling.

#### Château de Javernand (Duboeuf)

*69115 Chiroubles. 30ha*

M Fourneau, president of the *cru*, owns this property. The wine is extraordinarily 'Chiroubles', with a 'floaty' taste but a lovely kernel of fruit. Sandy topsoil and steep slopes.

#### Domaine Méziat Père et Fils

*69115 Chiroubles*

Delightful Chiroubles, and true to the appellation's role as a giver of pleasure.

#### Domaine Alain Passot (Eventail)

*69915 Chiroubles. 8.5ha*

A divine, scented Chiroubles nose and a lovely mouthful of ethereal fruit. La Grosse Pierre is always one of the best wines of the appellation.

#### Château de Raousset (Duboeuf)

*69115 Chiroubles*

The property possesses 20ha of Chiroubles, as well as 12ha of Fleurie and 13ha of Morgon. The vineyards area largely granite-based, and the soil here has a little less clay than that at Morgon. The average age of the vines at this estate is 25 to 30 years. The Duboeuf bottling of this well-known property is impeccable – just as you would expect.

#### Domaine René Savoye (Eventail)

*69115 Chiroubles*

Another Chiroubles which gives real lift-off.

**Eventail de Vignerons Producteurs (Chiroubles)**
*Corcelles-en-Beaujolais, 69220 Belleville*
Other excellent examples of this particular AC, available through the Eventail, are those of Philippe Gobet, La Fontenelle and La Seigneronce.

## ● MORGON

**1996 production:**

| | |
|---|---|
| *Morgon* | *64,064hl* |

Morgon makes the most wine, after Brouilly, among the ten Beaujolais *crus*. The actual village of Bas-Morgon is not nearly as important as Villié-Morgon, but between the two lies the splendid Mont du Py, whence come the most exciting wines. The underlying soil is granite, but a distinctive feature of Morgon is the disintegrating schist called *roche pourrie*.

The wines from the best parts of the appellation have such an individual bouquet that they have their own verb – *morgonner*. But this pronounced nose is a product of the best sites and finest winemaking; it needs time to develop, because very young Morgon (for example, in the spring after the vintage) tends to be rather dumb of bouquet in comparison with the other *crus*. But given time in bottle, the robust, generous, fleshy character of the *cru* really shows its paces. There are rich, fine flavours at two to four years old and, in great years, exotic flavours in wines far older. Descriptions such as wild cherry and sherry are bandied about, but if I ever found a taste of sherry in my mature Morgon, I think I would be worried! The best *climats* are Le Py, La Roche Pilée, Bellevue, Les Pillets and Les Charmes, but frequently the wines are mixed between these favoured sites and others.

### *The Principal Morgon Producers*

**Domaine Georges Brun/Le Clachet (Eventail)**
*69910 Villié-Morgon*
Morgon Le Clachet which is terrific at two years.

**Domaine de la Chanaise**
*69910 Villié-Morgon. 13ha*
Dominique Piron emphasises fruit perhaps more than body.

**Domaine Paul Collonge/Domaine de Ruyère**
*Les Pillets, 69910 Villié-Morgon. 9ha. Morgon: Les Charmes, Morgon; Régnié; Beaujolais-Villages*
The vineyards are well-placed, facing south and southeast. The wines are robust, generous and keep well – M Collonge calls the bouquet 'kirsch and *framboise*', which is typically Morgon. Direct selling in France and exports.

**Domaine de Colonat**
*69910 Villié-Morgon*
Bernard Collonge produces very fruity wine which likes some bottle-age to show its paces.

## Domaine Jean Descombes (Duboeuf)

*69910 Villié-Morgon*

This is, obviously, one of the best Morgons, with three-quarters of the vines more than 30 years old. Bottle-aged Descombes wines taste of chocolate, truffles and warm cocoa! Exciting stuff.

## Domaine Louis Claude Desvignes

*La Voûte-au-Bourg, 69910 Villié-Morgon. 12ha. Vines are scattered over the commune: 4.5ha are in the best climats of Morgon Côte du Py and Morgon Javernières*

A family domaine, worked *de père en fils* for seven generations since 1712. Follows traditional methods and aims for keeping wines typical of Morgon. Bottled after six to 12 months. Serious wine.

## Domaine Louis Genillon (Eventail)

*69910 Villié-Morgon. 33ha*

Good Morgon, which lasts well. Jean-Louis Brun is another member of the *équipe de l'Eventail*, with his Château Gaillard.

## Domaine Lieven (Duboeuf)

*69910 Villié-Morgon*

Associated with Château de Raousset (*qv*); owned by the Princesse de Lieven (Madame Charles Piat). Her delightful, raspberry-scented Morgon-Charmes is bottled at the domaine by Georges Duboeuf. The wine is also sold under the Château de Bellevue label. Another Duboeuf bottling is the solid, full Domaine des Versauds.

## Domaine Jacky Passot

*Fontriante, 69910 Villié-Morgon. 10ha*

Archetypal, confidence-giving Morgon made here.

## Domaine des Pillets

*69910 Villié-Morgon*

Gérard Brisson produces Morgon with a lovely, fruity, deep bouquet, and a highly commendable, full, juicy taste. In ripe vintages, the wines are splendid at three to four years.

## Château de Pizay

*69220 St-Jean-d'Ardières. 50ha. Morgon; Régnié; Beaujolais Rouge, Blanc*

A beautiful property, with vineyards partly in Morgon, partly in Beaujolais-Villages territory. The Côte du Py is lighter than the wine of Pierre Savoye (*qv*), but has great finesse. The reason is that the Pizay vineyards are on the other side of the Côte, near the foot of the slope – Morgon from St-Joseph is like that, too. The Château also makes 2,500 cases of enticing Beaujolais Blanc each year.

## Domaine Savoye/Pierre Savoye

*'Sur la Côte du Py', 69910 Villié-Morgon. 14ha. Morgon: Côte du Py, Morgon; Beaujolais*

This is a splendid domaine, principally on the Côte du Py, where the schistous rock is called *pierre bleue*, which in effect becomes ochre in colour as it decomposes and gives that elusive quality to the wine – *un vin qui 'morgonne'*. Pierre Savoye, the son-in-law of Jean Descombes (*qv*) (who could be called the honorary grandfather of Morgon) makes splendid Côte de Py here. It has a wonderful colour and formidable taste, an experience for all who wish to taste 'true' Morgon. These wines keep. They even *terroitent*, due to the mineral content of the soil.

### Domaine Jacques Trichard

*Les Charmes, 69910 Villié-Morgon. 9ha*

Typical Morgon. Fine fruit; a bit hard in youth but promising well.

## ● REGNIE

**1996 production:**

*Régnié* 31,409hl

Régnié was officially granted status as Beaujolais' tenth *cru* in December 1988. The appellation lies between Morgon and Brouilly, and is based on a relatively light soil, a sandy granite similar to that in Chiroubles. It claims to be the first Beaujolais location where the Romans planted the vine, indeed the name derives from an early Roman resident, a nobleman called Reginus. The best Régniés are supple, delicate, scented wines, redolent of strawberries and redcurrants. Those from the southern end of the commune, near Brouilly, are the lightest and freshest; those coming from closer to Morgon in the north have more substance.

*The Principal Régnié Producers*

### Château du Basty

*69430 Lantignié. 12ha (5ha en métayage). Régnié; Beaujolais-Villages*

The Perrouds make light but stylish Beaujolais Régnié.

### Domaine Jean-Claude Braillon (Eventail)

*69430 Régnié-en-Beaujolais*

Domaine du Laboreur that is light and elegant.

### Domaine des Braves

*Les Braves, 69430 Régnié-Durette. 7ha*

One of the best of this *cru*, deep and vibrant. Paul Cinquin is an advocate and a practitioner of high-heat fermentations.

### Domaine Jean & Yves Durand

*Ponchon, 69430 Régnié-Durette. 16ha*

Light but well-crafted Régnié and Brouilly.

### Domaine de la Gérarde

*69430 Régnié-Durette. 5.7ha*

Stylish wine, a regular medal-winner at competitions.

### Domaine Joel Rochette

*Le Chalet, 69430 Régnié-Durette. 5ha (1.7ha en métayage)*

Flowery, appealing Régnié and Beaujolais-Villages.

### Château de la Tour Bourdon (Duboeuf)

*69430 Régnié*

Old vines, but the wine is delicious for the summer after the vintage.

## ● COTE DE BROUILLY

**1996 production:**

*Côte de Brouilly* *17,608hl*

In the context of the Côte d'Or, anything that is 'Côte de' is not as good as the straight name: in other words, Côte de Beaune is not as good as Beaune itself. Côte de Brouilly is, however, most certainly one up the ladder from plain Brouilly, due to the fact that its vineyards are on the slopes of Mont Brouilly. But, as there is far less Côte de Brouilly than Brouilly, not so many people discover it. It is interesting to note that Côte de Brouilly has a higher minimum alcohol level than the other *crus* – 10.5 per cent instead of ten per cent – but in all cases, if the name of the *climat* (vineyard) is added, it has to be 11 per cent. Mont Brouilly rises to 500m (1,640ft), with vines on all sides (therefore some sites are better exposed than others), on a base predominantly of granite.

The appellation is spread over the communes of Cercié, Odenas, Quincié and St-Lager. I have seen Mont Brouilly described as a sort of giant mole-hill placed like a lighthouse at the head of the Beaujolais – the person who coined that mixed metaphor must have imbibed a good deal of its wine. Côte de Brouilly has tremendous projection of fruit: rich, savoury and grapey.

## *The Principal Côte de Brouilly Producers*

### Domaine L Bassy

*Odenas, 69830 St-Georges-de-Reneins*

Deliciously juicy Côte de Brouilly.

### Domaine de Chavanne

*69460 Brouilly*

Claudius Geoffray makes excellent wine, with massive fruit on the nose and the impression of crunching grapes as you drink.

### Domaine de Conroy

*69460 Brouilly*

Wine of balance and charm and great drinkability made by Jean de St-Charles. The vines are right on the *pierre bleue*, the porphyry of the old volcano that is now Mont Brouilly.

### Domaine Delachanal

*Brouilly, 69460 Odenas. 5.2ha, half of which are in Brouilly, half on the Côte de Brouilly. Three-quarters are old vines on the southern side of the hill of Brouilly. 20,000 bottles per annum, 7,500 magnums from Côte de Brouilly*

Traditional vinification in wooden vats and bottling in March of the following year. Vatting is usually for six to seven days (M Charmette describes it as *vinification type Bordelaise*!), so this is not ephemeral Côte de Brouilly. Delachanal makes a speciality of amusing labels: 'personalised' presents for customers, such as the Cuvée des Pompistes, Cuvée des Douaniers, and even the Cuvée des Bordelais! The wines sell to *négociants*, as well as to private clients; exports are to Switzerland.

### Domaine André Large (Eventail)

*Mont Brouilly, 69460 Odenas. 3.8 ha*

Delicious, gulpable wine, as cheerful in itself as it makes you after drinking it.

### Domaine du Petit Pressoir (Eventail)

*69460 Brouilly*

Marcel and Daniel Mathon make juicy, tempting wine.

### Domaine Sanvers & Cotton

*Odenas, 69830 St-Georges-de-Reneins. 8.5ha*

Lovely wines with fruit and guts.

### Château Thivin

*69460 Odenas. 20ha*

Claude-Vincent Geoffray is responsible for superb Côte de Brouilly. It has a wonderful gutsy, fruity nose, lovely fruit and no hardness – yet body – on the palate. Terrific wine.

### Domaine Lucien & Robert Verger

*69220 St-Lager*

Verger's L'Ecluse has a nose of violets, which is very marked in this vineyard – another wine of superb fruit. The name is curious, with its evocation of running water, because the vineyard is right on the slopes and there has never been a stream here.

## ● BROUILLY

**1996 production:**

| | |
|---|---|
| *Brouilly* | *72,098hl* |

Brouilly produces much more wine than any other of the ten *crus* and so it inevitably has a high profile in cafés, bistros and brasseries. Some say, rather cruelly, that it is just a glorified Beaujolais-Villages, but good Brouilly has more substance and finish, and more solid examples keep longer than a straight villages. The appellation is spread over six communes: Cercié, Charentay, Odenas, Quincié, St-Etienne-la-Varenne and St-Lager. In fact, many producers make Brouilly and Beaujolais-Villages. Brouilly is a totally legitimate *cru*, because the vines grow on granite and schist, called locally *gore* and *morgon*. It is frank and without complication, a heady glass of the grape in liquid form.

### *The Principal Brouilly Producers*

### Château du Bluizard

*St-Etienne-la-Varenne, 69460 St-Etienne-les-Ouillières. 39.2ha*

Jean de St-Charles makes round, rich wines, supple and tempting – he also produces Beaujolais-Villages.

### Château de la Chaize

*69460 Odenas. 94ha (60ha en métayage). All vineyards are within the parish of Brouilly.Brouilly Château de la Chaize*

The Marquise de Roussy de Sales reigns over the largest integrated private wine estate in the Beaujolais and Burgundy, which includes extensive woods. The château, built in 1676 following the plans of Mansart and Le Nôtre, is of great classical symmetry. On form (for it is occasionally inconsistent), the wine is no less impressive, sold at a premium price, but luscious and full, brimming with Brouilly fruit. Enormous attention to detail goes into making this fine Brouilly, which has the body and fruit in good vintages to last three to five years. Length of vatting is five to seven days, and the wine is stocked in wooden *foudres* and then in stainless steel for optimum freshness. Pierre Martray is the accomplished manager.

### Domaine Fabrice Ducroux (Eventail)

*Charentay, 69220 Belleville*

Really rich Brouilly Bonnège, no doubt due to the many old vines.

### Vins Fessy

*69220 St-Jean-d'Ardières*

A bit patchy, but certainly some good wines.

### Domaine Jean Lathuilière

*69220 Cercié-en-Beaujolais. 5.8ha (4.5ha en métayage)*

Seductively fruity, prizewinning Brouilly-Pisse-Vieille, much prettier than its horrid name.

### Domaine de la Roche (Duboeuf)

*69460 St-Etienne-la-Varenne*

This vineyard is on steep slopes 420m (1,380ft) high; yields are small and work difficult on a mixture of gravel and sand. The wine is relatively light, for young drinking. Also makes Beaujolais-Villages.

### Domaine Ruet

*69220 Cercié-en-Beaujolais*

Jean-Paul Ruet makes most respectable wine.

### Domaine Patrick & Martine Vermorel/ Domaine de la Fully

*Chambon, 69460 Blacé. 14ha*

Really wonderful fruit – all that a beautifully handled, frank wine should be. The Beaujolais-Villages also excels.

### Domaine de Vuril

*Charentay, 69220 Belleville.*

Georges Dutraive is responsible for quite commendable Brouilly.

### Eventail de Vignerons Producteurs (Brouilly)

*Corcelles-en-Beaujolais, 69220 Belleville*

André Large, Daniel Mathon and the Domaine J Tatoux make fine, typical examples of the appellation.

## ● BEAUJOLAIS-VILLAGES

**1996 production:**

*Beaujolais-Villages* *363,290hl*

The following villages have the right to the appellation. In the Saône-et-Loire: Chânes, La Chapelle-de-Guinchay, Leynes, Pruzilly, Romanèche-Thorins, St-Amour-Bellevue, St-Symphorien d'Ancelles and St-Vérand; in the Rhône: Arbuissonnas, Les Ardillats, Beaujeu, Blacé, Cercié, Charentay, Chénas, Chiroubles, Denicé, Durette, Emeringes, Fleurie, Juliénas, Jullié, Lancié, Lantignié, Marchampt, Montmelas, Odenas, Le Perréon, Quincié, Régnié, Rivolet, St-Etienne-la-Varenne, St-Etienne-des-Oullières, St-Lager, St-Julien, Salles, Vaux, Vauxrenard and Villié-Morgon. All these villages lie between Villefranche-sur-Saône in the south and the border with the Mâconnais in the north. It is by far the best zone for Beaujolais; although the Villages wines do not have the individuality of the *crus*, they have more projection and body than straight Beaujolais.

It is a ravishingly pretty area, with rolling, vine-covered hills and somewhat sleepy villages, particularly in the afternoon. The roads twist and turn and dip, and no one should attempt high speeds. There is granite, schist and pebbles, with sandstone and limestone breaking out more often in the southern villages. Beaujolais-Villages is delicious in the spring following the vintage and for the next two years.

### *The Principal Beaujolais-Villages Producers*

### Château de Corcelles

*Corcelles-en-Beaujolais, 69220 Belleville. 100ha*

Light, pretty wine, in a well-designed bottle. The vineyards are on flat land and not in the best part of the hills.

### Domaine Dalicieux

*Vernette, 71570 Leynes. 10ha Mâcon-Villages; Beaujolais-Villages*

Excellent wines, both white and red.

### Georges Duboeuf

*Romanèche-Thorins, 71570 La Chapelle-de-Guinchay. 5ha. Pouilly-Fuissé (commune of Chaintré) 4ha, 25,000 bottles; Beaujolais Blanc (commune of Chaintré) 1ha, 8,000 bottles*

The domaine, good as it is, must inevitably be dwarfed by the vast Duboeuf *négociant* empire, one of the great wine trade success stories of this century. Georges Duboeuf, through sheer hard work, a deep knowledge of his region and a sure touch for the genuine, has done more than anyone else for the spread of the true taste of Beaujolais and Mâconnais wines. Stocks now run to four to five million bottles. Some of the wines he chooses are bottled at the individual domaines, the rest go to his ultra-modern plant. What are the secrets? He buys all his requirements very early, and so tends to get top quality. He also practises no *acténisation*, or flash pasteurisation, and relies on kieselguhr membrane filters and cold sterile bottling. As a result, Duboeuf wines are always fresh and fruity.

### Château de la Grand'Grange

*Le Perréon, 69830 St-Georges-de-Reneins*

M Chamussy at Le Perréon produces round, ripe wine.

### Domaine Claude & Michelle Joubert

*Lantignié, 69430 Beaujeu. 13ha. Juliénas; Régnié; Côte de Brouilly; Beaujolais-Villages Lantignié*

A reliable domaine built up lovingly by Claude and Michelle Joubert. The average age of the vines undoubtedly contributes to the full, deep fruit of the wines. The Beaujolais-Villages is made by semi-carbonic maceration, while the Juliénas receives a traditional vatting of eight to ten days. The Jouberts were first known for their rich, full Villages, but the Juliénas is rapidly catching up.

### Château de Lacarelle

*69460 St-Etienne-des-Oullières. 150ha (100ha currently planted in the communes of St-Etienne-des-Oullières and St-Etienne- La-Varenne)*

The family of the Comte Durieu de Lacarelle has been making wine here for more than 200 years. They produce aromatic and supple wines which are delicious to drink when young.

### GAEC René et Christian Miolane

*Le Cellier, 69460 Salles-Arbuissonnas. 11ha. Beaujolais-Villages: Classique, Cuvée des Chasseurs, Cuvée de la Côtebras, Rosé*

The Miolanes have had vineyards on the same slope for three centuries. René Miolane now runs the property with his son, his daughter and his son-in-law. The wines are solid for Villages and are not ephemeral, selling across the board to private clients and wholesalers, with exports accounting for 60–70% of total volume.

### Domaine Monternot

*69460 Blacé-en-Beaujolais. 11ha*

This is excellent Villages from Blacé, with fruit, style and body.

### Domaine de Montmeron (Duboeuf)

*69430 Lantignié*

More old vines give a wine of individuality.

### Domaine Jean-Charles Pivot

*69430 Quincié. 12ha*

Very seductive Villages is made by this astute producer.

### Domaine St-Sorlin

*Le Bourg, 69640 Montmelas-St-Sorlin*

René Jacquet makes wine which finishes with a fruity flourish.

### Louis Tête

*St-Didier-sur-Beaujeu, 69430 Beaujeu. 3.5ha. Moulin-à-Vent; Régnié; Beaujolais-Villages*

This is the small family property of Louis Tête, the highly respected *négociant* in Beaujolais wines, whose selection of wines are always prime examples of their kind. The wines at Tête's estate are produced at low temperatures – not only in order to conserve maximum fruit, but so that the finished bottles have good structure, too.

### Domaine des Trois Coteaux

*69430 Quincié*

Jean-Philippe Perron makes very frank, fruity Villages at Quincié.

### Château Varennes (Piat)

*69430 Quincié*

The wines here are totally tempting, with a glorious bouquet and a really attractive flavour.

### Georges Duboeuf (Beaujolais-Villages)

*Romanèche-Thorins, 71570 La Chapelle-de-Guinchay*

These include the Domaine des Buillats, Domaine du Colombier, Domaine du Potet, which ages well, Château de la Tour, Château des Vierres and the Domaine de la Treille, again a Villages which can be kept a year or two.

### Eventail de Vignerons Producteurs (Beaujolais-Villages)

*Corcelles-en-Beaujolais, 69220 Belleville*

The Eventail produces high-quality Beaujolais-Villages from André Depardon, Paul Fortune, André Jaffre, Jacques Montange, Guy Patissier, Jean-Louis Chagny and Roger & Jean-Luc Tissier.

# A–Z of Burgundy producers

The A–Z is an alphabetical list of some 600 Burgundy producers: growers, *négociants, négociant-éleveurs* or *caves coopératives.*

It can be used as an index for looking up producers from Burgundy's five viticultural areas (the area in which the producer is located is indicated in italics at the beginning of each entry).

When looking up a producer from the Yonne, Côte Chalonnaise, the Mâconnais and Beaujolais, the reader is referred to the relevant area and village/appellation in the Wines and Villages (W&V) section. There, details can be found of holdings (where available) and winemaking methods, together with an assessment of the wines.

For Côte d'Or producers, the address, total area of land cultivated, details of vineyard holdings and a description of the winemaking and wine styles are included here in the A–Z.

(Figures for holdings *en métayage* or *en fermage*, in the entries, are in addition to the main holdings figure.)

## Domaine Bertrand Ambroise *Côte d'Or*

*Prémeaux-Prissey, 21700 Nuits-St-Georges. 7ha (8ha en métayage)*
***Grands Crus:*** *Vougeot: Clos de Vougeot; Aloxe-Corton: Corton*
***1ers Crus:*** *Nuits-St-Georges: Rue de Chaux, Vaucrains*
***AOC Communales:*** *Nuits-St-Georges, Pommard, Vosne-Romanée.*
***AOC Régionales:*** *Côte de Nuits-Villages; Bourgogne Rouge, Blanc and Aligoté*

I have not liked the wines I have tasted, but maybe I have not seen enough. The temptation was not there.

## Domaine Bernard Amiot *Côte d'Or*

*21220 Chambolle-Musigny. 5.5ha (1.5ha en métayage)*
***1ers Crus:*** *Chambolle-Musigny: Les Charmes, Les Châtelots, Chambolle-Musigny.* ***AOC Communale:*** *Chambolle-Musigny*
***AOC Régionales:*** *Bourgogne Rouge and Aligoté*

Good straight Chambolle-Musigny. An easy style.

## Domaine Pierre Amiot et Fils *Côte d'Or*

*Morey-St-Denis, 21220 Gevrey-Chambertin. 7ha (3ha en métayage)*
***Grands Crus:*** *Gevrey-Chambertin: Charmes-Chambertin; Morey-St-Denis: Les Bonnes Mares, Clos des Lambrays, Clos de la Roche, Clos St-Denis*
***1ers Crus:*** *Gevrey-Chambertin Les Combottes; Morey-St-Denis: Aux Charmes, Les Millandes, Les Ruchots*
***AOC Communales:*** *Gevrey-Chambertin; Morey-St-Denis*
***AOC Régionales:*** *Bourgogne Aligoté; Bourgogne Grand Ordinaire*

Often remarkably good wines with a bouquet of undergrowth and truffles. The Clos de la Roche is particularly fine and Les Combottes can be a very good buy. Occasionally the wines are just good and fail to 'flash lights' at you, perhaps because of high yields. The grapes are destemmed and the wines aged in 15% new wood overall.

## Domaine Amiot-Bonfils *Côte d'Or*

*13 rue du Grand-Puits, Chassagne-Montrachet, 21190 Meursault*
*9ha (7.4ha en métayage)*
***Grand Cru:** Puligny-Montrachet: Le Montrachet. **1ers Crus:** Puligny-Montrachet Les Demoiselles; Chassagne-Montrachet: Les Caillerets, Les Champgains, Clos St-Jean (red and white), Les Macherelles, La Maltroie, Les Vergers (red and white). **AOC Communale:** Chassagne-Montrachet. **AOC Régionales:** Bourgogne Blanc and Aligoté*

Traditionally vinified wines aged in 25% new oak. Red wines and Le Montrachet are unfiltered. I hardly ever see these (occasionally in France which accounts for 45% of Guy Amiot's market) but the wines are well made.

## Domaine Robert Ampeau & Fils *Côte d'Or*

*6 rue du Cromin, 21190 Meursault. 9.7ha*
***1ers Crus:** Savigny-lès-Beaune: Fourneaux, Lavières; Beaune Clos du Roi; Volnay Santenots; Blagny La Pièce sous le Bois; Auxey-Duresses Les Ecusseaux; Meursault: Charmes, La Pièce sous le Bois, Perrières; Puligny-Montrachet Les Combettes*
***AOC Communales:** Pommard; Meursault*

Robert Ampeau and his son Michel work immensely hard and produce some astonishing wines. Great care is taken in the vineyard, and natural yeasts, late chaptalisation and stirring of the lees in the white wines are favoured. At first, it was the whites which were renowned, but now the reds are excellent, too. The whites last beautifully, with explosive flavours, heady bouquets and vanillin textures – they are frequently in full flight while other wines of the same appellation are tiring.

The reds ooze gamey fruit – I like the Blagny and Auxey, and even the Savignys, while they are still young and precocious, but obviously the Pommard, Beaune Clos du Roi and Volnay Santenots last longer. An Ampeau bottle is always a treat, but they are not seen as much as they should be as the family does not much like selling its wines!

## Pierre André/Château du Corton-André *Côte d'Or*

*Château de Corton-André, 21420 Aloxe-Corton. 50ha*
***Grands Crus:** Vougeot: Clos de Vougeot; Pernand-Vergelesses: Corton-Charlemagne; Aloxe-Corton: Corton Château de Corton-André, Corton Clos du Roi, Corton-Combes, Corton Hautes Mourottes, Corton-Pougets. **1ers Crus:** Aloxe-Corton Les Chaillots; Savigny-lès-Beaune Clos des Guettes. **AOC Communales:** Gevrey-Chambertin; Pernand-Vergelesses; Ladoix: white, Clos des Chagnots; Savigny-lès-Beaune: Clos des Godeaux, Clos des Guettottes. **AOC Régionale:** Côte de Nuits-Villages*

Pierre André is both a *négociant* and an important proprietor of vineyards. The labels depict the beautiful, flamboyantly tiled roofs of Burgundy. M André founded and owns the *négociant* firm of la Reine Pédauque in Beaune. I am afraid that I find most of the *négociant* wines common and lacking appellation definition. Sales in France are big, but exports are much smaller. The red domaine wines are often jammy and burnt-tasting, right across the range, but the whites are more palatable. The reds go through the *chapeau immergé* method of vinification, a rare occurrence in Burgundy, for ten days and the *grands vins* are matured in oak barrels, a third of which are renewed each year. The Corton-Charlemagne is vinified in new oak barrels. They bottle early as they believe this conserves the maximum amount of fruit, but it is the lack of appellation individuality and rather 'commercial' taste that worry me.

## Domaine Marquis d'Angerville *Côte d'Or*

*Volnay 21190 Meursault. 14ha*
***1ers Crus:*** *Volnay: Caillerets, Champans, Clos des Ducs, Fremiets, Taillepieds; Meursault Santenots.* ***AOC Communale:*** *Pommard*
***AOC Régionales:*** *Bourgogne Rouge and Blanc*

This was one of the first great Burgundy estates to domaine-bottle and its standards have never slipped. The emphasis is on finesse and elegance, and the wines usually have a long, lingering finish. Yields are low and old vines are left as long as possible. There is total destemming and a maximum of one-third new oak is used for the best wines. Exports account for 65% of the estate's turnover, and are to all the traditional markets. The d'Angerville family has contributed enormously to both quality and authenticity in wine production in Burgundy, and for that, burgundy-lovers must always be grateful. The Marquis d'Angerville is the sole owner of the Clos des Ducs, which can age magnificently.

## Domaine de l'Arillière *Mâconnais*

*See* W&V, Mâconnais, Pouilly-Fuissé.

## Domaine Arlaud Père & Fils *Côte d'Or*

*21700 Nuits-St-Georges. 11ha*

Wines perhaps made to attract a commercial following, rather than for someone seeking real individuality. The grandest are, naturally I suppose, better.

## Domaine de l'Arlot *Côte d'Or*

*Prémeaux, 21700 Nuits-St-Georges. 14ha*
***Grand Cru:*** *Vosne-Romanée: Romanée-St-Vivant*
***1ers Crus:*** *Nuits-St-Georges: Clos de l'Arlot (red and white), Clos des Forêts St-Georges, Vosne-Romanee: Les Suchots, Beaune: Les Greves.* ***AOC Régionale,*** *Côte de Nuits-Villages*

A relatively new domaine owned by the company Axa Millésimes, who also own Château Pichon-Longueville-Baron and Château Petit-Village (among others) in Bordeaux. There is clearly a similar dedication to quality here at their Burgundy estate, with very skilled winemaking from Jean-Pierre de Smet, who produces refined red and white Nuits-St-Georges. Very small quantities of organic fertilisers, low yields, natural yeasts, long *cuvaisons* and no filtration lead, in this case, to wines of great fruit intensity and appellation character. A star that can only rise further.

**Domaine Comte Armand** *Côte d'Or*

*21630 Pommard. 10ha*

The domaine's sole vineyard is Pommard Clos des Epeneaux, which includes both Grands and Petits Epenots. French-Canadian Pascal Marchand makes wine of great extract from low-yielding vines that are maintained according to bio-dynamic principles. There is complete destemming, long maceration and 35% new wood is used. The result is beautiful, intense wines that need time to develop.

**Domaine Arnoux Père & Fils** *Côte d'Or*

*21200 Chorey-lès-Beaune. 22ha (including 10ha in Chorey)*

Somewhat rustic reds, but the whites show better.

**Domaine Robert Arnoux** *Côte d'Or*

*Route Nationale, 21670 Vosne-Romanée. 12ha*

***Grands Crus:*** *Vougeot: Clos de Vougeot; Flagey-Echézeaux: Echézeaux; Vosne-Romanée: Romanée-St-Vivant*

***1ers Crus:*** *Vosne-Romanée: Les Chaumes, Les Suchots; Nuits-St-Georges: Corvées Pagets, Les Procès.* ***AOC Communales:*** *Vosne-Romanée Hautes Maizières, Vosne-Romanée; Nuits-St-Georges*

Rewarding wines on the whole. Occasionally they could have had more natural concentration. The domaine is now run by the son-in-law, Pascal Lachaux, and the future looks promising.

**Domaine d'Auvernay** *Côte d'Or*

*21190 St-Romain. 3.6ha*

***Grands Crus:*** *Gevrey-Chambertin: Mazis-Chambertin; Chambolle-Musigny: Bonnes Mares; Puligny-Montrachet: Chevalier-Montrachet, Criots-Bâtard-Montrachet.* ***1ers Crus:*** *Puligny-Montrachet: Les Folatières.* ***AOC Communales:*** *Auxey-Duresses; Meursault*

This estate is Madame Bize-Leroy's own home and domaine. *See* Domaine Leroy.

**Auvigue-Burrier-Revel et Cie** *Mâconnais*

*See* W&V, Mâconnais, Pouilly-Fuissé.

**Domaine Bernard Bachelet et Fils** *Côte d'Or*

*Dezize-lès-Maranges, 71150 Chagny. 37ha*

Improvements have seemed to coincide with the change to premises in Chassagne for vinification.

**Domaine Denis Bachelet** *Côte d'Or*

*Rue de Beaune, 21220 Gevrey-Chambertin. 3ha*

Denis Bachelet likes old vines and low yields, 100% new oak casks for the Charmes, 50% for the Premier Cru. The wines here are excellent and the Charmes is a treasure – try some, if you can find it.

**Domaine Jean-Claude Bachelet** *Côte d'Or*

*21190 St-Aubin. 8 ha*

Pretty, well-made St-Aubin whites and reds.

**Domaine Bachelet-Ramonet Père et Fils** *Côte d'Or*
*11, rue de Parterre, Chassagne-Montrachet, 21190 Meursault*
*12.75ha*
***Grands Crus:*** *Puligny-Montrachet: Bâtard-Montrachet, Bienvenues-Bâtard-Montrachet.* ***1ers Crus:*** *Chassagne-Montrachet (red and white).* ***AOC Communales:*** *Puligny-Montrachet (white); Chassagne-Montrachet (red and white)*
***AOC Régionales:*** *Bourgogne Aligoté and Bourgogne Passe-Tout-Grains*
A domaine with very well-situated vineyards, but unfortunately producing disappointing wines. Perhaps the new generation will make a difference.

**Domaine Ballot-Millot et Fils** *Côte d'Or*
*9 rue de la Goutte d'Or, 21190 Meursault. 14ha*
Good-quality Meursaults in particular, using only a modest proportion of new wood (about 25%). The domaine seems to be equally at home with red and white wines, in a range embracing myriad appellations.

**Domaine Daniel Barraud** *Mâconnais*
*See* W&V, Mâconnais, Pouilly-Fuissé.

**Domaine Bart** *Côte d'Or*
*24 rue de Mazy, 21160 Marsannay-la-Côte. 13.5ha (3.85ha en métayage)*
***Grands Crus:*** *Morey-St-Denis: Bonnes Mares; Gevrey-Chambertin: Chambertin Clos de Bèze*
***1er Cru:*** *Fixin-Hervelets.* ***AOC Communales:*** *Chambolle-Musigny; Santenay (red and white).* ***AOC Régionale:*** *Côte de Nuits-Villages*
In the past, uninspiring wines, but Martin Bart has taken a grip on things and this is now a good address.

**Domaine Barthod-Noëllat** *Côte d'Or*
*Chambolle-Musigny, 21220 Gevrey-Chambertin. 6.6ha*
***1ers Crus:*** *Chambolle-Musigny: Les Charmes, Chambolle-Musigny.* ***AOC Communale:*** *Chambolle-Musigny*
***AOC Régionale:*** *Bourgogne Rouge*
Ghislaine Barthod has totally revived this estate, with a preference for low yields, selection and the real exploitation of *terroir* in each *cru* that is produced. Highlights here are the ripe, supple Bourgogne Rouge and lovely, scented Chambolle-Musigny, unfiltered and modestly oaked. There were exceptional wines produced here in 1990 and (happily) the progress is continuing right into the 90s.

**Thomas Bassot** *Côte d'Or*
*5 quai Dumorey, 21700 Nuits-St-Georges*
*Négociant. See* Jean-Claude Boisset.

**Domaine L Bassy** *Beaujolais*
*See* W&V, Beaujolais, Côte de Brouilly.

**Château de Beauregard** *Mâconnais*
*See* W&V, Mâconnais, Pouilly-Fuissé.

**Domaine Adrien Belland** *Côte d'Or*
*Place du Jet-d'Eau, 21590 Santenay. 12ha*
***Grands Crus:*** *Gevrey-Chambertin: Chambertin; Aloxe-Corton: Corton Clos de la Vigne au Saint, Corton-Grèves, Corton-Perrières.* ***1ers Crus:*** *Chassagne-Montrachet Morgeot Clos Charreau; Santenay Clos des Gravières, Santenay Comme*
***AOC Communales:*** *Aloxe-Corton; Puligny-Montrachet; Santenay*
Belland's is an archetypal, fragmented Burgundian domaine from southern Santenay right up to Chambertin. Adrien Belland is now helped by one of his sons, Jean-Claude, and they follow a policy of de-stalking, long vatting, fermentation with *chapeau flottant* and *pigeage* twice a day, ageing in oak casks and bottling after 20 to 22 months. The Santenay wines are better than the grander appellations.

**Domaine Roger Belland** *Côte d'Or*
*21590 Santenay. 23ha*
A domaine that is definitely on an upward curve.

**Domaine Belleville** *Côte Chalonnaise*
*See* W&V, Côte Chalonnaise, Rully.

**Bénas Frères** *Mâconnais*
*See* W&V, Mâconnais, Mâcon.

**Domaine Paul Bernard** *Beaujolais*
*See* W&V, Beaujolais, Fleurie.

**Domaine Berrod** *Beaujolais*
*See* W&V, Beaujolais, Fleurie.

**Domaine Bertagna** *Côte d'Or*
*21640 Vougeot. 11ha (17ha en métayage)*
***Grands Crus:*** *Gevrey-Chambertin: Chambertin; Morey-St-Denis: Clos St-Denis; Vougeot: Clos de Vougeot; Aloxe-Corton: Corton, Corton-Charlemagne.* ***1ers Crus:*** *Chambolle-Musigny; Vougeot: Clos de la Perrière, Les Cras, Petit Vougeot, Vougeot (white); Vosne-Romanée Les Beaux Monts; Nuits-St-Georges Murgers*
***AOC Communales:*** *Chambolle-Musigny; Vougeot Clos Bertagna*
***AOC Régionales:*** *Hautes-Côtes de Nuits (red); Bourgogne Rouge, Vtémant de Bourgogne*
A fine clutch of Vougeot vineyards that have been rather up and down in quality in the past two decades. The Reh family (of the Von Kesselstatt estate in Trier, Germany) acquired the domaine in 1982 and the wines look very promising once again from 1988. The Premiers Crus Vougeot Clos de la Perrière and Vosne-Romanée Les Beaux Monts are wines of finesse and breed, regularly among their best bottles. Their white Vougeot Premier Cru is enticing.

**Domaine Vincent et Denis Berthaut** *Côte d'Or*
*9 rue Noisot, 21220 Fixin. 8ha (5ha en métayage)*
***1er Cru:** Fixin. **AOC Communales:** Fixin; Gevrey-Chambertin*
***AOC Régionale,** Bourgogne Rouge*
Vinification with long *cuvaison*; the wines are on the rustic side. Some find that they are becoming more refined.

**Domaine Bertheau et Fils** *Côte d'Or*
*Chambolle-Musigny, 21220 Gevrey-Chambertin. 7ha*
I have limited experience, but this is a serious domaine making good wine at all levels.

**Domaine Besancenot** *Côte d'Or*
*78 faubourg St-Nicolas, 21200 Beaune. 6ha (5ha en métayage)*
***Grand Cru:** Pernand-Vergelesses: Corton-Charlemagne*
***1ers Crus:** Beaune: Bressandes, Cent-Vignes, Clos du Roi, Grèves, à l'Ecu, Theurons, Toussaints*
***AOC Communales:** Pernand-Vergelesses (red and white); Aloxe-Corton; Beaune. **AOC Régionales:** Bourgogne Rouge and Aligoté*
An important domaine with some classic Beaune, and wines showing very good *typicité* between *climats*. Occasional bottles are not quite clean, which should not happen.

**Maison Albert Bichot** *Côte d'Or*
*6 bis boulevard Jacques-Copeau, 21200 Beaune. 41.36ha*
*Domaine du Clos Frantin, Vosne-Romanée, 15ha*
***Grands Crus:** Gevrey-Chambertin: Chambertin; Vougeot: Clos de Vougeot; Flagey-Echézeaux: Echézeaux, Grands Echézeaux; Vosne-Romanée: Richebourg; Pernand-Vergelesses: Corton-Charlemagne; Aloxe-Corton: Corton. **1ers Crus:** Vosne-Romanée Les Malconsorts; Aloxe-Corton Les Fourniers. **AOC Communales:** Vosne-Romanée; Gevrey-Chambertin; Nuits-St-Georges*
A huge firm concentrating on exports, with numerous *sous-noms*, including Paul Bouchard and Jean Bouchard (not to be confused with other Beaune Bouchards), Léon Rigault, Rémy Gauthier and Lupé-Cholet (*qv*). Many are very dreary burgundies indeed, although some Lupé-Cholet (*qv*) wines are considerably better and some Grands Crus survive their bottling with honour. I am happiest with the firm's Chablis from Domaine Long-Depaquit (*qv* and *see also* W&V, Chablis), especially the splendid La Moutonne.

**Domaine Billard-Gonnet** *Côte d'Or*
*21630 Pommard. 12ha*
Beaune and Pommard in a very firm style. Keepers, but not really up to the class of their appellations, especially at Pommard Rugiens level – but then I expect much more from such *terroir*.

**Domaine Pierre Bitouzet** *Côte d'Or*
*21420 Savigny-lès-Beaune. 45ha*
***Grand Cru:** Pernand-Vergelesses: Corton-Charlemagne*
***1ers Crus:** Aloxe-Corton Valozières; Savigny-lès-Beaune: Lavières, Les Talmettes; Chablis: Beauroy; Pommard: Platière; Volnay: Santenots*

***AOC Communales,*** *Chablis; Savigny-lès-Beaune (red and white); Mercurey; Ladoix-lès-Beaune (red and white); Meursault; Pommard*
Huge, newly formed estate. I have tasted exceptional Corton-Charlemagne; also good white Savigny-lès-Beaune. Fairly oaky wines, although M Bitouzet says he only uses one-third new wood.

### Domaine Bitouzet-Prieur *Côte d'Or*
*Volnay, 21190 Meursault. 9ha*
Vincent Bitouzet makes quality Meursaults, as well as Volnay-Taille Pieds which repay cellaring.

### Domaine Simon Bize & Fils *Côte d'Or*
*Rue Chanoine Donin, 21420 Savigny-lès-Beaune. 22ha*
***1ers Crus:*** *Savigny-lès-Beaune: Fournaux, Aux Guettes, Les Marconnets, Talmettes, Les Vergelesses*
***AOC Communales:*** *Savigny Grands Liards, Savigny-lès-Beaune (red and white).* ***AOC Régionales:*** *Bourgogne Rouge and Blanc*
An extremely serious family estate, passed from father to son for 150 years. Patrick Bize makes the wine, with great respect for the fruit and no excess weight or camouflage. He seems to have the right formula for this style of wine – long vatting and about 18 months in oak before bottling – he has upped the new oak, but it is absorbed by the fruit. Snap up the Savigny Les Vergelesses if you can. Entrancing white, too, Bourgogne Champlains from Chardonnay and Pinot Beurot.

### Domaine Blain-Gagnard *Côte d'Or*
*21190 Chassagne-Montrachet. 7.7ha*
***Grands Crus:*** *Puligny-Montrachet: Bâtard-Montrachet; Chassagne-Montrachet: Criots-Bâtard-Montrachet*
***1ers Crus:*** *Chassagne-Montrachet: La Boudriotte, Cailleret, Clos St-Jean, Morgeot.* ***AOC Communales:*** *Pommard; Volnay; Chassagne-Montrachet (red and white)*
Small amounts of wine from many appellations. Linked with Delagrange-Bachelet (*qv*), Jean-Marc Blain makes refined, perfumed, concentrated white wines with maximum lees contact, and also a stylish red Clos St-Jean with no new oak.

### Château du Bluizard *Beaujolais*
*See* W&V, Beaujolais, Brouilly.

### Domaine Jean Boillot et Fils *Côte d'Or*
*21190 Volnay. 13.5ha*
Henri Boillot is building himself a reputation that aspires to be as impressive as his vineyard holdings.

### Domaine Jean-Marc Boillot *Côte d'Or*
*21630 Pommard. 10ha*
***1ers Crus:*** *Beaune Montrevenots; Pommard: Jarolières, Rugiens, Saucilles; Volnay: Carelle sous la Chapelle, Pitures, Ronceret; Puligny-Montrachet: Champ Canet, Combettes, Referts, Truffières*

***AOC Communales:*** *Pommard; Volnay; Meursault; Puligny-Montrachet; Chassagne-Montrachet.*
***AOC Régionales:*** *Bourgogne Rouge and Aligoté*
Well-made wines. I have been impressed by Pommard Jarolières and Rugiens. True-to-type perfumed Volnays in a lighter style, which show that *macération à froid*, fermentation temperatures up to 32°C (90°F) and three *pigeage*s a day do not have to produce heavy wines; and broad, supple Côte de Beaune whites which could do with less oak at the *village* level, but which respect the appellation character nonetheless. Some of Domaine Sauzet has enlarged this estate from 1991.

## Domaine Lucien Boillot & Fils *Côte d'Or*

*1 rue Docteur Magnon-Puho, 21220 Gevrey-Chambertin.*
*6.5ha (7ha en fermage and en métayage)*
***1ers Crus:*** *Gevrey-Chambertin: Champonnets, Cherbaudes, Les Corbeaux, les Evocelles; Nuits-St-Georges Prûliers; Beaune Epenottes; Pommard: Les Croix Noires, Fremiers; Volnay: Les Angles, Caillerets, Brouillards*
***AOC Communales:*** *Fixin; Gevrey-Chambertin; Volnay; Pommard*
***AOC Régionales:*** *Côte de Nuits-Villages; Bourogne Rouge and Blanc*
Pierre and Louis Boillot are making strides here and quality is clearly improving. Pure, fruity, Pinot-style Beaune Epenottes and Volnay Les Angles, and solid, workmanlike Gevrey-Chambertins, with a distinctive, concentrated Premier Cru Les Corbeaux.

## Domaine Pierre Boillot *Côte d'Or*

*21190 Meursault. 2.5ha*
Low yield Meursaults of considerable concentration and judicious oaking. The whites can hit the bull's-eye. The domaine has a mass of private customers.

## Jean-Claude Boisset *Côte d'Or*

*2 rue des Frères-Montgolfier, 21700 Nuits-St-Georges*
A *négociant* with only 35 years behind it and sales of over 13 million bottles a year. Names now under the Jean-Claude Boisset aegis include: Thomas Bassot, Bouchard Aîné & Fils, Lionel J Bruck, Delaunay, Jaffelin (*qv*), Morin, Pierre Ponnelle, Marcilly, Chauvenet, Ropiteau (*qv*), Roland Thévenin, Charles Viénot (*qv*) and, more recently, Mommessin-Thorin (*qv*), Cellier des Samsons and J Moreau & Fils in Chablis. (Domaine Claudine Deschamps wines are sold entirely by Boisset, mostly to French wholesalers.) Many of these wines give me absolutely no lift at all and appellation character seems at a premium. Boisset is a big buyers of grapes, but its wine purchases for blending are much more important.

## Domaine Boisson-Vadot *Côte d'Or*

*21190 Meursault. 7ha*
Meursaults from old vines, with extended lees contact and ageing in up to a third new wood. If the *village* wines are sometimes too lean, the Genevrières can be particularly refined with real texture on the palate.

## Domaine André Bonhomme *Mâconnais*

*See* W&V, Mâconnais, Mâcon.

## Domaine Bonneau du Martray *Côte d'Or*

*Pernand-Vergelesses, 21420 Savigny-lès-Beaune. 11ha*
***Grands Crus:** Pernand-Vergelesses: Corton-Charlemagne; Aloxe-Corton: Corton*

Well-run domaine, with vineyards mid-slope on the Montagne de Corton. Owned by the le Bault de la Morinière family; the estate is now run by son Jean-Charles. For the great Corton-Charlemagne, stainless-steel vats are used for the first tumultuous stage of the fermentation, thus keeping the temperature below 20°C (68°F); the wines finish fermenting in one-third new-oak barrels and are bottled relatively early to retain fruit and freshness. The Corton-Charlemagne is rich and nutty; all the expected years are superb, but even modest vintages like '84 and '87 are intense, wonderful drinking after more than a decade. The Corton is vinified in open oak vats and the *élevage* is in a mixture of new, second- and third-year oak *pièces*. These are elegant wines, but more concentration and definition could perhaps be attained by lower yields and longer vatting. Up to 92% is exported to 19 countries, but in France the only sales are to restaurants awarded Michelin stars.

## Château Bonnet *Beaujolais*

*See* W&V, Beaujolais, Chénas.

## Domaine Bonnot-Lamblot *Côte d'Or*

*21420 Savigny-lès-Beaune. 8ha*

Roger Bonnot makes solid Savigny-lès-Beaune; forceful rather than refined.

## Bouchard Aîné & Fils *Côte d'Or*

The firm now belongs to Jean-Claude Boisset (*qv*).

## Bouchard Père & Fils/Domaines du Château de Beaune *Côte d'Or*

*Au Château, 21200 Beaune. 93ha*
***Grands Crus:** Gevrey-Chambertin: Chambertin; Vougeot: Clos de Vougeot; Chambolle-Musigny: Bonnes Mares; Vosne-Romanée: La Romanée; Pernand-Vergelesses: Corton-Charlemagne; Aloxe-Corton: Le Corton; Puligny-Montrachet: Chevalier-Montrachet, Le Montrachet.*
***1ers Crus:** Nuits-St-Georges: Clos St-Marc, Clos des Argillières; Aloxe-Corton; Savigny-lès-Beaune Les Lavières; Beaune: Cent Vignes, Clos de la Mousse, Clos St-Landry, du Château (red and white), Grèves Vigne de l'Enfant Jesus, Marconnets, Teurons; Pommard: Les Rugiens, Les Combes; Volnay: Caillerets Ancienne Cuvée Carnot, Fremiets, Clos de la Rougeotte, Taillepieds; Meursault-Genevrières*
***AOC Communales:** Savigny-lès-Beaune; Pommard*
***AOC Régionale:** Bourgogne Aligoté Bouzeron*

In spring 1995, the dynamic Joseph Henriot bought Bouchard Père, thereby ending family ownership, although Christophe Bouchard remains as technical director. This is, of course, an amazing domaine and a very important *négociant* house and Joseph Henriot is committed to restoring both to their former glory. He began by declassifying a large amount of wine. There is a state-of-the-art vinification plant which may be more suitable for vinifying large amounts of bought-in grapes rather than obtaining the maximum quality and individuality from Bouchard's won-derfully exciting domaine vineyards. However, Joseph Henriot's reputation for fostering quality, so evident during his time as head of Veuve Clicquot, leads one to believe that we should expect exciting developments at Bouchard, and the 1995 vintage should give him and his team the chance they seek. Much will depend on how they seize it. In 1996 they took over management of the 30ha domaine Ropiteau-Mignon.

## Domaine Jean-Marc Bouley *Côte d'Or*

*21190 Volnay. 12ha*

***1ers Crus:** Beaune: Reversées; Pommard: Fremiers, Pezerolles, Rugiens; Volnay: Caillerets, Carelles, Clos des Chênes, Ronceret, Volnay.* ***AOC Communales:** Pommard; Volnay*

***AOC Régionales:** Bourgogne Hautes-Côtes de Beaune, Bourgogne Rouge, Blanc and Aligoté; Bourgogne Passe-Tout-Grains*

The estate's wines were sold in bulk until Jean-Marc Bouley started domaine-bottling in 1985. He now makes wines from 17 appellations, but principally from Volnay and Pommard. Vinification aims at maximum extract and colour to make *vins de garde*, and the *village* and Premier Cru wines are aged in 30–50% new oak. In cask, perfumed Volnays, Pommards appropriately with more muscle; all the wines have plenty of *matière*, but perhaps not enough fruit. Recent tastings of the '88s and '89s have been disappointing, showing a rustic, dry quality. I have had rustic, dry bottles, but the strike rate has improved.

## Pierre Bourée & Fils/Vallet Frères *Côte d'Or*

*21220 Gevrey-Chambertin. 4.5ha*

***Grand Cru:** Gevrey-Chambertin: Charmes-Chambertin*

***1er Crus:** Beaune: Epenottes; Gevrey-Chambertin: Les Champaux*

***AOC Communale:** Gevrey-Chambertin Clos de la Justice monopole*

A small *négociant* now run by Pierre Bourée's nephew, Bernard Vallet. A large number of appellations are made from both Côtes, the *négociant* wines (the vast majority) being vinified from purchased grapes. People 'discover' the wines every few years, but they are not really to my taste – too alcoholic and top-heavy. The firm is sole owner of Gevrey-Chambertin Clos de la Justice, which is usually of a higher quality than its *village* designation implies.

## Domaine Denis Boussey *Côte d'Or*

*Monthelie, 21190 Meursault. 10.9ha*

Well-made red and white wines.

## Domaine Gilles Bouton *Côte d'Or*

*21190 St-Aubin. 12ha*

This is a good source of supply.

**Domaine Michel Bouzereau et Fils** *Côte d'Or*
*3 rue Planche-Meunière, 21190 Meursault. 11ha en métayage*
***1ers Crus:*** *Beaune: Les Epenottes, Les Vignes Franches; Meursault-Genevrières; Puligny-Montrachet Les Champs-Gains*
***AOC Communales:*** *Pommard Les Cras; Volnay Les Auxy; Meursault Les Grands Charrons, Meursault Les Tessons*
***AOC Régionales:*** *Bourgogne Rouge, Blanc and Aligoté*
Bouzereau et Fils produced some good quality wines in the 1990s. There are some fine Meursault-Genevrières and flavoursome Puligny-Montrachet Les Champs-Gains, but Meursault Les Tessons is the best-value wine, with a bouquet of limes and plenty of sheen and finesse.

**Domaine Philippe Bouzereau** *Côte d'Or*
*15 place de l'Europe, 21190 Meursault. 12ha*
I am afraid that I have been underwhelmed by the wines being produced by this domaine, especially as the Meursault tastes no more lofty than Bourgogne Blanc. Perhaps the future will bring some improvement.

**Domaine Hubert Bouzereau-Gruère** *Côte d'Or*
*21190 Meursault. 12ha*
Middle-of-the-road white wines, but the red Santenay has impressed in the past, as has the Corton-Bressandes.

**Domaine Yves Boyer-Martenot** *Côte d'Or*
*7 place de l'Europe, 21190 Meursault. 8.5ha*
***1ers Crus:*** *Meursault: Charmes, Genevrières, Perrières.*
***AOC Communales:*** *Pommard; Auxey-Duresses; Meursault: Les Narvaux, l'Ormeau, Le Pré de Manche*
***AOC Régionales:*** *Bourgogne Rouge, Blanc and Aligoté*
Rather hit and miss. A *village* Meursault Les Narvaux was elegant and attractive, but the Premier Cru Genevrières suggested was flat and dirty. Things may be improving, however.

**Domaine Guy Braillon** *Beaujolais*
*See* W&V, Beaujolais, Chénas.

**Domaine des Braves** *Beaujolais*
*See* W&V, Beaujolais, Régnié.

**Domaine Jean-Claude Brelière** *Côte Chalonnaise*
*See* W&V, Côte Chalonnaise, Rully.

**Domaine Bressand** *Mâconnais*
*See* W&V, Mâconnais, Pouilly-Fuissé.

**Domaine Michel Briday** *Côte Chalonnaise*
*See* W&V, Côte Chalonnaise, Rully.

**Lionel J Bruck** *Côte d'Or*
*See* Jean-Claude Boisset (*qv*).

**Domaine Jean Brugne/Le Vivier** *Beaujolais*
*See* W&V, Beaujolais, Moulin-à-Vent.

**Domaine Georges Brun/Le Clachet** *Beaujolais*
*See* W&V, Beaujolais, Morgon.

**Domaine des Brureaux** *Beaujolais*
*See* W&V, Beaujolais, Chénas.

**Domaine Alain Burguet** *Côte d'Or*
*18 rue de l'Eglise, 21220 Gevrey-Chambertin. 6ha*
***1er Cru:*** *Gevrey-Chambertin Les Champeaux*
***AOC Communales:*** *Gevrey-Chambertin, Gevrey-Chambertin Vieilles Vignes.* ***AOC Régionale:*** *Bourgogne Rouge*
Very good rather than great; evidence of great care in the vineyard and old vines. Alain Burguet vinifies with *pigeage* and long *cuvaisons* (two to three weeks), aiming for wines which can be drunk, as he puts it, 'at ten, 20 or 40 years of age, depending on the vintage'.

**Cave Coopérative de Buxy** *Côte Chalonnaise*
*See* W&V, Côte Chalonnaise, Montagny.

**Domaine Patrice Cacheux-Sirugue et Fils**
*58 route Nationale, 21700 Vosne-Romanée. 4.5ha*
***Grand Cru:*** *Flagey-Echézeaux: Echézeaux.* ***1er Cru:*** *Vosne-Romanée Les Suchots.* ***AOC Communales:*** *Vosne-Romanée, Nuits-St-Georges*
Formerly Jacques Cacheux, but now son Patrice is in charge.

**Domaine Roger Caillot-Morey** *Côte d'Or*
*21190 Meursault. 8ha*
Some earthy, workaday '89 Meursault Les Tessons and a *village*-quality Puligny-Montrachet Les Folatières hardly inspire confidence. Others have been more impressed.

**Domaine Camus Père & Fils** *Côte d'Or*
*21 rue Maréchal de Lattre de Tassigny, 21220 Gevrey-Chambertin. 17.5ha*
***Grands Crus:*** *Gevrey-Chambertin: Chambertin, Charmes-Chambertin, Latricières-Chambertin, Mazis-Chambertin, Mazoyères-Chambertin.*
***AOC Communale:*** *Gevrey-Chambertin.* ***AOC Régionales:*** *Bourgogne Rouge, Rosé and Aligoté; Bourgogne Grand Ordinaire*
Occasionally passable wines. I have never had a wine from this domaine that reflected the magnificence of the vineyard holdings. Long *élevage* may be one course, but this domaine needs a dramatic overhaul to capture the magnificence of the vineyard plots.

**Domaine Lucien Camus-Bruchon** *Côte d'Or*
*21420 Savigny-lès-Beaune. 7ha*
***1ers Crus:*** *Savigny-lès-Beaune: Gravains, Lavières, Narbantons; Beaune Clos du Roi; Pommard: Les Arvelets*
***AOC Communales:*** *Savigny-lès-Beaune (red and white)*
***AOC Régionales:*** *Bourgogne Rouge, Blanc and Aligoté*

Camus-Bruchon produces Bourgogne Blanc with a good depth of fruit and a firm, vivid Savigny-lès-Beaune Vieilles Vignes with plenty of character.

### Domaine François Capitain et Fils *Côte d'Or*

*21550 Ladoix-Serrigny. 16ha*

Can be good value in the more modest appellations.

### Domaine Capron-Charcousset *Côte d'Or*

*21420 Savigny-lès-Beaune. 4ha (3ha en fermage)*

***1ers Crus:*** *Savigny-lès-Beaune: Les Lavières, Les Peuillets*

***AOC Communales:*** *Pernand-Vergelesses (white); Savigny-lès-Beaune (white and red).* ***AOC Régionale:*** *Bourgogne Aligoté*

White and red Savigny which have increased in elegance and assurance. Top wines age well, but straight Savigny is better young. The owners seem to have captured the essence of Savigny.

### Domaine Louis Carillon & Fils *Côte d'Or*

*21190 Puligny-Montrachet. 12ha*

***Grand Cru:*** *Puligny-Montrachet: Bienvenues-Bâtard-Montrachet*

***1ers Crus:*** *Puligny-Montrachet: Les Champs Canet, Les Champs Gains, Les Combettes, Les Perrières, Les Referts.*

***AOC Communales:*** *Puligny-Montrachet; Chassagne-Montrachet (red and white); Mercurey.* ***AOC Régionales:*** *Côte de Beaune-Villages; Bourgogne Rouge and Aligoté*

Members of the Carillon family have been making wine since at least 1632 and know their *métier* very well. They sell direct, export and deal with *négociants.* White wines are matured in oak barrels for a year, then spend three to six months in stainless-steel or enamel-lined containers before bottling. The red grapes are entirely or partially destalked, according to the year, vatting takes at least two weeks, and the *élevage* is the same as for the whites. The Pulignys have elegance and style, while the Bienvenues can be magnificent.

### Domaine Denis Carré *Côte d'Or*

*Meloisey, 21190 Meursault. 11ha*

***1ers Crus:*** *Pommard; Auxey-Duresses.*

***AOC Communales:*** *Meursault Les Tillets; St-Romain (red)*

***AOC Régionales:*** *Hautes-Côtes de Beaune (red and white)*

Rather lean and sturdy style of reds; Carré's best wine is his broad, earthy *village* Meursault Les Tillets.

### Domaine Guy Castagnier *Côte d'Or*

*20 rue des Jardins, Morey-St-Denis, 21220 Gevrey-Chambertin. 5ha*

Mainly good wines in the scrumptious, fruity style, even in less than propitious years – therefore drink relatively young.

### Domaine Sylvain Cathiard *Côte d'Or*

*Vosne-Romanée, 21700 Nuits-St-Georges*

Sylvain Cathiard is a domaine that is emerging as quality-driven and worthwhile.

**Domaine des Caves/Famille Delore** *Beaujolais*
*See* W&V, Beaujolais, Moulin-à-Vent.

**La Chablisienne** *Chablis*
*See* W&V, Chablis.

**Château de la Chaize** *Beaujolais*
*See* W&V, Beaujolais, Brouilly.

**Domaine Jean-Noël Chaland** *Mâconnais*
*See* W&V, Mâconnais, Mâcon.

**Domaine Yves Chaley** *Côte d'Or*
*Curtil-Vergy, 21220 Gevrey-Chambertin. 13ha*
***AOC Régionales:*** *Bourgogne Hautes-Côtes de Nuits Rouge, Blanc and Pinot Beurot; Bourgogne Aligoté*
A well-situated domaine, vital in the Hautes-Côtes. Traditional methods. Reds kept for 18 months in a combination of oak *foudres* and up to one-third new barrels. The white wines are in stainless-steel tanks, and are slowly fermented at 18°C (64°F) in order to obtain both maximum perfume and freshness. Good-value wines.

**Château de Chambolle-Musigny /Jacques-Frédéric Mugnier** *Côte d'Or*
*21220 Chambolle-Musigny. 4ha*
***Grands Crus:*** *Morey-St-Denis: Bonnes Mares; Chambolle-Musigny: Musigny.* ***1ers Crus:*** *Chambolle-Musigny: Les Amoureuses, Les Fuées.* ***AOC Communale:*** *Chambolle-Musigny*
Frédéric Mugnier makes the wines here in a style which brings out all that is best in Chambolle: scent, subtlety, laciness of texture and great persistence. His wines are now at the top of the ladder; the '87s were excellent, and '88, '89 and '90 are a very great trio and the '93s look excellent. Low yields and stringent sorting of the grapes ensure, however, that the wines are in short supply.

**Domaine du Château de Chamilly** *Côte Chalonnaise*
*See* W&V, Côte Chalonnaise, Mercurey.

**Domaine du Château de Chamirey** *Côte Chalonnaise*
*See* W&V, Côte Chalonnaise, Mercurey.

**Domaine Louis Champagnon** *Beaujolais*
*See* W&V, Beaujolais: Chénas, Moulin-à-Vent.

**Champy Père & Cie** *Côte d'Or*
*5 rue du Grenier-à-Sel, 21200 Beaune. 2.5ha*
Until 1990, Champy Père was both a *négociant* and a proprietor (founded in 1720, it might be the oldest *négociant* of all), but now it operates solely as a *négociant/éleveur.* Louis Jadot (*qv*) purchased Champy in 1989 and, while retaining the vineyard holdings, sold the *négociant* side of the business in 1990. The principal owners are now Henri and Pierre Meurgey, although

Jadot retains an 18% interest. The wines used to be rather thick and heavy, but they were made in a much lighter style during the 1980s, when, however, if they were correct, they were also rather unexciting. The first vintage produced under the new ownership is the 1990, and, with the Meurgeys now supervising purchase and *élevage*, the wines already have more polish and elegance than their predecessors.

**Domaine de la Chanaise** *Beaujolais*
*See* W&V, Beaujolais, Morgon.

**Emile Chandesais** *Côte Chalonnaise*
*See* W&V, Côte Chalonnaise, Rully.

**Domaine Chandon de Briailles** *Côte d'Or*
*21420 Savigny-lès-Beaune. 13ha*
***Grands Crus:*** *Aloxe-Corton: Corton (white), Corton-Charlemagne, Corton Clos du Roi, Corton-Bressandes, Corton Les Maréchaudes*
***1ers Crus:*** *Pernand-Vergelesses, Pernand Ile des Vergelesses, Les Vergelesses, Les Fourneaux; Aloxe-Corton Les Valozières; Savigny-lès-Beaune Les Lavières*
***AOC Communale:*** *Savigny-lès-Beaune*
Owned by the Nicolay family, who are related to the Chandons of Champagne fame, this is an aristocratic wine estate with some excellent vineyards (and a magnificent French garden). Nadine and Claude Nicolay are transforming the wines in the 1990s and we are clearly in a new era for the domaine. The emphasis seems to be on finesse allied to character. I shall watch development in bottle with interest.

**Chanson Père & Fils** *Côte d'Or*
*10 rue Paul-Chanson, 21420 Beaune. 44ha*
***1ers Crus:*** *Pernand-Vergelesses: Les Caradeux, Les Basses Vergelesses; Savigny-Dominode, Savigny-Marconnets (red and white); Beaune: Champimonts (red and white), Clos des Fèves, Clos des Marconnets, Clos des Mouches (red and white), Clos du Roi, Grèves, Teurons*
Chanson is one of those Beaune houses which combine an important *négoce* business with ownership of some very fine vineyards. Recent vintages of the domaine wines have, in my opinion, seemed very good, although some of the *négociant* wines are dull in comparison. Much more could be done here and it is to be hoped that François and Philippe Marion will take up the challenge.

**Chanut Frères** *Beaujolais*
*See* W&V, Beaujolais.

**Chanzy Frères/ Domaine de l'Hermitage** *Côte Chalonnaise*
*See* W&V, Côte Chalonnaise, Bouzeron.

### Domaine Maurice Chapuis *Côte d'Or*

*21420 Aloxe-Corton. 11ha*

***Grands Crus:*** *Aloxe-Corton: Corton, Corton-Languettes, Corton-Perrières; Pernand-Vergelesses: Corton-Charlemagne*

***1er Cru:*** *Aloxe-Corton*

***AOC Communales:*** *Aloxe-Corton, Savigny-lès-Beaune and Chorey-lès-Beaune*

***AOC Régionale:*** *Bourgogne Blanc*

Maurice and Claude Chapuis are in charge of this highly respected domaine, which combines selling to *négociants* with direct selling locally and on the export markets. There has been modernisation and construction of new cellars. Total destalking for Pinot Noir, ten-day fermentations on average, and *élevage* in barrels (15% new each year) for 18 months to two years. Obviously, there is a rush to buy his excellent Corton-Charlemagne (drink earlier than the Louis Latour (*qv*) or Bonneau du Martray (*qv*) versions). Less-successful reds.

### Domaine François Charles *Côte d'Or*

*21190 Nantoux. 11ha (1ha en métayage)*

***1ers Crus:*** *Beaune Les Epenottes; Volnay Les Frémiets*

***AOC Communales:*** *Pommard; Meursault*

***AOC Régionales:*** *Bourgogne Hautes-Côtes de Beaune (red, white and rosé); Bourgogne Aligoté; Bourgogne Passe-Tout-Grains*

Notably good Hautes-Côtes de Beaune.

### Domaine Philippe Charlopin-Parizot *Côte d'Or*

*21220 Gevrey-Chambertin. 5ha (5.5ha en fermage)*

***Grands Crus:*** *Gevrey-Chambertin: Charmes-Chambertin; Morey-St-Denis: Clos St-Denis.* ***AOC Communales:*** *Marsannay (red and white); Gevrey-Chambertin; Morey-St-Denis; Chambolle-Musigny; Vosne-Romanée.* ***AOC Régionale:*** *Bourgogne Rouge*

A somewhat puzzling domaine, with highs and lows of quality. Destalking and early bottling seem to have produced a better 'strike rate' with more fruit added to the weight of the wines.

### Château de la Charrière *Côte d'Or*

*21590 Santenay*

Concentrated, long-lived Santenays of very good quality are made by Jean Girardin; look for Santenay Les Gravières especially.

### Domaine Chartron/ Chartron & Trébuchet *Côte d'Or*

*13 Grande-Rue, Puligny-Montrachet, 21190 Meursault. 8.2ha*

***Grand Cru:*** *Puligny-Montrachet: Chevalier-Montrachet*

***1ers Crus:*** *Puligny-Montrachet: Clos de la Pucelle, Clos du Cailleret (red and white), Les Folatières*

***AOC Régionales:*** *Bourgogne Rouge, Blanc, Aligoté*

Created in 1984, Chartron & Trébuchet specialises in white wines and distributes the wines of Domaine Chartron. The *négociant* wines are good, if not long-lasting; they are vinified in a light but elegant style and bottled early. In lesser vintages, however, they can be light to a fault, and there is also, occasionally, a slight oiliness in the flavour. My favourite wines from the domaine are the Premier Cru Clos de la Pucelle and the Chevalier-Montrachet. The *négociant* side produces Le Montrachet with a finish of nougat.

**F Chauvenet** *Côte d'Or*

Now part of Jean-Claude Boisset (*qv*).

**Domaine Jean Chauvenet** *Côte d'Or*

*Rue de Gilly, 21700 Nuits-St-Georges. 9.5ha*

Chauvenet makes fullish, solid Nuits-St-Georges; good (Les Bousselots and Les Vaucrains) on the whole without being top class.

**Domaine de Chavanne** *Beaujolais*

*See* W&V, Beaujolais, Côte de Brouilly.

**Domaine Gérard Chavy et Fils** *Côte d'Or*

*Puligny-Montrachet, 21190 Meursault. 11.5ha*

Good domaine-bottled whites and a reliable source.

**Domaine Chavy-Chouet** *Côte d'Or*

*21190 Meursault. 5ha*

Straightforward Meursaults, often rather angular.

**Domaine des Chazelles** *Mâconnais*

*See* W&V, Mâconnais, Mâcon.

**Château de Chénas** *Beaujolais*

*See* W&V, Beaujolais, Chénas.

**Maurice Chenu**

*21200 Montagny-lès-Beaune. 28ha*

A *négociant* since 1978 and now owning estates all over Burgundy, where the wines are domaine-bottled.

**Domaine de Chervin** *Mâconnais*

*See* W&V, Mâconnais, Mâcon.

**Domaine Chevalier** *Côte d'Or*

*Buisson, 84110 Ladoix-Serrigny. 11ha*

*See* W&V, Côte d'Or, Ladoix-Serrigny.

**Domaine Georges & Michel Chevillon** *Côte d'Or*

*21700 Nuits-St-Georges. 6.5ha (2ha en métayage)*

***1ers Crus:*** *Nuits-St-Georges: Aux Champs Perdrix, Porets, St-Julien, Nuits-St-Georges, Les St-Georges*

***AOC Communales:*** *Vosne-Romanée; Nuits-St-Georges*

***AOC Régionales:*** *Bourgogne Rouge; Bourgogne Passe-Tout-Grains*

Georges and Michel Chevillon are cousins of Robert Chevillon (*qv*), who also makes Nuits-St-Georges. The wines have a good reputation, though without the class of Robert's. Some seem to show a need for new wood.

## Domaine Robert Chevillon *Côte d'Or*

*68 rue Félix Tisserand, 21700 Nuits-St-Georges. 13ha*

***1ers Crus:*** *Nuits-St-Georges: Les Cailles, Les Perrières, Les Roncières, Les St-Georges, Les Vaucrains*

This is a comparatively new estate, which established an excellent reputation for itself during the 1980s. Traditional vinification is the order of the day, with long fermentations depending on vintage, followed by a maceration of the wine and skins for several days. Open *cuves*; *pigeage* and *remontage* every day. Of total production, 80% is bottled at the domaine; the rest is sold to local *négociants*. The domaine exports to a spread of countries. Chevillon's wines are at the top of the Nuits-St-Georges ladder, consistently elegant and fascinating expressions of vintage and *terroir*. Impressive white Nuits from Pinot Blanc.

## Domaine Cheysson *Beaujolais*

*See* W&V, Beaujolais, Chiroubles.

## Domaine Georges Chicotot *Côte d'Or*

*21700 Nuits-St-Georges. 5ha*

***1ers Crus:*** *Nuits-St-Georges: Les Rues de Chaux, Les Pruliers, Les Vaucrains, Les St-Georges*

***AOC Communales:*** *Nuit-St-Georges*

***AOC Régionales:*** *Bourgogne*

Chicotot produces strong, dark wines based on the methods of Guy Accad (long cold maceration before fermentation and then a prolonged vatting on the skins). They are flattering when tasted young, but they have yet to convince me that they will ultimately age gracefully.

## Domaine Michel Chignard *Beaujolais*

*See* W&V, Beaujolais, Fleurie.

## La Maison des Vignerons à Chiroubles *Beaujolais*

*See* W&V, Beaujolais, Chiroubles.

## Domaine Jean Chofflet-Valdenaire *Côte Chalonnaise*

*See* W&V, Côte Chalonnaise, Givry.

## Domaine Chopin & Fils *Côte d'Or*

*Comblanchien, 21700 Nuits-St-Georges. 11.5ha*

Chopin et Fils makes quite firm wines, but tastings of its wares are not frequent enough to allow a real pattern to emerge.

## Domaine Daniel Chopin-Groffier *Côte d'Or*

*Comblanchien, 21700 Nuits-St-Georges. 7ha*

Clean, frank, well-made wines are the hallmark of this estate, with the emphasis placed firmly on elegance rather than on concentration. Warmly fruity Côte de Nuits-Villages. The Clos Vougeot has a good reputation, but the Bourgogne Rouge may be the better bet. Son-in-law Hubert Chauvenet in Nuits is gradually taking over here.

**Domaine Bruno Clair** *Côte d'Or*

*5 rue du Vieux-Collège, 21160 Marsannay-la-Côte. 20ha*
***Grand Cru:*** *Gevrey-Chambertin: Chambertin Clos de Bèze*
***1ers Crus:*** *Gevrey-Chambertin: Clos de Fontenay monopole, Clos St-Jacques, Les Cazetiers, Gevrey-Chambertin; Savigny-lès-Beaune La Dominode*
***AOC Communales:*** *Marsannay Rouge, Blanc and Rosé; Fixin; Morey-St-Denis en la Rue de Vergy (red and white); Chambolle-Musigny Veroilles; Vosne-Romanée Champs Perdrix*
***AOC Régionales:*** *Bourgogne Rouge, Blanc and Aligoté; Crémant de Bourgogne*

The team here – consisting of Bruno Clair, André Geoffroy and Philippe Brun – is a prime example of the most encouraging aspects of contemporary Burgundian winemaking, being unblinkered, hardworking and conscientious in everything it does. The resulting wines are extremely pure in their Pinot character, stressing refinement and aromatic persistence rather than sheer puissance, and the use of oak is accordingly moderate: 35% is the maximum allowed for the Grands Crus. Bruno Clair feels that there is a potential for more white wine production in the northern Côte de Nuits, and many appreciate his white Marsannay made from Chardonnay and Pinot Beurot. Overall, this domaine is one of the best examples in Burgundy of where the vineyard sites are truly (and rightfully) respected by the men who own and work them.

**Domaine Michel Clair** *Côte d'Or*

*21590 Santenay. 5.53ha (5.17ha en fermage)*
***1ers Crus:*** *Santenay: Clos de Beaurepaire, Clos de la Combe, Clos de Tavanne, Gravières, Passe-Temps*
***AOC Communales:*** *Santenay: red, white, Clos Genets*
***AOC Régionales:*** *Bourgogne Aligoté; Crémant de Bourgogne*

Michel Clair produces quite a pretty style at this domaine, and the wines (thankfully) do not tend to become as earthy as some Santenays do.

**Domaine Henri Clerc et Fils** *Côte d'Or*

*Puligny-Montrachet, 21190 Meursault. 25ha*
***Grands Crus:*** *Puligny-Montrachet: Bâtard-Montrachet, Bienvenues-Bâtard-Montrachet, Chevalier-Montrachet*
***1ers Crus:*** *Puligny-Montrachet: Combettes, Folatières*
***AOC Communales:*** *Blagny La Pièce sous le Dos d'Ane; Puligny-Montrachet (red and white)*
***AOC Régionales:*** *Bourgogne Rouge, Blanc and Aligoté*

Form at this domaine can at times be something of a hit-and-miss affair, but, when on target, Bernard Clerc's *village* and Premier Cru Pulignys are definitely enjoyable, with a soft, full and peachy style. In a good vintage, the Grands Crus often have considerable weight and opulence to them; nonetheless, they lack the breeding necessary to place them in the top rank. I would call these quixotic rather than classic wines, but they are worth the effort of seeking out.

## Domaine Christian Clerget *Côte d'Or*

*Gilly-lès-Cîteaux, 21640 Vougeot. 5ha*
***Grand Cru:** Flagey-Echézeaux: Echézeaux*
***1ers Crus:** Vougeot; Chambolle-Musigny: Les Charmes.*
***AOC Communales:** Morey-St-Denis; Chambolle-Musigny; Vosne-Romanée Les Violettes*
***AOC Régionale:** Bourgogne Rouge*

Small domaine. His best wines can be a lovely combination of gamey Pinot and Côte de Nuits spice. Choose carefully.

## Domaine Raoul Clerget *Côte d'Or*

Now owned by Maurice Chenu (*qv*).

## Domaine Yvon Clerget *Côte d'Or*

*Rue de la Combe, Volnay, 21190 Meursault. 6ha*
***1ers Crus:** Pommard Rugiens; Volnay: Caillerets, Clos du Verseuil, Carelle Sous la Chapelle, Santenots, Volnay*
***AOC Communale:** Meursault. **AOC Régionale:** Bourgogne Rouge*

This must be the family of growers with the oldest history in Burgundy – with skills which have been passed down from father to son in Volnay since 1268. Clergets abound, but this branch goes right back to the source. The domaine's red wines have the balance and style to keep well, especially in the loftier *climats*. However, Meursault Chevalières can be coarse. The domaine uses 25% new wood for all its wines.

## Cave Coopérative de Clessé *Mâconnais*

*See* W&V, Mâconnais, Mâcon.

## Domaine Alain Coche-Bizouard *Côte d'Or*

*21190 Meursault. 8ha*

Good quality without being exciting; the Premiers Crus are more reliable than the *village* wines. Alain Coche makes wines for keeping and robust reds.

## Domaine Jean-François Coche-Dury *Côte d'Or*

*21190 Meursault. 6ha (8.5ha en métayage)*
***Grand Cru:** Pernand-Vergelesses: Corton-Charlemagne*
***1ers Crus:** Monthelie; Volnay; Auxey-Duresses; Meursault-Perrières. **AOC Communales:** Meursault (red and white)*
***AOC Régionales:** Bourgogne Rouge, Blanc and Aligoté; Bourgogne Grand Ordinaire*

This domaine has sold wine under its own label since 1973 and now must be considered in the Meusault's top rank. Jean-François Coche-Dury favours old vines, low yields and natural yeasts, allowing long fermentations to start in their own time and practising *bâtonnage*. He prefers not to make wines of over 13% alcohol and carefully balances new oak according to the vintage and the wine itself. The whites are stunning – '82s and '86s drunk recently have been heavenly – and the red Premier Cru Auxey-Duresses is almost a miracle from relatively young vines. This winemaker has a magic touch and his wines have extraordinary dimension.

### Domaine Pierre Cogny *Côte Chalonnaise*

*See* W&V, Côte Chalonnaise, Rully.

### Domaine Michel Colin-Deléger *Côte d'Or*

*3 impasse des Crêtes, Chassagne-Montrachet,*
*21190 Meursault. 18.8ha*

***Grand Cru:*** *Puligny-Montrachet: Chevalier-Montrachet*
***1ers Crus:*** *Puligny-Montrachet Les Demoiselles; Chassagne-Montrachet: Les Chaumées, Les Chenevottes, La Maltroie (white and red), Morgeot (white and red), En Remilly, Les Vergers*
***AOC Communales:*** *Chassagne-Montrachet (red and white)*
***AOC Régionales:*** *Bourgogne Rouge and Aligoté*

Colin-Deléger's wines also appear under the simpler name of Michel Colin. This is classy winemaking, producing stylish, beautifully balanced white burgundies which show real breeding and refinement, as well as the capacity to age; the Chassagne-Montrachet Les Chaumées is particularly good. All vines are worked *en métayage; élevage* is in 20% new oak; eight to ten months for whites, 12 to 15 for reds, which are good, though not of the same standard as the whites.

### Domaine Jean Collet & Fils *Chablis*

*See* W&V, Chablis.

### Domaine Paul Collonge/ Domaine de la Ruyère *Beaujolais*

*See* W&V, Beaujolais, Morgon.

### Domaine de Colonat *Beaujolais*

*See* W&V, Beaujolais, Morgon.

### Château de Juliénas/François Condemine *Beaujolais*

*See* W&V, Beaujolais, Juliénas.

### François Condemine *Mâconnais*

*See* W&V, Mâconnais, Mâcon.

### Domaine Jean-Jacques Confuron *Côte d'Or*

*Prémeaux, 21700 Nuits-St-Georges. 7ha*

***Grands Crus:*** *Vosne-Romanée: Romanée-St-Vivant; Vougeot: Clos de Vougeot*
***1ers Crus:*** *Vosne-Romanée Les Beaux Monts; Nuits-St-Georges: Boudots, Chaboeufs; Chambolle-Musigny*
***AOC Communales:*** *Chambolle-Musigny; Nuits-St-Georges*
***AOC Régionales:*** *Côte de Nuits-Villages; Bourgogne Rouge and Aligoté*

Confuron makes sturdy wines whose extract and 'thickness' have tended to blur their appellation characters. There is now sometimes 100% new wood for the Grands Crus, 40% for the Premiers Crus and *villages*. New cellars have coincided with noticeable improvement at this domaine, and Alain Meunier is definitely 'on the up', as they say. There is also a small *négociant* business, Féry-Meunier.

## Domaine Confuron-Cotétidot *Côte d'Or*

*Vosne-Romanée, 21700 Nuits-St-Georges. 11ha*

***Grands Crus:** Vougeot: Clos de Vougeot; Gevrey-Chambertin: Charmes-Chambertin, Mazis-Chambertin; Flagey-Echézeaux: Echézeaux. **1ers Crus:** Vosne-Romanée Les Suchots; Nuits-St-Georges: Les Murgers, Les Vignes Rondes. **AOC Communales**: Gevrey-Chambertin; Chambolle-Musigny; Vosne-Romanée; Nuits-St-Georges*

Jacky Confuron and his oenologist son, Jean-Pierre, are both dedicated winemakers and well-known supporters of the controversial oenologist, Guy Accad, (who seems recently to have disappeared from the Burgundian scene). They make their wines from old vincs and very ripe whole grapes which are cold-macerated for eight to ten days before undergoing a relatively cool fermentation (25–28˚C/77–82˚F), and barrel-ageing is in a maximum of 20% new wood. The wines' 'showiness' from cask (the sweetness of bouquet in particular) has led to doubts as to whether they will be true-to-type burgundies when mature. However, they have plenty of backbone, and an '85 Nuits-St-Georges had both the seductive ripeness of the vintage as well as the distinctive 'earthiness' wanted from a good Nuits. Especially good Echézeaux, which is lacy, layered and with a lovely projection of flavours.

## Domaine de Conroy *Beaujolais*

*See* W&V, Beaujolais, Côte de Brouilly.

## Château de Corcelles *Beaujolais*

*See* W&V, Beaujolais, Beaujolais-Villages.

## Domaine Cordier Père et Fils *Mâconnais*

*See* W&V, Mâconnais, Pouilly-Fuissé.

## Château de Coreaux *Mâconnais*

*See* W&V, Mâconnais, St-Véran.

## Domaine Claude Cornu *Côte d'Or*

*21 Magny-lès-Villers. 14ha*

Claude Cornu is making thoroughly respectable wines here, with a few disappointments along the way.

## Domaine Edmond Cornu *Côte d'Or*

*21550 Ladoix. 8ha (4.15ha en métayage)*

***Grand Cru:** Aloxe-Corton: Corton-Bressandes. **1ers Crus:** Ladoix Corvées; Aloxe-Corton Moutottes. **AOC Communales:** Ladoix; Aloxe-Corton; Savigny-lès-Beaune; Chorey-lès-Beaune (red and white). **AOC Régionales:** Bourgogne Rouge, Bourgogne Aligoté*

Rather variable in quality, but some good buys at this domaine.

## Coron Père & Fils *Côte d'Or*

*21200 Beaune. 6ha*

Both a domaine and a *négociant*. Past bad experiences have not led me to explore further.

**Domaine Corsin** *Mâconnais*
*See* W&V, Mâconnais, Pouilly-Fuissé.

**Domaine Coste-Caumartin** *Côte d'Or*
*Rue du Parc, 21630 Pommard. 12ha*
***1ers Crus:*** *Pommard: Clos des Boucherottes, Les Fremiers*
***AOC Communales:*** *Pommard; St-Romain (white)*
***AOC Régionales:*** *Bourgogne (white and red)*
Jérôme Sordet scoops up medals with great regularity, and there are definitely some good things to be sampled here. However, choose with care.

**Domaine Jean Coulon** *Côte Chalonnaise*
*See* W&V, Côte Chalonnaise, Rully.

**Domaine de Courcel** *Côte d'Or*
*Place de l'Eglise, 21630 Pommard. 8.4ha*
***1ers Crus:*** *Pommard: Epenots, Croix Noires, Grand Clos des Epenots, Fremiers, Rugiens*
***AOC Communale:*** *Pommard.* ***AOC Régionale:*** *Bourgogne Rouge*
This old-established family domaine is designed to make the parvenus shudder; more than four centuries lie behind this estate. Extraordinary wine, deeply coloured and intensely concentrated, the result of long vatting and several *pigeages* each day to obtain the maximum extraction. Partial destalking, according to the year, and up to two years in new wood before bottling. These are wines with a good heart of flavour even in lesser vintages; in great years they require, and repay, keeping. I wish I had more Rugiens '78 in my cellar.

**Domaine Alain Creusefond** *Côte d'Or*
*Auxey-Duresses, 21190 Meursault. 12ha*
Creusefond is quite a good source of supply for both red and white wines.

**Domaine Michel Crozet** *Beaujolais*
*See* W&V, Beaujolais, Chénas.

**Domaine Louis Curveux** *Mâconnais*
*See* W&V, Mâconnais, Pouilly-Fuissé.

**Domaine Dalicieux** *Beaujolais*
*See* W&V, Beaujolais, Beaujolais-Villages.

**Domaine Pierre Damoy** *Côte d'Or*
*Le Tamisot, 21220 Gevrey-Chambertin. 12ha*
***Grands Crus:*** *Gevrey-Chambertin: Chambertin, Chambertin Clos de Bèze, Chapelle-Chambertin*
***AOC Communale:*** *Gevrey-Chambertin Clos du Tamisot*
Pierre Damoy is a domaine owning untold riches: the biggest single share of Clos de Bèze plus Chapelle and the Gevrey-Chambertin monopole, Clos du Tamisot. Memorable old wines. Occasional good

bottles recently, but far too many misses. Perhaps the current Pierre Damoy can take the improvements further – he has made a good start.

**Domaine Darnat** *Côte d'Or*
*20 rue des Forges, 21190 Meursault. 3ha (1ha en métayage)*
***1ers Crus:*** *Meursault: Clos Richemont monopole, Gouttes d'Or; St-Aubin: En Rémilly*
***AOC Communales:*** *Meursault: Les Pelles, Les Charrons, Le Meix Tavaux*
***AOC Régionales:*** *Bourgogne Blanc and Aligoté*
Darnat has belonged to the same family for more than a century. Henri Darnat seems to be reversing some of the past practices and everything appears 'cleaner' in style. Clos Richemont can be rewarding.

**Domaine Jean Dauvissat** *Chablis*
*See* W&V, Chablis.

**Domaine René & Vincent Dauvissat** *Chablis*
*See* W&V, Chablis.

**Domaine du Château de Davenay** *Côte Chalonnaise*
*See* W&V, Côte Chalonnaise, Montagny.

**David & Foillard** *Beaujolais*
*69830 St-Georges-en-Beaujolais.*
This is a very large *négociant* firm which occupies itself in selling in bulk as well as bottle. Jean-Louis Foillard owns three estates in the Beaujolais *crus*.

**Domaine Jean Defaix** *Chablis*
*See* W&V, Chablis.

**Domaine Delachanal** *Beaujolais*
*See* W&V, Beaujolais, Côte de Brouilly.

**Domaine Delagrange-Bachelet** *Côte d'Or*
*Chassagne-Montrachet, 21190 Meursault. 1ha*
This tiny, good-quality wine estate has already been handed down to the next generation, although 86-year-old Edmond Delagrange still has a few ares of vines under his supervision. The rest of the vineyards have gone to Blain Gagnard (*qv*), where the Delegrange-Bachelet's wines are made, Fontaine-Gagnard (*qv*) and Gagnard-Delagrange (*qv*).

**Domaine Marius Delarche** *Côte d'Or*
*21420 Pernand-Vergelesses. 6.5ha (1.5ha en métayage)*
***Grands Crus:*** *Pernand-Vergelesses: Corton-Charlemagne; Aloxe-Corton: Corton-Renardes*
***1ers Crus:*** *Pernand-Vergelesses: des Vergelesses, Ile des Vergelesses*

***AOC Communales:*** *Pernand-Vergelesses (red and white)*
***AOC Régionales:*** *Bourgogne Rouge and Aligoté*
Produces reliable Corton-Charlemagne/Renardes in good vintages.

**Edouard Delaunay et ses Fils** *Côte d'Or*
Now part of the Boisset empire (*qv*).

**André Delorme** *Côte Chalonnaise*
*See* W&V, Côte Chalonnaise, Rully.

**Domaine Lucien Denizot** *Côte Chalonnaise*
*See* W&V, Côte Chalonnaise, Montagny.

**Domaine Jacques Depagneux** *Mâconnais*
*See* W&V, Mâconnais, Mâcon.
Distributed through the SVGC.

**Domaine André Depardon** *Mâconnais*
*See* W&V, Mâconnais, St-Véran.

**Domaine Michel Derain** *Côte Chalonnaise*
*See* W&V, Côte Chalonnaise, Givry.

**Domaine Jean Descombes** *Beaujolais*
*See* W&V, Beaujolais, Morgon.

**Domaine Desmures Père & Fils** *Beaujolais*
*See* W&V, Beaujolais, Chiroubles.

**Vins Dessalle** *Beaujolais*
*See* W&V, Beaujolais, Beaujolais-Villages.

**GFA Domaine Desvignes** *Beaujolais*
*See* W&V, Beaujolais, Moulin-à-Vent.

**Louis Claude Desvignes** *Beaujolais*
*See* W&V, Beaujolais, Morgon.

**Propriété Desvignes** *Côte Chalonnaise*
*See* W&V, Côte Chalonnaise, Givry.

**Domaine des Deux Roches** *Mâconnais*
*See* W&V, Mâconnais, St-Véran.

**Domaine Jean-Pierre Diconne** *Côte d'Or*
*Auxey-Duresses, 21190 Meursault. 7ha*
***1er Cru:*** *Auxey-Duresses Les Duresses.*
***AOC Communales:*** *Auxey-Duresses; Meursault.*
***AOC Régionales:*** *Bourgogne Rouge, Blanc and Passe-Tout-Grains*
Old-fashioned approaches to many aspects of winemaking here, but when that includes old vines, that is not all bad. Characterful, rich whites and burly reds – I have been lucky.

## Domaine Diochon *Beaujolais*

*See* W&V, Beaujolais, Moulin-à-Vent.

## Maison Doudet-Naudin *Côte d'Or*

*21420 Savigny-lès-Beaune. 4.83ha*
***Grands Crus,*** *Pernand-Vergelesses: Corton-Charlemagne; Aloxe-Corton: Corton Les Maréchaudes*
***1ers Crus:*** *Pernand-Vergelesses Fichots; Aloxe-Corton; Savigny-lès-Beaune Les Guettes, Savigny-lès-Beaune Redrescul; Beaune Clos du Roy.* ***AOC Communales:*** *Aloxe-Corton Les Boutières; Savigny-Liards.* ***AOC Régionale,*** *Bourgogne Blanc*
Known above all for its *négociant* wines, which tend to divide opinion. The style is big, rich, dark and jammy, with alcoholic backbone – so the wines last, but I find it easier to recognise a Doudet-Naudin wine than to identify its commune. Their own wines receive long vinifications in oak *cuves*, with partial de-stalking according to the character of the year.

## Jean-Paul Droin *Chablis*

*See* W&V, Chablis.

## Maison Joseph Drouhin *Côte d'Or/Chablis*

*7 rue d'Enfer, 21200 Beaune. 63ha. Côte d'Or 24.7ha Chablis 35.3ha*
***Grands Crus:*** *Chablis Les Clos Vaudésirs; Gevrey-Chambertin: Chambertin Clos de Bèze, Griottes-Chambertin; Morey-St-Denis: Bonnes Mares; Chambolle-Musigny: Musigny; Vougeot: Clos de Vougeot; Flagey-Echézeaux: Echézeaux, Grands Echézeaux; Pernand-Vergelesses: Corton-Charlemagne; Aloxe-Corton: Corton-Bressandes; Puligny-Montrachet: Le Montrachet (Domaine Marquis de Laguiche)*
***1ers Crus:*** *Chablis; Chambolle-Musigny, Chambolle-Musigny Amoureuses; Beaune, Beaune Clos des Mouches (red and white); Volnay Clos des Chênes; Nuits-St-Georges*
***AOC Communales:*** *Chablis; Chorey-lès-Beaune; Meursault*
Maison Joseph Drouhin, run by Robert Drouhin in combination with his extremely capable and technically trained children, is a highly reputed Beaune *négociant*, but also an important domaine proprietor – many people forget how much it owns in Chablis. The maison combines tradition with new developments and is always willing to try fresh techniques if they are improvements. Red wines are fermented in open *cuves* with floating *chapeau*, natural yeasts, and go through long, temperature-controlled macerations. The white grapes are pressed slowly, the last pressings not used, and fermentation takes place in 228-litre casks. The white and red Beaune Clos des Mouches are flagships, but all wines are to be highly recommended. The Chablis is influenced by oak and is delicious. The *négoce* business buys in grapes and turns them into wine with the same care it gives those of its own domaine. The business only sells AC Bourgogne and has never created a *vin de marque*. *See also* W&V, Chablis.

**Domaine Drouhin Laroze** *Côte d'Or*
*20 rue de Goizot, 21220 Gevrey-Chambertin. 12ha*
***Grands Crus:*** *Chambertin Gebrey-Chambertin: Clos de Bèze, Latricières-Chambertin, Chapelle-Chambertin; Vougeot: Clos de Vougeot; Morey-St-Denis: Bonnes-Mares*
***1ers Crus:*** *Gevrey-Chambertin, Chambolle-Musigny, Morey-St-Denis*
This estate has well-placed parcels of vineyards in Latricières-Chambertin, Chapelle-Chambertin and Chambertin Clos de Bèze, as well as plots in some of the best parts of the Clos de Vougeot. Recently, however, the Clos de Vougeots have been weak (over-cropping?) and the Chambertins are also light. Some of the wines age well, for eight to ten years anyway, but most are at their prettiest when young. However, Grands Crus should not be merely pretty.

**Georges Duboeuf** *Beaujolais*
*See* W&V, Beaujolais, Beaujolais-Villages. For *négociant* details, *see* Beaujolais: St-Amour, Fleurie, Beaujolais-Villages.

**Roger Duboeuf** *Mâconnais*
*See* W&V, Mâconnais, Pouilly-Fuissé.

**Domaine Jean Dubois** *Côte d'Or*
*21370 Plombières-les-Dijon. 6ha*
Good red and Bourgogne, made on the outskirts of Dijon.

**Domaine Robert Dubois & Fils** *Côte d'Or*
*Prémeaux, 21700 Nuits-St-Georges. 9ha*
*(9ha en fermage and en métayage)*
***1ers Crus:*** *Chambolle-Musigny Les Combottes; Nuits-St-Georges: Clos des Argillières, Les Porêts St-Georges; Beaune Blanche Fleur*
***AOC Communales:*** *Vosne-Romanée Les Chalandins; Nuits-St-Georges; Savigny-lès-Beaune Les Golardes*
***AOC Régionales:*** *Côte de Nuits-Villages; Bourgogne Rouge, Blanc, Rosé and Aligoté; Bourgogne Passe-Tout-Grains*
This is yet another Burgundian family domaine, with Régis Dubois currently in charge; he (along with the rest of the family) would like to widen the appellation range even further. Dubois heats the must to 40°C (104°F) for four hours before fermentation in order to extract colour and aromas, then cools it to 28°C (82°F) for a traditional Burgundian vinification. The wines are certainly keepers, but I have not appreciated them as much as some, always finding something slightly tainted about them (I am not sure whether it is the heating or tastes from some barrels). Exports account for 60%, but there is also an important private clientele in France.

**Domaine P Dubreuil-Fontaine Père & Fils** *Côte d'Or*
*Pernand-Vergelesses, 21420 Savigny-lès-Beaune. 21ha*
***Grands Crus:*** *Pernand-Vergelesses: Corton-Charlemagne; Aloxe-Corton: Corton-Bressandes, Corton Clos du Roi, Corton-Perrières*

***1ers Crus:*** *Pernand Ile des Vergelesses; Savigny-Vergelesses*
***AOC Communales:*** *Pernand-Vergelesses: (red and white), Clos Berthet (red and white); Aloxe-Corton*
***AOC Régionales:*** *Bourgogne Rouge and Aligoté*
Bernard Dubreuil manages this excellent domaine, which sells half its wines on the export markets and half in France. Vinification is traditional in wood *cuves*, with a floating *chapeau* of skins which is pushed down into the fermenting must (*pigeage*) twice each day. The aim is for wines which will keep, but only in those years with ageing potential. His family knows all there is to know about Pernand, and is especially proud of its Clos Berthet (which the family owns in its entirety) and of its Corton-Bressandes. Daughter Christine is now here too and the red Clos Berthet has just been replanted.

## Domaine Michel Duchet — *Côte d'Or*

*21200 Beaune. 5ha*
***Grands Crus:*** *Aloxe-Corton: Corton-Charlemagne*
***1ers Crus:*** *Beaune: Bressandes, Cent Vignes, Pertuisots, Theurons, Grèves; Savigny-lès-Beaune: Les Peuillets*
***AOC Communales,*** *Beaune, Pommard*
The red wines have a reputation for keeping well and younger wines look promising.

## Domaine des Duc — *Beaujolais*

*See* W&V, Beaujolais, St-Amour.

## Domaine Fabrice Ducroux — *Beaujolais*

*See* W&V, Beaujolais, Brouilly.

## Dufouleur Frères — *Côte d'Or*

*1 rue de Dijon, 21700 Nuits-St-Georges. 8ha*
***Grands Crus:*** *Vougeot: Clos Vougeot Les Grands Maupertuis; Chambolle-Musigny: Musigny*
***1ers Crus:*** *Nuits-St-Georges: Les St-Georges; Gevrey-Chambertin, Chambolle-Musigny, Vosne-Romanée*
***AOC Communales:*** *Mercurey, Mercurey Champs Martin, Mercurey Clos l'Evêque*
***AOC Régionale:*** *Côte de Nuits-Villages Les Vaucrains*
Dufouleur is a name that is certainly *du métier* because a *fouleur* is a man who treads the grapes in order to crush them. This is a large *négociant* business, exporting all over Europe, with the domaine activity somewhat dwarfed by the *négociant* side. Vinification is traditional in oak vats, with long vatting and floating *chapeau* of skins. Destalking only takes place in certain, well-defined cases. Some of the wines are kept in *fûts* – the firm selects and buys the oak two years beforehand so that it can be aged. It is particularly proud of its Clos Vougeot.

## Dufouleur Père & Fils — *Côte d'Or*

*17 rue Thurot, 21700 Nuits-St-Georges. 48ha*
This *négociant* markets a very wide range of wines and spirits

from Burgundy, the Rhône and Bordeaux. The *négociant* wines are fairly dull, but the firm does distribute the wines of Guy Dufouleur (*qv*).

**Domaine Guy Dufouleur** *Côte d'Or*

*19 place Monge, 21700 Nuits-St-Georges. 20ha*

***1ers Crus:*** *Nuits-St-Georges: En-La-Châine-Carteaux, Clos des Perrières, Les Crots, Les Poulettes.* ***AOC Communales:*** *Nuits-St-Georges; Santenay Clos Genêts.* ***AOC Régionales:*** *Bourgogne Hautes-Côtes de Nuits; Bougogne Grand Ordinaire*

The Santenay Clos Genêts and Bourgogne Hautes-Côtes de Nuits are to be recommended.

**Domaine Dufour** *Beaujolais*

*See* W&V, Beaujolais, St-Amour.

**Domaine Bernard Dugat-Py** *Côte d'Or*

*21220 Gevrey-Chambertin. 6ha*

***Grand Cru:*** *Gevrey-Chambertin: Charmes-Chambertin.*

***1er Cru:*** *Gevrey-Chambertin Champeaux*

***AOC Communale:*** *Gevrey-Chambertin*

The wines ferment in open cement vats with a manual *pigeage*, and age between 50-100% new oak at top level. Very well-made wines, full yet elegant and concentrated.

**Domaine Claude Dugat** *Côte d'Or*

*21220 Gevrey-Chambertin. 4ha*

Serious, powerful wines with real ageing potential.

**Domaine Dujac** *Côte d'Or*

*7 rue de la Bussière, Morey-St-Denis, 21220 Gevrey-Chambertin. 11.5ha*

***Grands Crus:*** *Gevrey-Chambertin: Charmes-Chambertin; Morey-St-Denis: Clos de la Roche, Clos St-Denis, Bonnes Mares; Flagey-Echézeaux: Echézeaux.* ***1ers Crus:*** *Gevrey-Chambertin Aux Combottes; Morey-St-Denis; Chambolle-Musigny.*

***AOC Communales:*** *Morey-St-Denis; Chambolle-Musigny.*

***AOC Régionale:*** *Bourgogne Rouge*

Jacques Seysses bought this domaine in 1968 and has built it up to one of the most notable on the Côte de Nuits through a combination of hard work and intelligent winemaking. He qualified as an oenologist at the University of Dijon and is always willing to modernise (he favours clones, for example), although he still conserves many traditional techniques. Harvesting is immensely careful here; there is no destalking. The Grands and Premiers Crus are matured in new barrels, the *village* wines in *fûts* that have been used only once. The wines are fined with egg whites and bottled after 15 months without filtration. Great character is preserved in all the appellations. The domaine exports 90% of production.

**Domaine Duperon** *Mâconnais*

*See* W&V, Mâconnais, St-Véran.

**Domaine Duplessis** *Chablis*
*See* W&V, Chablis.

**Domaine Jean & Yves Durand** *Beaujolais*
*See* W&V, Beaujolais, Régnié.

**Domaine Dureuil-Janthial** *Côte Chalonnaise*
*See* W&V, Côte Chalonnaise, Rully.

**Jean Durup/Domaine de l'Eglantière** *Chablis*
*See* W&V, Chablis.

**Domaine Duvernay Père et Fils** *Côte Chalonnaise*
*See* W&V, Côte Chalonnaise, Rully.

**Domaine Maurice Ecard Père & Fils** *Côte d'Or*
*11 rue Chanson Maldant, 21420 Savigny-lès-Beaune. 12.5ha*
***1ers Crus:*** *Savigny-lès-Beaune: Les Cloux, Les Jarrons, Les Narbantons, Les Peuillets, Les Serpentières, Les Hauts Jarrons (blanc)*
***AOC Communale:*** *Savigny-lès-Beaune*
Savigny-lès-Beaunes which have been very impressive recently, aged in up to 25% new barrels. The Serpentières lasts well and all the wines combine great red-fruit quality with sound structure. The Savigny Blanc issues from Pinot Blanc.

**Domaine René Engel** *Côte d'Or*
*Vosne-Romanée, 21700 Nuits-St-Georges. 6ha*
***Grands Crus:*** *Vougeot: Clos Vougeot; Flagey-Echézeaux: Echézeaux, Grands Echézeaux.* ***1er Cru:*** *Vosne-Romanée Les Brûlées*
***AOC Communale:*** *Vosne-Romanée*
A domaine which includes precious land in a very good part of Clos Vougeot. There are great old bottles of Engel wines, and Philippe Engel has restored the estate's fine reputation. A stainless-steel sorting table is state-of-the-art and Grands Crus are put into 50% new barrels. There are both open and closed vats for fermentations – the enamel-lined vats give elegant, austere wines, while the wooden *cuves* contribute richness. There is often an abundance of tannin, but with the richness to match.

**Domaine Frédéric et André Esmonin** *Côte d'Or*
*21220 Gevrey-Chambertin. 3ha (5ha en métayage)*
***Grands Crus:*** *Gevrey-Chambertin: Griottes-Chambertin, Mazy-Chambertin, Ruchottes-Chambertin.* ***1ers Crus:*** *Gevrey-Chambertin: Les Corbeaux, Estournelles St-Jacques, Lavaux St-Jacques.* ***AOC Communale:*** *Gevrey-Chambertin Clos Prieur*
Usually wines of great extract and promise. Expressive, concentrated Estournelles.

**Domaine Michel Esmonin et Fille** *Côte d'Or*
*'Clos St-Jacques', 1 rue Neuve, 21220 Gevrey-Chambertin. 7ha*
Very good Gevrey-Chambertin Clos St-Jacques from 100% destalked grapes and knowledgeable, highly trained winemaking.

**Eventail de Vignerons Producteurs** *Beaujolais*
*See* W&V, Beaujolais: Chiroubles, Brouilly, Beaujolais-Villages.

**Maison Joseph Faiveley** *Côte d'Or/Côte Chalonnaise*
*8 rue du Tribourg, 21700 Nuits-St-Georges. 97ha (13ha en fermage)*
***Grands Crus:*** *Gevrey-Chambertin: Chambertin Clos de Bèze, Latricières-Chambertin, Mazis-Chambertin; Vougeot: Clos de Vougeot; Flagey-Echézeaux: Echézeaux; Pernand-Vergelesses: Corton-Charlemagne; Aloxe-Corton: Corton Clos des Cortons Faiveley; Chambolle-Musigny: Le Musigny*
***1ers Crus:*** *Gevrey-Chambertin La Combe aux Moines Les Cazetiers; Chambolle-Musigny: Les Fruées, La Combe d'Orveau, Aux Chaignots, Les Vignerondes; Nuits-St-Georges: Clos de la Maréchale, Les Porêts St Georges, Les St-Georges*
***AOC Communales:*** *Rully Les Villeranges; Mercurey Clos Rochette, Mercurey Clos des Myglands, Mercurey La Framboisière*
François Faiveley has taken the domaine wines of this important *négociant* right to the top. He starts off with careful soil analysis and choice of rootstock. Then there are very long, cool vinifications with natural yeasts (three weeks, even a month in some years), avoiding high temperatures in order to preserve aroma. Fermentation takes place in enamel-lined metal *cuves* which are equipped with a cooling system by means of running water down the sides of the *cuves* (seen more often in Bordeaux than in Burgundy). The wines are aged in oak *pièces* for 18 months, with Grands and Premiers Crus in varying proportions of new oak. There is light fining with egg white, and the Grands and Premiers Crus are mostly bottled unfiltered and by hand from cask. The aim is to make aromatic wines which keep, and the results are often spectacular.

Maison Faiveley is a very large owner in Mercurey, on the Côte Chalonnaise, its properties including the Clos des Myglands. The firm also buys in grapes and makes wine itself – notably in Morey-St-Denis and Vosne-Romanée, and on the Côte de Beaune, other than Corton and Corton-Charlemagne. (Only 25–30% of total production is not from the domaine.) Faiveley wines have great flavour and appellation character, and the Mercureys are very good value. The house has existed since 1825, and France takes just over half the production. I would like to take the other half personally!

**Domaine Jean Faurois** *Côte d'Or*
*Vosne-Romanée, 21700 Nuits-St-Georges*
This domaine has shrunk as Jean Faurois has retired, and the Clos de Vougeot has reverted to its owner, Domaine Méo-Camuzet (*qv*). For the moment, there is good Chaumes.

**Pierre Ferraud & Fils** *Beaujolais*
*See* W&V, Beaujolais.

**Domaine Jeanne Ferret** *Mâconnais*
*See* W&V, Mâconnais, Pouilly-Fuissé.

**Domaine William Fèvre /Domaine de la Maladière** *Chablis*
*See* W&V, Chablis.

**Domaine Jean-Philippe Fichet** *Côte d'Or*
*2 rue Sudot, 21190 Meursault. 5ha en métayage or en fermage.*
***1ers Crus:** Volnay Champans. **AOC Communales:** Meursault; Volnay. **AOC Régionales:** Bourgogne Rouge and Blanc*
Little track record as yet from this new, young producer, but early efforts look promising, especially his whites. Distinctive 'stony' Meursault Les Perrières, slightly austere style in the Monthelie, good Bourgogne Rouge and even better Bourgogne Blanc. The Perrières has gone but there will be Puligny.

**Cave des Producteurs de Fleurie** *Beaujolais*
*See* W&V, Beaujolais, Fleurie.

**Domaine Fleurot-Larose** *Côte d'Or*
*21590 Santenay. 6.8ha*
***1ers Crus:** Chassagne-Montrachet Abbaye de Morgeot (red and white); Santenay*
A diminishing domaine. It can make a good red Santenay Clos du Passetemps, but it is not always consistent.

**Domaine de la Folie** *Côte Chalonnaise*
*See* W&V, Côte Chalonnaise, Rully.

**Domaine Fontaine-Gagnard** *Côte d'Or*
*19 route de Santenay, 21190 Chassagne-Montrachet. 6.1ha (1.9ha en métayage)*
***Grands Crus:** Puligny-Montrachet: Bâtard-Montrachet; Chassagne-Montrachet: Criots-Bâtard-Montrachet*
***1ers Crus:** Chassagne-Montrachet: Caillerets, Clos St Jean (red), La Maltroie, Morgeot (red and white), Vergers, Chassagne-Montrachet; Pommard Rugiens; Volnay Clos des Chênes*
***AOC Régionales:** Bourgogne, Bourgogne Pass-Tout-Grains*
Good-quality wines, whites especially; they spend about a year in wood and the reds 18 months, with a maximum of 25% new oak. Richard Fontaine is in charge.

**Domaine Michel Forest** *Mâconnais*
*See* W&V, Mâconnais, Pouilly-Fuissé.

**Domaine Forey Père & Fils** *Côte d'Or*
*2 rue Derrière-le-Four, 21700 Vosne-Romanée. 4.5ha (3ha en métayage)*
***Grand Cru:** Flagey-Echézeaux: Echézeaux*
***1ers Crus:** Vosne-Romanée: Les Gaudichots, Les Petits Monts; Nuits-St-Georges: Les Perrières, Les St-Georges*
***AOC Communales:** Vosne-Romanée; Nuits-St-Georges*
***AOC Régionales:** Bourgogne Rouge, Blanc and Passe-Tout-Grains*
The red wines spend 12–18 months in 30–40% new oak. Good, rich wines, especially from Vosne-Romanée.

## Domaine Fougeray de Beauclair *Côte d'Or*

*21160 Marsannay. 20ha*

This domaine has interesting but fragmented vineyard holdings.

## Domaine Jean-Claude Fourrier *Côte d'Or*

*7 route de Dijon, 21220 Gevrey-Chambertin. 8.5ha*

***Grand Cru:** Gevrey-Chambertin: Griotte-Chambertin*

***1ers Crus:** Gevrey-Chambertin: Clos St-Jacques, Combe aux Moines, Aux Echézeaux; Morey-St-Denis: Clos Sorbé; Vougeot: Les Petits Vougeots. **AOC Communales:** Gevrey-Chambertin, Morey-St-Denis, Chambolle-Musigny*

The wines are not nearly as wondrous as in the time of Fernand Pernot, great-uncle of the current owner (whose '69 Griotte and Clos St-Jacques are among the most amazing burgundies of my life). A few have breeding and cherry-like qualities; however, there is a hit-and-miss element here, and often the cellars seem to give the wines a taint. A real pity, as the vineyards are so superb. More concentration and cleanliness are urgently needed and will perhaps be provided by Jean-Marie Founier.

## Société Civile du Château de Fuissé *Mâconnais*

See WGV, Mâconnais, Pouilly-Fuissé.

## Domaine Jean-Noël Gagnard *Côte d'Or*

*21190 Chassagne-Montrachet. 8.5ha*

***Grand Cru:** Puligny-Montrachet: Bâtard-Montrachet*

***1ers Crus:** Chassagne-Montrachet: Les Caillerets, Les Chenevottes, Clos de la Maltroye, Clos St-Jean (red), Morgeot (red and white), Chassagne-Montrachet; Santenay Clos de Tavannes (red)*

***AOC Communale:** Chassagne-Montrachet Les Mesures*

***AOC Régionales:** Bourgogne Rouge and Aligoté*

The great white wines have always been exceptionally good from this domaine, but the reds deserve attention, too. The whites are bottled quite late and they keep splendidly. M Gagnard is a true guardian of his region's winemaking reputation and I have always had wonderful bottles here. His daughter Caroline is now helping him run the domaine.

## Domaine Jacques Gagnard-Delagrange *Côte d'Or*

*26 rue Charles Paquelin, Chassagne-Montrachet, 21190 Meursault 2.35ha (2.5ha en métayage)*

***Grands Crus:** Puligny-Montrachet, Le Montrachet, Bâtard-Montrachet*

***1ers Crus:** Volnay-Champans; Chassagne-Montrachet La Boudriotte, Clos St-Jean, Morgeot*

***AOC Communales:** Chassagne-Montrachet (red and white)*

Jacques Gagnard no longer looks after all the vineyards at this estate as he has given some parcels to members of his family (Domaine Blain-Gagnard (*qv*) and Domaine Fontaine-Gagnard [*qv*]) *en métayage*. Nonetheless, this is a renowned estate, where standards remain high, with natural yeasts, plenty of lees stirring and minimum new wood.

**Vincent Gallois** *Chablis*
**/Domaine de la Vallée aux Sages**
*See* W&V, Chablis.

**Domaine des Gandines** *Mâconnais*
*See* W&V, Mâconnais, Mâcon.

**Domaine Jean Garaudet** *Côte d'Or*
*21630 Pommard. 5ha*
Garaudet produces very good Pommards in addition to Beaune Clos des Mouches.

**Domaine Paul Garaudet** *Côte d'Or*
*Monthelie, 21190 Meursault. 9ha*
Reliable wines from this domaine.

**Domaine du Gardin** *Côte Chalonnaise*
*See* W&V, Côte Chalonnaise, Givry.

**Domaine François Gaunoux** *Côte d'Or*
*23 rue du 11-novembre, 21190 Meursault. 8.4ha*
***Grand Cru:*** *Aloxe-Corton: Corton-Renardes*
***1ers Crus:*** *Beaune Le Clos des Mouches;*
*Pommard: Les Grands Epenots, Les Epenots, Les Rugiens;*
*Volnay Les Clos des Chênes; Meursault La Goutte d'Or*
***AOC Communales:*** *Pommard; Meursault Le Clos de Tavaux monopole*
***AOC Régionales:*** *Bourgogne Rouge and Blanc*
Brother of Michel Gaunoux (*qv*) of Pommard.

**Domaine Jean-Michel Gaunoux** *Côte d'Or*
*21190 Meursault. 6ha*
A new, breakaway domaine and one worth watching.

**Domaine Michel Gaunoux** *Côte d'Or*
*Rue Notre-Dame, 21630 Pommard. 10ha*
***Grand Cru:*** *Aloxe-Corton: Corton-Renardes*
***1ers Crus:*** *Beaune: Les Boucherottes, Les Epenottes; Pommard: Les Arvelets, Les Charmots, Les Combes, Grands Epenots, Rugiens*
***AOC Communale:*** *Beaune*
***AOC Régionale:*** *Bourgogne Les Sorbins*
Those wishing to try the wines of this domaine will probably have to go to France, as very little is exported; top French restaurants and a following of private customers get there first. Methods are more than traditional, with treading carried out by a *pigeur* in each wooden *cuve*. Many growers say they wish to produce *vins de garde*, but Gaunoux achieves it, especially with the very good Pommard Grands Epenots. Mme Gaunoux deserves much credit.

**Domaine Gay Père & Fils** *Côte d'Or*
*21200 Chorey-lès-Beaune*
*See* W&V, Côte d'Or, Chorey-lès-Beaune.

**Domaine Geantet-Pansiot** *Côte d'Or*
*3 route de Beaune, 21220 Gevrey-Chambertin*
*0.5ha (10.5ha en fermage)*
***Grand Cru:** Gevrey-Chambertin: Charmes-Chambertin*
***1er Cru:** Gevrey-Chambertin Le Poissenot; Chambolle-Musigny*
***AOC Communales:** Marsannay Champs Perdrix;*
*Gevrey-Chambertin Vieilles Vignes*
***AOC Régionales:** Bourgogne Rouge and Passe-Tout-Grains*
Rich and classy Le Poissenot; all the wines seem to have moved up a gear with the excellent '90s. Elegance and scent.

**Domaine Pierre Gelin** *Côte d'Or*
*2 rue du Chapitre, 21220 Fixin. 11ha*
***Grands Crus:** Gevrey-Chambertin: Chambertin Clos de Bèze, Mazis-Chambertin. **1ers Crus:** Fixin: Clos Napoléon (monopole), Les Hervelets. **AOC Communales:** Fixin; Gevrey-Chambertin*
***AOC Régionales:** Bourgogne Aligoté and Passe-Tout-Grains*
Good wines, but they do not, personally, engender much enthusiasm. This may be stylistic preference.

**Domaine Louis Genillon** *Beaujolais*
*See* W&V, Beaujolais, Morgon.

**Château Génot-Boulanger** *Côte d'Or*
*25 rue de Cîteaux, 21190 Meursault. 23ha*
***Grands Crus:** Aloxe-Corton: Corton-Charlemagne, Le Charlemagne*
***1ers Crus:** Aloxe-Corton: Clos du Chapitre; Beaune: Grèves, Montrevenaux; Meursault: Clos de Cromin; Pommard: Clos Blanc; Volnay: Les Aussy; Chassagne-Montrachet: Les Vergers; Mercurey (red)*
***AOC Communales:** Pommard; Volnay; Meursault; Mercurey (white)*
Whites which need a few years to look their best – Les Vergers is floral and smoky, becoming plumper on contact with air. The wines can be a bit patchy, however, and I have been unimpressed with the reds under this banner.

**Domaine Alain Geoffroy** *Chablis*
*See* W&V, Chablis.

**Domaine de la Gérarde** *Beaujolais*
*See* W&V, Beaujolais, Régnié.

**Domaine François Gerbet** *Côte d'Or*
*Place de la Mairie, 21700 Vosne-Romanée. 16ha*
***Grands Crus:** Vougeot: Clos de Vougeot. Flagey-Echézeaux: Echézeaux*
***1ers Crus:** Vosne-Romanée: Aux Réas,*
*Les Petits Monts; Chambolle-Musigny: Les Plantes*
***AOC Communale:** Vosne-Romanée*
***AOC Régionale:** Bourgogne Hautes-Côtes de Nuits*
Marie-Andrée and Chantal Gerbet make very good wines at this domaine; many of them are sold to private clients. Old vines, low yields and balanced new oak all add up to good quality and good ageing potential.

**Domaine Henri Germain et Fils** *Côte d'Or*
*Rue des Forges, 21190 Meursault. 5ha*
I have not yet experienced the true *frisson* of tasting a fine wine here, but others have had more luck.

**Domaine Jacques Germain** *Côte d'Or*
*Château de Chorey-lès-Beaune, 21200 Beaune. 16.5ha*
***1ers Crus:*** *Beaune: Les Boucherottes, Cent-Vignes, Les Cras, Les Teurons, Vignes-Franches.* ***AOC Communales:*** *Pernand-Vergelesses (white); Château de Chorey-lès-Beaune*
***AOC Régionales:*** *Bourgogne Château Germain (red and white)*
François Germain makes the wines at this domaine, which was established over 100 years ago by his great-grandfather. The wines are uniformly excellent, whether they be simple Chorey-lès-Beaune or grand Beaune Les Teurons. The emphasis is on finesse and perfume – a fact that makes every vintage a pleasure to drink. Yields are low and vinification is in wood *cuves* with quite long vattings of ten to 15 days. The *élevage* is partly in new wood – the amount varies with the *cru*, with the Beaune Premiers Crus being matured in 50% new barrels, the Chorey-lès-Beaune in 25% and the Pernand-Vergelesses in 20%. Exports account for 75% of total sales, with Switzerland and the UK being the best customers.

**Maison Jean Germain** *Côte d'Or*
*9 rue de la Barre, 21190 Meursault. 0.76ha (1ha en métayage)*
***AOC Communales:*** *St-Romain Clos sous le Château; Meursault: La Barre, Meix Chavaux; Puligny-Montrachet: Corvées des Vignes, Les Grands Champs*
This is an impeccably run small domaine with a man at the helm who really knows how to make fine white Côte de Beaune wines. There is a handmade quality about the enterprise, with a very old press but new oak barrels for ageing. M Germain is not a devotee of unnecessarily high alcohol: he likes his wines to be around 12.8%. The wines are bottled at 11–18 months, and they are fruity and supple when quite young, but last beautifully due to the perfect techniques of *élevage*. Jean Germain is also a *négociant* and exports under the name of the Société l'Elevage et Conditionnement des Vins Fins. In this instance, the wines really merit the term *fins*! But it may be the end of an era here.

**Domaine Emilian Gillet** *Mâconnais*
*See* W&V, Mâconnais, Mâcon.

**Domaine Armand Girardin /Le Royer Girardin** *Côte d'Or*
*Route d'Autun, 21630 Pommard. 5ha (1.5ha en métayage)*
***1ers Crus:*** *Beaune: Montrevenots, Clos des Mouches; Pommard: Charmots, Epenots, Grands Epenots, Rugiens*
***AOC Communale:*** *Pommard.* ***AOC Régionale:*** *Bourgogne Rouge*
The running of this estate is being taken over by Armand Girardin's daughter, Aleth Le Royer Girardin, and the latter name will be seen increasingly on the labels. Rich and fruity Pommard

Grands Epenots '89; not absolutely top class, but this is a very good drink nonetheless. However, the same year's Rugiens (under the Royer Girardin name) was weak and dull by comparison. So, tread (or drink) warily, but hopefully, especially when well into the '90s.

**Domaine Jacques Girardin** *Côte d'Or*
*21190 Santenay. 6.5ha*
Wines that mostly age in a dependable fashion.

**Domaine Vincent Girardin** *Côte d'Or*
*Château de la Charrière, route de Chassagne-Montrachet, 21590 Santenay. 14ha*
***1ers Crus:*** *Santenay: Les Gravières, La Maladière, Clos du Beauregard (blanc); Beaune: Clos des Vignes Franches; Chassagne-Montrachet: Les Morgeots.* ***AOC Communales:*** *Savigny-lès-Beaune; Santenay; Maranges; Pommard*
Very good, well-made wines from the domaine and the *négociant* house is also reliable.

**Domaine Yves Girardin** *Côte d'Or*
*21590 Santenay. 11ha*
Good wines, in the same family 'complex'.

**Domaine Girard-Vollot et Fils** *Côte d'Or*
*21420 Savigny-lès-Beaune. 17ha*
***1ers Crus:*** *Savigny-lès-Beaune Les Peuillets, Les Rouvrettes, Les Lavières, Les Serpentières; Pernand-Vergelesses*
***AOC Communales:*** *Pernand-Vergelesses; Aloxe-Corton; Savigny-lès-Beaune.* ***AOC Régionales:*** *Bourgogne Rouge and Blanc*
This domaine produces straight Savigny and Les Peuillets which both have good fruit projection on the nose and a very satisfying taste. All of which means that Girard-Vollot is a very old family domaine worthy of our respect.

**Domaine Bernard et Louis Glantenay** *Côte d'Or*
*route de Vaut, Volnay, 21190 Meursault. 1ha (7ha en fermage).*
***1ers Crus:*** *Pommard: Rugiens, Saussilles; Volnay: Brouillards, Caillerets, Clos des Chênes, Santenots; Puligny-Montrachet: Les Folatières*
***AOC Communales:*** *Pommard; Volnay*
***AOC Régionales:*** *Bourgogne Rouge and Aligoté; Bourgogne Passe-Tout-Grains*
Bernard Glantenay makes very good wine from a fine array of vineyards. They are fairly firm in style, and need several years before they begin to show well.

**Domaine Georges Glantenay et Fils** *Côte d'Or*
*21190 Volnay. 9ha*

**Domaine Michel Goubard** *Côte Chalonnaise*
*See* W&V, Côte Chalonnaise, Montagny.

**Domaine Goud de Beaupuis** *Côte d'Or*
*Château des Moutots, 21200 Chorey-lès-Beaune. 10ha*
***1ers Crus:*** *Ladoix Les Hautes Mourottes; Aloxe-Corton Valozières; Savigny-Vergelesses; Beaune: Clos Ste-Anne, Clos des Vignes Franches, Grèves; Pommard: Epenots, La Chanière*
***AOC Communales:*** *Aloxe-Corton; Chorey-lès-Beaune*
***AOC Régionales:*** *Bourgogne Château des Moutots and Aligoté*
Beaupuis has been a family domaine since 1787, there seems to be a thriving direct sale business to the public from here, although the wines are also exported and sold to restaurants within France. The firm believes in the virtue of old vines to 'assure quality'. Vinification is in oak *cuves* with slow maceration to develop aromas. The grapes are destalked and the wines aged in oak barrels for two years before bottling. The domaine's wines are not to my taste, as the alcohol seems to be all-dominant, masking appellation character.

**Domaine Henri Gouges** *Côte d'Or*
*7 rue du Moulin, 21700 Nuits-St-Georges. 14.5ha*
***1ers Crus:*** *Nuits-St-Georges: Les Chaignots, Clos des Porets monopole, La Perrière, Les Pruliers, Les St-Georges, Les Vaucrains*
***AOC Communale:*** *Nuits-St-Georges*
***AOC Régionales:*** *Bourgogne Rouge and Blanc*
For a number of years, up to and including 1988, this domaine was making weak and uninspiring wines. Since 1989, however, things have improved enormously, and the wines (in '89, '90 and '91) once again have the depth and class that made this name so famous in the first place.

Christian and Pierre Gouges now preside over older vines and have raised their fermentation temperatures (initially in closed vats) and extended maceration time in order to create intense wines that really show the differences between the great Premiers Crus of Nuits. New wood is not part of the scheme of things – the individual *terroirs* and sensitive care do the speaking.

**Château de la Grand'Grange** *Beaujolais*
*See* W&V, Beaujolais, Beaujolais-Villages.

**Domaine des Granges** *Mâconnais*
*See* W&V, Mâconnais, Mâcon.

**Domaine Alain Gras/René Gras-Buisson** *Côte d'Or*
*21190 St-Romain. 14ha*
***AOC Communales****: Meursault; Auxey-Duresses (red and white) and St-Romain (red and white)*
Alain Gras is a proficient winemaker – which is precisely why you can easily lap up both red and white wines from this domaine with impunity.

**Château de la Greffière** *Mâconnais*
*See* W&V, Mâconnais, Mâcon.

**Domaine Albert Grivault** *Côte d'Or*
*7 place du Murger, 21190 Meursault. 4.8ha*
***1ers Crus:** Meursault: Clos des Perrières (monopole), Perrières, Meursault; Pommard Clos Blanc*
Michel Bardet, the son of the owner Mme Bardet-Grivault, now runs this property. Its whites are fermented at 16°C (61°F) and aged in one-third new oak. Classy Meursaults with Puligny-like finesse.

**Domaine Jean Grivot** *Côte d'Or*
*6 rue de la Croix-Rameau, 21700 Vosne-Romanée. 11.26ha (2.77ha en métayage)*
***Grands Crus:** Vougeot: Clos de Vougeot; Flagey-Echézeaux: Echézeaux; Vosne-Romanée: Richebourg. **1ers Crus:** Chambolle-Musigny La Combe d'Orvaux; Vosne-Romanée: Beaux Monts, Brûlées, Chaumes, Les Reignots, Les Rouges, Suchots; Nuits-St-Georges: Boudots, Lavières, Pruliers, Roncières. **AOC Communales:** Vosne-Romanée; Nuits-St-Georges. **AOC Régionales:** Bourgogne Rouge; Bourgogne Grand Ordinaire; Bourgogne Passe-Tout-Grains*
Etienne Grivot was among the first to recognise that Burgundy's soil was over-exploited and he went for a more biological, healthy approach. Guy Accad advised on viticulture here from 1982, and on vinification for the 1987–1991 vintages, but in autumn 1994, he appeared to have left Burgundy. Very good wines, although the Grands Crus can sometimes lack the gloss and opulence of the finest. A maximum of 20% new wood is used for the first year's ageing. Etienne Grivot aims to make wines with the structure to age well, but which are harmonious enough to be drunk young too. Not surprisingly, it is difficult to satisfy both of these aims, but nearly all the domaine's wines achieve this feat. However, genuine burgundy-lovers will be watching how the bottles from the Accad years develop; we shall learn much as a result. It would be difficult to find a domaine with more integrity than this.

**Domaine Robert Groffier Père et Fils** *Côte d'Or*
*4 route des Grands-Crus, 21220 Morey-St-Denis. 7ha*
***Grands Crus:** Gevrey-Chambertin: Chambertin Clos de Bèze; Morey-St-Denis: Bonnes Mares. **1ers Crus:** Chambolle-Musigny: Les Amoureuses, Les Hauts-Doix, Les Sentiers*
***AOC Communale:** Gevrey-Chambertin. **AOC Régionale:** Bourgogne*
This is a domaine that has been on top form from the late 1980s. Much thought and a flexible attitude aid vinification, where controlled high temperatures are sought for maximum colour and extract. 80% new wood is used for the Grands Crus and Les Amoureuses. The recipe works well and the wines are rich and elegant, with long flavours.

**Domaine Gros Frère & Soeur** *Côte d'Or*
*21700 Vosne-Romanée. 15ha*
***Grands Crus:** Vougeot: Clos Vougeot; Flagey-Echézeaux: Grands Echézeaux; Vosne-Romanée: Richebourg*
***AOC Communale:** Vosne- Romanée*
***AOC Régionale:** Bourgogne Hautes-Côtes de Nuits*

The *frère et soeur* here are the brother and sister of Jean Gros (*qv*): Gustave (deceased) and Colette, but the domaine is now run by Bernard, Jean Gros' second son. Very good wines, if not quite up to the superb quality of Domaine Jean Gros.

## Domaine Anne & François Gros *Côte d'Or*

*11 rue des Communes, 21700 Vosne-Romanée. 4.5ha*

***Grands Crus:*** *Vougeot: Clos Vougeot; Flagey-Echézeaux: Echézeaux; Vosne-Romanée: Richebourg.* ***1ers Crus:*** *Vosne-Romanée: Les Barraux; Chambolle-Musigny: La Combe d'Orveau.* ***AOC Communales:*** *Vosne-Romanée; Chambolle-Musigny.* ***AOC Régionale:*** *Bourgogne Rouge*

François is the second brother of Jean Gros (*qv*); his daughter Anne makes the wine here and runs the property with her father. (There is some vexation at the recent appearance of the wines of Domaine Anne-Françoise Gros [*qv*] under that name.) The recent wines are most appealing.

## Domaine Anne-Françoise Gros *Côte d'Or*

*La Garelle, Route d'Ivry, 21630 Pommard. 11.37ha*

***Grands Crus:*** *Flagey-Echézeaux: Echézeaux; Vosne-Romanée: Richebourg.* ***1ers Crus:*** *Vosne-Romanée: Maizières, Aux Réas; Savigny-lès-Beaune: Le Clos des Guettes.* ***AOC Communale:*** *Chambolle-Musigny.* ***AOC Régionale:*** *Bourgogne Hautes-Côtes de Nuits*

Anne-Françoise Gros is the only daughter of Jean Gros (*qv*). She is married to François Parent (Domaine Parent-Gros, Pommard) but produces the Côte de Nuits wines from the vineyards she inherited under her maiden name: an understandable source of confusion with the wines of her cousin Anne and uncle François! Only the Richebourg is made and bottled by Michel Gros – everything else happens at Pommard.

## Domaine Jean Gros/Domaine Michel Gros *Côte d'Or*

*3 rue des Communes, 21700 Vosne-Romanée. 10ha (8ha en fermage)*

***Grands Crus:*** *Vougeot: Clos Vougeot; Vosne-Romanée: Richebourg.* ***1er Cru:*** *Vosne-Romanée Clos des Réas (monopole)* ***AOC Communales:*** *Vosne-Romanée; Chambolle-Musigny; Nuits-St-Georges.* ***AOC Régionales:*** *Bourgogne Hautes-Côtes de Nuits; Bourgogne Rouge*

An excellent domaine (now managed by Jean's son, Michel) where your expectations of grand names are fulfilled. Inevitably the vineyards have been split up in true Burgundian fashion so that even the Burgundians are confused. The large (7ha) Hautes-Côtes de Nuits vineyard was planted some 20 years ago, and its wine is sold under the label of Michel Gros. Traditional methods are followed (except for the use of cultured yeasts), with 100% new oak used in the Grands Crus and Premiers Crus, while 30–50% is the preferred choice for the *villages*. Do try to obtain some of these superb wines as they are distinguished, signature burgundies – well worthy of the praise.

## Domaine Thierry Guerin *Mâconnais*

*See* W&V, Mâconnais, St-Véran.

**Domaine Guffens-Heynen** *Mâconnais*
*See* W&V, Mâconnais, Pouilly-Fuissé.

**Domaine Adrien Guichard** *Mâconnais*
*See* W&V, Mâconnais, Mâcon.

**Domaine Pierre Guillemot** *Côte d'Or*
*21420 Savigny-lès-Beaune. 7.6ha*
***1ers Crus:*** *Savigny-lès-Beaune: Les Jarrons, Les Narbantons, Les Serpentières.* ***AOC Communales:*** *Savigny-lès-Beaune (red and white).* ***AOC Régionale:*** *Bourgogne Rouge*
This estate is reliably consistent in that it produces some very good wines which display a pure Savigny taste of strawberries. Which is, of course, a good indication that Pierre and Jean-Michel Guillemot (who run the estate) really know exactly what the appellation should represent.

**Domaine Guillemot-Michel** *Mâconnais*
*See* W&V, Mâconnais, Mâcon.

**Domaine Antonin Guyon /Domaine Dominique Guyon** *Côte d'Or*
*21420 Savigny-lès-Beaune. 47ha*
***Grands Crus:*** *Gevrey-Chambertin: Charmes-Chambertin; Pernand-Verglesses: Corton-Charlemagne; Aloxe-Corton: Corton-Bressandes, Corton Clos du Roy, Corton-Renardes*
***1ers Crus:*** *Pernand-Vergelesses; Aloxe-Corton; Volnay Clos des Chênes; Meursault-Charmes.* ***AOC Communales:*** *Gevrey-Chambertin; Chambolle-Musigny; Pernand-Vergelesses; Savigny-lès-Beaune; Chorey-lès-Beaune, Beaune*
***AOC Régionales:*** *Hautes-Côtes de Nuits; Bourgogne Aligoté*
In the past, I often found wines of finesse and appellation style from this domaine. However, recent red wines have not had the concentration or style one could expect, while the whites have been better. A disappointing showing from what was an interesting domaine.

**Domaine Haegelen-Jayer** *Côte d'Or*
*47 rue Croix-Rameau, 21700 Vosne-Romanée. 5ha*
***Grands Crus:*** *Vougeot: Clos de Vougeot; Flagey-Echézeaux: Echézeaux.* ***1er Cru:*** *Nuits-St-Georges Les Damodes*
***AOC Communales:*** *Chambolle-Musigny; Vosne-Romanée*
Alfred Haegelen aims to make wines with plenty of extract, with four days' *macération à froide* and three weeks' *cuvaison*. The wines spend 18 months in 50% new wood, are given a light egg-white fining and are not filtered. They are well made. The *village* and Premier Cru wines are fruity and solid without being coarse; the Echézeaux and Clos de Vougeot are rich and supple; very good without being in the grandest league.

**Domaine Thierry Hamelin** *Chablis*
*See* W&V, Chablis.

### Les Caves des Hautes-Côtes *Côte d'Or*

*Route de Pommard, 21200 Beaune. 470ha in 40 appellations.*
*Principal holdings in Hautes-Côtes de Nuits and Hautes-Côtes de Beaune*

The *caves* is a group of 200 producers who sell to *négociants*, the export markets and directly to the public. Their vinification has improved greatly in recent years, and the *élevage* now includes the use of 2,000 oak *pièces*. The wines are fruity, fresh and charming – and good value. The group is a very good source of supply for Burgundy's generic wines, but you can do better elsewhere with your grander appellations.

### Domaine Heresztyn *Côte d'Or*

*27 rue Richebourg, 21220 Gevrey-Chambertin. 11ha*
***Grand Cru:** Morey-St-Denis: Clos St-Denis. **1ers Crus:** Gevrey-Chambertin: Les Champonnets, Les Corbeaux, Les Goulots, La Perrière; Morey-St-Denis Les Millandes. **AOC Communale:** Gevrey-Chambertin. **AOC Régionales:** Bourgogne Rouge and Blanc*

A domaine that is 'on the up', although my experience of its wine is, for the moment, limited.

### Hospices de Beaune *Côte d'Or*

*See* W&V, Côte d'Or, Hospices de Beaune.

### Domaine des Hospices de Nuits-St-Georges *Côte d'Or*

*Rue Henri-Challand, 21700 Nuits-St-Georges. 11.3ha*
*(8.5ha is Nuits-St-Georges); also owns Vosne-Romanée and Prémeaux-Prissey vineyards*
***1er Cru:** Nuits-St-Georges Les Didiers*
***AOC Communale:** Nuits-St-Georges*

The Hospices de Nuits is a charitable foundation dating from the year 1270 and, as with the Hospices de Beaune, its principal concern is the provision of retirement homes for the elderly. The main financial support for this comes from the annual sale of fine wines, which usually takes place on the Sunday before Palm Sunday. As with its far larger counterpart in Beaune, much depends on the *élevage*. When tasting the wines from barrel, they can seem too heavily chaptalised, and I wonder whether the use of 100% new oak, irrespective of the vintage, is wise.

### Domaine Bernard Hudelot /Domaine de Montmain *Côte d'Or*

*21700 Villars-Fontaine. 10ha*
*See* W&V, Côte d'Or, Hautes-Côtes de Nuits.

### Domaine Alain Hudelot-Noëllat *Côte d'Or*

*21640 Vougeot. 10ha*
***Grands Crus:** Vougeot: Clos Vougeot; Vosne-Romanée: Richebourg, Romanée-St-Vivant. **1ers Crus:** Vosne-Romanée: Les Malconsorts, Les Suchots; Chambolle-Musigny Les Charmes; Nuits-St-Georges Les Murgers; Vougeot*
***AOC Communales:** Vosne-Romanée; Chambolle-Musigny*

Absolutely lovely wines. Old vines, no green-pruning, maceration before fermentation and 100% new wood for the Grands Crus seem to be the recipe for these remarkable, deeply fruity wines – plus some genius, too. Instinct seems to guide this man to such excellence, plus respect for the raw material with which he works.

## Cave Coopérative d'Igé *Mâconnais*

*See* W&V, Mâconnais, Mâcon.

## Jaboulet-Vercherre *Côte d'Or*

*5 rue Colbert, 21200 Beaune. 12ha*

***Grand Cru:*** *Aloxe-Corton: Corton-Bressandes.* ***1ers Crus:*** *Beaune: Clos de l'Ecu monopole, Bressandes (white); Pommard Clos de la Commaraine monopole; Volnay-Caillerets; Puligny-Montrachet Les Folatières (white); Santenay Grand Clos Rousseau (red)* ***AOC Communales:*** *Savigny-lès-Beaune Les Vermots (red and white); Pommard Les Petits Noizons*

*Négociant* and domaine owner. I find it hard to identify appellation character in the *négoce* wines: a case of house style dominating the nuances.

## Domaine Lucien Jacob *Côte d'Or*

*21420 Echevronne. 14ha en fermage.*

***1ers Crus:*** *Savigny-Vergelesses (red and white); Beaune: Les Toussaints, Les Cent Vignes.* ***AOC Communale:*** *Savigny-lès-Beaune.* ***AOC Régionales:*** *Bourgogne Hautes-Côtes de Beaune; Bourgogne Aligoté, Bourgogne Rosé*

Well-made, fruity wines; good quality without being exceptional. The Hautes-Côtes de Beaune, however, is excellent.

## Château des Jacques *Beaujolais*

*See* W&V, Beaujolais, Moulin-à-Vent.

## Domaine Paul & Henri Jacqueson *Côte Chalonnaise*

*See* W&V, Côte Chalonnaise, Rully.

## Maison Louis Jadot *Côte d'Or*

*5 rue Samuel-Legay, 21200 Beaune. 62ha*

***Grands Crus:*** *Gevrey-Chambertin: Chambertin-Clos de Bèze, Chapelle-Chambertin; Chambolle Musigny: Le Musigny, Bonnes Mares; Bougeot: Clos de Vougeot; Flagey-Echézeaux: Echézeux; Morey-St-Denis: Clos-St-Denis.* ***1ers Crus:*** *Gevrey-Chambertin: Clos St-Jacques, Les Cazetières, La Combe aux Moines, Lavaux St-Jacques, Estournelles St-Jacques, Les Possenots; Chambolle-Musigny: Les Amoureuses, Les Fuées, Les Feusselottes, Les Baudes; Savigny-lès-Beaune: la Dominode, Les Narbantons, Les Vergelesses, Les Lavières; Beaune: Les Avaux, Les Theurons, les Boudots, Les Cent Vignes, Les Grèves; Puligny-Montrachet: Les Referts, Clos de la Garenne, Champ Gain; Chassagne-Montrachet: Morgeot; Pommard: Clos des Poutures monopole; Volnay: Close de la Barre monopole.* ***AOC Communales:*** *Marsannay, Chambolle-Musigny.* ***AOC Régionale:*** *Côte de Nuits-Villages*

A very important *négociant* business, sold to the owner of its American importer Kobrand in 1985. However, M André Gagey remained in charge, which was a good thing for everybody. After 45 years with the company – he made his first wine there in 1947 and took over as chairman in 1954 – he has handed over the running of Louis Jadot to his equally capable son, Pierre-Henry, who has inherited a tradition of intelligence and integrity. The Jadot family owns plots in some very prestigious vineyards on the Côte de Beaune, and these were substantially enlarged during the 1980s through the acquisition of a large portion of the Clair Daü vineyards on the Côte de Nuits in 1985, and of Maison Champy's vineyards in 1989. Jadot also makes and markets the wines of the Domaine du Duc de Magenta (*qv*).

The white wines are fermented in oak barrels and aged similarly for 12–18 months. The red wines are traditionally vinified in open wooden vats with long vatting, natural yeasts and a floating *chapeau* of skins, *pigeage* and ageing in oak barrels for 18 months to two years. Jacques Lardière, Jadot's technical director, is a 'minimal-interventionist' where winemaking is concerned, and produces wines that nearly always age well. He, rather originally, favours high temperatures for red wine vinification and little new oak, anywhere. Louis Jadot are rebuilding and extending their new winery in time for the 1997 harvest which will allow them to make a much higher proportion of their *négociant* wines themselves.

The almost always excellent results are exported around the world, as well as being sold in France. The grandest names are much sought after, and justifiably, but I have a particular weakness for the Beaune Boucherottes and the Chouacheux. The quality of the reds is perhaps less even than that of the whites; the latter are consistently fine and the best of them are quite glorious. Overall, this is one of Burgundy's most impressive operations.

## Maison Jaffelin — *Côte d'Or*

*Caves du Chapitre, 2 rue Paradis, 21200 Beaune*

The firm now belongs to Boisset (*qv*). It remains to be seen if it can retain a separate identity of any significance.

## Domaine Jacky Janodet — *Beaujolais*

*See* W&V, Beaujolais, Moulin-à-Vent.

## Château de Javernand — *Beaujolais*

*See* W&V, Beaujolais, Chiroubles.

## Domaine Patrick Javillier — *Côte d'Or*

*7 impasse des Acacias, 21190 Meursault. 8.2ha*

***AOC Communales:*** *Savigny-lès-Beaune; Pommard; Meursault; Puligny-Montrachet*

***AOC Régionales:*** *Bourgogne Rouge and Blanc*

Excellent village Meursault wines from a variety of *climats*. A questing attitude to vine-growing and winemaking results in wines that often surpass their category and that repay keeping. There is also a small *négociant* business.

**Domaine Henri Jayer** *Côte d'Or*
**/Domaine Georges Jayer/Domaine Lucien Jayer**
*21700 Vosne-Romanée. 7ha*
***Grands Crus:*** *Flagey-Echézeaux: Echézeaux; Vosne-Romanée: Richebourg.* ***1ers Crus:*** *Vosne-Romanée: Les Brûlées, Cros Parantoux; Nuits-St-Georges Les Murgers*
***AOC Communales:*** *Vosne-Romanée; Nuits-St-Georges*
Retired or not, Henri Jayer continues to advise a number of domaines and fortunately, his rich, opulent wines will be around for a long time. Jayer is a veritable magician: he has made some of the most exciting wines on the entire Côte d'Or. The depth of flavour and sheer impact of fruit are remarkable. His recipe appears simple: grapes are sorted on the vine; complete destalking; cold-maceration for five days before the start of fermentation (natural yeasts only); fining with fresh egg whites; maturing of all wines, except for the straight *villages*, in new oak; bottling by gravity; five analyses during *élevage*. Above all, perhaps, yields are kept low, which is the secret of concentration in fine burgundy. Jayer also made the wines of his brother Georges, but the vines are now with Jayer's nephew, Emmanuel Rouget (*qv*), who runs the Jayer domaine as well as his own. In addition, the Méo-Camuzet domaine (*qv*) is advised by Henri Jayer. Another brother, Lucien, made his own wines, but they are under Rouget control, too. All four labels appear.

**Domaine Jacqueline Jayer** *Côte d'Or*
*21700 Vosne-Romanée.*
Under Domaine Jean Grivot (*qv*); the wines are made by Etienne Grivot. Choose mature bottles with the Jacqueline Jayer name.

**Domaine Robert Jayer-Gilles** *Côte d'Or*
*21700 Magny-lès-Villers. 11ha*
***Grand Cru:*** *Flagey-Echézeaux: Echézeaux.* ***1er Crus:*** *Nuits-St-Georges Les Damodes, Hauts Poirets.* ***AOC Régionales:*** *Côtes de Nuits-Villages; Hautes-Côtes de Nuits, Hautes-Côtes de Beaune, Bourgogne Aligoté, Bourgogne Passe-Tout-Grain*
Robert Jayer makes exemplary wines, even at modest AC level. The prices are far from modest, but this producer always 'delivers the goods'; lots of new oak, but the fruit and character to take it in most, if not all, bottles.

**Domaine Jeannin-Naltet Père & Fils** *Côte Chalonnaise*
*See* W&V, Côte Chalonnaise, Mercurey.

**Domaine François Jobard** *Côte d'Or*
*2 rue de Leignon, 21190 Meursault. 4.91ha*
***1ers Crus:*** *Blagny La Pièce sous le Bois; Meursault: Les Charmes, Les Genevrières, La Pièce sous le Bois, Les Poruzots.* ***AOC Communale:*** *Meursault.* ***AOC Régionales:*** *Bourgogne Blanc, Rouge and Aligoté*
Serious winemaker with flavoursome, elegant Meursaults. No cultured yeasts here; fermentations are not hurried. Sometimes the length of time in cask creates a lack of balance when young. For maximum pleasure, bottles should not be broached too early.

**Domaine Joblot** *Côte Chalonnaise*
*See* W&V, Côte Chalonnaise, Givry.

**Domaine Jean Joliot et Fils** *Côte d'Or*
*Nantoux, 21190 Meursault. 10.5ha*
***1er Cru:*** *Beaune-Boucherottes.* ***AOC Communales:*** *Pommard; Meursault.* ***AOC Régionales:*** *Hautes-Côtes de Beaune; Bourgogne Aligoté, Bourgogne Passe-Tout-Grains; Crémant de Bourgogne*
A highly regarded domaine in the Hautes-Côtes de Beaune. The Joliot family has always had vines: *le souvenir se perd dans la nuit des temps*, as they say. Apart from the Hautes-Côtes wines, there are also small slices of grander appellations, but there is no doubt that the more modest wines are very good value, with the authentic taste of burgundy. Traditional methods are the order of the day, but modified each year according to the quality of the vintage. The aim is to make wines of perfume and finesse allied to reasonable body, maintaining balanced alcohol, tannin and acidity so that the wines can age according to their place in the hierarchy; in other words, keep a Pommard longer than an Hautes-Côtes de Beaune.

**Domaine Philippe Joliet** *Côte d'Or*
*Manoir de la Perrière, 21220 Fixin. 6ha*
***AOC Communale:*** *Fixin Clos de la Perrière*
Both the *manoir* and the Clos de la Perrière vineyard were created by the monks of the Abbey of Cîteaux during the 12th century. Methods at this estate are traditional, with partial destalking according to the year (20–60%). Long vatting (18–20 days) produces wines which keep. *Négociants* receive 35%, 35% is sold on export markets and 30% goes in direct sales. You won't find delicacy, but rather a wine to be drunk in cold weather from big glasses.

**Domaine Claude & Michelle Joubert** *Beaujolais*
*See* W&V, Beaujolais, Beaujolais-Villages.

**Manoir des Journets** *Beaujolais*
*See* W&V, Beaujolais, Chénas.

**Domaine Michel Juillot** *Côte Chalonnaise/Côte d'Or*
*See* W&V, Côte Chalonnaise, Mercurey/Côte d'Or, and Pernand-Vergelesses.

**Caves des Producteurs de Juliénas** *Beaujolais*
*See* W&V, Beaujolais, Juliénas.

**Château de Juliénas/François Condemine** *Beaujolais*
*See* W&V, Beaujolais, Juliénas.

**Labouré-Roi/Cottin Frères** *Côte d'Or*
*21700 Nuits-St-Georges*
A successful *négociant* and important distributor of domaines, dynamically run by the Cottin brothers. Wines are reliable, not exciting, but some of the domaine wines are good. I have been

impressed by the wines of the René Manuel estate, which the firm distributes. The Meursault is oaky and rich, and the unusual red Meursault has a gamey, fruity character to it. Labouré-Roi also usually has a good white Auxey-Duresses, an appellation which is worth finding when Meursault and Puligny look too expensive.

## Domaine Maurice Labruyère *Beaujolais*

*See* W&V, Beaujolais, Moulin-à-Vent.

## Château de Lacarelle *Beaujolais*

*See* W&V, Beaujolais, Beaujolais-Villages.

## Domaine Henri Lafarge *Mâconnais*

*See* W&V, Mâconnais, Mâcon.

## Domaine Michel Lafarge *Côte d'Or*

*Volnay, 21190 Meursault 10ha*
***1ers Crus:*** *Beaune-Grèves; Volnay: Clos du Château des Ducs, Clos des Chênes, Volnay; Pommard: Pézerolles*
***AOC Communales:*** *Volnay; Meursault*
***AOC Regionales:*** *Bourgogne Rouge, Aligoté and Passe-Tout-Grains*

This is a meticulous family domaine, making wine with care and intelligence allied to a strong ecological bias. Complete destalking is practised, and rigorous selection of the grapes if there is an element of rot in the vintage. Vinification lasts approximately ten days and the wine is aged in oak *pièces* for 18 months; about a third of the crop goes into new barrels. Connoisseurs of fine burgundy around the world know that a Volnay from Michel and Frédéric Lafarge is a treat indeed. But then, this family has been domaine-bottling for over 50 years. In years like 1988 and 1995, a comparison between the Clos du Château des Ducs and the Clos des Chênes is revelatory.

## Domaine des Comtes Lafon *Côte d'Or*

*Clos de la Barre, 21190 Meursault. 13.5ha*
***Grand Cru:*** *Puligny-Montrachet: Montrachet*
***1ers Crus:*** *Monthelie Les Duresses; Volnay: Champans, Clos des Chênes, Santenots du Milieu; Meursault: Charmes, Genevrières, Goutte d'Or, Perrières; Puligny-Montrachet: Les Champ Grains*
***AOC Communales:*** *Meursault: Clos de la Barre, Désirée, Meursault*

Lafon is a superb domaine making just the kind of burgundy I like, with an emphasis on organic viticultural methods where possible and a researcher's attitude to winemaking policy. Late harvesting is favoured as well as low yields. Reds age for two years in 30% new wood, whites in up to 40% new oak for 21 months – in one of the coolest cellars in Burgundy. There is no filtration here, and reds and whites usually need years to be at their best. Dominique Lafon is continuing the fine winemaking tradition of his father, René, and there is no greater reputation in Burgundy to uphold.

**Domaine Jean et Gilles Lafouge Père et Fils** *Côte d'Or*
*Rue du Dessous, 21190 Auxey-Duresses. 7ha*
***1ers Crus:*** *Auxey-Duresses: La Chapelle, Le Val, les Duresses, Les Grands Champs, Les Ecusseaux; Meursault Les Chanlins.*
***AOC Communales:*** *Auxey-Duresses red and white; Meursault*
***AOC Régionales:*** *Bourgogne Aligoté; Bourgogne Passe-Tout-Grains*

**Domaine Marquis de Laguiche** *Côte d'Or*
*Puligny-Montrachet, 21190 Meursault. 4.75 ha*
*See* W&V, Côte d'Or, Puligny-Montrachet. The domaine owns the largest parcel of Le Montrachet (*see* Joseph Drouhin [*qv*]). The vineyard is a combination of the domaine itself and Drouhin, but the Beaune team pick the fruit and make the wine. Some of the greatest, most exotic white burgundy comes from here.

**Domaine Laleure-Piot** *Côte d'Or*
*Pernand-Vergelesses, 21420 Savigny-lès-Beaune. 9ha*
***Grands Crus:*** *Pernand-Vergelesses: Corton-Charlemagne; Aloxe-Corton: Corton-Bressandes, Corton-Rognet.*
***1ers Crus:*** *Pernand- Vergelesses: Les Vergelesses, Ile des Vergelesses, Pernand-Vergelesses (red and white); Savigny-lès-Beaune Vergelesses*
***AOC Communales:*** *Pernand-Vergelesses (red and white); Chorey-lès-Beaune.* ***AOC Régionales:*** *Côte de Nuits-Villages Les Bellevues; Bourgogne Aligoté; Bourgogne Passe-Tout-Grains*
Particularly attractive white wines, but good all round. The top wines need an extra bit of inspiration.

**Domaine Lamarche** *Côte d'Or*
*9 rue des Communes, 21700 Vosne-Romanée. 8.5ha (8ha worked)*
***Grands Crus:*** *Vougeot: Clos de Vougeot; Flagey-Echézeaux: Echézeaux, Grands Echézeaux; Vosne-Romanée La Grand'Rue.*
***1ers Crus:*** *Vosne-Romanée: Les Chaumes, Les Malconsorts, Les Suchots, Le Croix Rameua.* ***AOC Communale:*** *Vosne-Romanée.* ***AOC Régionales:*** *Bourgogne Rouge and Aligoté; Bourgogne Passe-Tout-Grains*
A remarkable estate, with some 'golden' land: it is sole owner of La Grand'Rue, sandwiched between La Tâche and the Romanées, and has Grands Echézeaux, Echézeaux and Premier Cru Les Malconsorts. It aims to make wines which keep, wherever possible. Some have appeared somewhat rustic when young, but I have had fine old bottles, and quality is certainly improving under François Lamarche. Recent wines are elegant, but with the underlying concentration of low yields and top *terroir*.

**Lamblin & Fils** *Chablis*
*See* W&V, Chablis.

**Domaine des Lambrays** *Côte d'Or*
*21220 Morey-St-Denis. 13ha*
***Grand Cru:*** *Morey-St-Denis: Clos des Lambrays.*
*1er Cru Morey St-Denis.* ***AOC Communale:*** *Morey-St-Denis*

The virtual monopole Clos des Lambrays (8.66ha) was purchased by Louis and Fabien Saier (*qv*) in 1979 and they started to replant the vineyard from 1980. Under the previous owners nothing had been done for decades, and the average age of the vines was 70 years – a most unhealthy state of affairs. The vineyard is very well situated and was granted Grand Cru status in 1981, but this elevation seems premature based on its performance during the 1980s. The '88, for instance, which should have been outstanding, was not a bad wine as such, but it certainly lacked both Grand Cru class and the quality of the vintage. We must live in hope, however, for there were some splendid vintages in the 1940s and 1950s. The manager here is Thierry Brouin who perhaps needs a little more freedom to make top-class wine. In December 1996, a German businessman bought the domaine.

## Domaine Hubert Lamy-Monnot *Côte d'Or*

*St-Aubin, 21190 Meursault. 9.5ha (4ha en métayage)*
***Grand Cru:*** *Chassagne-Montrachet: Criots-Bâtard-Montrachet.* ***1ers Crus:*** *St-Aubin: Les Castets, Les Frionnes, En Remilly, Les Cortons, Clos de la Chatenière, les Murgers des Dents de Chien: Chassagne-Montrachet: Les Macherelles.* ***AOC Communales:*** *St-Aubin (red and white); Puligny-Montrachet; Chassagne-Montrachet (red and white); Santenay.* ***AOC Régionales:*** *Côte de Beaune-Villages; Hautes-Côtes de Beaune; Bourgogne Rouge, Aligoté and Passe-Tout-Grains*

The Lamy family have been *vignerons* since 1640, and in this case experience has resulted in knowledge of the subject. They know that St-Aubin is ignored by many, so are committed to 'reducing quantity to increase quality'. In this they succeed quite admirably, whether it is in the *village* wines or in the grander appellations. Whites have a stylish, acacia-like quality, while the reds are tannic when young, maturing to become a delicious mouthful. Red grapes are partially destalked, and vatting lasts for ten to 15 days, so you can safely lay down some bottles. They sell to private customers in France, Belgium and Switzerland, but England and the US are also the happy recipients of some of these wines.

## Domaine Lamy-Pillot *Côte d'Or*

*31 route de Santenay, 21190 Chassagne-Montrachet.*
*6ha (12ha partly owned, partly en fermage or en métayage)*
***Grand Cru:*** *Puligny-Montrachet: Le Montrachet.* ***1ers Crus:*** *Blagny La Pièce sous le Bois; St-Aubin: Les Castets, Les Combes; Chassagne-Montrachet: Boudriotte, Clos St-Jean, Morgeot.* ***AOC Communales:*** *St-Aubin: Argillières, Les Pucelles; Chassagne-Montrachet, Chassagne-Montrachet Champs de Morgeot; Santenay Les Charrons; Beaune.* ***AOC Régionales:*** *Bourgogne Rouge; Bourgogne Aligoté La Capitaine; Bourgogne Bas de Madrid; Crémant de Bourgogne*

René Lamy built up this domaine via a succession of plots scattered over a wide variety of appellations. Some wines are rather hard when young and need ageing. There could be a problem with barrels here, which would explain some rather 'off' odours. But other wines have been successful, and there are old vines in the Boudriotte.

**Domaine Hubert Lapierre** *Beaujolais*
*See* W&V, Beaujolais, Chénas.

**Domaine André Large** *Beaujolais*
*See* W&V, Beaujolais, Côte de Brouilly.

**Domaine Laroche** *Chablis*
*See* W&V, Chablis.

**Domaine Jean Lathuilière** *Beaujolais*
*See* W&V, Beaujolais, Brouilly.

**Maison Louis Latour** *Côte d'Or*
*18 rue des Tonneliers, 21200 Beaune. 47ha*
***Grands Crus:*** *Gevrey-Chambertin: Chambertin; Vosne-Romanée: Romanée-St-Vivant Les Quatre Journaux; Pernand-Vergelesses: Corton-Charlemagne; Aloxe-Corton: Corton: Bressandes, Chaumes, Clos de la Vigne au Saint, Clos du Roi, Grancey, Grèves, Perrières, Pougets; Puligny-Montrachet: Chevalier-Montrachet Les Demoiselles*
***1ers Crus:*** *Pernand-Vergelesses: Ile des Vergelesses, Pernand-Vergelesses; Aloxe-Corton: Les Chaillots, Les Fournières, Les Guérets; Pommard: Epenots; Beaune: Clos du Roi, Cras, Grèves, Perrières, Vignes Franches; Volnay-Mittants*
***AOC Communales:*** *Aloxe-Corton; Volnay; Pernand-Vergelesses*
A *négociant* and a domaine owner, dedicated to producing fine bottles of burgundy for the French market and around the world. Their methods have not changed with the times: the grapes are still harvested and transported in traditional wicker baskets; the vinification of the reds takes place in open wooden vats with treading of the floating cap; and they are aged for approximately 18 months in 20% new oak barrels. The whites are fermented in 80% new oak barrels and bottled after approximately 12 months. But if the methods are traditional, all the modern techniques of oenological analysis are also called upon.
Apart from the illustrious domaine wines (which make up about ten per cent of turnover), Côte d'Or red wines are bought young, in barrel, while the whites are bought as grapes and vinified by the firm. The *élevage* of these wines then takes place in Latour's cellars, side-by-side with the wines of the domaine.

Latour's white wines are superlative and, while the reds can go through tricky moments, many age well. Sometimes the reds taste disappointing after bottling – perhaps it is over-zealous filtration. The firm has pasteurised its red wines since the early part of this century. I think it is worth commenting that I have tasted many Burgundian wines which were not pasteurised but which were also perfectly disgusting! On the other hand, I do question whether pasteurisation is really necessary, and would find it very interesting to make a study of similar wines, made with and without the process, tasting them over a number of years to monitor their development. *See also* W&V, Côte Chalonnaise, Montagny.

**Domaine Latour-Giraud** *Côte d'Or*
*21190 Meursault. 10ha*
***1ers Crus:** Meursault: Bouchères, Caillerets (red), Charmes, Genevrières, Perrières, Poruzot; Puligny-Montrachet Champ Canet; Pommard: Refène; Volnay Clos des Chênes; Maranges La Fussière*
***AOC Communale:** Meursault. **AOC Régionale:** Bourgogne Blanc*
Some good wines, but far too patchy, with evidence of oxidation at bottling and perhaps sloppy cellar work. White wines best, especially in the Premiers Crus. Things seem to be looking up, however, with son Jean-Pierre Latour.

**Dominique Laurent** *Côte d'Or*
*21701 Nuits-St-Georges*
A new, small *négociant* with high standards. My experience is too limited to proffer more comment at this stage.

**Domaine Philippe Leclerc** *Côte d'Or*
*Rue des Halles, 21220 Gevrey-Chambertin. 7.34ha*
***1ers Crus:** Gevrey-Chambertin: Les Cazetiers, La Combe aux Moines, Les Champeaux, Les Platières*
***AOC Communales:** Gevrey-Chambertin, Chambolle-Musigny Les Babillaires. **AOC Régionale:** Bourgogne Rouge*
A span of very good, big-impact (too big?), Gevrey wines, with the Premiers Crus kept in 100% new oak, sometimes for over two years. Compare them with brother René Leclerc's (*qv*) domaine, where there is very little new wood. Late harvests are another feature here, as well as a policy of no filtration.

**Domaine René Leclerc** *Côte d'Or*
*28 route de Dijon, 21220 Gevrey-Chambertin. 9ha*
A range of Gevreys which has left me much less impressed than those of brother Philippe (*qv*), some tasting 'dirty'. However, others have had much more pleasant experiences, so I must keep trying.

**Domaine Leflaive** *Côte d'Or*
*Place des Marronniers, 21190 Puligny-Montrachet. 22ha*
***Grands Crus:** Puligny-Montrachet: Le Montrachet, Bâtard-Montrachet, Bienvenues-Bâtard-Montrachet, Chevalier-Montrachet. **1ers Crus:** Puligny-Montrachet: Les Combettes, Clavoillon, Folatières, Les Pucelles*
***AOC Communale:** Puligny-Montrachet*
***AOC Régionales:** Bourgogne Rouge and Blanc*
This is a great, if not *the* great, old family domaine of white burgundy. The legendary Vincent Leflaive died in 1993, and this author would like to pay tribute to his skill, integrity and unmatched *joie de vivre*. The domaine is now admirably run by his daughter, Anne-Claude, a qualified oenologist, with Pierre Morey (*qv*) as winemaker.

Absolute cleanliness in the cellar is a Leflaive maxim, as well as perfectly healthy fruit. Experiments with biodynamics in the vineyards aim to reduce the use of chemical treatments, and considerable effort now goes into reducing yield. The wines are bottled after about 18 months following an *élevage* in oak *pièces* and small stainless-steel vats. Let yourself be seduced by their honeyed smoothness – if you have not already succumbed to the heady bouquet, that is! I do not agree with criticism over a lack of concentration in wines of the late 1980s; we need to see them with the bottle-age they deserve. Leflaive wines are often reined in when young, but they develop into harmonious complexity after a decade. Personally, I have never been disappointed with a wine from the domaine. However, I have been both thrilled and uplifted by countless bottles, in all their aristocratic and multi-dimensional glory. The latest was an extraordinary, gingery Chevalier 1992 at five years old.

## Olivier Leflaive Frères *Côte d'Or*

*Place du Monument, 21190 Puligny-Montrachet. 7.5ha*
***Grand Crus:** Puligny-Montrachet: Montrachet, Chevalier-Montrachet, Criots-Bâtard-Montrachet, Bâtard-Montrachet, Bienvenue-Bâtard-Montrachet; Aloxe-Corton: Corton-Charlemagne*
***1ers Crus:** Puligny-Montracher: Les Pucelles, Les Folatières, Les Champs Gains, Le Champ Canet, Les Referts, Hameaux de Blagny, Les Garennes, Sous le Puits: Meursault: Les Perrières, Les Genevrières, Charmes, Poruzots; Chassagne-Montrachet: La Romanée, les Ruchottes, les Caillerets, les Chaumées, les Vergers, Morgeot; St-Aubin: En Remilly, Le Charmois, Chatenière; Pommard: Rugiens, Epenots, Charmots; Volnay: Caillerets, Clos des Angles, Fremiets; Monthelie; Rully; Montagny*
***AOC Communales:** Auxey-Duresses, St-Romain, Santenay, Pernand-Vergelesses, Puligny-Montrachet, Meursault, Chassagne-Montrachet, Pommard, Volnay, Santenay, Rully, Mercurey*
Olivier Leflaive manages his own *négociant* business and small domaine, specialising in white wines, which are excellent, but producing a few very good reds, too. Franck Grux buys and vinifies the grapes with the utmost care.

## Domaine François Legros *Côte d'Or*

*7 rue François Mignotte, 21700 Nuits-St-Georges.*
*5ha (2ha en métayage, 2ha en fermage)*
***1ers Crus:** Nuits-St-George: les Bousselots, La Rue de Chaux, La Roncière, Les Perrières; Chambolle-Musigny: les Noirots; Morey-St-Denis: Clos Sorbé, Les Millandes, La Riotte; Vougeot: Les Gras*
***AOC Communales:** Nuits-St-Georges, Chambolle-Musigny.*
***AOC Régionales:** Bourgogne red and white*
Barely a track record, as Legros made his first vintage in 1988. He is clearly committed, although consistency may not be there yet.

## Domaine Lejeune *Côte d'Or*

*La Confrérie, 21630 Pommard. 7ha*
***1ers Crus:** Pommard: Rugiens, En Largillière, Poutures*
***AOC Communale:** Pommard. **AOC Régionales:** Bourgogne Rouge, Blanc, Aligoté and Passe-Tout-Grains*

Unusual vinification method using part *macération carbonique*, which gives the wines a very marked 'fruit', but also long *cuvaison* and a high proportion of new oak, both of which make for a fairly tannic frame as well. Wines which will keep and give much pleasure, but classic they are not.

## Domaine Louis Lequin Roussot — *Côte d'Or*

*21590 Santenay. 7ha*
***Grands Crus:*** *Aloxe-Corton: Corton Les Languettes, Corton-Charlemagne; Puligny-Montrachet: Bâtard-Montrachet*
***1ers Crus:*** *Chassagne-Montrachet Morgeot (red and white); Santenay: La Comme, Clos Rousseau, Le Passe-Temps*
***AOC Communales:*** *Nuits-St-Georges; Pommard; Santenay*
***AOC Régionales:*** *Côte de Beaune-Villages; Bourgogne Rouge*
This is a classic example of a fragmented Burgundian vineyard – the Lequins have to rush up and down the Côte at vintage time, which accounts for some patchy quality perhaps. But they make fine wines as well, and that is quite a feat. Fermentations are relatively long, with *foulages* and *remontages*. The *élevage* is in oak barrels, a fifth of which are new. The wines have plenty of verve and keep well, and their AC character is not masked by an excess of oak. Since 1993 the original Lequin Roussot domaine has been split between René and Louis Lequin and we shall see if different styles emerge.

## Domaine René Lequin-Colin — *Côte d'Or*

*10 rue de Lavau, 21590 Santenay. 8ha*
***Grands Crus:*** *Aloxe-Corton: Corton Les Languettes, Corton-Charlemagne; Puligny-Montrachet: Batârd-Montrachet*
***1ers Crus:*** *Chassagne-Montrachet: Morgeot, les Vergers, Caillerets; Nuits-St-Georges: les Brûlées; Pommard: les Noizons; Santenay: Le Passe-Temps, la Comme.* ***AOC Communales:*** *Chassagne-Montrachet, Santenay.* ***AOC Régionale,*** *Bourgogne Rouge*
I have yet to try wines from this newly separate domaine, but it augurs well.

## Etablissements Leroy — *Côte d'Or*

*Auxey-Duresses, 21190 Meursault*
A high-profile *négociant* which also distributes the wines of Domaine Leroy (*qv*). Lalou Bize-Leroy has made a speciality of the *élevage* of fine wines from everywhere in Burgundy. Stocks and prices are high, the style is fairly massive and long-lasting.

## Domaine Leroy — *Côte d'Or*

*21700 Vosne-Romanée. 22ha*
***Grands Crus:*** *Aloxe-Corton: Corton-Charlemagne, Corton-Renardes; Vosne-Romanée: Romanée-St-vivant, Richebourg; Vougeot: Clos the Vougeot; Chambolle-Musigny: Le Musigny; Morey-St-Denis: Clos de la Roche; Gevrey-Chambertin: Latricières-Chambertin; Chambertin*
***1ers Crus:*** *Volnay: Santenots; Savigny-lès-Beaune: Les Narbantons; Nuits-St-Georges: Les Vignerondes, Les Boudots; Vosne-Romanée: Aux Brûlées, les Beaux Monts; Chambolle-Musigny: Les Charmes; Gevrey-*

*Chambertin: Les Combottes.* ***AOC Communales:*** *Auxey-Duresses, Pommard, Nuits-St-Georges, Vosne-Romanée, Chambolle-Musigny, Gevrey-Chambertin.* ***AOC Régionales:*** *Bourgogne Rouge, Blanc, Aligoté*
A formidable new domaine principally created from what was the Domaine Charles Noëllat in Vosne and the Domaine Remy in Gevrey. Lalou-Bize Leroy immediately put her stamp on these remarkable vineyard holdings. These emphatic, expensive wines are a reflection of her commitment and personality. Reducing yields is a religion and bio-dynamic viticultural methods the route to heaven. No de-stemming and long vattings add to the almost essence-like intensity. The 1990s are a legend before their lifetime, in wine-ageing terms, and all the vintages of the 1990s will be fascinating to see develop in bottle. *See also* Domaine d' Auvernay.

## Domaine Thierry Lespinasse *Côte Chalonnaise*

*See* W&V, Côte Chalonnaise, Givry.

## Cave Coopérative de Liergues *Beaujolais*

*See* W&V, Beaujolais, Juliénas.

## Domaine Lieven *Beaujolais*

*See* W&V, Beaujolais, Morgon.

## Domaine Xavier Liger-Belair *Côte d'Or*

*21700 Nuits-St-Georges. 3.5ha*
Owned by Dufouleur Père et Fils, the domaine includes some excellent parcels in Clos Vougeot, Richebourg and Nuits-St-Georges les St-Georges. I do not know the wines.

## Domaine Georges Lignier *Côte d'Or*

*41 Grande-Rue, 21220 Morey-St-Denis. 14ha (15ha en métayage)*
***Grands Crus:*** *Morey-St-Denis: Bonnes Mares, Clos de la Roche, Clos St-Denis.* ***1ers Crus:*** *Gevrey-Chambertin Les Combottes; Morey-St-Denis Clos des Ormes.* ***AOC Communales:*** *Gevrey-Chambertin; Morey-St-Denis; Chambolle-Musigny*
***AOC Régionales:*** *Bourgogne Rouge, Aligoté and Passe-Tout-Grains*
Traditional methods (but total destemming) and *élevage* in 50% new oak for the Grands Crus, 20% for the Premiers Crus. The Premier Cru Clos des Ormes is particularly good value. Usually, but not always, lovely wines which taste delicious from youth.

## Domaine Hubert Lignier *Côte d'Or*

*45 Grande-Rue, 21220 Morey-St-Denis. 6.2ha (1.4ha en métayage)*
***Grands Crus:*** *Gevrey-Chambertin: Charmes-Chambertin; Morey-St-Denis: Clos de la Roche.* ***1ers Crus:*** *Gevrey-Chambertin; Morey-St-Denis; Chambolle-Musigny.* ***AOC Communales:*** *Gevrey-Chambertin; Morey-St-Denis; Chambolle-Musigny.* ***AOC Régionales:*** *Bourgogne Rouge and Aligoté; Bourgogne Passe-Tout-Grains*
Morey-St-Denis of quality, with excellent Clos de la Roche. Hubert Lignier seems to use much more new wood for his Premier Cru and village wines than Georges Lignier (*qv*), and I sometimes feel that the new oak masks the Pinot. But this is a serious domaine.

**Domaine Long-Depaquit** *Chablis*

*See* W&V, Chablis.

**Loron & Fils** *Beaujolais*

*See* W&V, Beaujolais.

**Cave Coopérative de Lugny** *Mâconnais*

*See* W&V, Mâconnais, Mâcon.

**Lupé-Cholet** *Côte d'Or*

*17 avenue Général-de-Gaulle, 21700 Nuits-St-Georges. 28.57ha*

***1ers Crus:** Chablis Vaillons; Nuits-St-Georges Château Gris monopole*

***AOC Régionale:** Clos de Lupé (Bourgogne Rouge monopole)*

A *négociant*, now merged with the huge Bichot (*qv*) of Beaune, the largest exporter of burgundy. But it also owns two monopoles on the Côte de Nuits, although one carries only the Bourgogne Rouge appellation. Methods are traditional, with fermentations in wood *cuves*, and storage in new oak barrels. Bottling, however, is *chez* Bichot in Beaune. Château Gris is an enclave in the Premier Cru Aux Crots, not a Grand Cru as stated on some of the older labels. The new wood is very evident in recent vintages, but the wines should age well. The *négociant* wines seem quite honourable, and its Savigny selections appear particularly successful.

**Domaine Roger Luquet** *Mâconnais*

*See* W&V, Mâconnais, Pouilly-Fuissé.

**Lycée Agricole et Viticole** *Côte d'Or*

*16 avenue Charles-Jaffelin, 21200 Beaune. 19.3ha*
*(8.6ha en fermage, 1ha en métayage)*

***1ers Crus:** Beaune: Les Bressandes, Les Champs Pimont, La Montée Rouge, Les Perrières, Beaune*

***AOC Communales:** Beaune (red and white); Puligny-Montrachet; Côte de Beaune*

***AOC Régionales:** Bourgogne Hautes-Côtes de Beaune (Savigny) (red and white); Bourgogne Aligoté; Bourgogne Passe-Tout-Grains (red and rosé)*

These are the wines made by the future guardians of the reputation of Burgundy, because so many growers' sons and daughters study here. But students of viticulture and oenology come from all over France and there are exchange programmes with other countries. The standard is high and great care is taken. They sell the wine direct by mail order in France, and a little is exported to Belgium and Switzerland, but some goes *en vrac* (in bulk) to the local *négoce*. They make excellent Beaune Premier Cru, such as Champs Pimont, Perrières and Montée Rouge. The Lycée Agricole et Viticole was founded in 1884.

**Domaine Bertrand Machard de Gramont** *Côte d'Or*

*21700 Nuits-St-Georges. 4ha*

Tiny quantities of very good-quality Nuits-St-Georges are made at this estate.

**Domaine Machard de Gramont** *Côte d'Or*
*6 rue Gassendi, 21700 Nuits-St-Georges. 20ha*
*(2.7ha en métayage)*
***1ers Crus:*** *Nuits-St-Georges: Damodes, Hauts Pruliers, Vallerots; Pommard Le Clos Blanc; Savigny-lès-Beaune: Vergelesses, Guettes; Beaune Les Chouacheux*
***AOC Communales:*** *Chambolle-Musigny; Nuits-St-Georges; Aloxe-Corton; Savigny-lès-Beaune; Beaune; Pommard; Puligny- Montrachet*
***AOC Régionales:*** *Bourgogne Rouge and Blanc*
This is a comparatively new domaine, which has gone through all the vicissitudes of Burgundian family troubles. But what remains of the original estate is hardly insignificant, and the wines are often models of what burgundy should be all about. The emphasis here is on fruit rather than acquired weight, and consequently there is always a lovely Pinot Noir bouquet that is not overwhelmed by alcohol. Vattings are long, with ageing in oak barrels, 30–50% of which are new. There is some good appellation character here. The cellars are in Prissey, and the wines are widely exported.

**Domaine du Duc de Magenta** *Côte d'Or*
*Abbaye de Morgeot, Chassagne-Montrachet, 21190 Meursault. 12ha*
***1er Cru:*** *Puligny-Montrachet Clos de la Garenne*
***AOC Communales:*** *Auxey-Duresses; Chassagne-Montrachet Clos de la Chapelle; Meursault Meix Chavaux*
Sole owner of the former monastic vineyard of Clos de la Chapelle beside the old abbey of Morgeot. The red Morgeot can last well but there are patchy bottles from this domaine. Maison Louis Jadot (*qv*) now supervises both the making and the marketing of 80% of the domaine's wines, so there is much greater consistency and quality here.

**Domaine Pierre Mahuet** *Mâconnais*
*See* W&V, Mâconnais, Mâcon.

**Domaine Maillard Père & Fils** *Côte d'Or*
*2 rue Joseph-Bard, 21200 Chorey-lès-Beaune. 18ha*
***Grand Cru:*** *Aloxe-Corton: Corton-Renardes, Corton*
***1ers Crus:*** *Aloxe-Corton, les Grandes Lolières; Beaune-Grèves*
***AOC Communales:*** *Aloxe Corton; Beaune; Savigny-lès-Beaune; Chorey-lès-Beaune; Ladoix Les Chaillots; Meursault*
***AOC Régionales:*** *Côte de Beaune-Villages, Aligoté*
This domaine makes Chorey-lès-Beaune which has a delicious red-fruit flavour. Sure value.

**Domaine de la Maladière /Domaine William Fèvre** *Chablis*
*See* W&V, Chablis.

**Domaine des Malandes** *Chablis*
*See* W&V, Chablis.

**Domaine Michel Mallard & Fils** *Côte d'Or*
*21550 Ladoix-Serrigny. 13ha*
***Grand Crus:*** *Aloxe-Corton: Corton Les Maréchaudes, Renardes*
***1er Crus:*** *Ladoix; Savigny-lès-Beaune: Serpentières*
Some good wines, especially those from Ladoix, but grander wines seem to fall down.

**Château de la Maltroye** *Côte d'Or*
*Chassagne-Montrachet, 21190 Meursault. 16ha*
***Grand Cru:*** *Puligny-Montrachet: Bâtard-Montrachet*
***1ers Crus:*** *Chassagne-Montrachet (red and white); Santenay (red and white).* ***AOC Communales:*** *Chassagne-Montrachet (red and white).* ***AOC Régionales:*** *Bourgogne Rouge and Aligoté*
There were many disappointments here in the '70s and '80s, but this domaine, in the hands of a new generation, is becoming a good source again, mainly for whites, although the reds can be worthwhile, too.

**Domaine Manciat-Poncet** *Mâconnais*
*See* W&V, Mâconnais, Mâcon.

**Domaine Manière-Noirot** *Côte d'Or*
*4 rue Grande Velle, Vosne-Romanée, 21700 Nuits-St-Georges*
*10ha (3ha en fermage)*
Cold maceration and new oak in style – a useful address.

**Domaine Maurice Maratray**
*21550 Ladoix-Serrigny. 12ha*
Maratray can often be a source of good wines, but choose carefully even so.

**Domaine Marchand-Grillot et Fils** *Côte d'Or*
*13 rue du Gaizot, 21220 Gevrey-Chambertin. 8ha*
***Grand Cru:*** *Gevrey-Chambertin: Ruchottes-Chambertin*
***1ers Crus:*** *Gevrey-Chambertin: Petite Chapelle, Perrières*
***AOC Communales:*** *Gevrey-Chambertin; Chambolle-Musigny; Morey-St-Denis*
At the time of tasting, these were well-made, supple, forward and fruity burgundies; drinkable with very little bottle-age, but all may not be rosy at present, for reasons I do not know.

**Jean Maréchal** *Côte Chalonnaise*
*See* W&V, Côte Chalonnaise, Mercurey.

**Domaine Maroslavac-Léger** *Côte d'Or*
*21190 Puligny-Montrachet. 8ha*
***1ers Crus:*** *St-Aubin: Les Murgers des Dents de Chien; Puligny-Montrachet: Les Champ Gains, Les Folatières, Les Combettes; Auxey-Duresses: Les Bretterins*
***AOC Communales:*** *Auxey-Duresses; Meursault; Puligny-Montrachet; Chassagne-Montrachet (red and white)*
***AOC Régionales:*** *Bourgogne Rouge, Blanc and Aligoté*

Quality somewhat up and down. I recently tasted a dull, one-dimensional '88 Puligny-Montrachet, but also a light, very pretty, honeyed Premier Cru Les Folatières. So, choose with care.

### Domaine Maroslavac-Trémeau *Côte d'Or*

*21190 Puligny-Montrachet. 15.5ha*

A pair of quite awful Puligny-Montrachets (*village* and Premier Cru Champs Gains) suggests this source may be best avoided – at least in association with the Compagnie des Vins d'Autrefois! Maybe I was unlucky.

### Domaine des Marronniers *Chablis*

*See* W&V, Chablis.

### Domaine Tim Marshall *Côte d'Or*

*47 rue Henri-Challand, 21700 Nuits-St-Georges. 1.9ha*

***1ers Crus:*** *Chambolle-Musigny: Les Cras, Les Feusselottes; Nuits-St-Georges: Argillats, Perrières*

***AOC Communale:*** *Chambolle-Musigny Les Athets*

***AOC Régionales:*** *Bourgogne Rouge, Blanc and Aligoté; Bourgogne Grand Ordinaire*

Tiny domaine, but the wines here have very good appellation character. Until 1989, the wines were aged in 100% new wood, but from 1990 onwards, only 40–50% is used. Nicely wrought, elegant and clear-cut medium-weight wines with especially distinctive flavours from the Nuits-St-Georges.

### Domaine Maurice Martin *Mâconnais*

*See* W&V, Mâconnais, St-Véran.

### Domaine Jean Mathias *Mâconnais*

*See* W&V, Mâconnais, Pouilly-Vinzelles.

### Domaine Joseph, Pierre et Thierry Matrot *Côte d'Or*

*21190 Meursault. 18ha*

***1ers Crus:*** *Volnay-Santenots; Meursault: Blagny, Charmes, Perrières; Blagny La Pièce sous le Bois; Puligny-Montrachet: Les Chalumeaux, Les Combettes.* ***AOC Communales:*** *Auxey-Duresses; Meursault.* ***AOC Régionales:*** *Bourgogne Blanc and Aligoté*

A typically Burgundian fragmented domaine, with the biggest parcel in straight Meursault, although the red Blagny La Pièce sous le Bois is also made in significant quantities, and is well worth finding. The red grapes are destalked, the amount varying between 60–100% according to the year. Vatting lasts for six to ten days in enamel-lined *cuves* for the reds and the wines are matured in oak barrels (with no new wood). The reds are fined with albumen, the whites with bentonite, and both are filtered before bottling. Sales in bottle are to private customers and restaurants in France, the US, England, Belgium, Germany, Holland, Switzerland, etc. The wines do not show great breeding, but often have full flavour and character and decisive appellation individuality.

**Prosper Maufoux** *Côte d'Or*
*21590 Santenay. Domaine St-Michel*
***1er Cru:*** *Santenay.* ***AOC Communales:*** *Puligny-Montrachet; Santenay; Château de Viré (Mâcon) monopole.* ***AOC Régionales:*** *Côte de Beaune-Villages; Bourgogne Rouge and Aligoté*
*Négociants-éleveurs* based in Santenay. Although the head of the firm, Pierre Maufoux, jointly runs the Domaine St-Michel with Michel Gutrin, he is also dedicated to selecting and maturing wines from all over the Côte d'Or. A firm believer in wood-ageing, he matures his white wines in oak barrels for 12–15 months, and the reds for a minimum of 18 months. Sales of red and white are equally divided – the reds are not always consistent, but some of the whites are gloriously rich. Maufoux wines are found throughout the world, and also appear under the name of Marcel Amance. At the end of 1994, the *négociant* house was sold to the American importer, Robert Fairchild.

**Domaine Maume** *Côte d'Or*
*56 route de Beaune, 21220 Gevrey-Chambertin. 4ha*
***Grands Crus:*** *Gevrey-Chambertin: Mazis-Chambertin, Charmes-Chambertin*
***1ers Crus:*** *Gevrey-Chambertin: Les Champeaux, Lavaux St-Jacques*
***AOC Communale:*** *Gevrey-Chambertin*
These wines are big, sometimes rather inky and tannic, but they last well, especially top Gevrey *crus* Lavaux St-Jacques and Mazis-Chambertin. Expect concentration and ripeness.

**Domaine Mazilly Père & Fils** *Côte d'Or*
*Meloisey, 21190 Meursault. 12ha*
***1ers Crus:*** *Beaune: Les Cent-Vignes, Les Montrevenots, Les Vignes-Franches; Pommard Les Poutures.* ***AOC Communales:*** *Pommard; Monthelie Le Clou des Chênes; Volnay; Meursault*
***AOC Régionales:*** *Bourgogne Hautes-Côtes de Beaune: red, white, Le Clos, Clos du Bois Prévot; Bourgogne Passe-Tout-Grains*
This is principally an Hautes-Côtes de Beaune domaine, with small parcels in grander appellations. Vinification is long and the wines are tannic when young. *Elevage* lasts 12–18 months, with the wines stored in barrels or bigger oak *foudres*. There have been generations of Mazillys owning vineyards and making wine here, only now they export half of production. Some of the Hautes-Côtes wines are Tastevinés and are very pleasant at two to three years; but quality can be rather patchy.

**Domaine du Meix-Foulot/ Yves de Launay** *Côte Chalonnaise*
*See* W&V, Côte Chalonnaise, Mercurey.

**Domaine Méo-Camuzet** *Côte d'Or*
*21700 Vosne-Romanée. 15ha (some vineyards partially en métayage)*
***Grands Crus:*** *Vougeot: Clos de Vougeot; Aloxe-Corton: Corton; Vosne-Romanée: Richebourg.* ***1ers Crus:*** *Vosne-Romanée: Cros Parentoux, Boudots, Les Brûlées, Chaumes; Nuits-St-Georges*

*Murgers.* ***AOC Communales:*** *Vosne-Romanée; Nuits-St-Georges* ***AOC Régionales:*** *Bourgogne Rouge; Bourgogne Hautes-Côtes de Nuits Blanc, Bourgogne Passe-Tout-Grains*

This is a domaine with excellent vineyards and a reputation as one of Burgundy's top sources. It is now managed by Jean-Nicolas Méo who carries out the vinification with the advice of Henri Jayer (*qv*), making impressive wines of similar depth of flavour and impact of fruit. Méo attaches great importance to low yields, which accounts for the concentration of his wines. He also uses, as Jayer did, 100% new oak, except for Bourgogne Rouge (50%) and Passe-Tout-Grains (second year oak). There is no filtering, and bottling is from each cask. Outstanding wines have been made in 1988, 1989 (drink this before the others), 1990 and 1991 and I place this domaine at the pinnacle of Burgundy's achievements.

## Domaine Prince Florent de Mérode *Côte d'Or*

*Château de Serrigny, 21550 Ladoix-Serrigny. 11.38ha*

***Grands Crus:*** *Aloxe-Corton: Corton-Bressandes, Corton Clos du Roi, Corton-Maréchaudes, Corton-Renardes.* ***1ers Crus:*** *Ladoix Hautes Mourottes; Aloxe-Corton.* ***AOC Communales:*** *Ladoix Les Chaillots; Pommard Clos de la Platière*

There are certainly some prime sites in this domaine. It was a maison forte in the time of the Ducs de Bourgogne; the Château de Serrigny was rebuilt in 1700 by Pierre Brunet, president of the Chambre des Comptes in Paris. Since then it has always been inherited, never sold. The grapes are sorted on arrival, eliminating anything that does not come up to standard, and destalked. The domaine itself considers that the wines should not be drunk before four to five years and they eschew filtering. In France and Belgium the wines are sold only through the Savour Club, a powerful force in mail-order sales. They are also exported to the principal markets. Perhaps the wines could be more impressive still, but they have certainly improved.

## Domaine Mestre Père & Fils *Côte d'Or*

*Place du Jet-d'Eau, 21590 Santenay. 18ha*

***Grand Cru:*** *Aloxe-Corton: Corton.* ***1ers Crus:*** *Ladoix Clou d'Orge; Chassagne-Montrachet: Morgeot, Tonton Marcel monopole; Santenay: Beaurepaire, Clos Faubard, Comme, Gravières, Gravières Clos Tavannes, Passe-Temps (red and white).* ***AOC Communales:*** *Ladoix Côte de Beaune; Aloxe-Corton; Chassagne-Montrachet; Maranges; Santenay.* ***AOC Régionale:*** *Bourgogne Rouge*

An important Santenay domaine, built up by the fifth generation of a family of *vignerons*. Particularly strong on Premiers Crus. Vinification lasts eight to ten days with quite high temperatures and *remontages* twice a day. Ageing lasts 12–24 months in oak barrels, some of which are new. They stress the fact that they bottle in strictly controlled, clean conditions – an imperative with all wines – but Burgundian grape varieties are noticeably vulnerable to sloppy handling. Half of the crop is sold in bulk to local *négociants*, and half is now sold in bottle, divided between sales to the home market and export. Some wines have appeared rather dry and tired at an early stage, with a marked lack of colour, but other tasters have been more lucky.

**Domaine du Château de Meursault** *Côte d'Or*
*21190 Meursault. 60ha*
***1ers Crus:*** *Savigny-lès-Beaune Peuillets; Beaune: Grèves, Cent-Vignes, Toussaint; Pommard: Clos des Epenots, Pommard; Volnay Clos des Chênes; Meursault: Charmes, Perrières, Château de Meursault; Puligny-Montrachet Champ Canet*
***AOC Communales:*** *Aloxe-Corton; Savigny-lès-Beaune (red and white); Beaune; Pommard; Meursault*
***AOC Régionales:*** *Bourgogne Clos du Château; Bourgogne Rouge; Bourgogne Aligoté*
A great domaine owned by Patriarche (*qv*), the large Beaune *négociant*. It combines the modern (stainless steel, the latest presses) with the traditional (maturing in new-oak casks). White grapes are pressed and then fermented in new barrels, and red grapes are crushed, partially destalked, fermented for eight to 12 days and then aged in new-oak barrels. The domaine sells direct, including to all those who visit the beautiful *caves*, or cellars, to restaurants and on the export market. It is a pity that all the Meursault is blended into the Château de Meursault – the quality is acceptable, but depth and individuality could be attained with a different policy.

**Domaine Méziat Père et Fils** *Beaujolais*
*See* W&V, Beaujolais, Chiroubles.

**Domaine Bernard Michel** *Côte Chalonnaise*
*See* W&V, Côte Chalonnaise, Montagny.

**Domaine Louis Michel/**
**Domaine de la Tour Vaubourg** *Chablis*
*See* W&V, Chablis.

**Domaine René Michel** *Mâconnais*
*See* W&V, Mâconnais, Mâcon.

**Domaine Alain Michelot** *Côte d'Or*
*21700 Nuits-St-Georges. 4.2ha (3.5ha en métayage)*
***1ers Crus:*** *Nuits-St-Georges: Les Cailles, Aux Chaignots, Aux Champs Perdrix, Les Porets St-Georges, La Richemone, Les St-Georges, Les Vaucrains; Morey St-Denis Les Charrières*
***AOC Communales:*** *Morey-St-Denis; Nuits-St-Georges*
***AOC Régionale:*** *Bourgogne Rouge*
Alain Michelot is a guardian of Nuits quality and character, and thus prefers long, slow fermentations and gradual chaptalisation (when needed) which are followed by 20 months in barrel. The amount of new wood varies with the year, and the balance of these wines reflects the sage winemaking that goes into them. The individual flavours of the best *climats* in Nuits are well-demonstrated at this domaine.

**Domaine Michelot** *Côte d'Or*
*21190 Meursault. 21ha (2ha en métayage)*
***1ers Crus:*** *Meursault: Charmes, Genevrières, Perrières; Santenay: Les Gravières, Poruzot; Puligny-Montrachet: Les Garennes, Les Folatières.* ***AOC Communales:*** *Puligny-Montrachet, Meursault.* ***AOC Régionales:*** *Bourgogne Rouge, Blanc and Aligoté*
This large domaine is now run by Bernard Michelot's son-in-law, Jean-François Mestre. It produces barrel-fermented white wines that are aged for 12 months in up to one-third new oak... In essence, they are excellent wines – some of my best Meursault experiences, as a matter of fact. The quality dipped a bit at one point but is now back on track.

**Domaine François Mikulski** *Côte d'Or*
*5 rue de Leignon, 21190 Meursault. 6ha*
***1ers Crus:*** *Volnay Santenots; Meursault: Caillerets, Charmes, Genevrières, Poruzots.* ***AOC Communales:*** *Meursault (red and white).* ***AOC Régionales:*** *Bourgogne Rouge, Blanc, Aligoté and Crémant de Bourgogne*
François Mikulski is Pierre Boillot's (*qv*) nephew. He founded this new domaine in 1992 with a small inheritance of vines. If Domaine Mikulski does not yet have a track record, it probably soon will.

**Domaine Pierre Millot-Battault** *Côte d'Or*
*7 rue Charles-Giraud, 21190 Meursault. 8ha*
Pierre Millot-Battault has a reputation for making good wines, especially the Meursault-Charmes. The reds are influenced by new oak.

**GAEC René & Christian Miolane** *Beaujolais*
*See* W&V, Beaujolais, Beaujolais-Villages.

**Château de Mirande** *Mâconnais*
*See* W&V, Mâconnais, Mâcon.

**Maison P Misserey** *Côte d'Or*
*3 rue des Seuillets, 21700 Nuits-St-Georges. 6ha*
***Grand Cru:*** *Vougeot: Clos de Vougeot.* ***1ers Crus:*** *Gevrey-Chambertin Lavaux St-Jacques; Nuits-St-Georges: Les Vaucrains, Les Cailles, Les St-Georges, Aux Vignesrondes, Aux Murgers*
This estate produces some big but, on the whole, rather unexciting wines. That they are keepers is indisputable – but be advised not to hold your breath!

**Domaine Thomas Moillard** *Côte d'Or*
*2 rue F-Mignotte, 21700 Nuits-St-Georges. 30ha*
***Grands Crus:*** *Gevrey-Chambertin: Chambertin, Chambertin Clos de Bèze; Morey-St-Denis: Bonnes Mares; Vougeot: Clos de Vougeot; Vosne-Romanée: Romanée St-Vivant; Pernand-Vergelesses: Corton-Charlemagne; Aloxe-Corton: Corton Clos du Roi*
***1ers Crus:*** *Vosne-Romanée: Les Beaux Monts, Les Malconsorts;*

*Nuits-St-Georges: Clos des Grandes Vignes, Clos de Thorey, Les Murgers, Les Porets St-Georges, Les Richemones; Beaune Les Grèves* **AOC Communales:** *Nuits-St-Georges, Savigny-lès-Beaune red and white.* **AOC Régionales:** *Bourgogne Hautes-Côtes de Nuits, Haute-Côtes de Beaune Blanc*

Moillard-Grivot is the large *négociant* business, but there does seem to be distinct improvement in the domaine wines (Thomas-Moillard), some of which combine structure with fat in quite a majestic way. However, I have not found progress to be uniform.

## Mommessin/Clos de Tart *Côte d'Or*

*21220 Morey-St-Denis. 7.5ha*

**Grand Cru:** *Morey-St-Denis: Clos de Tart.*

**1er Cru:** *Morey-St-Denis La Forge*

Mommessin is first and foremost an important *négociant* firm dealing in wines from the Mâconnais and the Beaujolais, as well as *vins de marque*. In 1994, the two firms of Mommessin and Thorin merged and now they are owned by Boisset (*qv*). The proverbial jewel in the crown is the Morey-St-Denis Grand Cru Clos de Tart, which it has owned since 1932 and is still owned by the Mommessin family (i.e. not by Boisset). Founded in the 12th century by the Benedictines de Tart le Haut, this is the only *clos* in Burgundy which has never been divided since its foundation. There is usually no destemming, with fermentation in cement *cuves* and *élevage* in 100% new oak. Clos de Tart can age magnificently, with heady tastes and aromas, but it also has finesse and elegance. However, there seems to be no real distinction here and one wishes the domaine could settle with a brilliant and proven winemaker – the *terroir* deserves it.

## Domaine de la Monette *Côte Chalonnaise*

*See* W&V, Côte Chalonnaise, Mercurey.

## Domaine Mongeard-Mugneret *Côte d'Or*

*14 rue de la Fontaine, 21700 Vosne-Romanée*

*21ha (partly en fermage)*

**Grands Crus:** *Vougeot: Clos Vougeot; Flagey-Echézeaux: Echézeaux, Grands Echézeaux; Vosne-Romanée: Richebourg*

**1ers Crus:** *Vougeot: Les Cras; Vosne-Romanée: Les Orveaux, Les Petits Monts, Les Suchots; Nuits-St-Georges Les Boudots; Savigny-lès-Beaune Les Narbentons.* **AOC Communales:** *Fixin; Vosne-Romanée; Nuits-St-Georges; Puligny-Montrachet, Savigny-lès-Beaune.* **AOC Régionales:** *Bourgogne Hautes-Côtes de Nuits; Bourgogne Rouge, Rosé and Blanc; Bourgogne Passe-Tout-Grains*

This domaine is making better and better wines. There are some old vines and chemical fertiliser is not used. Maceration is carried out before fermentation, which lasts 13–15 days. Now, only natural yeasts are used and fermentation temperatures can go high; extensive *pigeage* always accompanies this stage. Half the barrels are new each year. The wines are incredible mouthfuls, if not the ultimate in breed. The Grands Crus are immensely spicy and concentrated, while Les Suchots often displays cherry notes.

**Domaine Elie Mongénie** *Beaujolais*
*See* W&V, Beaujolais, St-Amour.

**Domaine de Mongrin** *Beaujolais*
*See* W&V, Beaujolais, St-Amour.

**Domaine Jean-Marc Monnet** *Beaujolais*
*See* W&V, Beaujolais, Juliénas.

**Domaine René Monnet** *Beaujolais*
*See* W&V, Beaujolais, Juliénas.

**Domaine Jean Monnier & Fils** *Côte d'Or*
*21 rue du 11 novembre, 21190 Meursault. 17ha*
***1ers Crus:*** *Beaune; Pommard, Pommard Epenots Clos de Cîteaux; Meursault: Charmes, Genevrières*
***AOC Communales:*** *Meursault (red and white); Puligny-Montrachet.* ***AOC Régionales:*** *Bourgogne Rouge, Blanc and Aligoté*
An impeccably run domaine, which has been gradually increasing in size through the acquisition of small parcels. In 1950, Jean Monnier bought the Clos de Cîteaux in Pommard Epenots – three hectares which once belonged to the monks of Cîteaux. Tradition is followed in the vinification, and all the wines, even the *petites appellations*, are aged in oak barrels, with a smallish proportion of new *fûts*. The result is wines which have immense finesse and style, although others seem to have surpassed them now.

**Domaine René Monnier** *Côte d'Or*
*6 rue du Docteur-Rolland. 21190 Meursault. 16ha*
***1ers Crus:*** *Beaune: Cent-Vignes, Toussaints; Volnay Clos des Chênes; Meursault Charmes; Puligny-Montrachet Les Folatières; Maranges Clos de la Fussière monopole*
***AOC Communales:*** *Pommard Les Vignots; Meursault Les Chevalières, Meursault Le Limozin; Puligny-Montrachet; Santenay Les Charmes.* ***AOC Régionales:*** *Bourgogne Rouge, Blanc and Aligoté*
This domaine has been built up through the shrewd acquisitions of each generation of Monniers. White wines are vinified and aged in barrels of three origins: Allier, Vosges and Nevers, with one-third new barrels for each *cuvée*. The wines are bottled around June. The reds undergo 12–14 days of fermentation, after about two-thirds of the stalks are removed, varying with the year. *Pigeage* takes place twice a day, after the must has started to ferment, with *remontages* which cause the yeasts to multiply through the process of oxygenation. The wines are then stocked in Limousin oak barrels until the end of the malolactic fermentation. Quality is good.

**Domaine Monrozier** *Beaujolais*
*See* W&V, Beaujolais, Fleurie.

**Domaine Monternot** *Beaujolais*
*See* W&V, Beaujolais, Beaujolais-Villages.

**Domaine de Montgenas** *Beaujolais*

*See* W&V, Beaujolais, Fleurie.

**Château de Monthelie** *Côte d'Or*

*21190 Monthelie. 9ha*

***1ers Crus:*** *Château de Monthelie-Monthelie sur la Velle; Rully Meix Caillet.* ***AOC Communale:*** *Rully Agneux*

The red wines here are aged for 18 months in ten to 15% new oak, the white sees much less new wood and for a year only. The red Château de Monthelie needs, and repays, keeping.

**Domaine Monthelie-Douhairet** *Côte d'Or*

*21190 Monthelie. 6ha*

***1ers Crus:*** *Pommard Fremiets; Volnay Champans; Meursault Santenots (white); Monthelie Les Duresses*

***AOC Communale:*** *Monthelie.* ***AOC Régionale:*** *Bourgogne Aligoté*

A new cellar manager and the advice of André Porcheret mean that the wines of Monthelie-Dourhairet are both cleaner and less rustic than they used to be. The Meursault Santenots is a light but honeyed wine, while the Volnay Champans is perfumed and gently oaky. The domaine's Aligoté can be good, too. All of which makes this a reliable producer.

**Domaine de Montille** *Côte d'Or*

*Volnay, 21190 Meursault. 7ha*

***1ers Crus:*** *Pommard: Grands Epenots, Pézerolles, Rugiens; Volnay: Champans, Mitans, Taille Pieds.* ***AOC Régionale:*** *Bourgogne Rouge*

This domaine specialises in tight, concentrated, tannic wines which need years to mellow but are well worth the wait. Hubert de Montille and his son, Etienne, make the wines by long *cuvaisons*, temperatures over 30˚C (86˚F), and ageing for 18 months to two years in 25% new wood. *Vins de garde* are the result, with low alcohol for burgundy and great evolving flavour. The essence of burgundy.

**Domaine de Montmeron** *Beaujolais*

*See* W&V, Beaujolais, Beaujolais-Villages.

**J Moreau & Fils** *Chablis*

*See* W&V, Chablis.

**Domaine Bernard Morey** *Côte d'Or*

*Chassagne-Montrachet, 21190 Meursault. 11ha*

***1ers Crus:*** *Beaune Les Grèves; St-Aubin Charmois; Chassagne-Montrachet: Les Caillerets, Les Embrazées, Morgeot, Les Baudines; Santenay Grand-Clos-Rousseau*

***AOC Communales:*** *Chassagne-Montrachet (red and white)*

***AOC Régionales:*** *Bourgogne Rouge and Blanc*

Bernard Morey is a firm advocate of late harvesting for maximum ripeness, and plenty of lees stirring for the white wines. Very good wines, the whites above all, but the reds are good, too. Both are aged in 25% new wood: reds for 18 months, whites 12 months.

## Domaine Jean-Marc Morey *Côte d'Or*

*21190 Chassagne-Montrachet. 6ha (2ha en métayage)*
***1ers Crus:** Beaune Grèves; Chassagne-Montrachet: Caillerets, Clos St-Jean (red), Champs Gains (red and white), Les Chaumées, Chenevottes; St-Aubin Charmois; Santenay: Grand Clos Rousseau, Les Cornières. **AOC Communale:** Chassagne-Montrachet (red)*
***AOC Régionales:** Bourgogne Rouge, Blanc and Aligoté*
Bernard Morey's (*qv*) brother, Jean-Marc, makes soft, full and perfumed white burgundies at his domaine, which spend one year in 20% new wood. The reds are usually also to be recommended. Both brothers dislike clones and favour natural yeasts.

## Domaine Marc Morey et Fils *Côte d'Or*

*3 rue Charles Pacquelin, 21190 Chassagne-Montrachet. 9ha*
***Grand Cru:** Puligny-Montrachet: Bâtard-Montrachet*
***1ers Crus:** Puligny-Montrachet Les Pucelles; Chassagne-Montrachet: Les Caillerets, Chenevottes, Morgeot (red and white), Vergers, Verindot; St-Aubin Charmois. **AOC Communales:** Beaune; Chassagne-Montrachet (red and white). **AOC Régionales:** Bourgogne Rouge, Blanc, Aligoté and Passe-Tout-Grains*
Marc Morey is a cousin of Jean-Marc (*qv*) and the domaine is run by his son-in-law, Bernard Mollard. Excellent Bâtard-Montrachet, and good quality whites. They spend one year, and the reds 15–18 months, in 25–30% new oak. This is now a very good address.

## Domaine Pierre Morey *Côte d'Or*

*9 rue Comte-Lafon, 21190 Meursault. 3ha (5ha en métayage)*
***Grand Cru:** Puligny-Montrachet: Bâtard-Montrachet*
***1ers Crus:** Meursault: Perrières; Pommard Grands Epenots*
***AOC Communales:** Monthelie; Meursault (red and white)*
***AOC Régionales:** Bourgogne Rouge, Blanc and Aligoté; Bourgogne Passe-Tout-Grains*
Pierre Morey's holdings have diminished considerably as a result of various *métayage* arrangements coming to an end – with Domaine des Comtes Lafon (*qv*) among others. This was the principal reason for his starting to work for Domaine Leflaive (*qv*) in 1989. His wines combine fruit, oak and breed in a lovely mouthful, the result of beautifully judged picking times, meticulous lees contact and bottling after 18 months. Pierre Morey also has a small *négociant* company, Morey-Blanc.

## Domaine Albert Morot *Côte d'Or*

*Château de la Creusotte, 21200 Beaune. 7ha*
***1ers Crus:** Beaune: Bressandes, Cent-Vignes, Grèves, Marconnets, Teurons, Toussaints*
***AOC Communale:** Savigny-Vergelesses La Bataillère monopole*
Old vines are a feature at this domaine. There is no departure from the vinification in oak vats/*élevage* in oak barrels formula and the resulting wines really are very good. The cellars, on two levels, are beside the vineyard. Although the domaine does export, there is a strong clientele of private customers, carefully nurtured by the estimable owner, Françoise Choppin.

### Domaine Denis Mortet *Côte d'Or*

*22 rue de l'Eglise, 21220 Gevrey-Chambertin*
*10ha (including métayage)*
***Grands Crus,** Gevrey-Chambertin: Chambertin; Vougeot: Clos Vougeot. **1ers Crus:** Gevrey-Chambertin: Les Champeaux, Lavaux St-Jacques; Chambolle-Musigny Les Beaux Bruns. **AOC Communales:** Gevrey-Chambertin, Gevrey-Chambertin Clos Prieur, Marsannay. **AOC Régionales:** Bourgogne Rouge, Blanc and Aligoté; Bourgogne Passe-Tout-Grains*

In 1991, Domaine Charles Mortet was divided between sons Denis and Thierry. Chambolle-Musigny Premier Cru Les Beaux Bruns can be really good, and the straight Gevrey-Chambertin Clos Prieur is elegant, perfumed and persistent. Delightful quality, with evidence of new wood. Set for a starring role in Burgundy.

### Domaine Thierry Mortet *Côte d'Or*

*21220 Gevrey-Chambertin. 4.5ha*

The family quality philosophy and attention to detail is also evident here. One to watch.

### Château du Moulin-à-Vent *Beaujolais*

*See* W&V, Beaujolais, Moulin-à-Vent.

### Clos du Moulin-à-Vent *Beaujolais*

*See* W&V, Beaujolais, Moulin-à-Vent.

### Moulin-à-Vent des Hospices *Beaujolais*

*See* W&V, Beaujolais, Moulin-à-Vent.

### Domaine Gérard Mouton *Côte Chalonnaise*

*See* W&V, Côte Chalonnaise, Givry.

### Domaine de la Moutonne *Chablis*

*See* W&V, Chablis.

### Domaine Denis Mugneret et Fils *Côte d'Or*

*Route Nationale, 21700 Vosne-Romanée. 8ha*
***Grands Crus,** Vosne-Romanée: Richebourg; Vougeot: Clos de Vougeot. **1ers Crus:** Nuits-St-Georges: Les St-Georges, Aux Boudots*

Quality seems on the up. It should be, given the vineyard sites.

### Domaine Mugneret-Gibourg /Domaine Georges Mugneret *Côte d'Or*

*Vosne-Romanée, 21700 Nuits-St-Georges*
*8.5ha (with much en métayage)*
***Grands Crus,** Gevrey-Chambertin: Ruchottes-Chambertin; Vougeot: Clos-Vougeot; Flagey-Echézeaux: Echézeaux. **1ers Crus:** Chambolle-Musigny Les Feusselottes; Nuits-St-Georges: Les Chaignots, Les Vignes Rondes. **AOC Communale:** Vosne-Romanée*

There are six families called Mugneret at Vosne-Romanée, all of them wine-producers, so things become rather complicated. The names of Mugneret-Gibourg and Georges Mugneret are both associated with the same domaine. Since Dr Georges Mugneret's death in 1988, wine has been made by his two daughters, Marie Christine and Marie-Andrée (both qualified oenologists).

Methods owe nothing to modernisation (except destemming and cultured yeasts) – open *cuves*, vattings of at least 15 days, first racking after the malolactic fermentation, then two others before bottling at 18 months to two years; *élevage* is in oak barrels, with a high proportion of new oak for the Grands Crus, thereafter cascading downwards to match the level. Fining is with egg whites (six for a barrel of 228 litres). The wines are very well made, stylish and perfumed, with good keeping potential. I love drinking them.

## Domaine André Mussy *Côte d'Or*

*21630 Pommard. 6ha*

***1ers Crus:** Beaune: Epenottes, Montremenots; Pommard: Epenots, Pézerolles, Saucilles.* ***AOC Communales:** Pommard; Volnay*

***AOC Régionale:** Bourgogne Rouge*

Mussy's reputation seems to be higher than my experience of the wine bears out. Sometimes there are tastes of old casks, which is disappointing with the arrival of some new oak. However, yields are low here, a factor that is very much on the plus side.

## Domaine Lucien Muzard et Fils

*21590 Santenay. 20ha*

Traditional wines of character are made at this domaine, which also boasts a useful address.

## Philippe Naddef *Côte d'Or*

*21160 Couchey. 4.5ha*

***Grand Cru:** Gevrey-Chambertin: Mazis-Chambertin*

***1ers Crus:** Gevrey-Chambertin: Cazetiers, Champeaux*

***AOC Communales:** Gevrey-Chambertin; Marsannay (red and white)*

Good quality, fairly rich, oaky wines. Being wary of snap judgements, I shall watch evolution in bottle with great interest.

## Domaine Henri Naudin-Ferrand *Côte d'Or*

*Magny-lès-Villers, 21700 Nuits-St-Georges. 15ha*

*See* W&V, Côte d'Or, Hautes-Côtes de Nuits/Beaune.

## Domaine Christopher Newman

*21220 Morey-St-Denis. 1.25ha*

A tiny, American-owned domaine. I hardly ever see the wines under this label. Linked with Guy Castagnier-Vadey (*qv*).

## Domaine Michel Niellon *Côte d'Or*

*1 rue du Nord, 21190 Chassagne-Montrachet. 6ha (3ha en métayage)*

***Grands Crus:** Puligny-Montrachet: Bâtard-Montrachet, Chevalier-Montrachet.* ***1ers Crus:** Chassagne-Montrachet: Clos St-Jean, Clos de la Maltroie, Les Vergers, Champ-Gain*

***AOC Communale:** Chassagne-Montrachet*

Taut, elegant, concentrated wines, aged in 25% new wood. The top end is very good, but unfortunately in short supply.

**Domaine Ninot** *Côte Chalonnaise*
*See* W&V, Côte Chalonnaise, Rully.

**Domaine Gilles Noblet** *Mâconnais*
*See* W&V, Mâconnais, Pouilly-Fuissé.

**Domaine Jean-Paul Paquet** *Mâconnais*
*See* W&V, Mâconnais, Pouilly-Fuissé.

**Domaine Michel Paquet** *Mâconnais*
*See* W&V, Mâconnais, St-Véran.

**Domaine du Paradis** *Beaujolais*
*See* W&V, Beaujolais, St-Amour.

**Domaine Parent** *Côte d'Or*
*21630 Pommard. 11ha (4ha en métayage)*
***Grand Cru:** Aloxe-Corton: Corton-Renardes. **1ers Crus:** Ladoix La Corvée; Beaune: Les Boucherottes, Les Epenottes; Pommard: Les Arvelets, Les Chanlins, Les Chaponnières, Les Epenots, Les Pézerolles. **AOC Communales:** Ladoix-Côte de Beaune; Pommard La Croix Blanche. **AOC Régionale:** Bourgogne Rouge*
There are no departures from traditional methods here, as befits a former supplier of Thomas Jefferson. The wines are usually good examples of their appellation and an exercise in the charms of the Pinot Noir. Just occasionally, when the year has given high yields, there is a lack of definition (especially vexing at high prices), but Premier Cru Pommard Les Epenots usually gives great pleasure.

**Parigot Père & Fils** *Côte d'Or*
*21190 Meloisey. 17ha*
***1ers Crus:** Beaune-Grèves, Les Aigrots; Pommard: Les Charmots, Les Epenots; Savigny: Les Peuillets; Chasssagne-Montrachet: Clos St-Jean. **AOC Communales:** Savigny-lès-Beaune; Beaune; Pommard; Volnay; Meursault. **AOC Régionales:** Bourgogne Hautes-Côtes de Beaune (red and white); Aligoté*
There are some good buys at this domaine.

**Domaine Jean Pascal & Fils** *Côte d'Or*
*Puligny-Montrachet, 21190 Meursault. 6ha (9ha en métayage)*
I have had some bland and disappointing wines, although there are signs of improvement here.

**Domaine Alain Passot** *Beaujolais*
*See* W&V, Beaujolais, Chiroubles.

**Domaine Guy Patissier** *Beaujolais*
*See* W&V, Beaujolais, St-Amour.

**Domaine Jean-Michel Patissier and Domaine Jean-Bernard Patissier** *Beaujolais*
*See* W&V, Beaujolais, St-Amour.

**Patriarche Père & Fils** *Côte d'Or*

*Couvent des Visitandines, 21200 Beaune. 40.46ha*

***1ers Crus:*** *Château de Meursault; Beaune*

***AOC Communales:*** *Château de Marsannay Rouge, Rosé and Blanc*

A huge concern, fuelled by sales of a non-appellation sparkling wine. They are also the owners of the great estate of the Château de Meursault (*qv*), where quality is quite good but could be much better. The Château de Marsannay is an even sadder story. The *négociant* wines are dull.

**Baron Patrick** *Chablis*

*See* W&V, Chablis.

**Domaine Jean-Marc Pavelot** *Côte d'Or*

*21420 Savigny-lès-Beaune. 4.43ha (10.7ha worked), half in the Premier Cru vineyards of the slopes*

***1ers Crus:*** *Pernand-Vergelesses Les Vergelesses; Savigny-lès-Beaune: La Dominode, Narbantons, Aux Gravains, Aux Guettes, Peuillets.* ***AOC Communales:*** *Savigny-lès-Beaune (red and white)*

Growers in Savigny since 1640. The red wines are very good with a lovely red-cherry fruit character to them. This domaine really gives confidence.

**Domaine Pelletier** *Beaujolais*

*See* W&V, Beaujolais, Juliénas.

**Domaine Pernin-Rossin** *Côte d'Or*

*7 route de Flagey, 21700 Vosne-Romanée. 7ha*

***Grand Cru:*** *Morey St-Denis: Clos de la Roche*

***1ers Crus:*** *Chambolle-Musigny; Morey-St-Denis Les Monts Luisants; Nuits-St-Georges Les Richemones; Vosne-Romanée: Les Beaumonts, Champs-Perdrix.* ***AOC Communale:*** *Vosne-Romanée*

***AOC Régionale:*** *Bourgogne Grand Ordinaire*

Guy Accad was the consultant oenologist at this domaine until 1988. It is an estate that needs to prove its worth over the distance, to use racing parlance, although these are opulent, intensely fruity wines.

**Domaine Paul Pernot et Fils** *Côte d'Or*

*Place du Monument, 21190 Puligny-Montrachet. 19ha*

***Grands Crus:*** *Puligny-Montrachet: Bâtard-Montrachet, Bienvenues-Bâtard-Montrachet*

***1ers Crus:*** *Puligny-Montrachet Les Folatières, Les Pucelles*

***AOC Communales:*** *Puligny-Montrachet, Beaune, Santenay*

***AOC Régionales:*** *Bourgogne Rouge and Blanc*

A wide range of whites from the Côte de Beaune, Puligny-Montrachet especially. Rich, smoothly textured, elegant wines, beautifully crafted. An address to remember. I wish they bottled more at the domaine, as then we would all benefit more directly.

**Domaine Maurice & Gilles Perroud** *Beaujolais*

*See* W&V, Beaujolais, Régnié, Château du Basty.

**Domaine du Petit Pressoir** *Beaujolais*
*See* W&V, Beaujolais, Côte de Brouilly.

**Piat** *Côte d'Or*
*71570 La Chapelle-de-Guinchay*
A large firm although I never seem to see their wines now.

**Domaine des Pillets** *Beaujolais*
*See* W&V, Beaujolais, Morgon.

**Domaine Fernand et Laurent Pillot** *Côte d'Or*
*13 rue des Champs Gains, 21190 Chassagne-Montrachet. 13.5ha*
***1ers Crus:*** *St-Aubin; Beaune Bucherottes; Chassagne-Montrachet: Champs-Gains (red), Grandes Ruchottes, Morgeot (white and red), Les Vergers, Vide-Bourse; Pommard: Refène, Clos des Vergers, Charmots, Rugiens.* ***AOC Communales:*** *Pommard; Puligny-Montrachet; Chassagne-Montrachet (red and white); Santenay; Volnay.* ***AOC Régionales:*** *Bourgogne Grand Ordinaire, Aligoté*
Honourable, straight white Chassagne-Montrachet and superb Grandes Ruchottes. Whites much better than reds at this domaine, although attention is turning to the latter.

**Domaine Jean et Jean-Marc Pillot** *Côte d'Or*
*21190 Chassagne-Montrachet. 10ha*
This is emerging as a very good domaine.

**Domaine Paul Pillot** *Côte d'Or*
*21190 Chassagne-Montrachet. 12ha*
***1ers Crus:*** *Chassagne-Montrachet: Les Caillerets, La Romanée, Champs-Gains, Clos St-Jean*
***AOC Communale:*** *Chassagne-Montrachet*
Lovely, lush white wines.

**Domaine Pinson** *Chablis*
*See* W&V, Chablis.

**Domaine Jean-Claude Pivot** *Beaujolais*
*See* W&V, Beaujolais, Beaujolais-Villages.

**Château de Pizay** *Beaujolais*
*See* W&V, Beaujolais, Morgon.

**Domaine du Point du Jour** *Beaujolais*
*See* W&V, Beaujolais, Fleurie.

**Château de Pommard** *Côte d'Or*
*21630 Pommard. 25ha*
The largest domaine in one single parcel on the Côte d'Or, producing 60,000 bottles per annum; the best barrels are kept back after tasting and sold under the exclusive label of the Château de Pommard. An impressive property, with the Château in the middle of the vineyard, which is entirely surrounded by

walls. Old vines, low yields and traditional vinification, with two years' ageing in 50% new oak casks before bottling. These are big, tannic and beefy wines, much beloved by the general public (mostly French, Swiss, German and Belgian), who buy direct. M Laplanche says a good winemaker should be able to make good wine in any year. Flashy bottle and label, but no fireworks for me on the palate.

## Maison Pierre Ponnelle

*See* Jean-Claude Boisset.

## Domaine Ponsot *Côte d'Or*

*Morey St Denis, 21220 Gevrey-Chambertin*
*9ha (1.2ha en métayage)*
***Grands Crus,*** *Gevrey-Chambertin: Chambertin, Chapelle-Chambertin, Griotte-Chambertin; Morey-St-Denis: Clos de la Roche, Clos St-Denis.* ***1ers Crus:*** *Morey-St-Denis Monts-Luisants*
***AOC Communales:*** *Gevrey-Chambertin; Morey-St-Denis*

The vineyards here produce some of the best Pinot Noir clones now used. Spicy wines of great breadth and richness in fine vintages, although they can be surprisingly weak in lesser ones (overcropping?). Grapes harvested very ripe, long *cuvaisons*, high fermentation temperatures, frequent *pigeages*, mainly old wood for ageing and no filtration make some splendid wines. Ponsot produces a white Morey-St-Denis – Monts-Luisants – from Chardonnay and Aligoté. This is a curiously 'flat' wine; I have never seen a memorable bottle, and wonder why they make it.

## Château Portier/Michel Gaidon *Beaujolais*

*See* W&V, Beaujolais, Moulin-à-Vent.

## Domaine Pothier-Rieusset *Côte d'Or*

*Route d'Ivry, 21630 Pommard. 7.5ha*
***1ers Crus:*** *Beaune-Boucherottes; Pommard: Charmots, Epenots, Rugiens, Clos de Verger, Pommard.*
***AOC Communales:*** *Pomard; Volnày; Meursault.*
***AOC Régionales:*** *Bourgogne Rouge and Blanc*

Usually very good Pommards are made at this estate; *vins de garde* which need years to show their best.

## Domaine de la Poulette *Côte d'Or*

*Grande-Rue à Corgoloin, 21700 Nuits-St-Georges*
*15ha(2ha en métayage)*
***1ers Crus:*** *Vosne-Romanée Les Suchots; Nuits-St-Georges: Les Brûlées, Chaboeufs, Les St-Georges, Les Poulettes, Les Vallerots, Les Vaucrains.* ***AOC Régionales:*** *Côte de Nuits-Villages (red and white); Bourgogne Rouge, Rosé and Aligoté; Bourgogne Passe-Tout-Grains*

A domaine where all the traditions are followed, including treading (after the treaders have showered, says M Lucien Audidier!). But modern innovations of improved presses and temperature control are also in evidence, as befits the cellars of a distinguished *ingénieur agronome*. There is a strong following for these wines in France, but Switzerland is also an important market. The domaine dates back to the 18th century and has been in the family since that time.

## Château des Poupets *Beaujolais*

*See* W&V, Beaujolais, Juliénas.

## Domaine de la Pousse d'Or *Côte d'Or*

*Volnay, 21190 Meursault. 13ha (0.4ha en métayage)*
***1ers Crus:*** *Pommard Les Jarollières; Volnay: Caillerets Dessus Clos des 60 Ouvrées monopole, Clos de la Bousse d'Or monopole, Clos d'Audignac monopole, En Caillerets; Santenay Les Gravières, Clos de Tavannes*

The late Gérard Potel ran this syndicate-owned domaine with admirable precision and a spirit of research; his highly-qualified son Nicolas is now in charge. There is some destalking, vinification in open vats, with *pigeage* every day and a vatting of ten to 15 days. *Elevage* takes place in oak barrels with about 20–30% new wood. Of the production, 70% is exported, with the 30% sales to the French market being divided between private customers and top restaurants. The wines combine fruit and appellation character together with a long, emphatic after-taste. The top *crus* last beautifully in bottle. I love the crunchiness of these wines, perfectly illustrated by the 1993 Clos de la Bousse d'Or.

## Domaine Jacques Prieur *Côte d'Or*

*21190 Meursault. 16ha*
***Grands Crus:*** *Gevrey-Chambertin: Chambertin, Chambertin Clos de Bèze; Chambolle-Musigny: Le Musigny; Vougeot: Clos Vougeot; Puligny-Montrachet: Chevalier-Montrachet, Montrachet; Flagey-Echézeaux: Echézeaux; Aloxe Corton: Corton-Charlemagne, Bressandes.* ***1ers Crus:*** *Beaune Clos de la Feguine, Grèves; Volnay: Champans, Clos des Santenots, Santenots; Meursault-Perrières; Puligny-Montrachet Les Combettes; Chambolle-Musigny: Combe d'Orveaux.* ***AOC Communales:*** *Meursault Clos de Mazeray (red and white).* ***AOC Régionales:*** *Bourgogne Rouge, Rosé and Blanc*

A famous estate, with excellent vineyards on the Côte de Nuits and the Côte de Beaune. To avoid the break-up of the domaine on his death, Jacques Prieur formed it into a private company in the early 1960s and the Prieur family now owns 50% of the shares. In 1988, the Mercurey firm of Antonin Rodet (*qv*) and other investors purchased 50% of the shares as well as the right to distribute 50% of the domaine's production; that year also saw another change when Martin Prieur (Jacques' son) took over management of the property. Martin is a qualified oenologist, young, energetic and dedicated to putting the firm back among the top Burgundy properties – where it ought to be, given its enviable array of vineyards. After many years in which wines were noticeably below par, the Prieur/Rodet combination is achieving a renaissance. The first vintage where the changes began to show was the 1990, with the Meursault-Perrières, Volnay Clos des Santenots and Le Musigny, to note three of the best, showing very well – one to watch.

**Domaine Prieur-Brunet** *Côte d'Or*
*21590 Santenay. 20ha*
***Grand Cru:** Puligny-Montrachet: Bâtard-Montrachet*
***1ers Crus:** Santenay: Comme, Maladière; Pommard Les Platières; Volnay-Santenots; Meursault-Charmes; Chassagne-Montrachet: Les Embazées, Morgeot (red)*
***AOC Communales:** Santenay Clos Rousseau, Santenay (red and white); Beaune Clos du Roi; Meursault (red and white)*
***AOC Régionales:** Bourgogne Rouge and Blanc*
Distinctive, reliable wines, with good appellation character. Both reds and whites are aged in ten per cent new wood, with the excellent Chardonnay wines being fermented in barrel as well.

**Groupement des Producteurs de Prissé** *Mâconnais*
*See* W&V, Mâconnais, St-Véran.

**Domaine Maurice Protheau & Fils /François Protheau & Fils** *Côte Chalonnaise*
*See* W&V, Côte Chalonnaise, Mercurey.

**Domaine Henri Prudhon & Fils /Gérard Prudhon** *Côte d'Or*
*Place de l'Eglise, 21190 St-Aubin. 12ha*
The wines of Domaine Henri Prudhon are also sold under the label Gérard Prudhon, Henri's son. Well-made, stylish red and white St-Aubin: intensely strawberryish reds, and delicious whites, marked by vanillin and clean oak and with a honeyed finish.

**Domaine Michel Prunier** *Côte d'Or*
*Auxey-Duresses, 21190 Meursault. 6ha (5ha en métayage).*
***1ers Crus:** Beaune Les Sizies; Volnay Caillerets; Auxey-Duresses Clos du Val, Auxey-Duresses. **AOC Communales:** Meursault; Auxey-Duresses (red and white). **AOC Régionales:** Bourgogne Hautes-Côtes de Beaune (red); Bourgogne Blanc*
This is probably the signature Auxey domaine and you are in very safe hands here.

**Domaine Pascal Prunier** *Côte d'Or*
*Rue Traversière, Auxey-Duresses, 21190 Meursault. 5ha*
***1ers Crus:** Auxey-Duresses: Les Duresses; Monthelie: Les Vignes Rondes; Beaune: Les Reversées, Les Siziés*
***AOC Communales:** Auxey-Duresses, Monthelie, Beaune, Pommard*
Another good *étape* in Auxey. The wines of Jean-Pierre Prunier are also under this hat.

**Château de Puligny-Montrachet** *Côte d'Or*
*21190 Puligny-Montrachet. 20ha*
***Grand Crus:** Puligny-Montrachet: Bâtard-Montrachet, Chevalier-Montrachet, Le Montrachet.*
***1ers Crus:** Puligny-Montrachet: Les Folatières; Meursault-Perrières; St-Aubin: En Remilly (red and white); Monthelie: Les Duresses; Pommard: Les Pézerolles*

***AOC Communales:*** *Puligny-Montrachet, Puligny-Montrachet Clos du Château, Les Chalumeaux; Monthelie; St-Romain; Meursault Les Chalumeaux; Chassagne-Montrachet; Pommard*
***AOC Régionales:*** *Bourgogne Rouge and Blanc*
An important domaine, owned by the Crédit Foncier de France. A good range of wines: supple, textured, fruity, harmonious reds, and stylish whites. The norm for Premiers Crus is 30% new wood for 18 months, with 20% for one year for *village* and regional. This ought to go into orbit with some fine tuning.

## Domaine des Quatre Vents *Beaujolais*
*See* W&V, Beaujolais, Fleurie.

## Domaine Ragot *Côte Chalonnaise*
*See* W&V, Côte Chalonnaise, Givry.

## Domaine Ramonet *Côte d'Or*
*Chassagne-Montrachet, 21190 Meursault. 17ha White wines, 8.8ha*
***Grands Crus:*** *Puligny-Montrachet: Le Montrachet, Bâtard-Montrachet, Bienvenues-Bâtard-Montrachet*
***1ers Crus*** *Chassagne-Montrachet: Les Caillerets, Les Ruchottes*
***AOC Communale:*** *Chassagne-Montrachet*
*Red wines, 8.8ha:* ***1ers Crus:*** *Chassagne-Montrachet: Clos de la Boudriotte, Clos St-Jean*
***AOC Communale:*** *Chassagne-Montrachet*
Noël and Jean-Claude Ramonet have a cult following, richly deserved. I have done many complete tastings and the wines are remarkable. Try Les Caillerets for value. Ramonet wines are keepers and quite different in style from Leflaive (*qv*). There has been an occasional lack of consistency, however, in bottles of the prized 100% new wood Le Montrachet, but the Bâtard never fails. Few rules here, just instinctive brilliance.

## Château de Raousset *Beaujolais*
*See* W&V, Beaujolais, Chiroubles.

## Domaine Rapet Père & Fils *Côte d'Or*
*Pernand-Vergelesses, 21420 Savigny-lès-Beaune. 19ha en fermage*
***Grands Crus:*** *Pernand-Vergelesses: Corton-Charlemagne; Aloxe-Corton: Corton.* ***1ers Crus:*** *Pernand-Vergelesses: Vergelesses, Ile des Vergelesses; Beaune.* ***AOC Communales:*** *Pernand-Vergelesses; Côte de Beaune (Pernand); Aloxe-Corton; Savigny-lès-Beaune; Beaune.* ***AOC Régionales:*** *Côte de Beaune-Villages (Pernand); Bourgogne Rouge and Aligoté*
Good to very good wines, with the test of time behind them. The Grands Crus are not really imposing examples, however, and the village and Premier Cru wines are the best value from this property.

## Domaine Gaston & Pierre Ravaut *Côte d'Or*
*21550, Ladoix-Serrigny. 14ha*
Red wines that often seem to have rather too much tannin for their underlying fruit.

## Domaine François & Jean-Marie Raveneau *Chablis*

*See* W&V, Chablis.

## Domaine Henri Rebourseau *Côte d'Or*

*10 place du Monument, 21220 Gevrey-Chambertin. 13.6ha*
***Grands Crus:*** *Gevrey-Chambertin: Chambertin, Chambertin Clos de Bèze, Charmes-Chambertin, Mazis-Chambertin; Vougeot: Clos de Vougeot.* ***1ers Crus:*** *Gevrey-Chambertin: Fonteny*
***AOC Communale:*** *Gevrey-Chambertin*

There have been wonderful bottles from this estate in the past, but the current form is very patchy. A pity – especially considering the quality of the vineyards. Perhaps Jean de Surrel will take up the challenge. One needs some concentration here, both in the wines and (maybe) in the philosophy.

## A Régnard & Fils *Chablis*

*See* W&V, Chablis.

## Remoissenet Père & Fils *Côte d'Or*

*21200 Beaune. 2.4ha*
***1ers Crus:*** *Beaune (including Grèves and Toussaints)*

Remoissenet is both a small domaine owner and an important *négociant*. The white wines, particularly the top appellations, can be very good – the Corton-Charlemagne, for example. The reds, however, are much less consistent; the style seems to be somewhat stewed rather than individual and vibrant, and I do not find much appellation character.

## Michel Rémon *Chablis*

*See* W&V, Chablis, A Régnard & Fils.

## Domaine Henri & Gilles Remoriquet *Côte d'Or*

*25 rue de Charmois, 21700 Nuits-St-Georges*
*5.5ha (2.5ha en métayage)*
***1ers Crus:*** *Nuits-St-Georges: Les Bousselots, Les Damodes, Rue de Chaux, Les St-Georges.* ***AOC Communales:*** *Nuits-St-Georges, Nuits-St-Georges Les Allots.* ***AOC Régionales:*** *Hautes-Côtes de Nuits; Bourgogne Aligoté; Bourgogne Passe-Tout-Grains*

This is a small domaine which has been slowly built up this century and where the wines are made with great care and respect for true taste and flavour. The grapes are semi-destalked and vatting is quite lengthy. *Elevage* is in oak barrels renewed 'as often as possible'. Bottling takes place at 22 months, after a fining with white of egg. The wines are good, without being special.

## Domaine de la Renarde *Côte Chalonnaise*

*See* W&V, Côte Chalonnaise: Rully, Givry.

## Domaine Armelle & Bernard Rion *Côte d'Or*

*8 Route Nationale 74, 21700 Vosne-Romanée. 7ha (1ha en métayage)*
***Grand Cru:*** *Vougeot: Clos Vougeot.* ***1ers Crus:*** *Chambolle-Musigny Les Gruenchers; Vosne-Romanée Les Chaumes;*

*Nuits-St-Georges Les Murgers, Les Damodes*
***AOC Communales:*** *Chambolle-Musigny; Vosne-Romanée; Nuits-St-Georges.* ***AOC Régionale,*** *Bourgogne Rouge*
There has been a big improvement at this domaine, now under the management of Bernard Rion. Long *cuvaisons* and manual *pigeage*, followed by 100% new oak for the Clos Vougeot, 50% for the Premiers Crus and 30% for the *villages* make for dark, sturdy, concentrated wines. Armelle and Bernard Rion are also truffle producers from October to January. Plan your visits accordingly!

## Domaine Daniel Rion & Fils /Domaine Patrice & Michèle Rion *Côte d'Or*

*Prémeaux, 21700 Nuits-St-Georges. 18.5ha (0.7ha en métayage)*
***1ers Crus:*** *Chambolle-Musigny Les Charmes, Les Cras; Vosne-Romanée: Les Chaumes, Les Beaux Monts; Nuits-St-Georges: Aux Vignerons, Clos des Argillières, Hauts-Pruliers, Nuits-St-Georges (red)*
***AOC Communales:*** *Chambolle-Musigny; Vosne-Romanée; Nuits-St-Georges Vignes Rondes (all red).*
***AOC Régionales:*** *Côte de Nuits-Villages; Bourgogne Rouge, Blanc and Aligoté; Bourgogne Passe-Tout-Grains*
Daniel Rion's son, Patrice, is quite a meticulous winemaker, and, on the whole, his wines reflect this, combining class with quite delicious fruit. This domaine had a string of notable successes in '88, '89 and '90 after a few disappointing results. The Vosne-Romanées are full of seductive black-cherry and spice flavours, while the Nuits-St-Georges are marked by the appellation's particular *goût de terroir*. And the wines of the 1990s have progressed still further.

## Domaine de Roally *Mâconnais*

*See* W&V, Mâconnais, Mâcon.

## Domaine Guy Robin *Chablis*

*See* W&V, Chablis.

## Domaine de la Roche *Beaujolais*

*See* W&V, Beaujolais, Brouilly.

## Domaine Joel Rochette *Beaujolais*

*See* W&V, Beaujolais, Régnié.

## Antonin Rodet *Côte Chalonnaise*

*See* W&V, Côte Chalonnaise, Mercurey.

## Domaine Rollin Père & Fils *Côte d'Or*

*21420 Pernand-Vergelesses. 11.65ha (1.44ha en métayage)*
***Grand Cru:*** *Pernand-Vergelesses: Corton-Charlemagne*
***1er Cru:*** *Pernand-Vergelesses: Ile de Vergelesses*
***AOC Communales:*** *Aloxe-Corton; Savigny-lès-Beaune; Pernand-Vergelesses (red and white), Chorey-lès-Beaune*
***AOC Régionales:*** *Bourgogne Hautes-Côtes de Beaune;*

*Bourgogne Aligoté, Passe-Tout-Grains*
I tend to find a mixed bag of wines at this estate. The white wines are lean (young vines, early picking, overcropping?), and even the Corton-Charlemagne lacks depth and breadth for the AC. The reds are better, however, with a good, pure Pinot character, if not a great deal of charm. However, the 1990 Ile de Vergelesses Premier Cru shows that Rémi Rollin can make reds with scent, richness and length. A new *cuverie* has been installed, so things are looking up. Perhaps in a year or two, I will have something altogether different to report.

## Domaine de la Romanée-Conti *Côte d'Or*

*Vosne-Romanée, 21700 Nuits-St-Georges. 25.54ha*
***Grands Crus:*** *Flagey-Echézeaux: Echézeaux, Grands Echézeaux; Vosne-Romanée: Richebourg, Romanée-Conti, Romanée-St-Vivant (rented en fermage from the Domaine Marey-Monge), La Tâche; Puligny-Montrachet: Le Montrachet*
The vineyard holdings are fabulous, some of the best sites in Burgundy. An increasingly 'ecological', non-chemical approach has been taken with regard to this precious soil and the average age of the vines is positively venerable, leading to low yields. The policy is for late picking, to achieve maximum possible ripeness. The domaine says it always practises rigorous grape selection in years where there is rot. Partial destalking (none at all in 1989) according to the vintage, and very long fermentations are also features of DRC practice. There is, naturally, the finance to use new oak barrels every year and racking and filtrations are kept to a minimum. The domaine aims for great longevity in its wines.

The domaine is owned by the de Villaine (*qv*) and Leroy (*qv*) families. While I have criticised some wines of the 1970s, the 1980s saw an enormous improvement, due largely, I feel, to the increasing influence of the modest and talented Aubert de Villaine. Even the 1984s are now showing exciting gamey tastes, and the great vintages of '85, '88, '89 and '90 are the stuff of dreams. The '91 reds look distinctly promising, while the '93s will be majestic. The '87s are tight, concentrated and small-yield. Some '83s are shedding their 'hail and rot' dryness (amazingly enough) and the '82s are drinking deliciously now. The sheer heady quality and persistence of flavour and bouquet of DRC wines is un-equalled and the multi-dimensional depth and longevity of the wines is mind-blowing, especially at the level of Romanée-Conti itself and of La Tâche, which can sometimes rival it.

## Ropiteau Frères *Côte d'Or*

*21190 Meursault*
***Grands Crus:*** *Clos Vougeot; Echézeaux.* ***1ers Crus:*** *Beaune: Grèves, Genevrières, Perrières; Puligny-Montrachet.* ***AOC Communales:*** *Chambolle Musigny; Pommard; Monthelie; Volnay; Meursault*
A *négociant* house with some estate wines. The whites are better than the reds; their Meursaults, for which they have always been known, are the best of the whites. In 1994, Jean-Claude Boisset (*qv*) acquired the firm.

### Domaine Philippe Rossignol *Côte d'Or*

*59 avenue de la Gare, 21220 Gevrey-Chambertin. 5ha*

Tannic wines which need time. Not entirely consistent, but I have been lucky on limited tasting acquaintance.

### Domaine Régis Rossignol-Changarnier *Côte d'Or*

*21190 Volnay. 7ha*

I see excellent wines from this domaine, which is always striving to do the best possible. What an example, even to the *jeunes loups* of the younger generation.

### Domaine Rossignol-Trapet *Côte d'Or*

*Rue de la Petite-Issue, 21220 Gevrey-Chambertin. 13ha*

***Grands Crus:** Gevrey-Chambertin: Chambertin, Latricières-Chambertin, Chapelle-Chambertin.*

***1ers Crus:** Gevrey-Chambertin: Clos Prieur, Petite Chapelle; Beaune: Teurons. **AOC Communales:** Gevrey-Chambertin; Morey-St-Denis; Savigny-lès-Beaune; Beaune. **AOC Régionales:** Bourgogne Rouge and Blanc; Bourgogne Passe-Tout-Grains*

This new domaine derives from the division of the old Domaine Louis Trapet where, broadly speaking, the holdings were simply halved (the other half is under Jean et Jean-Louis Trapet, *[qv]*). It is too early to make any judgements about consistent quality here, but the '90s had lovely extract and oak. The vineyards are exceptional, so the potential is there. Keep a close eye on this one.

### Domaine Joseph Roty *Côte d'Or*

*24 rue du Maréchal-de-Lattre-de-Tassigny, 21220 Gevrey-Chambertin. 8.5ha*

***Grands Crus:** Gevrey-Chambertin: Charmes-Chambertin, Griottes-Chambertin, Mazis-Chambertin. **1er Cru:** Gevrey-Chambertin Les Fontenys. **AOC Communales:** Gevrey-Chambertin: La Brunelle, Champ Chenys, Clos Prieur; Marsannay. **AOC Régionale:** Bourgogne Rouge*

Small but good grower, with prices positively at boutique level. Wines with an abundance of ripe fruit and an almost port-like concentration in good vintages, but with disappointments in lesser years. Old vines and low yields, natural yeasts and cool fermentation temperatures plus masses of new wood. The '90s are incredibly good and the Grands Crus, will keep for decades, as will those from '88 and '89.

### Domaine Marc Rougeot *Côte d'Or*

*Rue André-Ropiteau, 21190 Meursault. 11.85ha*

***1ers Crus:** Meursault: Les Charmes, Volnay-Santenots (red) **AOC Communales:** Ladoix; Pommard; Monthelie; Meursault Monatine; St-Aubin. **AOC Régionales:** Bourgogne Rouge and Aligoté; Bourgogne Passe-Tout-Grains*

Marc Rougeot's whites are better than his reds: Les Charmes is rich in good years, but his Meursault Monatine is his best-value and most reliable wine. If rarely very concentrated, it is always elegant and stylish.

## Domaine Emmanuel Rouget *Côte d'Or*

*21700 Flagey-Echézeaux. 7ha (includes Jayer vineyards)*
***Grand Cru:** Flagey-Echézeaux: Echézeaux*
***1ers Crus:** Vosne-Romanée: Les Beaumonts, Cros Parantoux*
***AOC Communales:** Vosne-Romanée; Nuits-St-Georges*
***AOC Régionales:** Bourgogne Rouge, Passe-Tout-Grains*

Emmanuel Rouget is Henri Jayer's (*qv*) nephew and his uncle's influence is clear for these are rich and flavoursome wines. Not yet perhaps Henri Jayer... but the '90s are splendid, especially the Cros Parantoux. All the Jayer wines are now made by Rouget.

## Domaine Guy Roulot *Côte d'Or*

*1 rue Charles-Giraud, 21190 Meursault. 12ha*
***1ers Crus:** Meursault: Charmes, Perrières*
***AOC Communales:** Monthelie; Auxey-Duresses;*
*Meursault: Les Luchets, Les Meix Chavaux, Tessons*
***AOC Régionales:** Bourgogne Rouge, Blanc and Aligoté*

An admirable domaine, now run by the late Guy Roulot's son, Jean-Marc. They were among the first growers in Meursault to vinify the different *lieux dits* separately. For me, these are wines of finesse and breed. Pressing is rapid and vinification is in oak barrels with a proportion of new wood: between one-third and one-quarter for the Meursaults. Bottling is, on average, after ten to 11 months. The results have silky texture and length on the palate, giving real joy to the taster.

## Domaine Georges Roumier et Fils *Côte d'Or*

*21220 Chambolle-Musigny. 13.7ha en fermage, 0.81ha en métayage*
***Grands Crus:** Gevrey-Chambertin: Charmes-Chambertin,*
*Ruchottes-Chambertin; Morey-St-Denis: Bonnes-Mares;*
*Chambolle-Musigny: Musigny; Vougeot: Clos Vougeot;*
*Pernand-Vergelesses: Corton-Charlemagne*
***1ers Crus:** Morey-St-Denis Clos de la Bussière monopole;*
*Chambolle-Musigny Amoureuses. **AOC Communale:** Chambolle-Musigny. **AOC Régionale,** Bourgogne Rouge*

Christophe Roumier now makes the wines with his father. He favours a 'natural', organic approach in the vineyard as he wishes to encourage a diversity of natural yeasts. Low yields are also a fixture here, but via strict pruning, rather than green harvest later in the season. Fermentation temperature is not allowed to exceed 30˚C (86˚F), there are one to two *pigeages* a day, and the wines are aged in a maximum of one-third new oak. The Ruchottes and Charmes will appear under Christophe Roumier's own label in future. Wines of purity and great class, allied to depth of flavour, made by a youthful guardian of the Burgundian Grail.

## Domaine Armand Rousseau *Côte d'Or*

*21220 Gevrey-Chambertin. 13.3ha*
***Grands Crus:** Gevrey-Chambertin: Chambertin, Charmes-Chambertin, Chambertin Clos de Bèze, Chambertin Clos des Ruchottes, Mazy-Chambertin; Morey-St-Denis: Clos de la Roche*
***1ers Crus:** Gevrey-Chambertin: Les Cazetiers, Clos St-Jacques,*

*Lavaux-St-Jacques.* ***AOC Communale:*** *Gevrey-Chambertin*

Apart from being one of the most engaging and generous characters in the entire Burgundy region, Charles Rousseau is a gifted winemaker. His son, Eric, is now at his right hand. The heritage of this estate is awe-inspiring, but present-day standards bow to no one, and many are the tastings where, in my opinion, Rousseau's wines come out on top.

The process starts with old vines, low yields, and a policy of strict selection of only healthy grapes at harvest. Most of the wines are aged in 60% new oak – except for the straight Gevrey, which is put into old wood only – and the Chambertin and Chambertin Clos de Bèze, which both mature in 100% new barrels. Many people would agree that the Clos St-Jacques is a Grand Cru in all but name and it has the same treatment. These wines are the very spirit of Burgundy, with each appellation and *climat* perfectly expressive of its character. Drinking a Rousseau wine is truly an exciting experience, and one to be savoured.

**Domaine Roux Père & Fils** *Côte d'Or*

*St-Aubin, 21190 Meursault. 18ha (8ha en métayage)*

***1ers Crus:*** *St-Aubin: La Chatenière, Les Frionnes, La Pucelle, Les Macherelles; Meursault Clos des Poruzots; Chassagne-Montrachet Clos St-Jean; Santenay*

***AOC Communales:*** *St-Aubin; Puligny-Montrachet Les Enseignères; Chassagne-Montrachet (red and white)*

***AOC Régionales:*** *Bourgogne Rouge and Aligoté; Bourgogne Passe-Tout-Grains; Bourgogne Les Grands Charmeaux*

A good domaine; the Roux family now also have a *négociant* business. The white wines receive long fermentations and show fruit and appellation style, the reds have become much less rustic and more harmonious. Go for the St-Aubins here.

**Domaine Dominique et Vincent Roy** *Côte d'Or*

*21190 Auxey-Duresses. 11ha*

The Premier Cru Le Val is a good advertisement for this domaine.

**Domaine Roy-Thévenin /Château de la Saule** *Côte Chalonnaise*

*See* W&V, Côte Chalonnaise, Montagny.

**Domaine Ruet** *Beaujolais*

*See* W&V, Beaujolais, Brouilly.

**Château de Rully** *Côte Chalonnaise*

*See* W&V, Côte Chalonnaise, Rully.

**Domaine de Rully St-Michel** *Côte Chalonnaise*

*See* W&V, Côte Chalonnaise, Rully.

**Domaine Fabien & Louis Saier** *Côte Chalonnaise*

*See* W&V, Côte Chalonnaise, Mercurey.

**Domaine Francis Saillant** *Beaujolais*
*See* W&V, Beaujolais, St-Amour.

**Château de St-Amour** *Beaujolais*
*See* W&V, Beaujolais, St-Amour.

**Domaine St-Sorlin** *Beaujolais*
*See* W&V, Beaujolais, Beaujolais-Villages.

**Domaine Ste-Claire (Jean-Marc Brocard)** *Chablis*
*See* W&V, Chablis.

**Domaine Santé Père et Fils** *Beaujolais*
*See* W&V, Beaujolais, Chénas.

**Société Coopérative des Viticulteurs de Saône et Loire** *Mâconnais*
*See* W&V, Mâconnais, Mâcon.

**Domaine PBI Sarrau** *Beaujolais*
*See* W&V, Beaujolais, Juliénas.

**Domaine Roger Saumaize** *Mâconnais*
*See* W&V, Mâconnais, Pouilly-Fuissé.

**Etienne Sauzet** *Côte d'Or*
*Puligny-Montrachet, 21190 Meursault. 8ha*
***Grands Crus:*** *Puligny-Montrachet: Bâtard-Montrachet, Bienvenues-Bâtard-Montrachet.* ***1ers Crus:*** *Puligny-Montrachet: Champ Canet, Les Combettes, Les Perrières, Les Referts*
***AOC Communales:*** *Puligny-Montrachet; Chassagne-Montrachet*
***AOC Régionale:*** *Bourgogne Blanc*
Impeccably made wines under the management of Gérard Boudot, the son-in-law of Etienne Sauzet's daughter. The Grands Crus are aged in up to 50% new wood, the Premiers Crus in one third, and both are bottled after about 14 months. The oak seems to show on these wines more than on those from Domaine Leflaive (*qv*) (although it is eventually absorbed) and occasional bottles have had reductive bouquets. I have had a few disappointments – '87s and '88s were not as good as expected – but the '89s and '90s were back on form, and there are glorious bottles from this property. The domaine's size decreased by nearly a third in 1991, when Jean-Marc Boillot (*qv*) took his 'share' of the vineyard holdings. All the original Sauzet wines will still be available – in smaller quantities – except for La Truffière (0.25ha), which went to M Boillot in its entirety. In order to combat this reduction in domaine size, the family company was created to allow grapes to be bought in and vinified with the estate produce. In the second half of the 1990s, this whole operation is in top form.

**Domaine Savoye/Pierre Savoye** *Beaujolais*
*See* W&V, Beaujolais, Morgon.

**Domaine René Savoye** *Beaujolais*
*See* W&V, Beaujolais, Chiroubles.

**Domaine Seguin** *Côte d'Or*
*15 rue Paul-Maldant, 21420 Savigny-lès-Beaune. 3.5ha*
***1er Cru:,*** *Savigny-Lavières*
***AOC Communales:*** *Savigny Godeaux, Savigny-lès-Beaune*
Pierre Seguin (whose grandfather invented the *wagon-citerne*, or road tanker) is both a domaine owner and a *négociant*. The domaine wines are fermented in oak *cuves* in a 14th-century Cistercian *cuverie*; the aim is to make wines that keep well. But that does not always mean heaviness – the wines have bouquet and (happily) plenty of supple fruit. The Seguin family has owned the house, cellars, *cuverie* and vineyards since the 18th century.

**Domaine de la Seigneurie de Juliénas** *Beaujolais*
*See* W&V, Beaujolais, Juliénas.

**Domaine Comte Daniel Senard** *Côte d'Or*
*21420 Aloxe-Corton. 8ha (15ha en métayage)*
***Grands Crus:*** *Pernand-Vergelesses: Corton-Charlemagne (red); Aloxe-Corton: Corton, Corton-Bressandes, Corton Clos des Meix, Corton Clos du Roi*
***1ers Crus:*** *Aloxe-Corton Valozières; Beaune Les Coucherias*
***AOC Communale:*** *Aloxe-Corton. Domaine Terregelesses;*
*Wines vinified by Philippe Senard:*
***Grand Cru:*** *Aloxe-Corton: Corton-Charlemagne*
***1ers Crus:*** *Savigny-lès-Beaune Les Vergelesses (red and white)*
***AOC Communales:*** *Savigny-lès-Beaune (red); Chorey-lès-Beaune (red and white); Beaune (red)*
Philippe Senard makes the wines, and comes from the fourth generation of *vignerons* in his family. The 14th-century cellars were built by the monks of the Abbaye de Ste-Marguerite and were forgotten for several centuries. Methods used are traditional, but there is great emphasis on late picking and automatic temperature control at the time of fermentation/vatting. There are both wooden *cuves* and enamel-lined steel vats, and *élevage* is in oak barrels, with 25% new wood. These were nearly always wines designed for long keeping, being bottled after two years, and tannic, even rustic, when young. From the 1988 vintage onwards, Guy Accad was the consultant oenologist here and we have yet to see how that affects the style, *typicité* and keeping potential of the wines in that period. Some tastings of young wines in 1997 disappointed. The white Aloxe-Corton is made from Pinot Gris.

**Domaine Sérafin Père et Fils** *Côte d'Or*
*21220 Gevrey-Chambertin. 4.5ha*
***Grand Cru:*** *Gevrey-Chambertin: Charmes-Chambertin*
***1ers Crus:*** *Gevrey-Chambertin: Les Cazetiers, Les Fonteny*
***AOC Communales:*** *Gevrey-Chambertin Vieilles Vignes, Gevrey-Chambertin*

Limited tasting experience has not been entirely convincing, with new wood sometimes masking real excitement, but Christian Sérafin can get it right.

## Domaine Bernard Serveau et Fils *Côte d'Or*

*21220 Morey-St-Denis. 7ha*
***1ers Crus:** Chambolle-Musigny, Les Chabiots; Morey-St-Denis Les Sorbets*
The winemaking here shows real respect for the raw materials and the appellations.

## Domaine Michel Serveau *Côte d'Or*

*21340 La Rochepot. 8.8ha*
***AOC Communales:** Chassagne-Montrachet (red and white); St-Aubin*
***AOC Régionales:** Bourgogne Hautes-Côtes de Beaune (red and white); Bourgogne Aligoté; Bourgogne Passe-Tout-Grains*
Michel Serveau makes particularly good Hautes-Côtes de Beaune at this estate.

## Simonnet-Febvre *Chablis*

*See* W&V, Chablis.

## Pierre Siraudin/Château de St-Amour *Beaujolais*

*See* W&V, Beaujolais, St-Amour.

## Domaine Robert Sirugue *Côte d'Or*

*21700 Vosne-Romanée. 9.5ha*
***Grand Cru:** Flagey-Echézeaux: Grands Echézeaux.*
***AOC Communales:** Chambolle-Musigny; Vosne-Romanée Les Petits Monts, Vosne-Romanée.*
***AOC Régionale:** Bourgogne Rouge*
Good Bourgogne Rouge and remarkable Grands Echézeaux – maybe I have been lucky.

## Paul Spay/Domaine de la Cave Lamartine *Beaujolais*

*See* W&V, Beaujolais, St-Amour.

## Domaine de Suremain *Côte Chalonnaise*

*See* W&V, Côte Chalonnaise, Mercurey.

## Domaine Talmard *Mâconnais*

*See* W&V, Mâconnais, Mâcon.

## Domaine Jean Tardy *Côte d'Or*

*21700 Vosne-Romanée. 4.79ha*
***Grand Cru:** Vougeot: Clos de Vougeot.*
***1ers Crus:** Vosne-Romanée Les Chaumes; Nuits-St-Georges Les Boudots*
***AOC Communales:** Chambolle-Musigny; Nuits-St-Georges*
***AOC Régionale:** Bourgogne Rouge*
Long, slow fermentations, *saignées* (literally, the 'bleeding off' of

the juice from the vats to make more concentrated red wines), 100% new wood for the best wines and no fining produce long-lasting wines that may be difficult to find, but are definitely rewarding when you do. I am increasingly impressed with the wines Tardy manages to turn out.

**Domaine Jean Taupenot-Merme** *Côte d'Or*
*33 route des Grands-Crus, 21220 Morey-St-Denis. 9ha*
***Grand Cru:*** *Gevrey-Chambertin: Charmes-Chambertin'; Morey-St-Denis: Clos des Lambrays*
***1ers Crus:*** *Gevrey-Chambertin Bel Air; Morey-St-Denis La Riotte; Chambolle-Musigny Combe d'Orvaux*
***AOC Communales:*** *Gevrey-Chambertin; Morey-St-Denis; Chambolle-Musigny*
***AOC Régionales:*** *Bourgogne, Bourgogne Passe-Tout-Grains*
Good wines on the whole, although they can sometimes be a touch rustic and lacking in concentration.

**Louis Tête** *Beaujolais*
*See* W&V, Beaujolais, Beaujolais-Villages.

**Société Civile du Domaine Thénard** *Côte Chalonnaise/Côte d'Or*
*See* W&V, Côte Chalonnaise, Givry/Côte d'Or, Puligny Montrachet.

**Jean Thévenet/Domaine de la Bon Gran** *Mâconnais*
*See* W&V, Mâconnais, Mâcon.

**Domaine Thévenot-le-Brun & Fils** *Côte d'Or*
*Marey-lès-Fussey, 21700 Nuits-St-Georges. 26ha*
***AOC Régionales:*** *Bourgogne Hautes-Côtes de Beaune (red); Bourgogne Hautes-Côtes de Nuits: red, white, Clos du Vignon (red and white), Les Renardes; Bourgogne Aligoté; Bourgogne Grand Ordinaire; Bourgogne Passe-Tout-Grains*
Father and two sons work this property, and they are particularly proud of their Clos du Vignon, revived after the vines had been completely abandoned. I have liked the red better than the white. There is rather a special Bourgogne Aligoté, Perles d'Or, which is bottled straight off the lees to give some fresh *pétillance*.

**Domaine Jacques Thévenot-Machal**
*21190 Meursault. 6ha*
The reds seem to be better than the whites here. Certainly I have not appreciated the Meursault Poruzot.

**Château Thivin** *Beaujolais*
*See* W&V, Beaujolais, Côte de Brouilly.

**Domaine Gérard Thomas** *Côte d'Or*
*21190 St-Aubin. 9.5ha*
***1ers Crus:*** *Meursault-Blagny; Puligny-Montrachet La Garenne; St-Aubin: Murgers des Dents de Chiens (white),*

*La Chatenière (white), Les Frionnes (red); Puligny-Montrachet; St-Aubin (red and white)*
***AOC Communales:*** *St-Aubin, St-Aubin Côte de Beaune*
***AOC Régionales:*** *Bourgogne Rouge and Blanc*
The whites here are better than the reds; that said, the Premier Cru Puligny-Montrachet, Meursault-Blagny and St-Aubins are worth trying and these wines generally offer very good value.

## Domaine de Thurissey/Les Vieux Ceps *Mâconnais*

*See* W&V, Mâconnais, Mâcon.

## Martine & Jean-Luc Tissier /Domaine des Crais *Mâconnais*

*See* W&V, Mâconnais, St-Véran.

## Domaine Tollot-Beaut & Fils *Côte d'Or*

*Rue Alexandre Tollot, Chorey-lès-Beaune, 21200 Beaune*
*18.3ha (21.88ha en fermage)*
***Grands Crus:*** *Pernand-Vergelesses: Corton-Charlemagne; Aloxe-Corton: Corton, Corton-Bressandes.* ***1ers Crus:*** *Savigny-Lavières, Champ-Chevrey; Beaune: Clos du Roi, Grèves; Aloxe-Corton: Les Vercots, Les Fournières.* ***AOC Communales:*** *Aloxe-Corton; Savigny-lès-Beaune; Chorey-lès-Beaune; Beaune: Blanche Fleurs*
***AOC Régionales:*** *Bourgogne Rouge, Blanc and Aligoté*
This is a renowned family domaine – the first vines were bought in 1880 – and now the fifth generation is hard at work. The immaculate cellars house cement vats for the relatively short vinification and one-third new wood *élevage*. The wines are aromatic and charming, with genuine appeal. The top *crus* last well and have a lovely, heady quality. The Chorey-lès-Beaune is a wine with a good *rapport qualité/prix*, a distinct asset to those on a budget. Two-thirds of the production is exported.

## Domaine Tortochot *Côte d'Or*

*12 rue de l'Eglise, 21220 Gevrey-Chambertin. 10ha*
***Grands Crus:*** *Gevrey-Chambertin: Chambertin, Charmes-Chambertin, Mazis-Chambertin; Vougeot: Clos de Vougeot*
***1ers Crus:*** *Gevrey-Chambertin: Champeaux, Lavaux St-Jacques*
***AOC Communales:*** *Gevrey-Chambertin: Champerrière, Les Corvées, Les Jeunes Rois, Gevrey-Chambertin; Morey-St-Denis*
A well-respected domaine, run by M Gabriel Tortochot. Half of the production is sold to local *négociants* in barrel, half in bottle direct from the domaine – Switzerland and Belgium are good customers. Grapes are destalked, and fermentations are long, up to 14 days. Only one-tenth of the barrels are bought new each year. The wines tend to be big, sometimes slightly rustic, but there are occasional grand bottles when aged. The strike rate should be higher.

## Château de la Tour/Domaine Pierre Labet *Côte d'Or*

*Clos de Vougeot, 21640 Vougeot. Château de la Tour, 5.5ha*
***Grand Cru:*** *Vougeot: Clos Vougeot.*

*Domaine Pierre Labet, 5ha:* ***1ers Crus:*** *Beaune Coucherias; Savigny-Vergelesses (white)* ***AOC Communales:*** *Beaune Clos des Monsnières (red and white).* ***AOC Régionale,*** *Bourgogne Rouge*
Guy Accad advised on the vinification here from 1987 to 1992. Although the '87 was drinking well at five years of age, I wonder if the Clos de Vougeot of these years really expresses the nature of the *cru*. We shall have to wait and see how the Accad wines develop in the long term but, from 1993, François Labet has 'flown solo'. However, I was not impressed by recent vintages shown.

## Domaine de la Tour du Bief/ Comte de Sparre *Beaujolais*

*See* W&V, Beaujolais, Moulin-à-Vent.

## Château de la Tour Bourdon *Beaujolais*

*See* W&V, Beaujolais, Régnié.

## Domaine Jean et Jean-Louis Trapet *Côte d'Or*

*21220 Gevrey-Chambertin*
This domaine was halved in 1990 (*see* Rossignol-Trapet) but Jean Trapet and his son Jean-Louis remain here, with some truly wonderful vineyard holdings. The greatest Latricières of my life came from this domaine, where they were made to exhibit fascinating delicacy and finesse. But over-cropping produced some weak wines, and, in the 1990s, one is looking for greater consistency to put both these new domaines in the front rank where they should be.

## Domaine Gérard Tremblay/Domaine des Iles *Chablis*

*See* W&V, Chablis.

## Trenel & Fils *Mâconnais*

*See* W&V, Mâconnais, Mâcon.

## Domaine Jacques Trichard *Beaujolais*

*See* W&V, Beaujolais, Morgon.

## Domaine des Trois Coteaux *Beaujolais*

*See* W&V, Beaujolais, Beaujolais-Villages.

## Domaine Truchot-Martin *Côte d'Or*

*43 Grande-Rue, 21220 Morey-St-Denis. 7ha*
***Grands Crus:*** *Gevrey-Chambertin: Charmes-Chambertin; Morey-St-Denis: Clos de la Roche*
***1ers Crus:*** *Chambolle-Musigny Les Sentiers; Morey-St-Denis Clos Sorbés, Les Blanchards; Gevrey-Chambertin: Aux Combott*
***AOC Communales:*** *Gevrey-Chambertin; Chambolle-Musigny; Morey-St-Denis*
***AOC Régionale:*** *Bourgogne Rouge*
Truchot-Martine produces moderately extracted wines aged in 25% new wood for the Premiers Crus, a bit more for the Grands Crus. These are clean, frank and supple wines, pure in their fruit

flavours. They are good rather than great, with the Grands Crus lacking a little scope for really top quality. They lack for nothing in immediate appeal, though, and are typical of their *terroirs*.

## Domaine Jean Vachet *Côte Chalonnaise*

*See* W&V, Côte Chalonnaise, Montagny.

## Château Varennes *Beaujolais*

*See* W&V, Beaujolais, Beaujolais-Villages.

## Domaine des Varoilles *Côte d'Or*

*11 rue de l'Ancien-Hôpital, 21220 Gevrey-Chambertin*
*11.9ha (2ha en métayage)*
***Grands Crus:*** *Gevrey-Chambertin: Charmes-Chambertin, Mazoyères-Chambertin; Morey-St-Denis: Bonnes Mares; Vougeot: Clos Vougeot.* ***1ers Crus:*** *Gevrey-Chambertin: Champonnets, La Romanée, Clos des Varoilles, Clos du Couvent, Clos Prieur, Clos du Meix des Ouches, Gevrey-Chambertin*
Half the domaine and the *négociant* business Naigeon-Chauveau are now owned by the Swiss group Hammel. Great '90s at the domaine. Top *crus* that need time to open up.

## Domaine Bernard Vaudoisey-Mutin *Côte d'Or*

*Rue du Mont, 21190 Volnay. 10ha*
***1ers Crus:*** *Volnay: Les Caillerets; Pommard: Les Chanlins Bas*
***AOC Communales:*** *Pommard; Volnay; Meursault*
***AOC Régionales:*** *Bourgogne Rouge, Blanc and Passe-Tout-Grains*
Sturdy *village* red wines that will keep. Half the wine is still sold to *négociants*.

## Domaine de Vauroux *Chablis*

*See* W&V, Chablis.

## Domaine Alain Verdet *Côte d'Or*

*Arcenant, 21700 Nuits-St-Georges. 8.5ha*
***AOC Régionales:*** *Bourgogne Hautes-Côtes de Nuits (red and white)*
The red wines undergo a long *cuvaison* and are aged in 30% new oak for two years; the white wines spend 12–15 months in wood. M Verdet's labels proudly proclaim his 'organic' methods: *Domaine en Agrobiologie depuis 1971 – Culture sans produit chimique ni de synthèse*. Both reds and whites have plenty of flavour; the bouquets can be problematic – 'organic' odours?

## Domaine Lucien & Robert Verger *Beaujolais*

*See* W&V, Beaujolais, Côte de Brouilly.

## Verget *Mâconnais*

*See* W&V, Mâconnais, Mâcon.

## Domaine Patrick & Martine Vermorel /Domaine de la Fully *Beaujolais*

*See* W&V, Beaujolais, Brouilly.

**Domaine Thierry Vigot-Battault** *Côte d'Or*
*21220 Messanges. 2ha (1.5 en métayage)*
***Grand Cru:*** *Flagey-Echézeaux: Echézeaux.* ***1er Cru:*** *Vosne-Romanée Les Gaudichots.* ***AOC Communale:*** *Nuits-St-Georges.* ***AOC Régionales:*** *Hautes-Côtes de Nuits, Bourgogne Aligoté, Passe-Tout-Grains*
A promising domaine using a modest proportion of new wood. Supple and pleasing Hautes-Côtes de Nuits and good, rather than great, Vosne-Romanée and Echézeaux. Pretty wines with ripe-cherry Pinot flavours, but occasionally the old wood shows.

**A&P de Villaine** *Côte Chalonnaise*
*See* W&V, Côte Chalonnaise, Bouzeron.

**Henri de Villamont** *Côte d'Or*
*Rue du Docteur-Guyot, 21420 Savigny-lès-Beaune. 10ha*
***Grand Cru:*** *Flagey-Echézeaux: Grands Echézeaux*
***1ers Crus:*** *Chambolle-Musigny; Savigny-lès-Beaune Clos des Guettes.* ***AOC Communales:*** *Chambolle-Musigny; Savigny-lès-Beaune Le Village.* ***AOC Régionale:*** *Bourgogne Rouge*
An important Swiss-owned *négociant*. The Savignys can be pleasant and I have had good Puligny Pucelles. In 1969 de Villamont bought the Barolet business, but of course the recent wines have nothing to do with the great collection of wines built up by the late Dr Barolet – now, unfortunately, mostly happy memories.

**Domaine Vincent** *Mâconnais*
*See* W&V, Mâconnais, St-Véran.

**Cave Coopérative de Viré** *Mâconnais*
*See* W&V, Mâconnais, Mâcon.

**Domaine Virely-Rougeot** *Côte d'Or*
*Place de l'Europe, 21630 Pommard. 8ha*
***1ers Crus:*** *Pommard Clos des Arvelets, Les Chanlins, Pommard; Meursault Charmes*
***AOC Communales:*** *Beaune; Meursault; Pommard*
***AOC Régionale,*** *Bourgogne Rouge*
Usually dependable, if lacking real impact.

**Domaine Michel Voarick** *Côte d'Or*
*21420 Aloxe-Corton. 5ha (4ha en fermage)*
***Grands Crus:*** *Pernand-Vergelesses: Corton-Charlemagne; Aloxe-Corton: Corton Clos du Roi, Corton-Languettes, Corton-Renardes*
***AOC Communales:*** *Pernand-Vergelesses; Aloxe-Corton*
***AOC Régionale:*** *Bourgogne Aligoté*
Among the vines tended by this domaine is the famous 2.5ha Hospices de Beaune (*qv*) vineyard, Cuvée Corton Docteur Peste. Where vinification is concerned, the old Burgundian rules are followed to the letter, including a policy of no destalking. The resulting wines last well and make sturdy bottles, although the style is really not to my liking. Perhaps there should be a dollop of new wood.

**Domaine Robert Vocoret & Fils** *Chablis*
*See* W&V, Chablis

**Domaine Comte Georges de Vogüé** *Côte d'Or*
*21220 Chambolle-Musigny. 12.5ha*
***Grands Crus:*** *Morey-St-Denis: Bonnes Mares; Chambolle-Musigny: Le Musigny, Musigny Blanc.* ***1er Cru:*** *Chambolle-Musigny Les Amoureuses.* ***AOC Communale:*** *Chambolle-Musigny*
Marvellous vineyards and some very fine wines in the past. Most of the '70s and '80s lacked the magic associated with the best from this property, but the '90s have gone up several gears. Meticulous attention to detail is clearly there and François Millet's winemaking is making waves. It all starts with low yields and adaptability to the conditions of the year. It ends with the excellent, classy wines we are seeing this decade.

**Domaine Joseph Voillot** *Côte d'Or*
*Volnay, 21190 Meursault. 8ha (2ha en métayage)*
***1ers Crus:*** *Pommard: Clos Micault, Epenots, Pézerolles, Rugiens; Volnay: Caillerets, Champans, Frémiets; Meursault Cras*
***AOC Communales:*** *Pommard; Volnay; Meursault Chevalier*
***AOC Régionales:*** *Bourgogne Rouge and Aligoté*
Vignerons in Volnay since the 14th century, the Voillots certainly display fidelity to their origins! They support warm fermentations, and one-third new oak barrels are used for the domaine-bottled wines. Two-thirds of production is sold in bulk, to Beaunois or Swiss *négociants*, who clearly love these very creditable wines.

**Château de Vosne-Romanée** *Côte d'Or*
*Vosne Romanée, 21700 Nuits-St-Georges. 3.5ha*
***Grand Cru:*** *Vosne-Romanée: La Romanée*
***1ers Crus:*** *Vosne-Romanée: les Reignots, Les Chaumes*
***AOC Communale:*** *Vosne-Romanée du Château*
La Romanée is entirely owned by the Liger-Belair family, but the wines are bottled and distributed by Bouchard Père et Fils (*qv*).

**Domaine de Vuril** *Beaujolais*
*See* W&V, Beaujolais, Brouilly.

# Index

Indexer's note: Wine estates, domaines, etc, and their proprietors are listed in the A–Z of Burgundy Producers (pages 161–251). Page numbers in italics indicate maps or tabulated material.

## *A*

Accad, Guy 179, 183, 200, 231, 244, 248
acidity 27,
*acquits* 36
ageing *see* maturation
alcohol levels 19
AC specifications 15; *see also* chaptalisation
Aligoté grape 22, *35*
Aloxe-Corton 88–91
ANTAV (Association Nationale Technique pour l'Amélioration de la Viticulture) 20
AOC Communale 19
AOC Régionale 19
appellation contrôlée system 14–19
area of production
AC specifications 15
area of vineyards *see* under ACs
aromas *see* flavours
auctions *see* wine auctions
Auxey-Duresses 103–4

## *B*

*Ballons* 40, *41*
Ban de Vendange 27
barrels, oak 31, 53
Bâtard-Montrachet *66*, 108, 109
Beaujolais *11*
cooperatives 142
exports *38*
faults 140
fermentation 139–40
grapes 139
négotiants 142
pasteurisation 140
production figures *14*
terroir 12
villages and wines 139–60
Beaujolais Blanc 142
Beaujolais Nouveau 140
Beaujolais Supérieur 141
Beaujolais-Villages 158–60
Beaune 93–6
Bèze, Clos de *66*
Bienvenues-Bâtard-Montrachet *66*, 108, 109
biodynamic viticulture *see* vineyard management: biological methods
Blanchot 50, *51*
Blagny 104–5
Bonnes Mares *66*, 71
Bordeaux mixture 24
bottles 39–40; *see also* labels
bottling 32, 33
Bougros 50, *51*
Bourgogne 19, 21
Bourgogne Mousseux 33
Bourgogne Passe-Tout-Grains 21
Bouzeron 116, 118
brokers *see courtiers*
Brouilly 156–7
buying wine 37

## *C*

Cellar temperatures 41
Centre Hospitalier 98
César grape 21
Chablis *11*
area under vine *54*
frost protection 50, 52
Grands Crus 50, *51*, 52
maturation in oak 53
planting density 20
Premiers Crus 51
production figures *14*
soils and terroir 9–10, 52
villages and wines 50–62
wine sales 53
yields *54*
Chambertin, Le *66*
Chambolle-Musigny 73–5
Chapelle-Chambertin *66*, 68, 69
chaptalisation 19, 30, 33
Chardonnay grape 21–2, *35*
Charmes-Chambertin *66*, 68
Chassagne-Montrachet 111–13
Chénas 146–7
Chevalier-Montrachet *66*, 108, 109
Chiroubles 150–2
Chitry-le-Fort 63
chlorosis 28

Chorey-lès-Beaune 93
climate *see terroir;* vintages *and under* ACs
*climats* 39
clones of vines 20, 21, 22, 28
Clos, Les 50, *51*
*commissionaires en vins* 37
cooperatives 37
  Beaujolais 142
Corton *66*, 86
Corton-Charlemagne *66*, 86, 87, 89
Côte Chalonnaise *11*
  grapes 116
  production figures *14*
  *terroir* 10
  villages and wines 116–27
Côte d'Or *11*
  area under vine 8
  climate 14
  Grands Crus *66*
  grapes 10
  planting density 20
  production figures *14*
  *terroir* 10, 12
  vatting times 30
  villages and wines 63–115
  yields *16–17*
Côte de Beaune 115
  harvest dates 27
  villages and wines 85–115
Côte de Beaune-Villages 115
Côte de Brouilly 155–6
Côte de Nuits
  villages and wines 63–85
Côte de Nuits-Villages 84–5
Coulanges-le-Vineuse 62–3
*coulure see* flower abortion
*court noué see* fan leaf
*courtiers* 36–7
Crémant de Bourgogne 33
Criots-Bâtard-Montrachet *66*, 111

## D

Decanting 41–2
DGI (Direction Générale des Impôts) 15
downy mildew *see* peronospora
drainage 13

## E

Echézeaux *66*, 77
*Elevage* 15, 34
enjoying burgundy 39–44
exports of burgundy *35*, *38*, 39

## F

Fan leaf (*court noué*) 21, 22, 23
faults of Beaujolais 140
*fermage* 34
fermentation 19, 29, 31, 32, 139–40
fertilisers 25
filtering 33
fining 32, 33
Fixin 66–7
Flagey-Echézeaux 77–8
flavours 42–3; *see also under* ACs
Fleurie 149–50
flower abortion (*coulure*) 26, 28
foliage trimming (*rognage*) 26
food
  matching with burgundy 43–4
*fouleurs* 189
'fourth leaf' 23
frost 13, 25
frost protection 13, 50, 52

## G

Gamay grape 8, 21, *35*
geology *see terroir and under* ACs
Gevrey-Chambertin 67–70
Givry 125–6
glasses 40–1
grafting 9, 25, 28
Grand Rue, La *66*, 80
Grands Crus 19; *see also* individual Grand Crus
Grands Echézeaux *66*, 77
grape caterpillars 24
grapes 10, 20–2, 116, 128, 139
  AC specifications 15
  structure 29
  and *terroir* 12
  varietal distribution *35*; *see also* vines
grass between vine rows 23
*greffe anglaise* 25
Grenouilles 50, *51*
grey rot 14, 21, 23
growers 34, *35*

## H

Hail 26
harvesting 27
Hautes-Côtes de Beaune 85–6
Hautes-Côtes de Nuits 85–6
history
  of vineyards 7–9
  of wine trade 37

Hospices de Beaune 96–8
Hospices de Nuits-St-Georges 203
hygiene during winemaking 32

*I*

INAO (Institut des Appellations d'Origine) 15, 19, 33, 36, 40
Irancy 62

*J*

Juliénas 144–5

*L*

Labels 40
Ladoix-Serrigny 88, *89*
Lambrays, Clos des *66*, 71
Latricières-Chambertin *66*, 68, 69
laying down burgundy 41
leaf curl 21
lees 32
Lichine, Alexis 36

*M*

Mâcon 129–34
Mâconnais *11*
  grapes 128
  production figures *14*
  *terroir* 10
  villages and wines 128–39
Maranges 115
*marc* 31
Marsannay 33, 64
maturation 15, 31, 53
Mazis-Chambertin *66*
Mazoyères-Chambertin *66*, 68
Melon de Bourgogne grape 22
merchants *see négotiants*
Mercurey 121–5
*métayage* 34
*méthode traditionnelle* 33
Meursault 105–7
microclimate *see terroir*
monastic vineyards 7–8
Montagny 126–8
Monthelie 102–3
Montrachet, Le *66*, 108, 109
Morey-St-Denis 71–3
Morgon 152–4
Moulin-à-Vent 147–9
Moutonne, La 50, *51*
Musigny, Le *66*

*N*

*Négociants* 34, 36–7, 142
Nuits-St-Georges 81–4

*O*

Oak barrels 31, 53
oidium (powdery mildew) 9, 24
ONIVIT (Office National Interprofessionnel des Vins de Table) 15
organic viticulture *see* vineyard management: biological methods
origins of vines 7
*ouillage* 53
ownership of vineyards 8–9

*P*

Pasteurisation 140
Pernand-Vergelesses 86–8, *89*
peronospora (downy mildew) 24
phylloxera 9
picking grapes *see* harvesting
pigeage *see* treading grapes
Pinot Beurot grape 22
Pinot Blanc grape 22, *35*
Pinot Gris *see* Pinot Beurot grape
Pinot Noir grape 8,20–1, 29
placenames 39
planting density of vines 20
planting methods 15
planting new vineyards 23
ploughing 28
Pommard 98–100
Pouilly-Fuissé 134–7
Pouilly-Loché 137
Pouilly-Vinzelles 137
powdery mildew *see* oidium
Premeaux 84
Premiers Crus 19; *see also* Premiers Crus *listed under* ACs
pressing 31, 32
Preuses, Les 50, *51*
*prise de mousse* 33
production area
  AC specifications 15
production figures *14, 35*; *see also under* ACs
pruning 15
  Cordon-de-Royat 25
  Gobelet (*la taille*

*courte*) 25, 27, 139
Guyot (*la taille longue*) 24, 139
pre-pruning 28
*taille à queue* 25
Puligny-Montrachet 108–10
pumping must (*remontage*) 30

## R

racking 31
rainfall 13–14
red wine
exports *38*
winemaking 29–32
Régnié 154–5
*remontage see* pumping must
*remuage see* riddling
Richebourg *66*
riddling (*remuage*) 33
*rognage see* foliage trimming
Roche, Clos de la *66*, 71
Romanée, La *66*
Romanée-Conti *66*, 79
Romanée-St-Vivant *66*, 79
rootstocks 28
rosé wines
winemaking 33
Ruchottes-Chambertin *66*
Rully 118–21

## S

sales of wine
by *négociants-éleveurs* 34, 36, 53; *see also* wine auctions
Santenay 113–14
Savigny-lès-Beaune 91–2
Shoonmaker, Frank 36
sediment 32, 33
serving burgundy 41–2
Société l'Elevage et Conditionnement des Vins Fins 197
soil analysis 23
soil disinfection 23
soil exhaustion 13
soils *see terroir and under* ACs
sparkling wines
winemaking 33
spiders, red and yellow 24, 25
spraying vineyards 23
SRFCQ (Service de la Répression des Fraudes et du Contrôle de la Qualité) 15, 19
St-Amour 143–4
St-Aubin 107–8
St-Bris-le-Vineux 63
St-Denis, Clos *66*, 71, 72
St-Romain 100–1
St-Veran 137–9
star wines 49
'straight' wine 19
sunshine, hours of 13

## T

Tâche, La *66*, 79
tannin 29, 30
Tart, Clos de *66*, 71, 72, 73, 224
tartaric crystals 33
tastevins 40
tasting burgundy
AC requirements 18–19
flavours 42–3
temperatures
cellars 41
climatic 13
fermentation 29, 32
serving 42
*terroir* 9–10, 12–14
*see also under* ACs
Tokay d'Alsace *see* Pinot Beurot grape
treading grapes (*pigeage*) 29
Tressot grape 21

## V

Valmur 50, *51*
vatting times 30
Vaudésir 50, *51*
*village* wines 19
*vin gris* 33
vine diseases and pests
chlorosis 28
fan leaf (*court noué*) 21, 22, 23
flower abortion (*coulure*) 26, 28
grape caterpillar 24
grey rot 14, 21, 23
leaf curl 21
oidium (powdery mildew) 9, 24
peronospora (downy mildew) 24
phylloxera 9
spiders 24, 25
vines
clones 20, 21, 22, 28
origins 7; *see also* grapes
vineyard management
biological methods 24, 54, 164, 200, 208, 212, 215, 239, 241, 249
fertilising 25
foliage trimming (*rognage*) 26
grafting 9, 25, 28
grass between vine rows 23
harvesting 27
planting 15, 23
ploughing 28
pruning 15, 24–5, 27, 28, 139